Arthur Machen

The Heptameron

Tales and Novels of Marguerite, Queen of Navarre

Arthur Machen

The Heptameron
Tales and Novels of Marguerite, Queen of Navarre

ISBN/EAN: 9783744692519

Printed in Europe, USA, Canada, Australia, Japan

Cover: Foto ©Thomas Meinert / pixelio.de

More available books at **www.hansebooks.com**

THE HEPTAMÉRON

BY

MARGUERITE D'ANGOULEME

CONTENTS.

———◦◦◦———

b

CONTENTS.

DAY THE FOURTH.

ON THE FOURTH DAY RELATION IS MADE FOR THE MOST PART OF THE VIRTUOUS PATIENCE AND LONG-SUFFERING OF WOMEN TO WIN THEIR HUSBANDS; AND OF THE PRUDENCE USED OF MEN TOWARDS THEIR WIVES FOR THE PRESERVING OF THE HONOUR OF THEIR HOUSES AND LINEAGE.

DAY THE FIFTH.

On the Fifth Day relation is made of the virtuousness of such maids and wives of whom honour hath been preferred before pleasure; of them likewise who have done the contrary thereto; and of the simpleness of certain others.

DAY THE SIXTH.

ON THE SIXTH DAY RELATION IS MADE OF THE DECEITS BETWEEN MAN AND
WOMAN, THROUGH COVETOUSNESS, VENGEANCE, AND CRAFTINESS.

DAY THE SEVENTH.

On the Seventh Day relation is made of them that have done what
they least desired.

DAY THE EIGHTH.

ON THE EIGHTH DAY RELATION IS MADE OF THE MOST LECHEROUS CASES
THAT CAN BE CONCEIVED.

TRANSLATOR'S PREFACE.

In attempting a new version of the "Heptameron" the translator has endeavoured—1, to preserve as closely as possible the sense of the original; 2, to give the work a thoroughly English dress, and not merely to transfer the idioms of one language into those of another. The Queen of Navarre made use of a style marked by a quaint redundancy, and every page teems with repetitions which would not be tolerated in a modern book. Indeed, the reader is now and again reminded of the Law Reports, so determined was the writer to be understood by posterity, a peculiarity which the translator has, to the best of his ability, reproduced. But though the work is calculated to remind readers rather of Walton than Macaulay, it by no means lays claim to an antiquarian accuracy; "thou," "thee," "hath," &c., would, if pertinaciously adhered to throughout, become tedious, and be resented as a needless and irritating piece of affectation.

The present translator was, indeed, all the more impelled to choose an older form of English, after examining the version of Mr. W. K. Kelly (now out of print), originally published by the late Mr. H. G. Bohn in 1855, and afterwards by Messrs. George Bell and Sons, in which, from one end of the book to the other, not the slightest attempt is made to reproduce the quaint diction of the original. Slipshod in style, erroneous and unscholarlike in rendering, this translation, besides its grievous sins of commission, to which we shall presently return, is guilty also of sins of omission, excusable only on the ground of parsimony on the part of the original

Mr. Kelly has dealt in a very summary manner with the poetical pieces occurring in four novels of the "Heptameron." In the first case (Novel XIII.) the amorous captain's epistle is dismissed thus :—"It was an elaborate declaration of the feelings which the writer had so carefully concealed, and in it was inclosed a large, handsome diamond, mounted in a black enamel ring, which the lady was supplicated to put on her fair finger." In Novel XIX. the pitiful lament of the monk is altogether suppressed, and no mention whatever made of it. In Novel XXIV. the Castilian's farewell to his cruel mistress is rendered into somewhat bald prose, and ends as follows :—"I take my leave of cruelty, pain, torment, scorn, hatred, and the burning fire with which you are filled, no less than you are adorned with beauty. I cannot better bid farewell to all woes and pains and intolerable distresses, and to the hell of the amorous woman, than in bidding farewell to you, madam, without the least prospect that wherever you or I shall be we shall ever look upon each other more." Lastly, in Novel LXIV., a poem of forty-five lines is compressed into five lines of prose! The arguments to each day's Entertainment are also omitted, while many words—such as *crémeau*, *cannettes*, *gouvernante**—are left untranslated. And a few instances, culled at random, of his phenomenal ignorance and portentous blundering will suffice and serve better than any vituperation to exhibit the extent of Mr. Kelly's incompetency for the task of translating a French classic into English. It will readily be confessed that "she sat down to read for hours until his return" is not a satisfactory rendering of "en disant ses Heures, attendoit le retour de son mary" (Novel XXXVII.); while the monk and nun would scarcely, with all their faults, have "shouted three hours, loud and long," into the ear of a dying man. Novel LXXII. "Bien cryé *leurs* Heures à l'oreille du pauvre homme." It would be difficult to say on what grounds

---

* "Gouvernante" is found in some authors, but Johnson notes "governess" as the better expression.

the legal title "Maitre des Requêtes" has been rendered into
"Referendary." Courts of Requests existed in England till the
reign of Charles I., and appear to have adjudicated on small
money claims, discharging the functions of our modern
County Courts. Herrick alludes to them in the lines:

> "There needs no Court for our Request,
>   Where all is rest.
> Where all Star-Chamber Bills do cease,
>   Or hold their peace."

The same strictures apply to other volumes of Bohn's
Series. The translator of Martial in this series, which is
described in the Preface as a faithful rendering into English,
positively translates a score or two of the Epigrams not into
English but Italian!

The earliest English translation of the "Heptameron" was
published as far back as 1654. The title-page runs as follows:—
"Heptameron; or, the History of the Fortunate Lovers: written
by the most Excellent and Virtuous Princess, Margaret de Valoys,
Queen of Navarre; Published in French by the Privilege and
Immediate Approbation of the King; Now made English by
Robert Codrington, Master of Arts. 1654." In the
address of "The Translator to the Reader," Codrington
says he has been informed "that the Queen had fully
finished the Ten Days' work, but the fryers and religious
men who have deprived us of the two last Journals and
the greater part of the eighth, would have deprived us also
of all the rest, if possibly they could have prevented it."
A translation of Claude Gruget's Dedication is followed by
"The true and lively Portraiture of the most Illustrious and most
Excellent Princess Marguerite of Valois," by Ronsard; and this
by two sonnets to the same effect. The translation itself does
not call for any particular remark; it seems a somewhat
careless and hasty performance, owing whatever merit it
may possess rather to the quaint phraseology of English at that
period, than to any ability on the part of the translator. The

poetical pieces are all omitted, and the Arguments are wanting (the latter had doubtless dropped out of the current French text which Codrington made use of); but such as it is the version gives a far better notion of the original than the bald and commonplace rendering of Mr. Kelly.

We now pass on to the bibliography of the "Heptameron." The first edition bears the title: "Histoire des Amans fortunez dediée à très-illustre princesse madame Marguerite de Bourbon, duchesse de Nivernois, par Pierre Boiastuau dit Launay. Paris. G. Gilles. 1558." This edition, now of the utmost rarity, contains only sixty-seven novels, not arranged in their proper order, or divided into Days. Proper names are also altered, and many passages offensive to the clergy suppressed.

The second edition is entitled: "L'Heptameron des Nouvelles de très-illustre et très-excellente princesse Marguerite de Valois, royne de Navarre, remis en son vray ordre, confus auparavant en sa première impression, dediée à très-illustre et très-vertueuse princesse Jeanne, royne de Navarre, par Claude Gruget, Parisien. Paris. Benoit Prevost. 1559." Here we have for the first time the title "Heptameron," which was invented by Gruget himself. The Queen of Navarre intended her book to be a "Decameron;" or, Entertainment for Ten Days, and this is the title of the MSS. But the scheme· being apparently interrupted by death, only seven days and two stories of the eighth day were completed; hence Gruget's title. In this edition the order of the tales is preserved, with the division into days, and the arguments before each day. But in place of Novels XI., XLIV., and XLVI., Gruget substituted three others, composed, according to M. Frank, by himself. The many audacious, and indeed blasphemous passages in the work (*e.g.*, see the Epilogue to Novel XLI.), suppressed by Boiastuau, are also omitted in the edition of 1559.

This impression of Gruget's served as a model for succeeding editors of the sixteenth and seventeenth centuries, who reproduced his text with more or less fidelity. But the Parisians of the closing years of the seventeenth century, to whom Boileau gave laws in poetry and Bossuet in prose, were not likely to endure the archaisms of the " Heptameron :" consequently the text underwent great changes, and fared somewhat like a good many of our old country-houses of the same period, whose oriel windows and arched porches gave way to square surfaces of glass, rows of Corinthian columns, and imposing flights of steps. The very name was often suppressed, and the title ran: "Contes et Nouvelles de Marguerite de Valois, Reine de Navarre, mis en beau langage." Many of these editions were published in the various literary centres of Europe, and some of them—especially a London edition—are still highly valued for the sake of their engravings. The first attempt to reissue the work as Marguerite wrote it was made by M. Paul Lacroix, who published in 1841 an edition* which follows the text of Gruget—the orthography, however, being modernised as an intermediate step between the "beau langage" of the eighteenth century and the thorough-going antiquarianism of the present age. This impression was eagerly bought up, and the editor having suggested in his Preface that an edition from the text of the MSS. would be acceptable, the Société des Bibliophiles Français took the hint, and deputed their secretary, M. Le Roux de Lincy, to carry out M. Lacroix's suggestion. After a careful examination of the various MSS.† M. de Lincy chose the most complete and authentic, and in 1853 published his edition,‡ which has not been equalled by any subsequent editor

---

* " L'Héptameron ; ou, Histoire des Amans fortunez."

† The MS. chosen by Le Roux de Lincy as the basis of his text is numbered 7,572 in the National Library of France. This, however, wants the *arguments* to the Days and Novels, which were supplied by MS. 7,576.

‡ " L'Héptameron des Nouvelles de trés-haute et trés-illustre princesse Marguerite d'Angoulême, reine de Navarre, sœur unique de François Iᵉʳ." 3 vols. 8vo.

for completeness and fullness of illustration. For the first time the old classic was given to the world as the authoress had written it; the suppressed novels, and all those passages which had fallen under the ban of the Index Expurgatorius, being restored to their proper positions. An Introductory essay upon the life and works of Marguerite, with notices of sixteen MSS. examined by the editors, on the various editions of the "Heptameron," and the unpublished poetical pieces of the Queen of Navarre, precede the text; while at the end of each volume are notes, "critical and explanatory," on the subject matter contained in it.

Next to this admirable edition of the "Bibliophiles Français" comes M. Paul Lacroix's edition of 1858, in which the text of Le Roux de Lincy is followed throughout, the three rejected novels—XI., XLIV., and XLVI.—introduced by Gruget, being restored. M. Lacroix also made some slight alterations in the orthography, and fixed the punctuation on a logical basis; but with these exceptions his text (from which the present translation has been made) is practically identical with that of the "Bibliophiles Français." Prefixed to the worki s an historical notice of Marguerite, and a list of her writings, with some valuable critical remarks.

In the "Petite Collection Elzevirienne" a three-volume edition of the "Heptameron" was published in 1879 by Liseux, who seems to have spared no pains to make the paper and printing worthy of the work and of the laborious editing of M. Felix Frank. Like Lacroix, the last-named editor has been contented to avail himself of the labours of the Bibliophiles Français, and, with the exception of including Gruget's three novels, the text of Frank is substantially the same as that of Le Roux de Lincy. The Introduction of 179 pages contains an essay on the character and life of "La Marguerite des Princesses," with a minute criticism on the "Heptameron," its plan, and the personages who tell the novels. Not the least interesting portion is the comparison of Mar guerite's work with the similar collections of Boccaccio, Sabadino degli Arienti, Massucio, Antoine de Sains Denis, Bonaventura des Periers, and, last but not least, of Geoffrey Chaucer. It is noteworthy that M. Frank couples Marguerite and Chaucer together as the only writers of the kind who have endowed their *devisants* with individuality, and sought to make them something more than mere pegs to hang so many novels upon. Remarkable also for its curious research is his investigation into the real personalities of *Dagoucin, Ennasuitte, Parlamente,* and their companions. Here M. Frank differs repeatedly from Le Roux de Lincy and Lacroix. M. Lacroix sees under the mask of Dagoucin a certain Comte d'Agoust; M. Frank has ten pages to prove that he is an ecclesiastic named Nicolas Dangu. M. Le Roux de Lincy will have Longarine to be Madam de Chastillon, the Queen of Navarre's governess, while M. Frank shows that Longarine "est la dame de Longrai ou Longray en Normandie," one of Marguerite's most intimate friends. A hundred pages are devoted to this identification of the *devisants,* and to the third volume are subjoined three Appendices, with notes on the novels.

We have also seen an edition published by Garnier, without any date, introduction, or memoir, in which Novels XI., XLIV., and XLVI. are omitted and replaced by Gruget's substitutes; while the arguments to the Days and Novels are altogether wanting. Geburon and Ennasuitte appear as Guebron and Emarsuitte. The language is modernised and the text very corrupt: it seems, in fact, to be nothing more nor less than a reproduction of an edition published in the last century.

Thus our text is identical with that which is unquestionably the best—namely, the "Bibliophiles Français." We have omitted annotations which seem only to provoke discussion on matters concerning which nothing definite is known, and which, to use a hackneyed phrase, rarely rise above the level of "scandal about Queen Elizabeth." Those, however, who wish to identify the personages of the "Heptameron" will find what they require in the edition of M. Paul Lacroix; while for the biography of the authoress our readers cannot do better than consult Miss Freer's "Life of Marguerite d'Angoulême, Queen of Navarre." *

Finally, our aim has been to present in a worthy dress what we claim to be the only complete English translation of the "Heptameron."

* London, 1854.   2 vols.

PROLOGUE.

On the first day in September, when as the springs of the Pyrenean mountains begin to put on their virtuousness, there came together at those of Cauterets much folk from France, Spain, and other countries; some to drink of the water, some to bathe therein, and others to take the mud-bath. And each and all of these are so marvellous in their operation that men given up by the doctors return from Cauterets whole and sound. Yet my aim is neither to show forth the place nor the virtuousness of these springs aforesaid, but only to relate that which appertaineth to the matter on which I am about to write. Now there tarried in this place for more than three weeks all the sick folk, until they discovered by the good case of their bodies that it was fit for them to return. But at the time appointed for their setting forth, there fell such great rains that it seemed as if God had forgotten the promise that he made to Noah, not again to destroy the world by water, since by it all the cottages of Cauterets were so filled that no one could dwell therein. And those who came from the land of Spain returned thither by the mountains, as best they could, and, trust me, they who had a good knowledge of the tracks were the ones to fare best. But the ladies and gentlemen of France, thinking to get them back to Therbes as easily as they came, found the rivulets so swollen, that they were hardly to be crossed. And having come to the Gave Bearnois, which when they went was not more than two feet deep, they found it so mighty and rushing a stream that they turned aside to seek for bridges, but these being but of wood had been carried away by the strength of the torrent. Some indeed, believing that they could withstand its force by fording it in a body, were so quickly borne away, that the rest, though they would fain cross, had small wish to do so; and so, as their inclination was, they separated and went in divers directions to seek for some new way. Some taking the mountain track, and passing

B

through Arragon, came to the county of Roussillon. and to Narbonne, and others fared straight to Barcelona, whence sailing they got to Marseilles and Aiguemorte.

But a certain widow, of much experience, named Oisille, determined to lay by all fear of the bad roads, and to journey to Our Lady of Serrance. Not that she was of so superstitious a mind as to think that the glorious Virgin would leave her session by the right hand of her Son, and dwell in that desert land, but only for her great desire of seeing that holy place of which so great a noise had come to her ears, and being assured likewise that if there were any way out of this peril, the monks would be advised thereof. And this she accomplished, yet traversing such a wild country and ways as hard to go up as to come down, that although she was old and slow in movement, she had to go the best part of the journey on foot. But of this the worst was that most of her folk and her horses died on the way, so she came to Serrance, having one man and one woman only, and was there taken in and kindly entreated by the monks.

Now there were among the French travellers two gentlemen who had gone to the springs, rather that they might accompany their ladies than for any failing in their health. And seeing that the company was setting forth, and that the husbands of their ladies were likewise taking them away, they thought fit to follow them from afar, without making anyone privy to their design. But it came to pass that one evening when the married gentlemen were lodged with their wives at the house of one who was more a robber than a churl, that the lovers of these ladies, who were also lodged in a cottage hard by, heard at night a great tumult. Whereupon they and their servants arose, and enquired of their host what this noise might be. And he, much afraid, told them that it was some Roaring Boys, who had come to take their share of the booty that was at the house of the robber, their comrade; at which the young gallants forthwith laid hold of their arms, and with their servants went to the succour of the ladies, death for whom they accounted far sweeter than life without them. And when they came to the place they found the outer gate broken in, and the two husbands with their servants defending themselves full bravely. But since the number of the robbers was great, and they were grievously wounded, having by this time lost the greater part of their servants, they were beginning to give way. The two gallants, seeing their ladies wailing and entreating at the windows, were worked by pity and love to such a point of courage that, after the fashion of two bears rushing down from the mountains, they burst upon the robbers and so handled them that many were killed, and those left alive would not stay for any more blows, but escaped to their hiding place as best they could. The two gallants, having put these villains to flight, and killed the host among the rest, heard that the hostess was worse than her mate, whereupon they, with the thrust of a sword, sent her to join him. Next, entering into one of the lower rooms they found therein one of the married gentlemen, who presently gave up the ghost. The other was scot-free of wounds, yet was all his vesture pierced with sword-thrusts, and his own sword broken in two. This poor man, beholding before him his rescue, prayed the young men, after both embracing and thanking them, by no means to leave him, which was to them a request mighty pleasant. And after they had buried the dead man, and comforted, after the best sort they could, his widow, they set forth again, not knowing which road to take but leaving it in God's hands. And if it be your pleasure to know the names of these three gentlemen, the one who was married was called Hircan, and his wife Parlamente, and the widow was Longarine. And the names of the two gallants were Dagoucin and Saffredent. And after that they had been all the day on horseback, toward evensong they made out a spire, whither, after much travail and labour, they arrived. Now this was the spire of the abbey of St. Savyn, and here they were taken in and well entreated by the abbot and his monks. And the abbot, who was of a noble house, gave them good lodging, and as he waited upon them to their rooms, enquired of them their hap. And having heard how bad it was he told them that they were not alone in tasting of misfortune, for he had in one of his rooms two ladies who had escaped equal, if not greater peril, since they had had to do not with men but with beasts, in whom there is no pity. For these poor ladies, when half a league on this side of Peyrechitte, had met a bear coming down from the mountain, from before which they had fled at such a rate that at the gate of the abbey their horses dropped dead under them, and two of their maids, who came in a long while after, told them that the bear had killed all their men-servants. Then did the two ladies and the three gentlemen go into the room where these unhappy ones were lodged, and found them weeping, and knew them for Nomerfide and Ennasiutte. So having embraced one another, they told what had befallen them, and in concert with the good abbot, comforted themselves for having again fallen into company. And in the morning they heard mass with much devotion, praising God for the perils which were overpast.

And while they were all at mass there came into the church a man clad only in his shirt, flying as if some one pursued him, and crying for help. Straightway did Hircan and the other gentlemen go forth to discover what the affair was; and there they beheld two men with drawn swords, who followed after him; and these seeing so great a number, would fain have fled; but Hircan and his company pursued them and put them to the sword. And when the aforesaid Hircan returned he found that the man clad in the shirt was Geburon, one of his comrades, who said that while he was in bed in a cottage near Peyrechitte there came upon him three men, and though he was in his shirt and armed only with a sword, he so shrewdly wounded one that he died upon the spot. And whilst the two others set themselves to succour their fellow, he, perceiving that he was naked and the robbers armed, thought he could scarcely win save by flight, being little impeded by his dress. And for the good event of this he gave thanks to God, and to those who had for him done vengeance.

After they had heard mass and dined, they went to see if it were possible to cross the Gave, and seeing that it was not they were in great affray, although the abbot many times entreated them to abide there until the waters were abated, and to this for the day they agreed. And in the evening, as they were going to bed, there came an old monk who, for many a year, had failed not to be present during September at Our Lady of Serrance. And on their asking him the news of his journey, he said that by reason of the floods he had come by the mountain tracks, and that they were the worst roads he had ever been on. But one most pitiful case he had to tell, and this was that he had found a young gentleman named Simontault, who, weary of the long time the floods took to abate, had determined to force the passage, trusting in the goodness of his horse, and having first placed all his serving-men around him, thereby to break the force of the water. But when they were in mid-stream, those who were badly mounted were borne headlong, men and horses, down stream and were never rescued. The gentleman finding himself alone, turned his horse to the bank whence he came, yet not so sharply as to avail anything. But God willed that he was so near to the shore as to be able, drawing himself on his hands and knees, and drinking a great deal of water, to reach the rough flint-stones on the bank, so weak and feeble that he could not stand. But it chanced well for him that a shepherd, bringing his sheep home at evening, found him lying there among the stones, soaking wet, and sad at heart as well for himself as for his folk whom he had seen perishing before his eyes. The shepherd, who perceived his case more by his look than by his words, took him by the hand and led him to his cottage, where he dried him with a fire of broken sticks as well as might be. And, that night, God led thither this good monk, who showed him the way to Our Lady of Serrance, and told him he would be lodged there in better fashion than in any other place, and that he would find there an aged widow called Oisille, who was indeed his equal in misfortunes. And when all the company heard of the good lady Oisille, and the gentle knight Simontault, that they were safe, a great joy fell on them, and they praised the Creator that, deeming the serving-men and maids sufficient sacrifice, he had kept alive their master and mistress; and above all did Parlamente give thanks unto God from the bottom of her heart, since for a long while had Simontault been accepted by her as a devoted lover. And having made careful enquiry of the road to Serrance, although the good old man showed them how difficult it was, yet none the less did they determine to journey there; and on that very day did they set forth without lack of anything, for the abbot had given them of the best horses that were in Lavedan, and goodly cloaks of Bearn, and abundant provaunt, and an escort to guide them safely across the mountains. And so, faring more on foot than horseback, with great sweat and travail they

came to Our Lady of Serrance, where the abbot, though he
was an inhospitable man, durst not refuse them lodging, for the
fear he had of the Lord of Bearn, by whom he knew them to
be well beloved; but he, being a well-taught hypocrite, put
on for them his most obliging face, and led them to see the
good lady Oisille and the gentle knight Simontault.

Now such delight was on the company, in such wondrous
wise gathered together, that to them all the night seemed short,
praising God in the church for the mercy he had showed
toward them.   And after that in the morning they had taken
some short rest, they all went to hear mass and to receive the
Holy Sacrament of concord, in which all Christians are united
into one body, imploring Him who had gathered them together
to perfect their journey to his glory.   After dinner they sent
to know if the floods were not yet abated, and finding that they
were rather increased, they determined to make them a bridge,
fixing it on two rocks which are very near to one another,
and where there are still planks for those on foot, who, coming
from Oleron, may wish to cross the Gave.   In much delight
was the abbot that they performed this at their own charges,
to the end that the number of pilgrims and gifts should be
increased for him, and so he furnished them with labourers, yet
not one farthing did he give of his own, for he was too miserly.
And since the labourers said that the bridge could not be
finished before ten or twelve days, both the men and women of
the company began to be very weary; but Parlamente, the
wife of Hircan, who was never listless or melancholy, having
asked of her husband leave to speak, spoke thus to the aged
lady Oisille: "Good mistress, I am amazed that you, who have
had so great experience, and who stand towards us women as a
mother, do not think of some pastime wherewith to subdue
this weariness of ours at the long delay; for if we do not get
some pleasant and seemly pursuit we shall be in danger of
growing sick."   To this added the young widow Longarine:
"And what is worse we shall grow peevish, and hardly to be
cured thereof; for if you will consider there is no man nor maid
amongst us but has occasion enough for sorrow."   Ennasiutte,
laughing, replied to her: "Not every one of us has lost a
husband as you have, and as for serving-men one need not
despair on their account, for others are to be had; natheless I

/

am well persuaded that we should have some pleasant pursuit to pass the time, or else we shall be dead by the morrow." All the gentlemen were of their mind, and would have the lady Oisille declare to them what they should do, and she thus replied: "My children, it is a hard thing this that you ask of me, to show you some pastime that will free you from your weariness. For this I have sought through my whole life, and only one pastime have I found—namely, the reading of the Holy Scriptures, where is found the true and perfect joy of the spirit, whence there cometh health and rest to the body. And if you ask how I, at my years, can be so cheerful and healthy, I tell you that when I rise in the morning I straightway take the Holy Scriptures and read therein, considering and meditating on the goodness of God in sending, for our sake, his Son upon the earth to make manifest those good tidings in which he doth promise forgiveness of all sins, and satisfaction for all trespasses through the gift of His love, passion, and merits. This it is that makes me to be glad, so that I take my psalter, and in most lowly fashion do sing from my heart and indite with my mouth those psalms and canticles with which the Holy Spirit hath inspired David and the other writers. And this delight that I have in them is so great that all mishaps the day can bring show to me but as blessings, seeing that I have in my heart by faith Him who hath borne my sorrows. In like manner before I sup I go apart to give my soul his pasture in the Scriptures, and then in the evening I recall to my mind all that I have done during the day that is past, asking of God pardon for my sins, and thanking Him for the grace which He hath bestowed upon me; so in His love, and fear, and peace, I take my rest well assured against all perils. Behold, then, my children, the pastime to which I am attached, and have been a long while, after having searched all others, and not finding contentment therein for my spirit. Methinks, therefore, that if in the mornings you would give an hour to reading, and this done, pray devoutly at mass, you would find in this desert place a greater beauty than there is in cities, for he who knoweth God beholds all things beautiful in Him, and without Him nothing is fair; wherefore I entreat you that you receive my counsel, if you would live joyously." Next did Hircan take up the discourse, and said: "Good mistress, those who have read

the Holy Scriptures, as I believe we all have, will agree that
what you say is altogether true. Natheless, you must consider
that these bodies of ours are not so mortified as not to need
also some exercise, for if we were at our houses we should
have hunting and falconry, to make us forget our idle thoughts ;
while the ladies have their housewifery, their tambour-work,
and sometimes dancing, wherein they can take seemly exercise.
And all this makes me say (speaking on behalf of the men)
that you, who are most in years, shall read to us in the
morning time somewhat of the life of our Lord Jesus Christ,
and of the mighty and admirable works that He hath done for
us ; but as to the hours between dinner and evensong we have
yet to find some pastime that may be wholesome for the soul
and pleasant to the body, and so with all this shall the day be
passed joyously."

The lady Oisille said she had had such toil to put out of
mind all worldly vanities that she feared any choice of hers
would be a bad one ; but it was necessary to put the matter to
the vote, and would have Hircan give his opinion first. " As
for me," said Hircan, " if I conceived that the pastime I would
fain chose were as agreeable to a certain one of this company
as it is to me, my vote would soon be given, but as it is I am
dumb, and wait to hear what others say." His wife Parlamente thereupon fell to blushing, thinking that his words were
for her, and betwixt a frown and a smile spoke to him thus :
" Peradventure, Hircan, that one whom you deem hard to be
contented could find contentments enough if it was her humour ;
but let us leave those games at which only two can disport
themselves, and think of some which all can play." Then
said Hircan to all the ladies : " Since this wife of mine has
understood so fairly what lay beneath my words, and since this
privy play is not to her liking, I am assured that she, better
than any other, can tell us of some pastime for all ; and I do
herewith profess myself of her mind, whatever it may be, and
will in this matter be led entirely by her." And to this
the whole company agreed. Whereupon Parlamente, seeing
that the lot was fallen upon her, spoke as follows : " If I felt
within me such parts as had the ancients, by whom were all
arts invented, I would invent some game to discharge the duty
that you have laid upon me ; but knowing my wit and my

power, how little it is, and scarce able so much as to call to mind how others have performed well this very thing, I shall esteem myself lucky if I can but follow in their steps. Among the rest I think that there is not one of you who has not read those Hundred Novels of Boccaccio, lately done from the Italian into French. These did King Francis, first of his name, his Highness the Dauphin, the Princess his wife, and my lady Margaret of Navarre, esteem at such a price that if old Boccaccio could have heard them from the place where he is, he would have been, through the praises of such mighty folk, well-nigh brought to life again. And I hear that these two illustrious ladies have determined to make likewise a Decameron, but yet in one thing they will have it different from Boccaccio's—namely, every history therein contained shall be the truth. And their intent was that they, and his Highness with them, should each make ten stories, and afterwards should bring together ten persons whom they rated as most capable of telling them; but they would have no schoolmen or practised men of books, for his Highness must have nature and not art, and was in fear lest the truth of the histories might fare badly through odd-becoming tricks of rhetoric. But divers high affairs of state, as the peace between the King and the King of England, the bringing to bed of the Princess, and other matters of great consideration, have given all this scheme to forgetfulness at court; but by reason of the long delay we shall be able to accomplish it by the ten days in which the bridge is to be brought to a completion. And if it please you, every day from noon to four o'clock we will go to that pleasant meadow that is stretched along the Gave, where so thickly do the trees grow that the sun cannot pierce them through with his heat. There, seated at our ease, let each of us tell some story that he has either seen with his eyes or heard from the lips of a faithful witness. At the end of ten days we shall have summed up the hundred, and if God grants that our relations be pleasing to those lords and ladies aforesaid, we will lay them at their feet on our return from this journey in place of images or paternosters, to which I am assured they will be greatly preferred. Yet if any of you shall bring out a more pleasant pastime than this, to him I will give my vote." But all the company replied with one voice that than this there

could be nothing better, and that they were weary for the
morning to come, whereon to make a beginning of it.

So was this day joyously passed, one telling to another such
notable things as he had seen in his life.   But as soon as the
morning was come, they went to the room of Oisille, whom
they found at her prayers.   And when for a full hour they
had attended to her reading, and after this had devoutly heard
mass, they went to dinner, it being now ten o'clock.   And at
noon they failed not, according to what had been determined,
to go to the meadow, which was of such a sort that it would
need Boccaccio himself to tell the pleasantness of it; but be
you contented and know surely that never was there meadow
to vie with it.   And when all this company was seated in
order on the grass, that was so fine and soft that no need was
there of rugs or carpeting, Simontault began to say, "Who
shall be the one to rule over us?"   To whom Hircan:
"Since you were the first to speak, it is fitting that you bear
rule, for in the game we are all equal."   "God knows," said
Simontault, "that I would desire no bliss in the world so much
as to bear rule over this company."   This speech of his
Parlamente understood so well that she was fain to cough that
Hircan might not perceive the colour that came on to her
cheeks; but she presently told Simontault to begin; and this
he did.

DAY THE FIRST.

IN WHICH DAY ARE RECOUNTED THE BAD TURNS DONE BY WOMEN TO MEN,
AND BY MEN TO WOMEN.

NOVEL I.

The misdeeds of the wife of a certain proctor, who had a bishop for her gallant.

Fair ladies, I have had such a poor reward for all my long
service that, to avenge me on Love, and her whose heart is so
hard toward me, I am about to recount to you the misdeeds
done of women on us poor men; and I will tell you nothing
but the whole truth.

In the town of Alençon, in the time of the last Duke
Charles, there was a proctor named St. Aignan, who had for
wife a gentlewoman of the country. And she, having more
beauty than virtue, and being of a fickle disposition, was
courted by the Bishop of Séez, who, to gain his ends, handled
the husband in such fashion that he not only did not perceive
the wickedness of the Bishop, but did even forget the love he
had for his master and mistress, and at last had dealings with
wizards, that thereby he might compass the death of the
duchess. For a long while did the Bishop have dalliance with
this evil woman, who received him not for the love she bore
him, but because her husband, being greedy of money, so
charged her. But her love she gave to a young man of
Alençon, son of the lieutenant-general, and him she loved to
madness; often obtaining of the Bishop to send her husband
away, that she might see Du Mesnil, the son of the lieutenant,
at her ease. And this fashion of life lasted a long while, she
having the Bishop for profit, and Du Mesnil for pleasure, for
she told the last that all the pleasaunce she did to the Bishop
was but for his sake, and that from her the Bishop only got
words, and he might rest assured that no man beside himself
got aught else.

One day when her husband had to go on some charges of
the Bishop, she asked him to let her go into the country,
saying that the town air was hurtful to her; and having got to

her farmstead, she straightway wrote to Du Mesnil, enjoining him not to fail in coming to her at nine in the evening. This the poor gallant did; but at the porch he found the maid who was wont to let him in, who thus addressed him: "Go farther, friend, for here your place is taken." And he, thinking the proctor was come, asked her how they fared. The serving-maid, having pity on him, for that he loved so much, and was so little loved in return, and seeing, moreover, that he was comely, young, and of an honourable address, showed to him the frailty of her mistress, believing that when he heard this the flame of his love would be somewhat quenched. And she told him how the Bishop Séez was hardly come, and was now in bed with her mistress, though it was appointed that he should not come till the morrow; but having kept the proctor at his palace, he had stole away by night to privily visit her. Who then was in despair but Du Mesnil; yet scarcely could he believe the tale, and hid himself in a house hard by, where, remaining till three hours after midnight, he then saw the Bishop come out, not so well disguised as not to be more easily recognized than he desired.

And in this despair he made his way back to Alençon, whither this evil woman having returned, she came to speak to him, and would fain have fooled him in her old fashion. But he told her that she was too good, since she had touched holy things, to speak to a poor sinner like himself, whose repentance, nevertheless, was so great that he hoped ere long his sin would be forgiven. So when she perceived that her case was known to him, and that excuses, oaths, and promises availed nothing, she made complaint of him to her Bishop. And after having well pondered the matter with him, this woman came to her husband and told him that she could no longer live in Alençon, since the son of the lieutenant, whom he had accounted for a friend, did incessantly lay assault to her honour, wherefore she entreated him to take her to Argentan, to do away with all suspicion. To this her husband, who let himself be ruled by her, agreed. But they had been but a short while at Argentan when this evil one sent to Du Mesnil, saying that of all men in the world he was most wicked, and that she was well advised of his publicly speaking ill of her and the Bishop of Séez, for which she would labour to call him to account.

The young man, who had spoken to her alone on the matter, yet fearing to get into disfavour with the Bishop, went forthwith to Argentan with two of his servants, and found his mistress at evensong at the Jacobins. He, kneeling by her side, spoke thus : " Mistress, I am come to this place to swear to you before God that I have spoken against your honour to no one save you yourself; and so evilly have you entreated me that what I told you was not the half of what you deserved. And if there be man or woman who will say that I have so spoken, here am I to give them the lie before your face." She, seeing that much folk were in the church, and that he had for companions two stout serving-men, constrained herself to speak to him in the most gracious sort she could, saying she made no manner of doubt but that he spoke the truth, and that she esteemed him too honourable to speak evil of any man, much less of her who had for him so great a love ; but some tales had got to her husband's ears, on which account she would have him make declaration before her husband, that he had not told them, and believed them not at all. This he freely granted, and thinking to accompany her home, he would have taken her by the arm, but she told him that it would not be well for him to come with her, since her husband might suppose she had put the words into his mouth. And taking one of his servants by the sleeve of his doublet, she said, " Leave this man with me, and when it is time I will presently send him for you, but meanwhile do you go and rest in your lodging." And he, who knew not that she conspired against him, did as he was ordered.

To the servant she had taken with her, she gave supper, and when he often asked her if it was not time to look for his master, she told him that it would shortly come. And when night had fallen she privily sent one of her own serving-men to seek Du Mesnil, who, not knowing the evil that was to befall him, went with bold face to the house of the aforesaid St. Aignan, where his mistress still kept his servant, so that he had only one with him. And when he came to the door of the house, the man who had brought him told him the lady wished much to speak with him before he came into the presence of her husband, and that she awaited him in a room with only his own servant with her, and that he would do well to send the other

to the door in front. This he did, and whilst he was going
up a small and gloomy stair, the proctor, who had laid an
ambush in a closet, hearing the noise of his steps, called out,
"What is that?" And they told him that it was a man
privily endeavouring to enter his house. Whereupon a fellow
called Thomas Guerin, an assassin by trade, who to this intent
had been hired by St. Aignan, rushed forth and dealt the
young man such blows with his sword that, for all the defence
he might make, he fell dead between their hands. His servant
who was with the lady said to her, "I hear my master talking
on the stairs, and will go to him." But she held him back,
saying, "Be not troubled, he will shortly be here." And a
little after, hearing these words in his master's voice, "I am
gone, and may God receive my soul," he would fain have
succoured him. But she held him back, saying, "Be not
troubled, my husband does but chastise him for these follies of
his youth; come, let us go and see what is being done." And
leaning against the balustrade of the stairs, she asked of her
husband, "Is it finished?" · And he said to her, "Come and
see, for in this hour I have avenged you on him who has done
you so much shame." So saying he gave with his dagger ten or
twelve strokes into the body of him whom, when alive, he
durst not have encountered.

     After that the murder was done, and the two servants had
fled to carry the news to the poor father, the aforesaid St.
Aignan considered how the thing might best be kept secret,
and perceived that the two servants could not be admitted to
bear witness, and that none in his house had seen it done, save
the murderers, an old serving-woman, and a young girl of
fifteen. The old woman he was fain privily to put away, but
she, finding means to escape, took refuge in the liberties of the
Jacobins. And her witness was the best on the matter of the
murder. The young girl stayed some days in his house, but
he, having caused one of the murderers to bribe her, put her
in a stew in Paris, to the end that her witness might not be
received. And, better to hide the murder, he had the body of
the dead man burnt; and the bones which the fire had not
consumed he made mingle with the mortar that was being used
in building. This done he sent with great speed to court to
ask for pardon, letting it be understood that he had many times

forbidden a man whom he suspected to enter his house. And this man, who would have dishonoured his wife notwithstanding that he was forbidden, had come secretly by night to speak to her, wherefore having found him at the door of her room, and wrath casting out reason, he had slain him. But for all his haste he was not able to dispatch this letter to the chancellor's before the Duke and Duchess, who had been advised of what had taken place by the father of the murdered man, likewise sent to the chancellor, that pardon might not be granted him. This wretch, seeing that he could not obtain pardon, fled beyond seas to England, and his wife with him, and many of his kinsfolk. Yet before he set out, he made known to the murderer who had dealt the blow that he had seen express letters from the King, to take him and put him to death. And since, in return for the service he had done him he would gladly save his life, he gave him ten crowns for him to fly the realm. This he did, and has not been found to this day. This murder was so confirmed by the servants of the dead man, by the old woman who had fled to the Jacobins, and by the bones which were found in the mortar, that the case was begun and brought to an end in the absence of St. Aignan and his wife. Judgment went by default, they were condemned to death, to pay fifteen hundred crowns to the father of the murdered man, and the rest of their goods were escheated to the crown. St. Aignan, seeing that though he was living in England, in France the law accounted him dead, accomplished so much by his services to some great lords, and by the favour of the kinsfolk of his wife, that the King of England entreated the King of France to grant him a free pardon, and to restore to him his goods and his offices. But the King of France being assured of the enormity of his crime, sent the case to the King of England, asking him if such a deed deserved pardon, and saying that to the Duke of Alençon alone it pertained to grant pardon for offences done in his duchy. But for all these excuses he could not satify the King of England, who so earnestly entreated him that at last the proctor gained what he desired and returned to his home. And there, to fill up the measure of his wickedness, he called to him a wizard, named Gallery, hoping by this means to escape the paying of the fifteen hundred crowns to the father of the dead man.

And to this end, he and his wife with him, went up to Paris in disguise. And she, perceiving him closeted for a long while with the enchanter Gallery, and not being told the reason of this, on one morning played the spy and saw Gallery showing to him five wooden images, of which three had their hands hanging down, and of the two others the hands were raised. And she heard the wizard : " We must have images made of wax like these, and they that have the hands drooping shall be made in the likeness of those that are to die, but they that have the hands uplifted shall be made in the likeness of those whose love and favour we desire." To whom the proctor : " This one shall be for the King whose grace I would gain, and this for my Lord Brinon, the chancellor of Alençon." And Gallery said to him, " We must lay these images beneath the altar, where they may hear mass, together with the words that you shall presently say after me." And speaking of them that had the drooping arms, the proctor said that one should be Master Gilles du Mesnil, father of him who was murdered, for he knew well that as long as he was alive he would not cease from pursuing him. And another, that was made in the likeness of a woman, should be for my lady the Duchess of Alençon, the sister of the King ; since so well did she love Du Mesnil, her old servant, and had so great a knowledge of the proctor's wickedness in other matters, that unless she died, he could not live. And the last image, that was also made in the likeness of a woman, should be his wife, since she was the beginning of all his evil hap, and he knew well that she would never amend the wickedness of her ways. But when this wife of his, who saw through a chink in the door all that was done, heard that she was numbered among the dead, it was her humour to send her husband on before her. And pretending to go and borrow money of an uncle of hers, named Neaufle, Master of Requests to the Duke of Alençon, she told him of her husband, and all that she had seen and heard him do. This Neaufle aforesaid, like a good old servant, went forthwith to the chancellor of the Duchy of Alençon, and showed him the whole of the matter. And since the Duke and Duchess chanced not to be at court on that day, the chancellor went and told this strange case to the Regent, mother of the King and of the Duchess, who straightway sought out La Barre, Provost és١

Paris; and such good diligence did he make that he clapped
up the proctor and his wizard Gallery, who confessed freely
the crime, without being put to the question, or in any way
constrained. And the matter of their accusation was made
out and brought to the King, whereupon some, willing to save
the lives of these men, would fain persuade him that by their
enchantments they sought nothing but his grace. But the
King, being as tender of his sister's life as of his own,
commanded that sentence should be given as if they had
attempted his own peculiar person. Nevertheless, the Duchess
of Alençon made entreaty for the life of this proctor, and
for the doom of death to be changed to some other punish
ment. So this was granted her, and the proctor, together
with the wizard, were sent to the galleys of St. Blancart
at Marseilles, where they ended their days in close imprisonment, having time wherein to consider their sins, how great
they had been. And the wife, when her husband was
removed, sinned more wickedly than before, and so died
miserably.

"I entreat you, ladies, consider well the evil that cometh of
a wicked woman, and how many mishaps proceeded from the
sin of this one I have told you of. You will find that from the
time Eve made Adam to sin, all women have been for the
torturing, killing, and damnation of men. As for me, such an
experience have I of their cruelty that I am well assured that
when I meet with death and damnation, it will be through
despair of her whom I love. Yet so besotted am I, that I
must needs confess that this hell delights me more coming
from her hand than would heaven from the hand of another."
Parlamente, feigning not to understand that it was of her that
he made this discourse, said to him: "Since this hell of yours
is as pleasant as you say, it skills not to fear the devil who sends
it." But wrathfully he replied to her: "If my devil should
become visible as black as it has made me unhappy, this company would be struck with as great fear as my delight is in
regarding it, but the fire of my love makes me to forget the
fire of my hell. So to speak no more of this matter, I will give
my vote to Mistress Oisille to tell the second novel, and sure
am I, that if she would tell that she knows of women, she
would be of my opinion." Instantly the company turned

c

toward her, praying her to make a beginning. To this she
agreed, and smiling began thus :

"It seems to me, ladies, that he who has given his vote to
me has made such an ill report of women by this true story of
a woman who was exceedingly wicked, that I shall have to call
to mind all these old years of mine, to find one woman whose
virtue shall give the lie to his judgment. And since there is
come into my mind the recollection of a woman well worthy of
being had in everlasting remembrance, I will tell you her
history."

NOVEL II.

The wife of a muleteer had rather death than dishonour.

In the town of Amboise there was a muleteer who served
the Queen of Navarre, sister to Francis the First. And she
being at Blois brought to bed of a son, this muleteer went
thither to be paid such monies as were owing to him, and his
wife stayed at Amboise, being lodged in a house beyond the
bridge. Now there was a servant of her husband who had
for a long while loved her so greatly, that one day he must
needs speak his mind to her. But she, being a woman of true
virtuousness, so sharply reproved him, threatening that he
should be beaten and sent away, that never after did he dare
to address her. But he secretly kept the fire of lust in his
heart, until one day when his master was abroad, and his
mistress at evensong in the castle church of St. Florentin, no
short distance from her house. So, since she was living alone,
he conceived the humour of taking by force that which he
could obtain by none of his prayers or good offices, to which
end he broke the boards that were between his room and that
of his mistress. And this was not perceived when she, having
with her a wench of eleven or twelve years, came to bed, by
reason of the curtains that were hung by the master's bed on
one side, and the servant's on the other. And when the poor
woman was in her first sleep, the fellow came in by the hole
he had made, clad only in his shirt, and with a drawn sword in
his hand. But as soon as she was aware of his being in the
bed with her, she leapt forth from thence, and implored him in
such wise as an honourable woman would. And he, whose

love was but beastly lust, better able to understand the noise
of his mules than fair conclusions, showed himself more brutal
than the brutes he had a long while tended; for seeing that so
swiftly did she chase round a table that he could not take her,
and that she had twice escaped from his very hands, he de-
spaired of being able to rape her alive, and so gave her a
shrewd stroke in the reins, thinking that pain would make her
do what fear could not.   Yet it had a contrary effect, for like
a good soldier who, when he sees his blood flowing, is stirred
up all the more to be avenged on his enemies, and gain for
himself glory, so her chaste heart made her fly yet more
swiftly from the hands of this wretch, making still more earnest
entreaty to him, if haply he might see the wickedness of his
purpose.   But in such furious case was he, that to nothing of
this would he give ear, and aimed at her more and more blows,
to avoid which she still kept running as fast as she was able.
And when, by reason of loss of blood, she felt death to be
near at hand, she raised her eyes to heaven, and with clasped
hands gave thanks to God, calling upon him as her strength,
her virtuousness, her long-suffering, and her purity; beseech-
ing him to favourably accept that blood of hers which she had
poured forth for the sake of his Son, by whom she steadfastly
believed all her sins were blotted out from his sight.   And
saying : "Lord receive my soul, which by thy loving kindness
hath been redeemed," she fell on her face to the floor, where
the wretch gave her several strokes, and her tongue having
lost speech and her body strength, he took that from her which
she was no more able to defend against him.

And when he had appeased his evil lust, he fled forth in
such hot haste that all pursuit was of no avail, for he was never
found.   The young wench who had been sleeping with the
muleteer's wife had, for the fear she was in, hidden under the
bed, but when she saw that the man was departed, she went
to her mistress, and finding in her no speech or movement,
called from the window to the neighbours to bring help. They,
holding her in as good love and repute as any woman in the
town, came presently to her, bringing with them chirurgeons,
who made out that she had on her body five-and-twenty mortal
wounds.   All the aid they could give her was of no avail, and
yet for more than an hour she languished on, showing by the

signs she made with her eyes and hands, that she knew what was passing. Being asked by the parson in what faith she died, she gave answer by signs as plain as words, that she put the hope of her salvation in Jesus only; and so with glad countenance, and eyes lifted up to heaven, she gave up her soul and body to the Creator. And when she was being taken out for burial, the company thereto appointed attending, her poor husband came up, and saw the body of his wife in front of his house before tidings had been brought to him that she was dead. And the manner of her death being reported to him, he had then a double cause for lamentation, which he made in such grievous sort that he was well-nigh amort. So was this martyr of chastity buried in the church of St. Florentin, and at the burial of her all the honourable women of the town failed not to do her honour by their presence; thinking it no small thing to live in a place which had contained so virtuous a woman. And moreover, such women as were queans determined to live henceforth in amendment of life.

"Behold then, ladies, a true relation, by the consideration of which we should be enabled to guard yet more straitly this excellent virtue of chastity. And we, being of gentle blood, should die with shame on feeling in our hearts that worldly lust, to avoid which the wife of a poor muleteer did not shrink from a cruel death. And let not any one esteem herself a virtuous woman who has not like this one resisted unto death. Wherefore we must humble ourselves, for God giveth not his grace to men for that they are of gentle blood and have great riches, but only according to his good will. For he is no regarder of persons, but chooseth whom he will, and him, whom he hath chosen, he filleth with all goodness. And often he chooseth the lowly, that he may confound those that are in great esteem with this world, according as it is written, 'Let us not rejoice for our merits, but rather that our names are written in the book of life.'"

Not one lady was there in that company who did not weep for the pitiful and glorious death of this woman; each one resolving within herself that, if like case were to come to her, she would strive likewise to gain martyrdom. And Oisille, seeing that time was being lost by their praises of the dead woman, said to Saffredent: "Unless you can devise some pleasant tale to make the company laugh, they will not, I think, forgive me for making them weep. Wherefore I give my vote to you to tell the third novel."

Saffredent, who heartily desired to make some pleasant relation that might please them all, and particularly one of the ladies, said that this right did not belong to him, seeing that there were others who had seen more and could tell more than he; yet as the lot had fallen on him, the sooner it was fulfilled the better, for the more good speakers that came before him, the worse would his story be found when it was told.

NOVEL III.

Of a lustful King of Naples, and how he met with his match.

Since, ladies, I have ofttimes desired to be a fellow in good-luck with him of whom I am about to tell you, I will declare to you that in the town of Naples, in the time of King Alfonso, to whom lust was as the sceptre of his kingdom, there lived a young gentleman of such honourable character and so fine an address, that for these merits of his an aged widow gave him her daughter to wife. And she yielded in nowise to her husband in beauty and graciousness, and there was great love betwixt these two. But on a day in Carnival time, the King, as his custom was, went masked about the different houses, each one striving to make for him the best fare and welcome. And when he came to the house of this gentleman aforesaid, he was received after a better fashion than anywhere else; so fine were the sweetmeats, so admirable the singing, and above all, the bravest lady the King had ever set eyes on. And she, at the end of the entertainment, sang a song with her husband in such sort that it did but increase her beauty. And he, beholding in that body of hers so many perfections, did not set such store on the good accord between her and her husband as not to ponder how he might best break it; but the difficulty lay in the great love that he perceived they bore one another, wherefore he kept this passion of his as secret as he was able. But in some way to ease it he gave many entertainments to all the lords and ladies of Naples, and at these the gentleman and his wife were by no means forgotten. · And since a man believes what he desires, it appeared to him that this lady's eyes promised well for him, if it were not that her husband was present. So to try how he stood with her, he sent the husband on some charges of his to Rome, so that he might be away fifteen days or three weeks. No sooner was he gone than his wife, who had never before been without him, was filled with great grief, in which she was so comforted by the sweet remonstrances and gifts of the King, that not only was she consoled for her husband, but more than this was well content to live without him. And before the three weeks were come to an end she was grown so amorous of the King, the thought of her husband's return gave her as much discontent as before did his departure. And so, as not to be altogether shut out from the presence of the King, they agreed together that when the gentleman went a-hunting to his country house, she should advise the King of it, so that he might safely come and see her, and so privily that her repute, of which she was more tender than her conscience, should take no hurt.

In this contentment the lady kept herself, and her husband being returned she received him in such sort that, though he had been told that while he was away the King had had to do with her, he would not have believed it. But as time went on, that fire which so hardly can be concealed began to show itself, and in such fashion that her husband began to suspect her for a strumpet, and keeping close watch, was well nigh assured of it. But for the fear he had that he who had done him this great harm might, if he showed any suspicion, do him a worse, he determined to dissemble, thinking secret grief better than to make hazard of his life for a woman who loved him not. All the same, in the dolour of his heart, he was fain, if it might be, to cry quits with the King, and knowing that women, and notably those of noble mind, are more easily to be moved by grief than love, he made free one day, in speaking to the Queen, to tell her it was a mighty pity she was not better beloved of the King. The Queen, who had heard about the King and his wife, said to him: "One may not have both honour and pleasure at once. I am well advised that I have the honour, and another the pleasure, but she who has the pleasure has not the honour that appertains to me." He, understanding well to what intent these words were spoken, replied to her: "My lady, with you honour is inbred, for you come of such gentle blood that no title, be it Queen or Empress, can increase your nobility; yet your beauteousness and gracious ways so well deserve that you should likewise enjoy pleasure, that she who has robbed you of it hath done more ill to herself than you, since for a glory which is in truth her shame, she misses as much delight as you or any woman in the realm could desire. And I dare swear that, if the King's crown was fallen off his head, he could satisfy a lady no better than myself; and sure am I that if he would satisfy such an one as you, he would do well to change his complexion for mine." Laughing, the Queen replied to him: "Though the King be of more delicate complexion than you, yet I am so well satisfied with the love he bears me that I prefer it to any other." Then said the gentleman: "My lady, if it were indeed so, you would by no means move my pity, for I know well that the honourable love of your heart would content you, if there were in the King an equal love toward you; but God has wisely taken this from you, so that not finding in him that which you desire, you may not make him your god on earth." "I confess to you," said the Queen, "that the love I bear the King is of such sort, that in no heart but mine can love be found like to it." "Pardon me," said the gentleman to her, "you have not sounded the depths of all men's hearts, for I say unto you there is one who hath toward you a love so great that your love for your husband beside it would show as nothing. And as he beholds the King's love failing you, his own grows and increases in such a fashion that, were it your pleasure, you would be paid in full for all your griefs."

The Queen began, as much from his words as from his countenance, to perceive that what he said was from the depths of his heart; and it came into her mind that he had longwhile striven to do her service, so that he was become sad and melancholic. And this she had thought to be by reason of his wife, but she was now well assured that it was for love of herself. And so love, that when it is not feigned is quickly to be discovered, let her know for certain that which had been concealed from all men. And looking upon the gentleman that he was by far more worthy of love than her husband, and seeing that he was forsaken of his wife as she was of the King, hard pressed by grief

and jealousy of her husband, and by her love for the gentleman, she began to sigh forth with tears in her eyes : " My
God, can it be that for vengeance' sake I shall grant that which
no love could win from me." The gentleman, understanding
well the intent of what she said, replied : " Vengeance is sweet,
and sweeter when it slayeth not an enemy, but giveth life to a
true friend. I think that the time is come for you to put
away that foolish love for one who regardeth you not ; and a
true and reasonable love shall drive from your heart all fear,
which never is able to dwell in a virtuous and noble soul. Let
us lay aside the grandeur of your estate, and see in ourselves
the man and woman who of all the world are most deceived,
betrayed, and mocked of those whom they loved with a perfect
love. Let us be avenged, not so much to give to our enemies
their deserts, as to satisfy that love which, for my part, I
cannot longer keep contained and live. And I think, if your
heart be not harder than rock or adamant, you must feel within
you some spark of that fire which I can no more keep concealed. And if pity for me, who am a-dying for love of you,
do not stir in you some love for me, natheless love of yourself
should do so. For so perfect are you, that you are well
worthy of the love of every honest heart, yet you are contemptuously entreated and abandoned by him for whose sake you
despised all others."

The Queen hearing these words was so confounded that,
for fear of showing by her face the trouble at her heart, she
took the gentleman's arm and went forth into a pleasaunce that
was nigh her chamber, where for a long while she walked up
and down without speaking a word to him. But the gentleman, seeing her to be half-won, when they reached the bottom
of the alley where none could see them, made declaration of his
love in a very effective sort of way, and finding themselves both
at one on this matter, they played their mystery of *Vengeance*,
and liked it better than the mystery of the *Passion*. And
there it was agreed and determined that, whenever the King
should be at the gentleman's house with his wife, he should be
at the palace with the Queen ; so the cozeners being cozened,
they would all four have a piece of that cake which two thought
to keep to themselves. This treaty executed, they gat them
back, the lady to her room and the gentleman to his house, each

with such a good satisfaction for what they had done that all old griefs were forgotten. And the mislike which they both had aforetime to the King's going to see the lady was turned to a good liking thereat, insomuch that the gentleman went more than his habit had been to his house in the country, which was distant about half-a-league. And as soon as the King was advised of his going away he straightway would go off to the lady; and the gentleman, when night was come, would go to the palace and enjoy the easements of the King's deputy with the Queen. And all this done so privily that none knew of it. Which going on some time, the King being of public estate, could not well contrive to conceal his share in the matter, and all the world was aware of it, and mighty compassionate toward the poor gentleman, so much so as to make horns of derision at him behind his back, which he saw very plainly. But, such was his humour, he took more delight in these horns of his than the King's crown; and the King one day seeing a stag's head in the gentleman's house, did himself take occasion to say, with a laugh, that the stag's head was very well placed. So the gentleman, who had as sharp a wit as the King's, made write beneath the head in this wise:

> "These horns I wear, and plainly show it,
> But one doth wear them and not know it."

And the King, when he came next to the house, inquired of the gentleman what was the intent of this, to whom he replied: "If the secret of the King be hidden from the stag, it is not fitting that the secret of the stag should be revealed to the King; but be content to know that not all they that wear horns have their hats lifted off thereby, for some are so soft, that they would distress no one, and he carries them best who knows not that he has them." The King easily perceived by these words that the gentleman knew of what passed between him and his wife, but not a tittle did he suspect him and the Queen, for the better that she liked the life the King led the more she pretended to the contrary. So for a long time they all lived in this fashion, till old age took order with them.

"See, ladies, this relation, in which I freely show you how, when your husbands give you buck's horns, you may give them hart's." . Ennasiutte began to laugh, and say: "Saffre-dent, I am well assured that if you loved as you did afore, you would bear to carry horns as high as oaks, if you might vent your passion; but now those hairs of yours are whitening, it is time for your desires to call a truce." "Fair mistress," said Saffredent, "although she whom I love hath taken from me every hope, and age hath weakened my strength, yet as great as ever is my goodwill. But since you have reproved me for this my honourable desire, I give my vote to you to tell the fourth novel, that we may see if you can draw any example therefrom wherewith to refute me." And during this dis-course a lady of the company must needs laugh, for she knew that the one who took the words of Saffredent to herself, was not in such wise beloved of him, that he should bear for her sake horns, or shame, or anything else. And Saffredent per-ceiving the lady laughing understood, and was content, and so let Ennasiutte talk as she would, and she thus began:

"Ladies, to the intent that Saffredent and this company may know that all women are not like to the Queen of his story, and that those who are ready to risk all, do not in every case gain all, and moreover that I may declare the judgment of a certain lady, who esteemed the grief of failure in love harder to bear than death itself, I will tell you this history, in which you will find no names, since it is so fresh in recollection that I should fear to displease some of those very near akin."

NOVEL IV.

Of a young man who attempted the honour of a princess, and the poor success of his adventure.

There was in the land of Flanders a lady of a most illustrious house, who had been twice married and was now a widow without any children. In the time of her widowhood she lived retired with her brother, who was a great lord, and married to a daughter of the King, and this brother loved his sister exceedingly. Now this prince was a man some-what enslaved to pleasure, having great delight in hunting, games, and women, as his youth led him, but having to wife one of a peevish disposition, to whom none of her husband's

contentments were pleasing, he would always have his sister
with him, for she was of a most joyous nature, and a good and
honourable woman withal.   And there was in the house of
this prince a gentleman whose beauty and grace did far surpass
that of his fellows ; and he beholding the sister of his master
that she was joyous and always ready for a laugh, thought that
he would assay how the offer of an honourable love would be
taken by her.   But her reply was by no means favourable to
him ; yet though it was such as became a princess and a
woman of honour, she, seeing him to be a handsome man and
of good address, easily pardoned to him his great boldness in speaking to her after such a fashion.   And moreover
she assured him that she bore him no displeasure for what he had
said, but charged him from henceforth to let her have no more
of it.   This he promised, that he might not lose the delight he
had in her company, but as time went on his love grew even
more and more, so that he forgot the promise he had given.
Not that he made a second trial of what words could do, for
he had found out the manner of her replies ; but he thought
that since she was a widow, young, lusty, and of a pleasant
humour, she might perchance, if he came upon her in a fitting
place, take compassion on him and her own flesh.

To which end, he said to his master that hard by his
house there was most excellent hunting, and that if in Maytime
he would be pleased to come and chase the stags, he could
promise him as good contentment as he could desire. The prince,
as much for the love he bore him as for his delight in hunting, granted his request, and going to his house found it most
bravely ordered, and as good as that of the greatest lord in the
land.   And the gentleman lodged his lord and lady on one
side, and opposite to them he appointed a room for her whom
he loved better than himself.   And so bravely was this room
decked out with tapestry above and matting below, that no
one could discover a trap-door contrived in the wall by the bed,
which led to where his mother was lodged.   And she, being
an old dame with an obstinate rheum, and troubled with a cough,
had made an exchange of chambers with her son, so as not to
annoy the princess.   And before curfew-time in the evening
this good lady would carry sweetmeats to the princess for her
supper, in which service she was assisted by her son, since

being well-beloved of the prince, it was not refused to him to be present at her *levee* and *couchee*, at which times he got fresh fuel for the fire that was in him.   And so late one night did he tarry there that she was well nigh asleep before he left her for his own room.   And having put on him the finest and best scented shirt he had, and a night-cap of surpassing device, he was well persuaded, on looking himself over, that there was not a lady in the world hard enough to refuse a man of such a grace and beauty.   Wherefore, promising to himself a good issue of his adventure, he lay down on his bed, hoping not to make thereon a long stay, but to change it for one more pleasant and honourable.   And as soon as he had dismissed his servants he got up and shut the door behind them, and afterwards listened for a long while if he should hear any noise in the room of the princess.   So when he was satisfied that all was quiet, he was fain to begin his pleasant travail, and little by little let down the trap-door, which, so well was it carpeted over, did not make so much as the least noise.   And so he got into the room by the bed of the princess, who was now asleep.   And straightway, heeding not the duty he owed her or the house from which she came, without with your leave, or by your leave, he got into bed with her, who felt herself in his arms, before she knew he was in the room. But she, being strong, got from between his hands, and having required of him who he was, fell to beating, biting, and scratching with such hearty good will that, for fear of her calling out, he would have stopped her mouth with the blanket; but in this he was foiled, since the princess, seeing that he spared none of his resources to rob her of her honour, spared none of hers to defend it. So she called at the top of her voice to her maid of honour, an ancient and prudent dame, who slept with her, and she, clad only in her nightgear, ran to the help of her mistress.

And when the gentleman saw he was discovered, so great a fear had he of being recognised, that as fast as might be he departed by his trap-door; and in like degree, as he had been desirous and well assured of a good reception when he was going, so now did he despair as he went back in such evil case. He found his mirror and candle upon the table, and beholding his countenance, that it was all bloody from the bites and scratches she had dealt him, he began to say: "Beauty! thou hast received a wage according to thy deserving; for by thine idle promise I attempted an impossible thing, and which, moreover, in place of increasing my happiness, hath made my sorrow greater than it was before; since I am well assured that if she knew that I, against my solemn undertaking, had done this foolish thing, I should be cut off from that close and honourable commerce I aforetime had with her. And this I shall have well deserved, for to make my beauty and grace avail me anything, I should not have hidden them in the darkness; I should not have attempted to carry that chaste body by assault; but striven to gain her favour, till by patience and long service my love had gained the victory; for without love all the power and might of men are as nothing."

So, in such wise that I cannot tell, passed the night in tears, and regrets, and griefs; and in the morning, so torn was his face, that he made pretence of great sickness, saying that he could not bear the light, even until the company was departed.

The lady who had come off conqueror knew that there was none other in the prince's court who durst set about such an enterprise save her host, who had already had the boldness to make a declaration of love to her. So she, with her maid of honour, made search around her chamber to find how he could have made an entry. And not being able to find any place or trace thereof, she said to her companion in great wrath : " Be assured that it was none other than the lord of the house, and in such sort will I handle him on the morrow with my brother, that his head shall bear witness to my chastity." The maid of honour, seeing her so angered, said to her : "My lady, I am well pleased at the price you set on your honour, since the more to exalt it you would make sacrifice of the life of one who, for his love of you, has put it to this risk. But in this way one ofttimes lessens what one would fain increase. Wherefore, my lady, I do entreat you to tell me the whole truth of this matter." And when the princess had made a full account of the business, the maid of honour said to her : " Do you verily assure me that he had nothing from you but only scratches and fisticuffs?" "I do assure you," said the lady, " and if he find not a rare mediciner, I am much mistaken if to-morrow his face do not bear evident witness to what I say." "Well, my

lady," said the maid of honour, "if it be as you say, it seems
to me that you have rather occasion to thank God than to
imagine vengeance; for you may conceive that since this
gentleman had a heart daring enough to attempt such a deed,
you can award to him no punishment, nay, not death itself,
that will not be easier to bear than his dolour at having failed
therein.   If you are fain to be revenged on him, leave him to
his love and to his shame, and from them he will suffer more
shrewdly than at your hands; and if you have regard for your
honour, beware lest you fall into the same pit as he, for in
place of gaining the greatest delight he could desire, he is in
the most shameful case that may hap to a gentleman.   So you,
good mistress, thinking to exalt your honour, may haply bring
it to the dust; for if you make advertisement of this affair, you
will cause to be blazed abroad what no one would ever know,
since the gentleman, trust me, will throw but little light on the
matter.   And when my lord, your brother, shall do justice on
him at your asking, and the poor gentleman goes forth to die,
it will be noised abroad that he had his pleasure of you, and
men will say that it is not to be believed a man could make
such an attempt, if he had not before had of you some good
matter of contentment.   You are young and fair, living gaily
amongst all, and there is no soul at court who has not seen
your commerce with this man you have in suspicion, so all
will determine that if he finished the work you began it.   So
your honour, which hitherto hath been mightily extolled, will
become common matter of dispute wherever this story is
related."

The princess, considering the fair conclusions of the maid
of honour, perceived that she had spoken the truth, and that
with just cause would she be blamed, since both openly and
privily she had always given a good reception to the gentleman,
and so would have her woman tell her what was best to be
done. And she answered her: "Good mistress, since it is your
pleasure, seeing the love from whence they come, to give ear
to my counsels, I think that you should be glad at heart, for
that the bravest and most gallant gentleman I have ever seen
hath not been able to turn you from the path of true virtuousness.   And for this you should humble yourself before God,
confessing that it is not your own strength or virtue, for women

leading, beyond compare, straiter lives than you, have been
brought to the dust by men less worthy of love than he. And
henceforth, do you avoid proposals of love and the like, for
many that at the first got off scot-free, the second time have
fallen into the pit. Be mindful that Love is blind, and a causer
of blindness, for it makes believe the path is sure, when in
truth it is most slippery. And it is my mind that you should
give him no sign as to what has taken place, and if he say
anything on the matter, feign to understand him not, and so be
quit of two perils; the one of vainglory for your victory, the
other of recalling to mind things that are pleasant to the flesh,
ay, so pleasant are they that the chastest have much ado to
quench all sparks of that fire they are most fain to avoid. And
moreover, I counsel you, that he think not he hath done you
any sort of pleasure, that you do, by small degrees, put a close
to your intimacy with him, so he may perceive your misliking
to what he hath done, and yet understand that so great is your
goodness that you are content with the victory God hath given
you, and desire no farther vengeance. And may God grant
you to abide in your virtuousness of heart, and seeing that all
good things are from Him, may you love and serve Him in
better sort than afore." And the princess, determined to abide
by these conclusions, gave herself to a sleep as joyful as her
lover's wakefulness was sad.

And on the morrow, the prince being about to depart,
asked for his host, but they told him he was so sick as not to
endure the daylight, or to speak with any one, whereat the prince
was astonished and would have seen him, but being advised that
he slept, he went forth from the house without so much as
good-bye, and took with him his wife and sister. But she,
hearing the put-offs of the gentleman, and that he would see
neither the prince nor the company, was assured that he was
the man who had so troubled her, and would not show the
marks she had stamped upon his face. And though his master
ofttimes sent for him, he would by no means return to court
till he was healed of his wounds; save those indeed that love
and shame had made upon his heart. And when he did return,
and found himself before his victorious foe, he blushed; nay,
he who was most bold-faced of all the company, was in such
case that, often in her presence, he was struck dumb. At this,

being quite persuaded that her suspicion was truth, she by little and little severed herself from him, yet not by such slow degrees that he was not aware of it, but could say nothing lest he should fare worse, and patiently bore this punishment which he so well deserved.

"Consider, ladies, this relation; and let those who would gain what is not for them be warned by it. And hereby let ladies be of good heart, beholding the virtue of the young princess, and the wise counsels of her maid of honour. If like hap fall to any, let them seek herein the remedy." "It appears to me," said Hircan, "that the gentleman of whom you speak was of so poor a heart, that he is not worthy to be had in memory, since having such an opportunity, neither the young woman nor the old one should have foiled him in his desire. And it is very evident his heart was not altogether filled by love, since there dwelt in it beside the fear of death and shame." Nomerfide replied to this: "But what would you have the poor gallant do, with two women against him?" "He had done well to have slain the old dame," said Hircan; "and when the maid found herself alone, she would have been half won." "To have slain her!" said Nomerfide, "you would then turn a lover into a murderer. Since you are of this advice, one should indeed fear to fall into your hands." "If I had brought it to such a point," said Hircan, "I should hold myself dishonoured if I did not bring it to an end." Whereupon said Geburon : "Truly is this a strange thing and marvellous in your eyes that a princess, nourished in all honour, should make strong resistance to a single man? All the more then shall you be astonished to hear of a poor woman who escaped from the hands of two." "Geburon," said Ennasiutte, "I give my vote to you for the fifth novel, for I am assured you have that to tell of this woman that will not weary us." "Since the lot is fallen upon me," said Geburon, "I will tell you a story which I know to be true, for in the place it occurred I myself have made inquisition concerning it. And by it you shall conclude that not only in princesses may virtue be discovered, and that they of great reputation in love-craft are sometimes found wanting therein."

NOVEL V.

How two Grey Friars were by one poor woman left in the lurch.

In the harbour of Coulon, hard by Niort, there lived a boatwoman, who, by day and night, carried people across the ferry. And it came to pass that two Grey Friars of the aforesaid Niort were crossing over by themselves in her boat, whereupon, seeing that the passage is one of the longest in France, they began to crave love-dalliance, to which entreaties she gave the answer that became her. But they, who for all their journeying were not aweary, nor by reason of the water were acold, nor by her refusal ashamed, determined to have her by force, and if she made an outcry to throw her into the river. And she, whose wit was as good and sharp as their's was gross and evil, said to them : "I have not so hard a heart as I seem to have, but I entreat you to grant me two things, and then you shall perceive that I am readier to obey than you to command." So the two Grey Friars swore by St. Francis that she should ask nothing of them that they would not grant, so long as she did them the pleasure they desired. "In the first place then," said she, "I require of you that you advertise no man of this matter." This they promised with great willingness. "And in the second place," she went on, "that you have your pleasure of me by turns, for this would be too great shame to have to do with the one before the face of the other. Determine, then, which shall first enjoy me." This likewise they deemed a reasonable thing, and the younger of the two granted his companion the prerogative. So when they drew near a small island she said to the former : "Holy father, do you tell your beads and tarry here, while I am gone with your companion to yonder island, and if, when he returns, he gives a good account of me, we will leave him, and you and I will go apart together." The young friar leapt on to the island, and awaited there his comrade's return, whom the boatwoman took off to another island. And when they had come alongside, the woman, making pretence to fasten her boat to a tree, said to him : "Do you go, sweetheart, and look for a place where we may dispose ourselves." The holy man got on to the island and searched about for some nook fit for the

D

purpose; but no sooner did she see him on firm ground than
she pushed off, and made for open water, leaving these two
holy fathers to their deservings, for all the clamour they made
to her. "Wait patiently, good sirs," said she, "for an angel
to come and console you, for to-day you will have of me no
pleasaunce."

Then the two poor friars, finding they were tricked, fell
down on their knees at the edge of the water, praying her not
to entreat them thus shamefully, and promising that, if she
would fairly bring them to port, they would ask nothing more
of her. But, rowing the while, she called to them : "Truly I
should be a thoroughpaced fool if, after escaping from your
hands, I put myself between them again." And when she
had got to the village, she went to call her husband, and the
constables, that they might take these two wolves, from
whose teeth, by the grace of God, she had escaped. And so
brave a company was made up that none stayed in the village,
either great or small, that was fain to have a part in the
delight of this hunting. But when the poor friars saw such a
sort of people coming against them, they hid themselves, each
one in his island, like Adam when he saw that he was naked.
For shame put their sin plainly before their eyes, and the fear
of what would befall them had made them to tremble so that
they were well-nigh amort. But nevertheless they were taken
prisoners, with many a flout and jeer from the men and women.
For the first would say : "These good fathers preach chastity,
and straightway attempt our wives," and the second : "They
are sepulchres whited without, but within full of death and
rottenness." Then another would cry out : "The tree shall be
known by his fruits." You may well conceive that all the
pleas of the Gospel against hypocrites were brought out for
these poor prisoners, who were succoured by their warden; he
coming in hot haste to this intent, and assuring the men of law
that he would punish them in severer sort than if they had
laymen for their judges. And to satisfy all he promised the
friars should say as many masses as might be desired of them.
The civil magistrate granted the warden's desire, and he, being
an upright man, they were used by him in such fashion that
never after did they pass over a ferry without making the sign
of the cross, and recommending themselves to God.

" I entreat you, ladies, to consider, if this poor boatwoman had the wit to cozen these evil men, what should be due from them who have both read and seen so many noble examples, and before whose eyes is ever the goodness of virtuous ladies; so that indeed the virtue of ladies of gentle upbringing is not so much to be named virtue as habit? But these women that know nothing, who do not hear in the twelve months more than two sermons, who have no leisure to think of aught else but gaining their daily bread, and who, when hard pressed, keep such ward over their virtue; it is in these that one discovers true purity, indwelling in the heart; for when man's wit is smallest, God's work is greatest. Unhappy is the woman who keepeth not strict watch over this treasure, which, well guarded, is her glory, but otherwise is her shame." Longarine said to him: " Methinks, Geburon, it needs not such great virtue to refuse a Grey Friar, but rather I should esteem such an one impossible to be loved." "Longarine," replied Geburon, "they that are not accustomed to noble lovers do by no means despise a Grey Friar, for they are fine men enough, and lusty, and have a sweet repose about them which we lack; they can talk like angels, and press maids as hard as the devil; wherefore these women of the poorer sort, who are not used to silk and plush, should be held virtuous if they resist the grey robe." Then in a loud voice said Nomerfide: " Faith, you may say what you list, but I had rather be thrown into the water than lie with a Grey Friar." Laughing, Oisille said to her: " Are you, then, so good a swimmer?" This Nomerfide took in bad part, thinking that Oisille held her not in that repute she desired, wherefore wrathfully she answered: " There are they that have refused more personable men than Grey Friars, without so loudly blowing their horn." Oisille, smiling to see her in a rage, said to her: " And there are they that have not refused, but yet do not beat the drum over loudly." Then said Geburon: " I am well assured that Nomerfide has somewhat to say, wherefore I give my vote to her, that she may make for us some good relation." " What has been said," Nomerfide replied, "touches me so little, that it gives me neither joy nor grief. But, since I have your vote, I beseech you to listen to me, and I will show you that if one woman used craft to a good end, another used it for an evil end. And for that we have sworn to speak the truth, I will conceal nothing, for since the virtuousness of the boatwoman brings not honour to woman, if she follow not her ensample, so the vice of another cannot dishonour her, unless she be herself vicious. Wherefore, give ear."

NOVEL VI.
A woman's craftiness.

Charles, last Duke of Alençon, had about his person an old body-servant, who had lost one eye, and had to wife a woman far younger than himself. And forasmuch as his master and mistress loved him as well as any of their folk, he was not able so often to see his wife as he desired, whence it fell out that she so far forgot her honour as to fall in love with a young man, which affair was so noised abroad that her husband was advertised of it. But even thus, he was fain to give the tale no belief, for the notable signs of love that his wife showed to him. All the same, one day he thought to put the matter to the touch, and to avenge himself, if he were able, on her who had done him this great shame. And to this intent he feigned to go away from that place for the space of three or four days. No sooner had he started out than the wife sent for her lover, who had scarce been half an hour with her when they heard the husband knocking at the door. But his wife, well knowing who it was, consoled her sweetheart, since in such affright was he that he had rather have been shut up in his mother's womb, and cursed the love that had brought him to such a pass. But she told him to fear nothing, inasmuch as she would find some manner of conveying him away without open shame, and would have him put on his gear as quickly as might be. All this while the husband kept knocking at the door, and calling upon his wife at the top of his voice. But she feigned not to recognise it, and cried to the people of the house: " Wherefore do you not arise, and put to silence those who are making such a clamour at the door? Is this the hour to come to the houses of honest people? If my goodman were at home he would presently see to it." The husband, hearing the voice of his wife, still more loudly called to her: " Wife, open I say; would you have me tarry here till dawn?" And when she perceived her sweetheart was ready to go forth, she threw open the door, and said to her husband: "Dear husband, with what contentment do I behold your return, for I have dreamt a marvellous dream, and was filled with great joy, since it was that you had recovered the sight of your eye." And embracing and kissing him she took him by the head and closed with one hand his good eye, saying to him: "See you not better than you are wont?" And at that moment, while he saw not at all, she signed her sweetheart to get him gone. But though the husband saw nothing yet he suspected a good deal, and said to his wife: "Of a verity, wife, I will keep no more watch over you, for thinking to cozen you, I myself have experienced a mighty pretty piece of cozenage. May God mend you, for no man in the world can put a close to the wickedness of a woman, save he kill her outright. But seeing my kind entreating of you has availed nothing, perchance the scorn I shall henceforth think of you will be in some sort a punishment." So saying he went forth and left his wife a widow; but nevertheless, through the prayers and tears of herself and her friends, he at last returned to her.

"Herein, ladies, you may discover how subtile a thing is a woman to escape danger. And if, for the concealing of evil, her wit is so sharp to find some means, I believe that, to avoid evil or to do good, it would be yet sharper, since, as I have always heard, the minds of the good are more powerful than the minds of the evil." To this Hircan said: "Extol your craftiness as you will, but I think this of you, that if you had been in this woman's place you could not have concealed the matter." "I had as lief," said Nomerfide, "that you thought me the most foolish woman upon earth." "Such," said Hircan, "was not my intent, but that if there were slander against you, you would be in great affray, and not consider how you could stop men's mouths." "You think," said Nomerfide, "that everyone is as you, who with one scandal patch up another. But the danger is that at last a patch make a rent where all is sound, and the foundations have such a weight of patch-work upon them that the whole house come to the ground. Yet, if you think that these schemes of yours excel those of women, I give place for you to tell the seventh novel. And if you bring yourself into it, I warrant me we'll hear enough of wickedness." "I am not here," said Hircan, "to make myself out worse than I am, for there are those who tell me that I am bad enough." And so saying he looked towards his wife, who straightway spoke to him: "Be not afraid to tell the truth for that I am here, since I can easier bear to hear the story of your crafty ways than see them done under my eyes, though indeed I think there is nothing that will lessen my love for you." Hircan replied: "On this account I make no complaint of all the lying tales you have believed concerning me. Wherefore, since we have so good a knowledge the one of the other, the future is made more secure. But I am not so foolish as to tell a tale of myself, the very truth of which would be your grief; natheless I will tell you one of a gentleman who was very dear to me."

NOVEL VII.

The ready wit of a Paris mercer.

In the town of Paris there lived a mercer, who was amorous of a young wench his neighbour, or, to speak by book, the wench was by far more amorous of him than he of her. For all his love-making and dalliance was but a pretence, whereby he concealed his love for a more honourable lady; but this wench, who let herself be cozened by him, loved him so hotly as to have quite forgotten the way to refuse. So the mercer, who before had taken much pains to go where he might find her, at last ended by making her come and find him. And this being brought to the mother, who was an honest woman, she straightly charged the wench to have no more dealings with the mercer, or she should be clapped up in a nunnery. But the girl, who had a love for the man greater than was her fear for her mother, sought him out all the more. And one day it fell out that, being all alone in a closet, the mercer came in unto her, and deeming the place a fitting one, fell to that kind of talk with her that wants two and not three. But a serving-maid, who saw him going in, ran quickly and advertised the mother of it, and she went thither in great wrath. And when the wench heard her coming, she said weeping to the mercer: "Alas, alas, sweetheart, this love of mine will cost me dear, for hither comes my mother, who will discover to be true that which she had always dreaded." The mercer, who was by no means troubled or affrayed, straightway left her, and going to her mother, caught her in his arms, and with the rage that was half-spent on the daughter threw the old woman on a small bed. And she, not knowing what to make of this device, could scarcely speak a word but: "What would you? Are you mad?" But for all that he pressed as hard and fast on her as if she had been the rarest beauty in the world, and had she not lifted up her voice and brought her servants to her rescue she would have gone the same gate she was afraid her daughter had passed through. However, by main force they wrenched the poor old dame from between the hands of the mercer, and to her dying day she could never find out for what reason she had been used in this fashion. As for the wench she got her away to a house hardby, where there was a wedding, and stayed there till all was quiet. And many an honest laugh did she and the mercer have together at the expense of the old dame, who never got any light on the matter.

"In which relation, ladies, you see how the subtilty of a man cozened an old dame and saved the honour of a wench. But anyone who could name names, and saw the face of the mercer, and the amazement of the old woman, would have to be very tender of his conscience, did he not laugh. It is enough for me to have clearly shown to you that the wit of men is as ready as that of women in their hour of need, wherefore fear not to fall into the hands of men, for if your own wit fail you theirs will not, and your honour shall be in no peril." "Truly, Hircan," said Longarine, "I do not deny that the relation is pleasant, and the wit beyond compare, but the wench's part is not an ensample to other girls. I doubt not you know maids whom you would fain have follow in her steps; but you are surely not fool enough to wish your wife, or any woman of whose honour you make more account than her pleasure, to play such games as these. I verily believe there is none who would more closely keep watch and ward upon them than you." "Pardy," said Hircan, "if she of whom you speak had gone and done likewise, I would think no worse of her, if I knew nothing about it. And indeed, for all I know, some one may have served me in this fashion. But knowing nothing, I care nothing." Parlamente could not refrain from saying : "Needs must be that the evil man is full of suspicion; but happy are they who have no suspicion, and give no occasion for it." Longarine said: "I have never seen a great fire from which there came no smoke; but I have plainly seen smoke arising from no fire. For one is as often suspected by the wicked when there is no cause as when there is." To whom replied Hircan : "Truly, Longarine, you have made so fine a defence of the honour of wrongly-suspected ladies, that I give you my vote for the eighth novel ; in which take heed that you make us not to weep, as did Oisille, by your marvellous praise of honourable women." Longarine, herself laughing mightily, began to speak: "Since you are fain for me to make you laugh, as is my custom, I will do so, yet not at the expense of women ; but my story shall be of how easy they are to be deceived, when jealousy is their humour, and they esteem themselves well able to deceive their husbands."

NOVEL VIII.

Of one who on his own head engrafted horns.

In the county of Alet, there was a man named Bornet, who being married to a woman of honour, had for her good name such a regard as I suppose all husbands here present have for that of their wives. But though he was fain for her to be without reproach, yet this law of his did not press on husband and wife with equal rigour, for he loved his serving-maid, from whom he could get no more delight than that arising from a diversity of meats. Now he had a neighbour named Sandras, a drum-maker and tailor ; and there was such friendship betwixt them that, except the wife, they had all things in common. So to this Sandras he made known the enterprise he had undertaken against the serving-maid, who not only thought well of it, but gave his friend all the aid in his power to bring matters to a conclusion, since he had good hope of dividing the spoil. The wench, who would by no means consent, seeing herself hard-pressed on every side, went to her mistress, and prayed her that she might go home to her kinsfolk, since she could no longer live in such torment. The wife,

who greatly loved her husband, and had before had some suspicion of him, was mightily pleased to hear this, thinking to show
him that her jealousy was not altogether without foundation;
and so said to the girl: "Do you, by little and little, entice
my husband and then make appointment with him to lie
with you in my closet, failing not to tell me the night agreed
upon; and above all take heed that none be advised of this."
All this the maid performed, and so much to the pleasing of
her master, that he went to his friend to make known the good
tidings. And he, since he had helped to fight the fight,
entreated a share in the victory. This being granted, and the
hour determined, the master went to lie, as he thought, with
his maid, but his wife, who had renounced the authority of
commanding for the pleasure of obeying, had put herself in
place of the serving-maid, and received her husband not after
the fashion of a wife, but like a timid and frightened girl.
And this she did so well that her husband perceived nothing.

I cannot tell you which of the two had most delight, he at
the thought of cozening his wife, or she at the thought of
cozening her husband. And when he had remained with her,
not according to his wish but according to his power, for he
began to feel that he was an old married man, he went outside
the house and found his friend, who was by far younger
and handsomer than he, and boasting to him that a sweeter
morsel he had never tasted, his friend said: "You know
what you promised me?" "Come then, and quickly," said
the master, "or she will have got up, or my wife may require
her." His friend went, and found still there the serving-maid,
who, taking him for her husband, refused him nothing he liked
to ask. Much longer stay did he make than the husband, at
which the wife was in amaze, for it was not her custom to have
such work of nights; all the same, she bore it patiently; fortifying herself with the discourse she would have with her
husband in the morning, and the jeers she would make at him.
But a little while before dawn he got up from her, and in
taking a last taste before he went, he snatched a ring off her
finger, the same with which her husband had espoused her.
And this ring of espousal the women of that country hold in
high honour, and have in great regard the woman who keeps
her ring even unto death. But on the other hand, if she loses

it, she is held in no account, and esteemed as one who has given her faith to another than her husband. And she was glad to see him take it, thinking it would be sure proof of the deceit she had laid upon him.

And when Sandras returned to Bornet, the latter asked of him what his hap had been, to whom he replied that he had fared excellently well, and that if it had not been that the day was breaking he would have stayed still longer. And then they betook them to a most hearty sleep. But in the morning, as they were dressing, the husband perceived the ring his companion wore on his finger made in the exact likeness of the one he had given his wife at their betrothal, and so required of Sandras whence it came. But when he heard that it was snatched from the finger of the serving-maid, he was in great affray, and fell to knocking his head against the wall, saying : " Oddsfish ! have I then made myself a cuckold, without the knowledge of my wife ?" His companion, for his consolation, said : " Perchance your wife gave the ring to the wench for her to take care of it." To this the husband had nothing to say, but gat him home straightway, where he found his wife prettier, gayer, and more frolicsome than was her custom, as was indeed to have been looked for in a wife who had saved her maid's conscience, and sounded her husband to the depths, at the small price of a sleepless night. He, seeing her with so pleasant a countenance, said within himself : " Did she but know of what has been done, she would have an otherguise visage." And making discourse on various concerns he took her by the hand, and perceived that she had not her ring, whereat in great affray, and with a tremor in his voice, he asked her : " What have you done with your ring ?" But she, glad that he had brought that matter into discourse, from which it was her mind to draw out some points to his edification, made this beginning : " O thou vilest of men ! From whom, think you, did you ravish it ? In good sooth from my maid, on whose behalf you poured forth more of your substance than ever fell to my share ; for the first time you were bedded with me I judged you to be as vigorous as you were able. But after you had gone out and come back again you seemed the incarnate devil of concupiscence. Wretch ! conceive your blindness in praising so much this poor body of mine, which you have enjoyed a year without placing it in any great esteem. It was not then the beauty or the breasts of the maid that gave you such great delight, but the deadly sin of lust which enflames your heart and so enfeebles your reason, that I verily believe in that mad heat of yours you would have taken a she-goat in a nightcap for a girl of surpassing comeliness. Of a truth, husband, it is time for you to cleanse your ways, and to be as content with what I can give you, in my proper person as a good wife and an honest woman, as you were when you took me for a naughty quean. This that I have done has been for the correction of your evil ways, and to the end that in our old age we may love one another with an honest love and a good conscience. For if you will still continue in your former manner of living, I had rather be severed from you than see from day to day before mine eyes the ruin of your soul, body, and substance. But if you will bring to mind the wickedness of your heart and live obediently to the law of God, faithfully observing his commandments, I will forget your sins that are past, as I trust God will forget my sin, who have not loved him as I ought." Who then was in despair but this poor husband? For he had abandoned this wise and chaste wife of his for a wench that loved him not, and, worse than this, had, without her knowledge, made her a strumpet, and caused another man to share in that delight which was for him alone. So well had he made him horns of everlasting derision. But seeing his wife, how wrath she was at his love for the serving-maid, he took good care to tell her nothing of the evil turn he had done her; and giving her back the ring, asked her pardon, and promised an entire amendment of his former iniquitous living. And he strictly charged his friend to tell no man anything; but since what is whispered in the ear is ere long proclaimed from the housetop, the whole truth became known, and making no account of his wife, all folk called him cuckold.

"It appears to me, ladies, that if all who have committed a like offence against their wives, should receive like punishment, Hircan and Saffredent would have shrewd cause for fear." At this Saffredent said: "What, Longarine, of all this company are Hircan and I alone married?" "Many there are married," quoth she, "but no other who would play a game like this." "Whence had you," said Saffredent, "that we have attempted our wives' serving-maids?"   "If they, whom this discourse pricks, were to speak the whole truth, they could tell us of many a wench that had notice of dismission and her quarterage." "Truly," said Geburon, "you are a fine lady who, in place of affording us our promised laughter, have given occasion of wrath to these two gentlemen."   "'Tis all one," replied Longarine, "so long as their swords are sheathed their anger will serve but to increase our diversion."   "Goodly diversion is this," said Hircan, "which, if our wives gave credit to her tale, would make an uproar in the best ordered household in the company."   "I know well what I am saying," answered she, "for so well do your wives love you that, if you were to give them horns as big as stags', they would willingly persuade themselves and all beside that they were garlands of roses." At this the whole company, and even the wives aforesaid, fell to laughing in such wise that the discourse came to an end. But Dagoucin, who hitherto had kept silence, must needs say : " Man is, in truth, irrational, since when he has good matter of contentment at home, he must needs go and search for it abroad.   For I have often seen men, through their lust of gaining more, and their ill-liking to what should suffice them, fall into far worse case than they were before, and so get their deserts, for fickleness is well worthy of blame."   Simontault said to this : " But what do you say as to those who have not found their other half?   Call you it fickleness to seek every quarter, if haply they may find it?"   "Ay, verily I do, and for this reason—that man knoweth not where to look for this other half, with whom there is such perfect union that the one differs not from the other.   Wherefore love should be stead-fastly fixed, and in whatever hap, change not its heart or inclination, for if she whom you love is like to yourself, so that there is but one will between you, then it is yourself you love and not her."   "Dagoucin," said "Hircan, this position of yours is false, as if we should bear love to women by whom we are not beloved."   "My intent is," answered Dagoucin, "to maintain that when love is bottomed merely upon the beauty, gracious ways, or wealth of a woman, and our aim be only pleasure, honour, or profit, that love will not long endure.   For, when that upon which we found our love becomes wanting, the love itself perishes.   But I am steadfast in my opinion, that he who loves, and desires nothing better than to love with a perfect love, will cling to this love while his soul clings to his body." "Pardy," said Simontault, "I cannot believe that you have ever been in love, for if you had felt this fire like other men, you would not treat us in this fashion with a Republic like Plato's, that has life only on paper." "Not so," said Dagoucin, "I have loved, do still love, and while I live, will love. But I have so great a fear lest, when I make manifest this love, I thereby do injustice to its perfection, that I conceal it even from her of whom I desire a like return. Hardly indeed do I suffer it to enter my thoughts, lest my eyes make revelation of it, for so much the more that I keep this fire hidden out of sight, so the more earnestly do I delight to know that it is perfect and without stain." "Yet," said Geburon, "I am well assured that to be loved in return would not be to your misliking." "This I acknowledge, but since my love is not lessened for that it is not returned, so it would not be increased if it were returned." Whereupon Parlamente, who held this fantasy in small favour, said: "Take care, Dagoucin, for I have seen others beside you who had rather die than speak." "These, mistress," answered Dagoucin, "I deem exceeding happy." "Even so," said Saffredent, "and well deserving a place among the Innocents, of whom the church sings : *Non loquendo, sed moriendo confessi sunt.* I have heard much of these feeble lovers, but never yet stood I at the death-bed of one of them. And since I have come scot-free from all my dolours, I believe not that another man will die of such woes." "How then," said Dagoucin, "do you expect to be loved? But lovers of your sort need never fear death. Yet have I known many an one to whom death came by no sickness but love." "Since you are advised of such," said Longarine, "I give you my vote for the telling some pleasant story that shall be the ninth novel." "To the intent," he replied, "that your faith may be confirmed by signs and miracles, I will tell you an authentic history, which came to pass not three years ago."

NOVEL IX.

A relation of a perfect love, and the pitiful end thereof.

In the coasts of Dauphiné and Provence there lived a gentleman whose riches stood rather in virtuousness, a brave address, and an honourable heart, than in gold or worldly gear. And he loved a maid, as to whose name I will say nothing, since she came of a most illustrious house; but be you none the less assured that my tale is the whole truth. And for that he came not of such gentle blood as she did, he was unwilling to make manifest his love to her, since this love of his was so perfect that he would rather die than cause her any dishonour. So perceiving that, compared with her, he was of low estate, he had no hope of marrying with her. Wherefore his love was bottomed upon this and this alone—to love her with all his whole might; and this he did, and for so long a time that at last she was advised thereof. And seeing that the love he bore her was honourable, and bore fruit in seemly and virtuous talk, she was well pleased to be loved by such an one, and carried herself so graciously toward him that he, who hoped for nothing better, was well contented therein. But malice, that suffers no one of us to be at rest, could not leave this goodly manner of living in peace, for certain ones must needs go tell the mother that it was matter of astonishment to them that this gentleman was made of such account in her house, that it was common talk that the daughter brought him there, and that she had often been seen to talk with him. The mother, who had no more doubt as to this gentleman's honour than that of her own children, was much troubled to hear his presence was taken in bad part, so that at last, fearing the scandalous tongues of men, she entreated him that for some while he would come no more to her house as his custom had been. And this he found tough matter of digestion, knowing that the honest talk he had with the maid deserved not this estrangement. All the same, to shut evil mouths, he kept away for some time, till the rumour was hushed, and then went as before, his love being in no wise lessened by absence. But one day, being in the house, he heard some talk of marrying his mistress to a gentleman who was not so rich as to rightly carry this point over him. So he forthwith took heart, and began to use his friends' offices on his behalf, thinking that if the lady had to choose he would be preferred. But the mother and kinsfolk chose the other man, for that he had the greater wealth, at which the poor gentleman took so much despair, knowing his sweetheart to be as much grieved as himself, that little by little, without any sickness, he began to consume away, and in a short time was so much changed that he seemed to have covered the beauty of his face with the mask of death, whither hour by hour he was joyously hastening.

Yet he could not restrain himself from going to speak as often as might be with her he loved so well. But at last, since his strength failed him, he was constrained to keep to his bed, not wishing his mistress to be advertised of this lest she too should have part in his woe. And giving himself up to black choler and despair, he left off both drinking and eating, sleep and rest, in such sort that for the wasting away of his countenance he could scarcely be known. And some one bringing tidings of this to the mother of the maid, she, being a woman full of charity, and liking the gentleman in such fashion that if the kinsfolk had been of her and her daughter's mind, she would have been better pleased with his honest heart than all the riches of another, went to see this unfortunate, whom she found more dead than alive. And perceiving that his end drew near, he had that morning made confession of his sins, and received the blessed sacrament, thinking to die without the sight of any one. But though he was within a span of death, when he saw her enter who was for him the resurrection and the life, he was so much revived that, starting up from his bed, he said to the mother: "What has brought you here, mistress, to visit him who has one foot in the grave, and of whose death you are the cause?" "How can it be," she said, "that you receive death from our hands, who love you so well? I pray you tell me wherefore you hold this manner of discourse." "Mistress," said he, "although I have, as far as lay within me, concealed the love I bore your daughter, yet my kinsfolk in speaking of our marriage have made too evident my thoughts. Hence I have lost hope, not on account of my privy pleasure, but because I know that at the hands of no other man will she receive as good love and contentment. Her loss

of the best and most affectionate friend she has in the world
does me more hurt than the loss of my life, which for her sake
alone I was fain to preserve.   But since it can now no more
avail her anything, the loss of it is to me great gain."   At this
discourse the mother and daughter laboured to console him, the
mother saying : " Take heart, my friend, for if it please God
to give you back your health, I promise you my daughter shall
be your wife.   See ! she is here, and I command her also to
make this promise to you."   And the daughter, with much
weeping, laboured to assure him of that her mother promised.
But he, well knowing that if he recovered his health, he could
not have her to wife, and that all this pleasant talk of theirs
was only in some sort to revive him, answered them that if they
had said all this three months ago he would be the stoutest
and the most happy of all the gentlemen in France, but that
help had come too late to him, for whom hope was no more.
And when he saw that they still laboured to persuade him he
spoke as follows : " Since you, on account of my feeble case,
promise to me that which, even if you would have it so, can
never pertain to me, I ask you to grant me somewhat less,
which I have never had the boldness to require at your hands."
Straightway they promised, and confirmed their promise with
an oath, whereupon he said : " I beseech you that you place
her whom you pledge me for a wife between my arms, and
charge her that she both embrace and kiss me."   The maid,
not accustomed to such dalliance, made some difficulty, but her
mother straightly charged her, seeing that the gentleman was
rather to be counted among the dead than the living, and she
went up to the bed of the sick man, saying to him : " Sweetheart, I pray thee be of good cheer."   Then this poor soul
stretched out his arms, all skin and bone, as well as he could,
and kissed with a fervent kiss the cause of his death, and holding her to his cold and bloodless mouth kept her there as long
as he could.   And furthermore he spoke to her : " The love I
have had towards you hath been so seemly and honest that I
have never desired more bliss of you than that I now possess,
by which, and with which I gladly commend my soul to God,
who is perfect love, who knoweth my soul that it is great, and
my love that it is without stain.   And now, since within my
arms I hold my desire, I entreat Him in His arms to take my

soul." And at this he pressed her between his arms with such good will that his enfeebled heart was not able to bear it, and was voided of its radical humours, which joy had so used that his soul fled her seat and returned to her Creator. And though the poor body had lain a long while without life, and was therefore unable any more to hold fast its treasure, the love which the maiden had always kept concealed was now made so manifest that her mother and the servants had much ado to draw them apart; but by force they took at last the living-dead from the dead, for whom they made honourable burial. And of this the crowning point was in the weeping and lamentations of that poor maid, who in like measure, as she had kept her secret while her lover was yet alive, so made it manifest when he was dead, as if in some sort to make satisfaction for the wrong she had done him. And notwithstanding that they gave her a husband for her contentment, never more, so the story goes, did she take any pleasure in her life.

"Do you not agree, gentlemen, though you would not before believe me, that this example suffices to prove that perfect love may bring men to death, if it be too much hidden from view? There is none amongst you who does not know the kinsfolk on both sides, wherefore there is no room for you to doubt that it is the truth." At this the ladies with one consent fell to weeping, but Hircan said to them : "Verily he was the greatest fool of whom I have ever heard. Is it according to reason, prithee, that we should die for women, who are made but for us? or that we should be afraid to require of them what God has commanded them to give us? I speak not for myself or married men, for I have as much as I desire, but my words are for those in need, whom I account fools to be afraid of those who should be afraid of them. And do you not mark how great was this maiden's regret for her folly? Since, if she would embrace the body of a dead man—a thing against nature—how much the more would she have embraced him when alive, had he had courage to require it of her." "All the same," said Oisille, "the gentleman most plainly displayed how honourable a love he had towards her, and for this he is worthy to be had in everlasting remembrance, for to find chastity in an enamoured heart, this, indeed, is mighty rare." "Mistress," said Saffredent, "to confirm the opinion of Hircan,

E

which is likewise mine, I would have you believe that fortune
favours the daring, and that there is no man beloved by
woman who, if he do his courting with wisdom and gracious
ways, will not attain at last to the desire of his heart; but
ignorance and a foolish fear makes us lose many a good chance,
and we then put down our loss to our mistress' virtue, when
we have not so much as touched her with the tips of our
fingers.   Believe me, a fortress assailed is a fortress gained."
"I am astonished," said Parlamente, "that you two dare hold
such discourse.   The ladies you have loved owe you but little
thanks, or you have done your service in so bad a quarter that
you think all women are like these queans of yours."   "I,"
replied Saffredent, "have the misfortune not to be able to
boast of any great success; but I lay my bad luck less to the
virtue of the ladies than to my own lack of wisdom and fore-
thought in going about the matter, and to this intent will put,
in the words of the old woman in the *Romance of the Rose:*
'We are all made, fair sirs, for one another; every woman
for every man, and every man for every woman.'   Wherefore I cannot believe but that, when love is once in
session on a woman's heart, her lover will bring matters to a
good conclusion, if he be not plainly a blockhead."   Parlamente
said: "But if I could name a woman, strongly beloved,
strongly importuned, and strongly pressed, and all the while an
honest woman, victorious over her flesh, her love, and her lover,
would you not believe it for the truth that it is?"   "Why
yes," said he.   "Then indeed," said Parlamente, "you would
be hard of faith and slow to believe if you were not won by an
example I could give you."   Dagoucin said to her: "Mistress,
since I have shown, by an example, how a virtuous man loved
even unto death, I beseech you, if you know any such relation
as to woman, to tell it and so bring to a close this day's
entertainment, and fear not to speak somewhat at length, for
there yet remains abundance of time to discourse many a pleasant
case."   "Since then," said Parlamente, "I am to bring a close
to the day, I will not make a long beginning to my story, for so
fine a history have I to relate that I am fain you as well as I
should know it.   And though my eyes have informed me
nothing concerning it, I was told it by one of my most familiar
friends to the praise of the man who had of all the world loved

most. And he enjoined me that, if I ever told it, I should change the name of the persons therein; so that it is, excepting names and places, the whole truth and nothing else."

NOVEL X.

Florida, hard pressed by her lover, virtuously resists him, and on his death takes the veil.

In the county of Aranda, in Aragon, there lived a lady who, while yet in her first youth, was left a widow by the Count of Aranda, with a son and a daughter, the daughter's name being Florida. This lady aforesaid laboured to bring up her children in all virtuousness of living as appertains to those of gentle blood, and in such sort that her household was commonly accounted one of the most honourable in all the coasts of Spain. She often went to Toledo, where the King held his court, and when she came to Sarragossa, which was not far from her house, she would tarry a long while with the Queen and the Court, amongst whom she was held in as great esteem as might be. On one day going, as her manner was, to stand in the presence of the King where he was near Sarragossa in his castle of Jasserye, she passed through a village pertaining to the Viceroy of Catalonia, who was not used to stir beyond the coasts of Perpignan, for the great wars between the Kings of France and Spain. But it so fell out that at this time there was peace, wherefore the Viceroy and all his captains had come to do their suit and service to the King. And the Viceroy, being advised that the Countess of Aranda passed through his domain, went to meet her both for the ancient friendship that was between them and to do her honour as a kinswoman of the King. Now he had in his company many honourable gentlemen, who by the long continuance of the wars had gained so much glory and good report that any one who could see them and resort to them counted himself happy on that account. And amongst the rest there was one named Amadour who, although he was but eighteen or nineteen years of age, had so well-assured a grace, and so good an understanding, that he would have been chosen out from a thousand as worthy the office of a governor. True it is that this good understanding was conjoined with such beauty that no eye could do but look upon him, and though this beauty was of so excellent a kind, yet it was hard pressed by his manner of speaking; so that men knew not where to bestow the palm, to his grace, his beauty, or the words of his mouth. But that for which he was most of all esteemed was his surpassing bravery, notwithstanding he was so young, for in so many places had he shown the strength of his arm that not only in all the coasts of Spain, but also in France and Italy, were his virtues held in great account, and with good reason, since in no fight did he spare himself; and when his own country was at peace he would seek for wars in foreign lands, where likewise he was beloved as well by enemies as friends.

This gentleman, for the love he bore his general, came with him to his domain, whither the Countess of Aranda was arrived; and as he looked upon the beauty and grace of her daughter Florida, then about twelve years old, he thought within himself that she was the sweetest he had ever beheld, and that could he gain her favour it would do him more pleasure than anything whatsoever he might win from another woman. And after for a long while fixing his regard upon her, he resolved to give her his love, although reason made plain to him that he desired impossible things, as much for that she was of a most noble house as for her tender years, which as yet were not fit to listen to the discourse he was fain to make to her. But against this fear he strengthened himself with hope, promising himself that time and patience would bring a happy issue to his undertaking, and from henceforth the great love that was entered into his heart assured him of means of attaining thereto. And to surpass the greatest difficulty of all, that was the remoteness of his own land, and his few opportunities of seeing Florida, he was resolved to marry, contrary to what he had determined while he was with the dames of Barcelona and Perpignan, where he was held in such account that few or none would have refused him. And so long had he tarried in these coasts, by reason of the wars, that his speech smacked rather of Catalonia than Castille, although he was born near Toledo of a wealthy and honourable house, but being a younger son, he had no inheritance. So, perchance, it came to pass that Love and Fortune, seeing

him abandoned of his kinsfolk, determined to make a
masterpiece of him, and by means of his virtuousness
and courage granted him what he could not obtain from
the laws of his country. Such good skill had he in the craft
of war, and so well-beloved was he by lords and princes,
that he more frequently refused their employ than asked
for it.

The Countess then has come to Sarragossa, and has been
graciously received by the King and his Court. The Viceroy
of Catalonia often came to visit her, and Amadour never failed
to accompany him, only that he might have the delight of looking upon Florida, for of speaking to her he had no opportunity.
So to make himself known in such good company he addressed
himself to the daughter of an old knight, his neighbour, whose
name was Aventurada, and who had such converse with Florida
that she knew what was in the depths of her heart. Amadour,
whether for the graciousness he found in her, or for the three
thousand ducats a year that was her dowry, determined to talk
to her as one he desired to marry. And willingly did she give
ear to him, but seeing that he was poor and her father rich,
she thought that he would never give her in marriage to
Amadour unless by the entreaty of the Countess of Aranda.
Wherefore she addressed herself to Florida, saying : "You
have seen that young gentleman of Castille often speaking with
me, and I am persuaded that his intent is to ask me in marriage.
You know too what kind of father I have, and that he will
never consent thereto, if he be not strongly entreated of the
Countess and yourself." Florida, who loved her as herself,
promised that she would lay this to heart as if it were for her
own peculiar good; and Aventurada accomplished so much as
to present Amadour to her, who on kissing of her hand was
like to have swooned away for joy. And he, who was accounted the readiest speaker in all Spain, was so affected in her
presence that he stood dumb; and this was matter of great
surprise to her, who, although she was but twelve years old,
had well understood that no man in Spain could say what he
wished more readily or with a better grace. So seeing that he
said nothing, she began thus : "The renown that you have won,
my lord, in all the coasts of Spain is so great as to make you well
known in this Court, and causes those who are of your acquaint-

ance to desire to employ themselves in your service; wherefore, if there is anything wherein I can aid you, I am at your command." Amadour fixing his eyes upon her beauty was thereby possessed with such a ravishment, that he could hardly find words to give her his hearty thanks, whereupon Florida, astonished to find him thus dumb, but putting it down to some fantasy and not to the power of love, went from his presence without another word.

Amadour, perceiving the goodness which even in early youth began to show itself in Florida, said to her whom he intended for his wife: "Marvel not that in the presence of Mistress Florida I lost all power of speech, since the virtues and the wisdom which are contained in one of so few years in such wise astonished me that I knew not what to say. But, prithee, tell me, Aventurada, who know all her secrets, whether every heart at Court is not in love with her, for verily they who know her and love her not are either hard as rocks or senseless as beasts." Aventurada, who by this time loved Amadour better than all the men in the world, would not conceal aught from him, and so told him that Florida was beloved of all, but by the custom of the land few spoke to her, and still fewer—nay, only two—paid any court towards her. And these two were Spanish Princes, of whom one was the son of the Fortunate Infante, the other the young Duke of Cardona. "Prithee, then, tell me which she loves best." "She is so prudent," said Aventurada, "that she would never confess to having any will besides her mother's in the matter; natheless, as far as my wit goes, I am persuaded she loves the son of the Fortunate Infante above the Duke of Cardona. But to her mother Cardona is most agreeable, since in the case of their being wed she would have her daughter always by her. And of such good judgment do I esteem you that this very day, if it is your pleasure, you may come to a conclusion, for the son of the Fortunate Infante is being nurtured in this Court, and is one of the bravest and most admirable young princes in Christendom. And if we maids had the disposing of the matter, he would be well assured of his bride, and we should have the fairest couple in all Spain. You must understand that, although they are both young, she twelve and he but fifteen, it is already three years since the courtship began, and if you would have her favour, I would counsel you to make yourself his faithful friend and follower."

Amadour was in great delight to hear she was in love with something, hoping that in time he might gain the place, not of husband but of lover, for it was not her virtue that he feared, but lest she should have no love whatever in her temperament. And soon after these passages he began to be constantly in company with the son of the Fortunate Infante, whose good graces he easily obtained, for in whatsoever pastime the young prince took delight he was well skilled, and above all in the practice of horsemanship, and in sword play, and to be short in all the games which it is becoming in a prince to know. But war broke out in Languedoc, and needs must that Amadour return with the governor, which indeed was great grief to him, since it took away the possibility of his seeing Florida ; wherefore on his setting out he told a brother of his, who was chamberlain to the King, of the good match he had made in the person of Aventurada, and prayed him that in his absence he would do all that lay within him to forward the marriage, thereto employing the favour he had with the King and Queen and all his friends.   The gentleman, who loved his brother not only for his kinsmanship but also for his excellent endowments, promised him to use his best endeavours, and moreover did so, inasmuch as the father, a surly old miser, laid by his natural complexion and paid some regard to the virtues of Amadour, which the Countess of Aranda, and above all Mistress Florida, took care to set before him.   Also in this they were aided by the young Count of Aranda, who as he grew in years began to esteem brave men.   So the marriage having been agreed upon by the kinsfolk on either side, the King's chamberlain sent for his brother, since a lasting truce had been made between the two Kings.

About this time the King of Spain betook himself to Madrid for the avoiding of the bad air that prevailed where he was, and at the advice of his Privy Council, and the request of the Countess of Aranda, he gave consent to the marriage of the Duchess of Medina-Celi with the young Count of Aranda, no less for their contentment and the union of their houses than for the love he bore towards the Countess ; and so was pleased that the marriage should be solemnised in his castle at

Madrid. And at the marriage feast was present Amadour, who used such good means on his own account that he was wedded to the lady whose love for him was beyond compare greater than his for her. But to be short, he held his wife only as a cloak to conceal his liking to another, and a means whereby he might be incessantly in Florida's company. After that he was married he entered into all the privity of the Countess of Aranda's household, where they paid no more heed to him than if he had been a woman. And though at this time he had not seen more than twenty-two years, yet so sage was he that the Countess would make known to him all her occasions, and enjoined her son to discourse with him and give ear to all his counsels. And having attained this high point in their esteem, he kept himself so prudently and coldly that even she whom he loved knew nothing of his thoughts. But since Florida loved his wife above all others, she trusted in him in such sort that she concealed from him nothing, and at this time opened to him all the love she had for the Fortunate Infante. So he, who sought but one thing, to gain her altogether for himself, talked to her always of the prince, for it mattered not one whit to him what the subject of their discourse might be so that it lasted a long time. There he stayed for a month after his marriage was concluded, and was then forced to go to the wars, whither he remained two years without returning to see his wife. And she lived all this while in the place where her nurture had been.

And during these two years he wrote often to his wife; but his letters consisted for the most part of messages to Florida, who on her side failed not to return them, and in every letter of Aventurada's sent him some pleasant piece of wit, and this made the husband unfailing in his writing. But with all this Florida discovered nothing save that he loved her as if he had been a brother. Now and again he would come home, but in such sort that in five years he only saw Florida for two months altogether; yet in despite of estrangement and the length of his absence his love did but increase. And it came to pass that he made a journey to see his wife, and found the Countess far removed from the Court, for the King was gone to Andalusia, bearing with him the young Count of Aranda, who was now beginning to carry arms. The Countess had

betaken herself to her pleasure-house on the coasts of Arragon
and Navarre, and was glad to see Amadour return, since for
nigh three years he had been away. He was made welcome
by all, and the Countess enjoined that he should be used as if
he had been her own son. While he was with her she
advertised him of all the charges of the household, and for the
most part took his judgment thereon, and so great esteem did
he win at this place, that whithersoever he would go the door
was opened to him, since they made such account of his
prudence that he was trusted like an angel or a holy man.
Florida, for the love she bore his wife and himself, sought him
out wherever he went, and had no suspicion of him, wherefore
she put no guard on her face, having no love to conceal, but
only feeling great contentment when he was by her. Amadour
was in great pains to escape the suspicion of those who can
discern a lover from a friend, for when Florida came privily to
speak to him the flame that was in his heart rose so high that
he could not hinder the colour rising on his cheeks or conceal
the flashing of his eyes. And to the end that nobody might
observe all this, he set himself to pay court to a mighty fine
lady named Pauline who, in her time, had such renown from
her beauty that few who saw her escaped her nets. And this
Pauline, hearing that Amadour had had some experience of the
love-craft in Barcelona and Perpignan, and had gained the affection
of the handsomest gentlewomen in the country, notably that of the
Countess of Palamos, who was accounted for the most beautiful
of all the Spanish ladies, told him that it was a great pity, after
such good fortune, to have taken to wife so ugly a woman.
But Amadour, understanding by her words that she had a
mind to help him in his hour of need, made as pleasant discourse to her as might be, thinking that, if he could cause her
to believe what was false, he should thereby hide from her the
truth. But she, of keen wit, well tried in the service of love,
was not to be contented with words alone, and being assured
that such kindness as he had for her did not suffice him, suspected
he would fain use her as a cloak, and on that account kept
good watch on his eyes. But these knew so well how to feign,
that any suspicion she might conceive was but dark and obscure,
yet it was matter of great toil to the gentleman, since Florida,
ignorant of all these plottings, used him in such familiar fashion

before Pauline that his eyes had a wondrous struggle with his
heart.   And for the avoiding of this, one day he spoke as
follows to Florida, while they were standing by a window:
"Prithee, sweetheart, tell me whether is it better to speak or
to die."   And Florida presently replied to him: "I would
counsel all such as are my friends to speak and not die, for 'tis
a bad speech that cannot be mended, but a life lost cannot be
recalled."   "You promise me then," said Amadour, "that
you will not only take in good part what I am going to say,
but even that you will not be astonished thereat till I have made
an end."   To this she replied: "Say what you will, for if you
astonish me, none can reassure me."   And so he began:
"Mistress, up to this time I have had no wish to speak of my
love towards you, and this for two reasons.   In the first place,
for that I desired to be well tried by you, and in the second
because I doubted whether you would esteem it for an honour
to be loved by me, who am but a poor gentleman.   And again,
though I were of as high estate as yourself, the steadfastness
of your heart would not allow you to listen to love-talk from
any but him who has gained your love, I would say the son of
the Fortunate Infante.   But just as in war, necessity makes
men sacrifice their own possessions, and cut down their own
corn lest the enemy enjoy it, so I dare to risk gathering before-
hand the fruit I hoped to pluck much later, lest it profit our
enemies and be to your loss.   Understand then that from your
youth until now I have been so given up to your service that I
have never wearied in seeking to gain your favour, and for that
cause alone did I wed her whom I thought you loved the best.
And knowing the love you bore to the son of the Fortunate
Infante, I have taken pains, as you are advised, to do him
service and to be frequently with him, and all this because I
fain would please you, and truly I have used to that end all my
power.   You know that I have gained the favour of your
mother and brother, and all whom you love, in such sort that I
am held in this house not as a servant but a son, and all the
pains that for these five years I have taken have been to no
other intent than that with you I may pass all my life.   Understand that I am not of those who would pretend by these
means to get anything from you to the hurt of your honour,
for I know that I cannot take you to wife, and if it were in my

power I would not do this thing against him whom you love, and whom I desire to see your husband. And so far removed am I from those who, by long service, hope for a reward against the honour of their ladies, and love with a vicious love, that I would rather see you dead than know you were less worthy of being loved, or that your virtue had, for my pleasure, been made of small account. For the end and reward of what I have done I ask alone one thing—that you be to me such a mistress as never to take your favour from me, that you continue me in my present case, trusting in me more than in any other, and being well assured that, if in any matter you need a gentleman's life, mine shall be with the heartiest good will at your service. And in like manner I would have you believe that whatever I do that is brave and honourable is done only for your sake. And if I have done for ladies of far less account than you things which have been thought worthy of regard, be assured that, you being my mistress, my bravery will grow in such fashion that deeds I aforetime found impossible shall become most easy to be performed. But if you will not accept me as wholly yours, it is in my mind to renounce arms, and the valour which helped me not in my hour of need. Wherefore, mistress, I entreat that my desire be granted me, forasmuch as your honour and conscience cannot fairly refuse it."

The maid, hearing this strange discourse, began to change colour and let down her eyelids, as a frightened woman is accustomed. Natheless, since she was wise and prudent, she said to him: "Wherefore is it, Amadour, that you ask of me what you have already? To what intent is all this talk? I greatly fear that beneath your honourable words there is concealed some hidden evil to deceive the ignorance of my youth. Wherefore I am in great doubt what to reply; for if I refuse the honourable friendship you offer me, I shall be doing the very contrary to what I have always done, since I have trusted you above all men. Neither my conscience nor mine honour forbid your desire, nor yet my love for the son of the Fortunate Infante, for that is bottomed upon marriage, to which you make no pretence. I know nothing to hinder me from replying to you according to your wish, if it be not the fear I have at heart arising from the small need you had to ask all this; for since you have what you require, what need to ask for it?" Amadour, who was not without an answer, said to her: "Mistress, you speak according to wisdom, and do me so great honour by the faith you put in me, that if I were not content with this reward, I should not be worthy of any other. But know that he who would build a house to last for ever must take care first to lay a strong and sure foundation; wherefore I, who would dwell for ever in your service, must take care not only of the means whereby I may always be near you but also that none other be advised of my great love towards you. For though it be honourable enough to be proclaimed from the housetops, yet those who cannot discern the hearts of lovers often judge falsely concerning them, and thereby come evil rumours, of which the event is likewise evil. And she who makes me say this and manifest my love towards you is Pauline, who has strong suspicions concerning me, and knowing well in her heart that I do not love her, makes it her chief concern to watch my face. And when you so familiarly come and speak to me before her, I am in great fear lest I make some sign for her to bottom her suspicion on, and so fall into the pit I am fain to escape. Wherefore it has been my intent to entreat you that before her, and before others whom you know to be as malicious as she is, you come not so suddenly to speak to me, for I had rather die than any man should come to a knowledge on these matters. And had I not been so tender of your honour I would not have had this discourse with you, since I deem myself sufficiently happy in your love and confidence towards me, and ask of you nothing more than to continue them unto the end."

Florida, who on hearing this was exceedingly glad, began to feel a somewhat at her heart she had never felt before, and considering the fair conclusions he had laid before her, replied that virtue and honour answered for her, and granted his desire. And who that has loved can be in doubt as to whether Amadour rejoiced thereat? But Florida more straitly followed his counsels than he would have her, for she, being afraid not only in the presence of Pauline but everywhere beside, no longer would seek him out as she had been accustomed; and whilst they were thus estranged she took in bad part his often going to Pauline, whom she thought so pretty that she could not believe but that he loved her.　　And for the consolation of her sadness she had much talk with Aventurada, who began to be exceeding jealous of her husband and Pauline, and so ofttimes made complaint to Florida, who comforted her as well as might be, she herself being stricken with the same plague.　Amadour before long perceiving how Florida was changed towards him, thought that she did not merely follow his counsels, but had mingled with them some peevish imagination of her own devising.　And one day, while they were going to evensong at a monastery, he said to her : " Prithee, mistress, what countenance is this you show me ?"　　" I suppose that which pleases you," said she.　Whereupon, having a suspicion of the truth, and willing to know if he was right, he began to say : " Mistress, I have so spent my days that Pauline thinks no more of you."　　To which she replied : " Than this you cannot do better, both for yourself and for me, for in serving your pleasure you preserve my honour." At which Amadour saw that she thought he took pleasure in parley with Pauline, and at this thought waxed so desperate that he could not contain himself, and wrathfully exclaimed : " Truly, mistress, these are early days to begin tormenting your poor slave and pelting him to death with bitter words, for I thought there could be no greater travail than to oblige myself to parley with one for whom I have no love.　And since what I have done in your service is taken by you in bad part, I will never again speak to her, come what will of it !　And that I may conceal my wrath as well as I have concealed my contentment, I will begone to some place hardby until your fantasy is overpast.　But I have good hopes while I am there to get tidings from my general that will take me back to the wars, where I will stay long enough to let you know that you alone have kept me here."　Thus saying, and without waiting for a reply, he forthwith left her.　At this Florida was filled with grief and sadness, and love by its repulse began to show her all its strength, in such wise that, knowing the ill she had done him, she wrote again and again to Amadour praying him to return, and this he did after that a space of some days had abated the bitterness of his anger.

　　I cannot make for you a particular account of the discourse by which they destroyed this jealousy.　At all events, he won the battle, inasmuch as she promised him to believe no more

that he was in love with Pauline, and also that she was assured
that to speak with Pauline or anyone else, save to do her a
service, was a martyrdom hardly to be borne.

And when love had conquered this first suspicion, and the two
lovers began to take more delight than ever in talking with one
another, tidings were brought that the King of Spain was drawing
his whole army to Salces. Wherefore Amadour, who was always
in the van of battle, lost not this chance of winning for himself
glory, yet it is true that he went with a regret that was not his
custom as much for the loss of pleasure as fearing to find some
change on his return. And this because he knew that Florida
was sought in marriage by great princes and lords, seeing she
was now come to the age of fifteen or sixteen years, wherefore
he thought that if she was married while he was away he
would no longer have any opportunity of seeing her, except the
Countess of Aranda should give her as a companion his wife
Aventurada. And so well did he manage his affairs amongst
his friends that the Countess promised that, let her daughter go
where she might, his wife should go with her. And though it
was intended that Florida should be married in Portugal, yet it
was determined that Aventurada should never forsake her; so
on this assurance, not without regret unspeakable, Amadour
went away and left his wife with the Countess. And when
Florida found herself alone after the departure of her slave, she
set herself to the doing of good works, whereby she would fain
get as much honour and repute as the most perfect women, and
show herself worthy of such a lover as Amadour. And he,
being arrived at Barcelona, received from the ladies such welcome
as he was wont, but so changed did they find him that they
would not have believed that marriage had such power over a
man as it had over him. For it was plain that the things in
which aforetime he had taken delight now wearied him; and
the very Countess of Palamos whom he had loved so well could
scarce find means to draw him to her lodging, on which account
he made but short stay at Barcelona, being weary for the fight
and the heat of battle. And when he had come to Salces,
there began that great and fierce war between the two kings
of which I do not propose to make any relation, not so much
of the mighty deeds done by Amadour, for if I did my tale
would be long enough to suffice for the entertainment of a

whole day.　But know that he far excelled in glory each and all of his fellows.　And when the Duke of Nagera came to Perpignan, being captain over two thousand, he entreated Amadour to be his lieutenant, who with this band did such service that in every fight the battle-cry was *" Nagera ! "*

At this time it came to pass that the King of ·Tunis, who for a long while had waged war with the Spaniard, hearing that the Kings of France and Spain were at odds together on the coasts of Perpignan and Narbonne, thought that he could find no better occasion of doing a displeasure to the King of Spain.　To this end he despatched a host of light galleys and other ships to pillage and destroy any badly-guarded place on the coasts of Spain.　The men of Barcelona, seeing a great number of vessels passing in front of the town, advertised the viceroy of the matter; and he, who was then at Salces, forthwith sent the Duke of Nagera to Palamos.　And the Moors, seeing the place guarded in such sort, feigned to go away, but returned about midnight and sent so many men on shore, that the Duke of Nagera was surprised by the enemy and taken captive.　Amadour, who kept good watch, hearing the tumult, drew together as great a company as he was able, and made snch defence that the enemy, for all their numbers, were for a long while unable to accomplish anything.　But at last, knowing the Duke of Nagera to be taken, and that the Moors were resolved to set Palamos afire, and with it the house he held against them, he preferred to render himself up than to be the cause of destroying the brave men who were of his fellowship.　Also he had hopes of being ransomed, and thus once more to see Florida.　So he presently gave himself up to a Moor named Dorlin, governor to the King of Tunis.　And this man took him to his master, by whom he was well received and better guarded, for the King, having him in his hands, thought he had taken the Achilles of the Spaniards.

And so abode Amadour nigh two years in the service of the King of Tunis.　Now the report of this mischance was brought to Spain, at which the kinsfolk of the Duke of Nagera were sore grieved; but they who laid the honour of their country to heart esteemed the capture of Amadour to be the greater loss.　And the news came to the house of the Countess of Aranda, where at this time lay Aventurada grievously sick.

The Countess, who had great suspicion of the love Amadour bore her daughter, but suffered it and concealed it for the virtues she discerned in him, called her apart and told her these pitiful tidings. Florida, who knew well how to feign, replied that it was a great loss for the whole house, and above all for his poor wife, who was now in such evil case. But seeing her mother weeping exceedingly, she too let a few tears drop to bear her company, fearing that by feigning too much her deceit might become apparent. And from this time the Countess often spoke to her of him, but could never bottom her suspicions on anything in Florida's face. I leave untold the pilgrimages, prayers, and fasts which Florida discharged in due order for the safety of Amadour, who no sooner got to Tunis than he sent tidings thereof to his friends, and by a trusty messenger advertised Florida that he was in good health and hope of seeing her again. And this was the poor lady's only means of sustaining her anguish, so doubt not that, since it was permitted him to write to her, she in return did her part so well that her letters of consolation came to Amadour thick and fast.

At this time the Countess was commanded of the King to go to Sarragossa, where he was come, and she found there the young Duke of Cardona, who so strongly urged the King and Queen that they prayed the Countess to give him her daughter in marriage. The Countess, who in nothing was disobedient to their will, agreed thereto, thinking that her daughter, who was still young, could have no will in the matter but her own. And when the agreement was determined upon she told her daughter that she had chosen as mate for her one she thought most fitting. And Florida, knowing that when a thing is done it skills not to give advice, said to her that for all things God was to be praised ; and seeing her mother bear herself coldly towards her, she had enough to do to obey without much pity of herself. And as matter of consolation for her woes, it was told her that the son of the Fortunate Infante was sick unto death ; but neither before her mother nor any beside did she ever make any appearance of grief. Indeed so strongly did she constrain herself that the tears driven inwardly into her heart caused such a flow of blood from the nose that her life was in jeopardy ; and that she might be restored they gave her as wife to him, than whom she would far rather have received

death.   And after the wedding was brought to a close Florida
went with her husband to the duchy of Cardona, taking with
her Aventurada, to whom she privily made her complaints both
of the rigour of her mother and the grief she had at the loss
of the son of the Fortunate Infante.   But of her grief at the
loss of Amadour she said nothing save by way of consolation.
And from this time she resolved to keep God always before
her eyes; and so well concealed her sorrows that none of
her people ever perceived that her husband was displeasing
to her.

So passed a long time, Florida living a life scarce better
than death.   And of all this she failed not to send news to her
lover, who knowing the greatness of her heart and the love she
bore to the son of the Fortunate Infante, thought it scarce
possible that she should continue to live, and mourned for her
as one worse than dead.   And by this dolour his own was
increased, since he would willingly have continued all his days
a slave, if Florida could but have a husband to her liking; so
did he forget his own woe in that which his sweetheart had.
And for that he heard, by a friend he had at the Court of the
King of Tunis, that the aforesaid King was resolved to give
him his choice of impalement or renouncing his faith, because
he greatly desired for him to become a good Mussulman and
continue in his service, he persuaded his master to let him go
on his parole.   And this master put upon his head so high a
ransom as he thought could never be found by a man of small
means.   So then, without speaking on the matter to the King,
his master let him go.   And when he had gone to Court and
stood in the presence, he went forth amongst all his friends to
the intent that he might get together the ransom, and straightway betook him to Barcelona, whither the young Duke of
Cardona, his mother, and Florida had gone on some charges.
And as soon as his wife Aventurada had tidings that her
husband was returned from captivity, she bore them to Florida,
who rejoiced thereat, as if for love of her.   But fearing lest
her joy upon seeing him might change the manner of her
countenance, and lest they who knew her not might take a bad
opinion of her, she withdrew herself to a window, that she
might see him coming from afar.   And as soon as she perceived him she went down by a stair so dark that no one

F

could see her change colour, and embracing Amadour she led
him to her room and that of her mother-in-law, to whom he
was unknown.   But he tarried there only two days, and in
that time made himself as much beloved by them all as he had
been in the household of the Countess of Aranda.

It is not my intent to tell you of all the talk that Florida
and he were able to have together, and the complaints she
made to him for the ills done her in his absence.   After much
weeping, both for that she was married to one against her
liking, and also that she had lost beyond hope of seeing again
him whom she loved so well, she determined to draw some
causes of consolation out of the love and firm trust she had in
Amadour, though she never durst declare it to him.   But he,
having some suspicions, lost neither time nor opportunity of
letting her know how great a love he had towards her.   And
just at that time, when she was ready to receive him not as a
servant but as a true and perfect lover, it fell out by evil hap
that the King, by reason of certain weighty charges, commanded the immediate presence of Amadour.   And this so
grieved his wife that, on hearing of the news, she swooned
away, and falling down a stair did herself such hurt that she
was not taken up alive.   Florida, who through this death lost
all consolation, made mourning as one who weeps for her
father and mother and all her kinsfolk.   But still more did
Amadour grieve, not alone that he had lost on his side one of
the best wives in the world, but also that he had lost all means
of seeing Florida; at which he fell into such sadness that he
was like to have died.   The old Duchess of Cardona came
often to speak with him, and drew from the philosophical
writings many good and solid reasons for him to bear this
loss with patience.   But this did not much avail him, for if
death itself was torment, love did but increase the agony.   So
Amadour, having beheld the burial of his wife and having no
more cause for delaying to perform the King's commands, was
filled with such despair that his brain wellnigh fell into some
distemperature.   But Florida, in endeavouring to console him,
spent a whole afternoon discoursing to him in the most
gracious sort to the intent of diminishing the extremity of his
grief, assuring him that she would find better means of seeing
him than he thought.   And since he was to set out on the

morrow, and was so weak that he could hardly stir from his
bed, he entreated her to come and see him in the evening after
every one had done so, which she promised, ignorant that his
love knew not bounds nor reason.   And he, who found himself
in despair of ever seeing her again whom he had served so long,
and having had of her no favours except what I have told you
of, was so torn asunder by hidden love and the loss of all means
of being in her company, that he was resolved to play at double
or quits, to win or lose it all, and to repay himself in one hour
as he thought to have deserved.   So he had his bed decked
with curtains in such fashion that those who came into the room
could not see him, and made more complaint than was his
custom, that the people of the house might not believe him to
have twenty-four hours to live.

After that every one had been to see him, Florida, her very
husband desiring her, went to him, intending as matter of consolation to declare her affection, and to assure him that, as far
as honour allowed, she would give him her love.   And she sat
herself down on the chair by the bedside, and began her consolation by weeping with him.   Amadour, seeing her grief,
thought that thereby he should more easily attain his ends, and
raised himself from the bed, whereupon Florida, thinking that
he was too weak, would have held him back.   But he fell on
his knees and began to say: "Must I for ever lose the sight of
you?" and so let himself fall into her arms as one whose
strength fails him.   Poor Florida for a long time embraced and
sustained him, doing all that lay in her power to console him,
but the medicine she gave to cure his sickness did but increase
it; for with the face of a man half-dead, and without a word,
he fell to seeking for that which the honour of the ladies for-
bids.   And though Florida perceived his evil intent, she could
hardly believe it, having in her mind all his honourable conversation, and so asked him what he would do; but Amadour,
fearing to hear her reply, which he knew well would be a chaste
and virtuous one, persisted with all his strength in the quest of
that he desired, whereat Florida, mightily astonished, suspected
rather that he had taken leave of his senses than that he was
attempting her dishonour.   Wherefore she called aloud to a
gentleman whom she well knew to be in the room, and at this
Amadour, in the bitterness of his despair, threw himself back

so suddenly upon the bed that the gentleman held him for a
dead man. Florida, having arisen from the chair, said to him :
"Go presently and get some vinegar." And this he did,
whereupon Florida began : "Amadour, what fantasy is mounted
to your brain? and what were you minded to have done?" He,
who by reason of love had lost all reason, replied : "Doth so
long a service as mine deserve so cruel a return?" "And
where is that honour," said Florida, "which you have so often
preached to me?" "Ah! mistress," said Amadour, "it is
not possible to be more tender of your honour than I have
been; for before that you were married I so conquered my
heart that you knew nothing of my desire ; but now that you are
married, and your honour is in safe keeping, what wrong is this
I do you in asking what is my own? For by the very force of
love I have won you. He who first had your heart, made such
poor assault on your body that he well deserved the loss of
both. He to whom your body now belongs is by no means
worthy of your heart, wherefore neither by right does the body
appertain to him. But I, mistress, who for these five or six years
have borne for your sake so many woes, you cannot deny that
it is I alone who deserve both your body and your heart. And if
you would call your conscience into court, be well assured that
when love presses hard on every side, sin shall by no means be
imputed. Those who in a fit of madness slay themselves are
not to be accounted sinners for what they have done, for passion and reason cannot dwell together. And being love is the
most unbearable of all the passions, and most of all blinds the
senses, what sin would you impute to him·who is carried along
by its irresistible might? I am about to go, having no hope of
seeing you any more. But if I had had before I set forth
that security from you which my great love hath deserved, I
should have gained strength to bear patiently the sorrow of
this long farewell. And if it be not your pleasure to grant
me my desire, you shall soon perceive that your hard heart has
caused me a most miserable and cruel death."

Florida, no less grieved than astonished at such discourse
from him, from whose lips she never thought to have heard
the like, said weeping : "Alas! Amadour, is this the virtuous
talk you had with me while I was yet young? Is this the
honour and the good conscience you have so often counselled

me rather to die than lose? Have you then forgotten your good examples of virtuous ladies, who made resistance to light love, and all your despising of wanton women? I cannot believe, Amadour, that you are so far from yourself that God, your conscience, and my honour are altogether dead within you. But if it indeed be as you say, I praise the Divine Goodness for that it has delivered me from the pit into which I wellnigh had fallen, and shown by your speech the wickedness of your heart. For having lost the son of the Fortunate Infante, not only because I am married, but also because I am advised he loves another, and seeing myself wedded to one to whom I cannot, take what pains I may, give my heart, I was resolved entirely and altogether to set my soul and my affections on loving you. And this love I founded on the virtuousness I perceived in you, and to which, by your help, I deem myself to have attained; and the manner of it is to love my honour and my conscience better than my life. Bottomed upon this rock of honour, I came here determined to make it yet more sure; but in a moment, Amadour, you have shown me that in place of pure and shining marble it would have been founded on a quaking sand, or a filthy mire. And though this my strong place, where I hoped to dwell for ever, has been in great part begun, you have suddenly brought it down, even to the dust. Wherefore you must now put aside every hope you had concerning me, and resolve yourself, in what place soever I be, not to address me by words or looks, nor ever deem that I can or will change this my determination. All this I say to you with great grief, but if I had so far gone as to swear with you eternal love, I know my heart, and am well assured that in that strife of the soul I should have died. And even now my sorrowful amaze for that you have deceived me is so great that I am persuaded it will make my life a short and sad one. And with these words I bid you farewell, but remember that it is for ever !"

I spare you the relation of the grief that Amadour felt at the hearing of these words, for it is not only impossible to write but even to conceive, except to those who have been in like case. And seeing that with this cruel conclusion she would leave him, he took her by the arm, since he well knew that if he suffered this bad opinion of him to remain in her, he would lose her for ever. Wherefore, having put on as solemn a countenance as he was able, he said to her: "Mistress, I have all my life desired to love a woman of honour, and since I have found but little of that commodity, I was fain to make trial of you, to see if you were as worthy to be held in esteem for your virtue as you are to be loved. And this I now know for a certainty, wherefore I give thanks to God, who has directed my love towards such perfection, entreating at your hands pardon for the folly of my endeavour, seeing that the issue thereof has been to your honour and my great contentment." Florida, who by his example began to perceive the wickedness of men, as she had been slow to believe the evil that was in him, so was now slow to believe the good that was not, and replied: "I would to God you spoke the truth! But I am not so simple that the estate of marriage in which I am does not let me know that the blindness of a strong desire made you do what you have done. For if God had slacked the reins, I am assured you would not have drawn in the bridle. Those who make search for virtue go on a different road to the one you have taken. But it is enough; if too lightly I believed in your virtue, it is time I should know the truth, which now delivers me from out of your hands." Thus saying, Florida went forth from the room, and while the night went on did nought else but weep, taking at this change so great grief that her heart had shrewd work to withstand the assaults of love and regret. For though, reason guiding her, she was resolved not to love him any more, yet the heart, which is lord over itself, would by no means allow this, so she was determined to satisfy her affection and continue to love him, and yet to satisfy her honour and never make any sign to him of her love.

And on the morrow Amadour went forth in such woe as you have heard; nevertheless his heart, which had not its equal in the world, would not suffer him to despair, but set him on some new means for seeing Florida again, and winning back her favour. Wherefore as he went to the King of Spain, who was at Toledo, he took his way through the county of Aranda, and came there one evening very late, and found the Countess in great sadness by reason of the absence of her daughter Florida. And when she saw Amadour she kissed and embraced him as if he had been her own son, as much for the love she

bore him as for the suspicion she had that he loved Florida, of
whom she made curious inquiry.   And he told her the best
news he could, but not all the truth, and confessed the love
that was between them, which Florida had always kept secret,
praying her to give him her help in having tidings of her
daughter, and soon to bring her to Aranda.   And on the
morrow he continued on his journey, and having performed the
charges of the King, went to the wars with so changed and
sorrowful a countenance that ladies, captains, and all of his
acquaintance scarcely recognised him.   And henceforth black
was his only wear, but of much coarser frieze than was due to
his dead wife, whose loss served to conceal what was in his
heart.   So Amadour passed three or four years without returning at all to Court.   And the Countess of Aranda hearing how
Florida was changed, and that to see her was pitiful, sent to
her, wishing her to return home.   But these tidings had the
opposite effect, for when Florida heard that Amadour had
made manifest the love that was between them to her mother,
and that her mother, all good and virtuous as she was, held
their love for an honest one, she was in great perplexity.   For
on the one hand she saw that if she told her mother the whole
truth, Amadour might get some hurt thereby, than which
death would have been preferred by her, for she felt herself to
be strong enough to punish him without calling her kinsfolk to
her aid.   But on the other hand she perceived that if she concealed the evil she knew of him she would be constrained
by her mother and all her kin to speak to him and show him a
good countenance.   And this she feared would but strengthen
him in his wicked purpose.   But inasmuch as he was far away,
she said nothing, and wrote to him when her mother charged
her so to do ; all the same these letters of hers let him know
pretty plainly that they came from obedience and not good
will, and so caused him as much sorrow in the reading as aforetime tidings from her had given him joy.

At the end of two or three years, having done so many and
so great deeds, that would scarcely be contained by all the
paper in Spain, he conceived a most daring imagination, not to
win the heart of Florida, which he held as lost, but to gain
the victory over his enemy, since it was in this manner she
showed to him.   He put behind him all the counsels of reason,

and even the fear of death, of which he would thus make
hazard, and this was his fixed resolve. He made himself
so esteemed of the Viceroy that he was sent to speak to
the King of a certain secret undertaking against Leucate; and
before that he had spoken to the King, he declared the matter
to the Countess of Aranda, to take her mind upon it. And
he came post haste to the county of Aranda, where he was
advised was Florida, sending a friend of his secretly to the
Countess to make known his approach, and praying her to keep
it in great privity, and for him to speak with her at night, so
that no one should be advertised thereof. The Countess, being
glad on account of his coming, told Florida, and sent her to
undress herself in her husband's room, to the intent that she
should be ready when the time was come and all others were
in bed. Florida, who was by no means recovered from her
first fear, made no sign to her mother, but went apart to an
oratory. There she commended herself into the keeping of
our Lord, praying Him to preserve her heart from all evil lust.
And it then came into her mind that Amadour had often praised
her beauty, which, though she had been for a long while sick,
was by no means diminished; so preferring to do hurt to this
beauty than to suffer the heart of so good a man by it to be
kindled with an evil flame, she took a stone that chanced to be
in the chapel and with it gave herself so hearty a blow that
her mouth, nose, and eyes were altogether put out of shape.
And to the intent that none should suspect that she herself
had done it, she, when summoned by her mother, let herself
fall with her face to the earth while she was going out of the
chapel, and cried with a loud voice. And when the Countess
came she found her daughter in a pitiful case, and straightway
had her face dressed and bound up.

After the Countess had led her to her room, she told her
to go and hold discourse with Amadour until the company was
departed; and this did Florida, thinking there were others with
him. But finding herself all alone and the door shut on her,
she was as much vexed as Amadour was glad, since he conceived that by persuasion or force he would get his desire.
And when he had spoken to her, and found her of the same
mind as afore, and that she would rather die than change it,
maddened with despair, he exclaimed: "I swear to you by

God that the fruit of my travail shall not be plucked from me
by your nice points of conscience; for since love, long-suffering,
and humble prayers have availed nothing, I will not spare my
strength to gain that without which I shall perish." And
Florida saw his eyes and the manner of his countenance that
they were changed, and the fairest face in the world was as red
as fire, and his most sweet and pleasant regard was so dreadful
to look upon that a consuming flame seemed to blaze within his
heart and on his face, and in this phrensy he took within one
of his mighty hands her two hands most delicate and weak.
She, seeing that all resistance was of no avail, since she was thus
straitly held a prisoner that she could not fly, much less make
defence, knew not what to do save to seek if there were not
in him some traces of his former love by the recollection of
which he might forget his cruelty; wherefore she said to him:
" Amadour, though you now hold me for an enemy, I entreat
you, by the honourable love I formerly thought you had for me,
to give ear before you begin your torture." And when she perceived that he gave ear to her, she went on with her discourse,
saying: " Alas, Amadour, to what intent do you seek from me a
thing whereby you will take no contentment, and will give me the
greatest of all pains? You made so good trial of my mind in
the time of my youth and beauty, by reason of which you might
take some excuse, that I am astonished in this season of my age,
and ugliness, and sorrow, you seek for what you cannot find.
I am well assured you know my mind that it is not changed,
wherefore you cannot gain save by force your desire. And if
you look upon my face, and, seeing the manner of it, forget its
beauty that was of old, you will not, I think, be wishful of
approaching nearer. And if there are in you any remains of
bygone love, I am persuaded that pity will conquer your
madness. And to this pity, which I have found in you, I make
my lamentation and pray for grace, to the intent that you will let
me live to the end of my days in peace, and in that honour, over
which, by your counsel, I am determined to keep watch and
ward. For though the love you bore me is turned to hatred,
and more for revenge than passion you would fain make me the
most wretched of all women, I assure you that this thing shall
not be, since against my desire you will compel me to make
manifest your wickedness to her who believes you to be so good,

and thereby your life shall be put in no small risk." Amadour, breaking into her words, said to her: "If I must needs die, then all the sooner shall I be quit of this torment; but your misshapen countenance, which I believe to be the work of your own hands, shall not hinder me from working my will, for though you were but bones I would hold them closely to me." And Florida, perceiving that sound reason, prayers, and tears availed nothing, and that in his cruelty he would endeavour to accomplish his wicked desire, called to her aid that help she feared as much as death, and cried in a sad and woeful voice for her mother. The Countess, hearing her daughter summon her in such a voice, had great suspicion of what was indeed the truth, and ran into the room as quickly as might be. Amadour, not being as near death as he would have Florida believe, so seasonably abandoned his enterprise, that the lady on coming in found him at the door and Florida far enough from him. Forthwith the Countess asked: "Amadour, what is it? Tell me the truth." And he, who was never devoid of invention, with a sad and solemn countenance, answered her: "Alas! mistress, into what case has Florida fallen? Never was I more astonished, for as I have told you, I thought to have had her favour, but now clearly perceive I have none of it. It appears to me that while she was with you she was no less wise and virtuous than she is now, but she did not then make it a point of conscience to speak with no one, and now that I would fain have looked upon her she would by no means suffer me. And seeing this change towards me, I was assured that it was but a dream, and required her hand that, after the manner of the country, I might kiss it, but this also she would not suffer me to do. I confess that I took her hand with a gentle compulsion and kissed it, and in this I did wrongfully and crave your forgiveness, but naught else did I ask of her. Yet she, as I believe, having determined my death, called you as you have seen; I know not wherefore, unless she feared some other intent, which I in truth had not. Natheless, mistress, however that may be, I acknowledge that I have done amiss, for though she ought to love them that serve her well, I alone, who am of all most devoted to her, am exiled from her favour. But I will still be towards you and her as I have always been, and I entreat you to continue me in your good will, since through no fault of mine

I have lost hers." The Countess, who half believed and was half in doubt, went to her daughter, and said to her: "Wherefore called you me after this fashion?" Florida replied that she was afraid. And although the Countess made particular inquiry of her, she got no other reply, for Florida, seeing herself escaped from the hands of her enemy, held his ill-success sufficient punishment.

After that the Countess had for a long while held parley with Amadour, she made him stay with Florida to see what face he would put on it. But he said little to his mistress, save that he thanked her for not telling her mother the truth, and prayed at least, since she had driven him from out her heart, she would not let another man take his place. And to the first matter of his discourse she thus replied: "If I had had other means of defending myself except my voice, you would not have heard it; and you shall have no worse thing from me if you cease to constrain me as you have done hitherto. And be not afraid lest I love another, for since in the heart which I deemed the most virtuous in the world I have not found that I desired, I believe not I shall find it in any other man." Thus speaking, she bade him farewell. Her mother, though she carefully regarded his face, could come to no conclusion, save that henceforth she was well assured her daughter had no love for Amadour, and held her so void of reason as to hate everything she herself loved. And from that hour she behaved in such sort towards Florida that she spoke not to her but chidingly for seven whole years, and all this on account of Amadour. So during this time Florida turned the fear she had of being with her husband to a desire not to stir from him, because of her mother's rigorous entreatment of her. But finding this of no avail, she resolved to put a deceit upon Amadour, and, laying aside for a day or two her cold aspect, advised him to make proposals of love to a lady who, she said, had spoken to her of the love that was between them. Now this lady was in the household of the Queen of Spain, and was called Loretta. Amadour, believing this story, and thinking hereby to regain the favour of his mistress, made love to Loretta, who was the wife of a captain, one of the King's viceroys. And she, exceeding glad for that she had gained such a lover, set such store by him, that the rumour of it was blazed abroad, and even the Countess of Aranda, since she was at Court, was advertised of it, wherefore she ceased henceforth to torment Florida as had been her custom. And one day Florida heard that this warrior husband of Loretta's was become so jealous that he was determined, as best he might, to kill Amadour; and she who, despite her altered countenance towards him, could wish him no ill, presently advised him of it. But he, who easily took to his old paths, replied to her that if it was her pleasure to give him three hours of her company every day, he would speak no more with Loretta; but this she would not grant. "Wherefore then," said Amadour, "since you are not willing to give me life, do you trouble yourself to guard me from death? Save, indeed, that you hope to cause me greater torments by keeping me alive than a thousand deaths. But though death escape me, I will seek till I find it, for the day of my death shall be the first of my rest."

About this time came news that the King of Granada had begun to make great war against the King of Spain, so that the King sent the Prince his son, and with him the Constable of Castille and the Duke of Alba, two old and prudent lords. The Duke of Cardona and the Count of Aranda were not willing to stay at home, and so entreated of the King to give them some command; and this he did according to the dignity of their houses. And for their safe keeping he gave them into the charge of Amadour, who during the war did such wondrous and mighty deeds as seemed to savour rather of despair than bravery. And to come to my story, I will show you how his great courage was proved by the manner of his dying; for the Moors, having made a show of giving battle, and seeing so large an army of Christians, feigned to retreat, whereupon the Spaniards began to pursue them; but the old Constable and the Duke of Alba, having a suspicion of their device, kept back against his will the Prince of Spain, so that he did not cross the river. But this, notwithstanding that it was forbidden them, the Duke of Cardona and the Count of Aranda did, and when the Moors perceived that they were pursued of a small company they wheeled round, and with one stroke of a scimitar the Duke of Cardona was slain, and so grievously was the Count of Aranda wounded that he was left where he fell for dead. At this Amadour came up so furiously enraged that he broke through all the press of battle, and made take the two bodies and carry them to the camp of the Prince, who grieved for them as if they had been his own brothers. But on searching out their wounds, the Count of Aranda was found to be still alive, and so was carried on a litter to his house, where he lay for a long while sick. And they bore to Cardona the dead body of the Duke. And after having in this manner rescued the two bodies, Amadour took so little heed for himself, that he was at last surrounded on every side by a host of Moors, and no more wishing capture to be made of his body than he had made capture of the body of his mistress, and not to break his faith with God as he had broken it with her; knowing that, if he was taken to the King of Granada, he would either be constrained to die a cruel death orrenounce Christianity, he was determined not to give his enemies the glory of his death or capture. And so kissing the cross of his sword, and commending his soul to God, he drove it home so deeply that it skilled not to give a second blow. So died Amadour, and the sorrow after him was that his valour deserved. And the news of it was noised abroad through all the coasts of Spain, and Florida, who was at Barcelona, where her husband had given command he was to be buried, heard the report thereof. And after that she had made for him honourable burial, without speaking to her mother or her stepmother, she became a nun of the Convent of Jesus, taking for her spouse Him who had delivered her from the burning love of Amadour, and from her weariness in the companionship of such a husband. Henceforth she turned all her affections to Godward, and, after for a long while living as a nun, gave up her soul with such gladness as when the bride goeth forth to meet the bridegroom.

"I am well aware, ladies, that this long novel may have been wearisome to some among you, but if I had wished to tell it after the manner of him who told it me, it would have been much longer. And I entreat you, while you make the virtue of Florida your ensample, to abate somewhat of her hardness of heart, and not to believe too much good of any man, lest when you know to the contrary you be the occasion to him of a cruel death, and to yourselves of a life of sorrow."

And after that Parlamente had had a long and attentive audience, she said to Hircan: "Is it your opinion that this woman was pressed to the bitter end, and made virtuous resistance?" "No," said Hircan, "for a woman cannot make a feebler resistance than crying out, and had she been where none could hear her I know not how she would have fared; and if Amadour had had more love and less fear, he would not for so little have left the work undone. And for all this case of yours I am not shaken from what I maintain—that no man who loves with a perfect love, or who is beloved of a lady, can fail to bring matters to a good issue, if he carry himself as he ought. Natheless, I must praise Amadour, insomuch that in some sort he did his duty." "What duty?" said Oisille. "Call you it duty for the servant to take by force his mistress, to whom he owes all reverence and obedience?" Whereupon Saffredent took up the discourse and said: "When our mistresses sit in state in chamber and hall, holding session upon us at their ease as our judges, then we fall on our knees before them; in fear and trembling we lead them forth to dance; so diligently do we serve them that we know their needs before they ask; so desirous are we to do suit unto them, and so fearful of their displeasure, that those who look upon us pity us, and often hold us as dull-witted as the beasts, and men forsaken of their understanding. Then do they give glory to our ladies, whose visage is so bold, and their speech so fair, that they make those that know them but on the outside both to fear, esteem, and love them. But when we are in some privy place, where love alone holds session over us, it becomes plain that they are women and we men, and then is *mistress* changed to *sweetheart*, and *servant* unto *lover*. To this consents the proverb:

> ' He that serves as best he can
> Maketh master out of man.'

They have such honour as men have, who can give it them and take it away, and they see our long-suffering that it is great; but it is reasonable that this should have its sure reward, when honour thereby can take no hurt." "You speak not of that true honour," said Longarine, "which is the best contentment for this life; for when all the world call me honourable woman, and I know that I am not, this praise does but increase my shame, and makes me still more to be confounded; and in like manner when men speak evil of me, and I know my innocency,

their blame is but my praise." "Whatever you have said,"
continued Geburon, "I am well persuaded that Amadour was an
honourable knight, and a virtuous, and without compare; and
though the names are feigned, I think I can recognise him. But
since it was not Parlamente's pleasure to name names, neither
is it mine. But be assured that, if he be the man I think, he knew
not fear, and his heart was still full of love and bravery."

Then Oisille said to them all: "So joyously do I esteem
this day to have been spent, that if we continue in like fashion
on the others, the time will pass all too quick. But see how
low is the sun, and the bells of the Abbey have this long while
rung to evensong. But I told no one of this since I had rather
hear the end of the story than the vesper music." At these words
all arose, and when they were come into the church they found
there the monks who had awaited them a good hour and more.
And when they had heard evensong, they took supper, with
much talk of the stories they had heard, each one searching
through the byways of his memory, that the following day
might be passed in as much delight. And after playing many
a game in the meadow, they went to bed, and with much
contentment brought to an end the first day.

DAY THE SECOND.

ON THE SECOND DAY EACH ONE TELLS THE FIRST CONCEIT THAT RISETH IN
HIS BRAIN.

PROLOGUE.

On the morrow they arose with a great desire of returning
to the place in which, on the day before, they had received so
great pleasure, for so ready was each one's tale that time passed
slowly for it to be told. After that they had heard Oisille's
reading, and also mass, where they all prayed God to the
intent that He might continue to put words into their mouths,
they went to dinner, recollecting meanwhile many a notable
relation.

But after dinner, when they had rested in their rooms, they
returned at the appointed time to the meadow, where all seemed
favourable to their undertaking, and being seated on the grass,

Parlamente began to say : "Since I brought yesterday to an end, it is my part to name one who shall begin to-day. And seeing that Oisille, the oldest and wisest of us was the first to speak, I give my vote to the youngest—I say not the most foolish, being assured that if we all follow her example we shall not keep evensong so long awaiting as we did yesterday. Wherefore, Nomerfide, do you make a beginning, but, prithee, let us not begin the day with tears." "Your entreaty skills nothing," said Nomerfide, "for one of our companions has made me chose a tale that has so got into my head that I can tell no other; and if it engender sadness in you, your complexion is in truth a melancholy one."

NOVEL XI.

Of a very privy matter.

In the household of Madame de la Tremoille there lived a lady named Roncex, who having one day gone with her mistress to the Grey Friars at Thouars, was compelled there to visit a place where she could not send her serving-maid in her stead. And she took with her a girl named La Mothe to keep her company ; but since she was shamefaced she left the wench in a room, and all alone entered a dark and gloomy privy. And this being held in common by all the Friars, they had given such a good account therein of all they had eaten, that the seat and the whole place were covered with the lees of Bacchus and the corn of Ceres, passed through the bellies of the Grey Friars. The poor woman, being so hard put to it that she had scarcely time to lift her dress, had the fortune to light upon the filthiest seat in the whole place, and found herself as well fastened to it as if she had been glued, with her thighs, dress, and feet in such case that she fell to crying at the top of her voice, "La Mothe, La Mothe, I am ruined and put to shame." The wench, having heard tales of the Friar's wickedness, thought some to be concealed within the privy who would fain rape her, and so ran full speed, crying to all she met : "Quick! succour Madame de Roncex, whom the Friars would ravish in the privy." And these running there hot-foot, found the poor lady, who called for help to the intent that she might get some woman to clean her. And all her hinder parts were bare, for she feared to let down her dress, lest it too should be covered with filth.   And on the entering of the gentlemen, they saw this sight, mighty pretty, but found no Grey Friar, but only the ordure on her thighs and fundament.   And to them this was great matter of laughter, but very shameful to the lady, who, in place of women-servants, was groomed down by men, and seen of them naked in the worst case possible for a woman.   And when she was well quit of this place of abominations, she must needs strip from top to toe, and change her whole dress before that she left the monastery, for when she saw the men she had let down her dress to cover her nakedness, forgetting the filth that was upon her in her shame at being seen of men.   Very wrath was she with the help La Mothe had brought her, but hearing that the poor wench believed she was in even worse case than she was, she put aside her anger and laughed with the rest.

"I think, ladies, that my tale has been neither long nor melancholy, and that you have had of me what you desired." But Oisille said to her : " Though it is a nasty tale and a dirty one, yet knowing those to whom it relates we cannot pronounce it tedious.   But I would have had great delight to see the countenances of La Mothe and the lady to whom she gave such fine assistance.   And since you have so soon made an end, give your vote to one whose thoughts run not so lightly in his head."   Nomerfide replied: " If you would have my fault repaired, I give my vote to Dagoucin, for so wise is he that he would rather die than make a foolish speech."   Dagoucin thanked her for the repute in which she held his good sense, and began to say: " The history which I will presently relate to you is to the intent that you may perceive how love blinds the greatest hearts and the noblest, and how difficult is wickedness to be conquered by means howsoever good."

NOVEL XII.

A Duke of Florence would have his friend prostitute his sister to him ; but in place of love meets with death.

Ten years are now overpast since there bore rule in Florence that Duke who had for wife Margaret, bastard daughter to the Emperor.   And for that she was so young,

that it was not lawful for him to lie with her till she grew of
riper age, he handled her mighty tenderly, for, while she slept
of nights, he would talk to very good purpose with other ladies
in the town.   Amongst the rest, he was amorous of a pretty,
wise, and virtuous lady, sister to a gentleman whom the Duke
loved as himself, and whose authority in his house was so
great that his word was feared and obeyed as if it were the
Duke's.   And the Duke had no secret he did not declare unto
him, in such sort that he might wellnigh be named his second
self.

And the Duke seeing his sister that she was so honourable
a woman that, after seeking every way, he could find no means
of declaring his love to her, came to the gentleman he loved so
well, and said to him: "If there were a thing in the world, my
friend, that I would not do for you, I should fear to make known
my mind to you, much less to ask your aid for the accomplish-
ing of my desire.   But so great a love do I bear you, that if I
had mother, wife, or child, who could be effectual for the saving
of your life, I would so use them rather than let you die in
torment; and I esteem your love towards me is like to mine,
and if I, who am master over you, love you so well, you at
least love me no less.   Wherefore I have a secret to manifest
to you, from concealing which I am fallen into the case you
now see, and from which I hope amendment either through
your offices or my death."

The gentleman hearing this discourse of his master, and
seeing his grief not feigned, and his face all covered with tears,
took so great compassion on him, that he said: "O, my lord, I
am your creature; all the contentments and all the honour I
have in the world come from you; you can speak to me as to
yourself, well assured that whatever is in my power is likewise
in yours."   Whereupon the Duke declared the love he bore
his sister, that it was so strong and fierce that if he did not, by
his means, have the enjoying of her, he saw not how he could
live any longer.   For he knew well that with her prayers and
gifts would not avail anything.   Wherefore he prayed the
gentleman, if he loved as he was beloved, that he would find
some means of getting for him this delight, which he never
hoped to have in any other way.   The brother, loving his
sister and the honour of his house better than the pleasure of

the Duke, would fain have made him some remonstrance, entreating him to use him in all other straits, but not to ask of him this abominable thing, the compassing the dishonour of his own blood, and saying that his heart and his honour alike forbade him take any part therein. The Duke, inflamed with unbearable displeasure, and biting his nails, replied in great wrath : "So be it then, and since I find no friendship at all in you, I know how to play my part." The gentleman, well advised of his master's cruelty, was afraid, and said to him : "My lord, since it is your pleasure, I will speak to her and bring you her reply." And the Duke returned : "As you love my life, so will I love yours," and so left him.

The gentleman knew well what was the intent of these words. And for a day or two he considered what was best to be done, without coming into the presence of the Duke. On the one hand there came before him all that was due to his master, the contentments and honours he had received of him ; on the other, the fame of his house, the virtuousness and chastity of his sister, whom he was well persuaded would not listen to this wickedness, unless by some cozenage of his own finding she was overcome by force, and this such an infamous deed that he and his would be for ever disgraced by it. And tossed from one side to the other, he at last determined rather to die than do his sister, one of the best women in all Italy, such an evil turn. But he thought to do still better if he delivered his country from such a tyrant, who would forcibly put this stain upon his house, for he held for certain that if he did not slay the Duke his own life and the lives of his kinsfolk would be in small security. Wherefore, without parley with his sister or any beside on the matter, he took counsel with himself how, by one blow, he might best save his life and avenge his shame. And at the end of two days he went to the Duke and told him he had used such order with his sister that, after much toil on his part, she had at last agreed to do him pleasure, if he would keep the matter so secret that none, save her brother, should be advertised thereof.

The Duke, desiring to hear this news, easily believed it, and embracing the messenger, promised him all he might ask for, and entreated him presently to bring affairs to a conclusion, and together they appointed a day. Whether the Duke was glad, it skills not to ask, and when he saw that the long-desired night drew near, on which he had good hopes of gaining the victory over her whom he aforetime deemed unconquerable, he went apart very early with the gentleman, forgetting not nightcaps and perfumed shirts, and such like gear, the best that he had.   And when all were gone away, he went with the gentleman to his sister's lodging, and entering in came into a bravely ordered chamber.   The gentleman having put his night-gear on him, and laid him in bed, said to him : "My lord, I go seek one who will not enter into this room without blushing, but before morning I hope she will be assured of you."   So saying he left the Duke and went to his own room, where he found one of his people, to whom he said : "Have you a heart bold enough to follow me whither I would be avenged on my greatest enemy ?"   The fellow, knowing not what he was called upon to do, replied : "Why, ay sir, were it against my lord Duke."   Whereupon the gentleman led him away so suddenly that he had no time to take other arms, but only a dagger, which he wore on him.   And when the Duke heard their return, thinking that the gentleman bore with him her for whom he lusted, he opened wide both the curtain and his eyes to look upon and receive the expected blessing ; but in place of seeing the preservation of his life, he beheld the instrument of his early death.   And this was a naked sword, which the gentleman held in his hands, and with which he struck the Duke, who was clad only in his shirt.   But he, wanting in arms and not courage, got behind the bed, and taking the gentleman by the middle, said to him : "Is it thus you keep your promise ?"   And having none other weapons save teeth and nails, he bit him in the thumb, and by the force of his arm so defended himself that they both fell on to the floor beside the bed.   Then the gentleman, not trusting overmuch in himself, called upon his follower, who, finding the Duke and his master intermingled so confusedly that he knew not which of the two to strike, pushed them with his feet into the middle of the room, and essayed to cut the Duke's throat for him.   But he still defended himself till loss of blood made him so weak as not to be able to do any more, whereupon the gentleman and his follower threw him on the bed, and there, with blows from the dagger, they made an end of killing him.   Then, drawing the curtain, they went forth and shut up the dead body in the chamber.

And when he saw himself victorious over his great enemy, by whose death he thought to have freed the commonwealth, his work seemed to him but half done, if he used not in like manner the five or six who were kinsfolk of the Duke. To which intent he spoke to his follower, that he should go seek them one by one, and do on them like vengeance. But his follower replied, having neither courage nor folly for such an undertaking : "It seems to me that for this present time you have achieved enough, and would do better to think of saving your own life than depriving others of their's. For if we take as much time to put an end to each one of them as we did to slay the Duke, the day will dawn upon our enterprise unfinished, even if we chance to find them undefended." The gentleman, whom a bad conscience rendered fearful, gave ear to his follower, and taking him alone, went to a Bishop, whose charge was that of Portreeve, to give authority for posting. To him the gentleman said : "This evening tidings came to me that my brother was at the point of death, and therefore I asked leave of the Duke to go to him, which he has granted me. So I pray that you give orders that I may have two good horses, and that the town gates may be opened to me." The Bishop, hearing his entreaty, and the command of the Duke his master, gave him forthwith a paper, by means of which the horses were granted him and the gates opened, even as he had desired. And in place of going to see any brother of his, he went straight to Venice, where he healed him of the bites the Duke had given, and after that journeyed to Turkey.

But on the morrow all the servants of the Duke, seeing how slow he was to return, had good suspicion that he was gone to see some woman, but since he tarried so long away made search for him in all the quarters of the town. And the poor Duchess, who began to bear her Duke great love, hearing that they searched and found him not, was exceeding troubled. But when the gentleman, his familiar friend, was seen no more than he, they went to his house and there sought for him. And finding blood at the door of his room, they entered in, but found no one who could give them any tidings. And following the trace of blood, these poor servants of the Duke came to the chamber where he lay, and the door was shut. And when it was broken open they saw the whole place that it was full of blood, and drawing aside the curtain they found the body stretched out upon the bed and sleeping its last sleep. Then were the servants sorely grieved, and having borne the body to the palace, they found there the Bishop, who told them how that the gentleman had last night fled the town on pretext of seeing his brother. Whereby it was clearly ascertained that it was he who had done this murder. And it was also proved that his sister had not so much as heard him speak of it, and she, although in great astonishment at what he had done, yet on account of it loved him all the more, since he had not spared to make hazard of his life, that she might be delivered from so cruel an enemy. And more and more honourably and virtuously did she continue in her former manner of living, for though, by reason of the escheatment of her goods, she was poor, yet did she and her sister get as honourable and rich husbands as were in Italy, and henceforth have always lived in good repute.

"By this, ladies, you may know what fear you should have of Love, since, though he is but a boy, he takes delight in tormenting prince and peasant, strong and weak, alike; blinding them all, so that they become forgetful of God and their conscience, and at the last, of life itself. And princes and those set in authority should beware of doing displeasure to those under them. For there is none so small that he cannot do hurt, if God would by him take vengeance on the sinner, and none so great that he should entreat evil those who are in his hands."

This relation was well listened to by all the company, but it engendered amongst them diverse opinions; for some maintained the gentleman to have done his duty in saving his life and the honour of his sister, and at the same time freeing his country from a tyrant; others said no, since it was foul ingratitude to put to death him who had given this gentleman so many honours. The ladies said he was a good brother and a good citizen to boot; the men, that he was a traitorous and wicked servant; and mighty pleasant hearing were the conclusions on both sides. But the ladies, as they are wont, spoke rather by

passion than sound logic, affirming the Duke to have been
worthy of death, and calling him who had given the blow
exceeding happy. Wherefore, seeing the great disputation
that was come of it, Dagoucin said to them : " Oddsfish, ladies,
enough of disputation about a thing gone-by and of the past ;
take you care lest your beauty bring about as dreadful murders
as that I have told you of." Whereupon Parlamente replied
to him : *La Belle Dame sans Mercy* would teach us that few
folk die of this pleasant sickness." " Would to God," said
Dagoucin, " that all you ladies here present were to know this
position how false it is ! And then I am assured they would
not desire to be named *Sans Mercy*, nor to be like that unbe-
lieving woman who, for fault of a gracious word, left her poor
lover to his death." " Would you then," said Parlamente,
" that, to save the life of one who affirms he loves us, we should
risk our honour and conscience ?" " That by no means is my
intent," answered Dagoucin, " for he who loves with a perfect
love had rather wound himself than his lady's honour. Wherefore I am of opinion that an honourable and gracious reply can
but increase virtue and better the conscience, and he is no true
lover who seeks aught else." " All the same," said Ennasuitte,
" all your prayers do but begin with honour and end with its
contrary. And if all who are here present will tell the truth, I
will believe them on their oath." Hircan swore he had never
loved another man's wife, but only his own. So said Simontault, and added that he had often wished all women to be
surly except his own wife. Geburon said to him : " Verily
you deserve that yours should be such as you desire others ;
but, as for me, I can with good conscience swear to you that I
have only loved one woman, whom I would rather see die than
that she should do anything to make me have less regard for
her. For my love was founded on her virtuousness alone,
wherefore I did not wish to see any stain thereon for the sake
of my pleasure." Whereupon Saffredent began to laugh,
saying : " I thought, Geburon, that your good sense. and your
love for your wife would have saved you from being a
gallant, but I see that it is not so, since you make use of
our terms of art, whereby we deceive the keenest and gain a
hearing from the most prudent. And where is the woman to
close her ears when we begin our passages with honour and

virtue? For if we were to plainly show them our hearts, a good many now welcome amongst the ladies would be poorly accounted of by them. But we cover our devil with the bravest angel we can find. And beneath this covering, before we are discovered, we have some mighty pretty entertainment. Perchance indeed we may so skilfully handle their hearts, that thinking they are on the straight road to virtue, they have neither means nor time to draw back their feet, when they find themselves on the threshold of vice." "Faith," said Geburon, "I thought you other than you are, and that virtue gave you more pleasure than pleasure itself." "What say you," replied Saffredent, "is there then a greater virtue than to love as God has commanded us? Methinks that it is much better to love a woman as a woman, than after the fashion of many to make of her an idol. And as for me I am fixed in this position; that use is better than abuse." But the ladies were all on the side of Geburon, and would have Saffredent keep silence. So he said: "To speak no more will be an easy burden to me, for I have been so evil entreated in your talk, that I wish not to return to it." "Your evil thoughts," answered Longarine, "are the cause of your evil treatment. For what virtuous woman would have you for her lover after the manner of your discourse?" "There have been women," he replied, "who have not found me tedious, and yet would not yield to you in virtue; but let us speak no more of it, so that my anger may displease neither you nor myself. Let us see to whom Dagoucin will give his vote." And he said: "I give it to Parlamente, for I think that she more than any beside ought to know what is honourable and perfect friendship." "Since I am chosen," said Parlamente, "for the third story, I will tell you what befell a lady who hath always been of my acquaintance, and all whose thoughts are open to me."

NOVEL XIII.

How a sea-captain served love with the sauce of religion.

In the household of the Regent, mother to King Francis, there lived a lady of great devotion, married to a gentleman in this point like to her. But otherwise they differed, for he

was old, and she was young and pretty; yet did she love
and serve him all as if he had been a brave young gallant.
And that he might have no cause for sorrow or weariness, she
set herself to live as a woman of his own age, putting from her
all company, fine gear, dances, and pastimes, in which young
women are wont to take delight; but all her delight and pleasure
was to do service to God, on which account her husband had
for her such love that she ruled as she would both him and his
household. And one day it chanced that he said that from his
youth up he had been desirous of journeying to Jerusalem, and
would have her mind on the matter. · She, who asked naught
but to please him, said: "Dear husband, since God has been
pleased to give us no children, and has granted us to enjoy a
sufficiency of worldly wealth, it would be much to my liking
that we should use a part of it in making this sacred journey;
for go where you may, I am determined never to leave you."
At this the good man was so contented that already he deemed
himself on the top of Calvary.

And while their talk ran on this, there came to Court a
gentleman who had often been in the wars against the Turks,
and was now forwarding with the King an enterprise against
one of their towns, which being taken would be greatly to the
advantage of Christendom. And the old gentleman asked him
about his journey. And when he had heard what the intent of
it was, he inquired whether, after this had been accomplished,
he had any purpose of making another to Jerusalem, whither
he and his wife had a great desire to go. The captain was
much pleased to hear of their intent, and undertook to conduct
them thither, and to keep the affair secret. Then the time
seemed long to the husband, till he should find his good wife
and tell her of these passages, since she had no less desire to
achieve the pilgrimage than he. And on that account she often
held parley with the captain, who, paying more regard to her
than to her words, fell so deep in love that often in his talk of
sea-voyages he would confuse Marseilles with the Archipelago,
and meaning to say ship would say horse, like one who is
ravished out of his senses; yet he found her of such a complexion that he durst not make any sign. And this concealment
bred such an inward fire, that he would often fall sick, in which
case the good lady was as careful of him, her guide, as of a

roadside cross; and would visit him so frequently that he, perceiving her to have a regard for him, was cured without need of medicaments beside. But certain folk, knowing the captain as rather famed for a brave and courtly comrade than a good Christian, marvelled within themselves how this pious lady could make such account of him. And seeing him to have quite changed his manner of living, and to often go to churches, sermons, and confession, they had a suspicion that all this was to the end that thereby he might gain the lady's favour, and could not restrain themselves from saying as much to him. Whereupon the captain, fearing that if anything of this came to her ears he should be banished from her presence, said to her and her husband that he was soon to be despatched by the King on his journey, and that he had several things for their hearing; but, to the intent that their own undertaking might be kept secret, he was fain not to hold parley with him and his wife in a public manner, and therefore entreated them to send for him when they were both gone to bed. And this the gentleman found reasonable, and failed not every evening to go to rest in good time, and make his wife also undress herself.

And when all their people were gone to bed, they would send for the captain, and make their plans for the journey to Jerusalem, in the midst of which, from sheer devotion, the husband would often go to sleep. The captain, seeing the old gentleman asleep in bed, and himself sitting on a chair near to her whom he held for the fairest and most virtuous woman in the world, was so cut to the heart by his fear of speaking and his longing thereto, that he would often altogether lose power of speech. But, lest the lady should see something of this, he would set himself to talk about the holy places of Jerusalem, where were such signs of the love Jesus Christ had towards us. And so by his talk of this love he concealed his own, looking upon the lady with sighs and tears, of which she understood nothing. But, beholding his devout visage, she held him for so holy a man, that she prayed him tell her what path it was he had taken, and by what means he had come to this so great love of God. He thereupon made the following declaration:—"He was a poor gentleman who, that he might attain to riches and honour, had forgotten his conscience, and had taken to wife a woman nearly akin to him by blood, for that she had great wealth, though she was old and ugly, and he loved her not; and when he had spent all her substance he had gone to sea to look for adventures, and had done so much by his toil that he was come to a good and honourable estate. But since he had been of her acquaintance, she had been the cause, by her holy words and good ensample, of a change in the manner of his life. And that above all he was determined, if he came back from his present enterprise, to take her husband and herself to Jerusalem; to satisfy in some sort his grievous sins past, which he had now brought to a close, save that he had not yet made satisfaction to his wife, but yet had good hope of soon being reconciled with her." All this discourse was mighty pleasant to the lady, but above all she rejoiced, inasmuch as she had drawn such a man to the love and fear of God. And until he set forth from Court, these long parleys continued each and every evening, without his ever opening his mind to her. And he gave her as a gift a crucifix, praying her that whenever she looked upon it she would be mindful of him.

So the hour of his departure drew nigh, and when he had taken leave of the husband, who was falling asleep, he came to bid farewell to the lady, in whose eyes he saw tears, for the honourable friendship she bore him. But this made his passion to be so unbearable, for that he might not make it manifest, that in bidding her farewell he fell, as if he had been a-swoon, into so great a sweat, that not only his eyes but his whole body seemed to pour forth tears. And so, without a word, he departed; and the lady marvelled greatly, for such a sign of regret she had never before seen. All the same for this she did not change her good opinion, and always made memorial of him in her prayers and orisons. But at the end of a month, as she was returning to her lodging, she fell in with a gentleman who gave her a letter from the captain, entreating her to read it by herself, and said that he had gone on board, well determined to accomplish something pleasing to the King and of service to Christendom; and as for himself, he was come back from Marseilles to put the affairs of the captain in order. And the lady went apart to a window, and opening the letter found it to be two sheets of paper covered on either side; and this was the manner of it:—

" My long delay and silence have left none,
Or hope or means of consolation,
Save that I speak and tell you all my mind,
And of the thoughts that are therein enshrined.
And now that I am all alone, and far
From you my hope, and have no guiding star
To rule the course ; needs must the words should go
And strive for me, since verily no moe
My eyes behold her who was all my life ;
Go, then, good letter, and make plain the strife
And clamours of my heart ; for if I keep
Them close concealed, then to my last long sleep
I shall begone.   O all too ready wit !
That wast most fearful, and the cause of it
Whereby I spoke not to you ; for I thought
Better to die in silence than give aught
Of grief to her I love, and was content
That for her good my poor life should be spent.
But yet again—what if I die and give
Some pain to her for whom alone I live ?
And this my promise was most certainly
That when the present toil was happily
Come to fulfilment, then I would fare back
And guide your footsteps on the sacred track ;
Until at last you made your orison
Upon that holy mountain named Sion.
But if I die no hand shall lead you there,
And seeing this. I will by no means dare
To bring to nothing what is next your heart.
And this thing done that holds us now apart
I will return and live then for your sake,
But doing so my heart is forced to make
Confession of my love, that it is sore.
O words most daring, fearful now no more,
What would you do ?   Or are you fain to show
The greatness of my love ?   Then you must know
You have not power to tell the thousandth part ;
But tell her this, her eyes have used my heart
In such sort that it takes its life alone
From her, unto such languor hath it grown.
Alas ! poor words and faint,
It is not yours to show her the constraint
Her eyes have on my heart.   At least say this,
Her high regard so strong and mighty is,
Than in her presence all words went astray,
And day was night, and night was full noon-day.
And when I fain would speak of my desire,
My words did run upon the Northern Fire.
And also say : my fear of thy displeasure,
This shut my lips, this put a bound and measure

Upon our parley, my supreme love
Full well deserving note in Heaven above,
For it in virtue had foundation,
Hence should not be a secret benison,
But open glory, being that your attire
Is always virtue, wherefore my desire
Is virtuous likewise.　No light love have I
Bottomed on beauty that one day must die;
Much less in me doth dwell of lust the flame
That would for pleasure work you sin and shame.
I had much rather die in this adventure
Than know your honour less by my calenture.
But if your love I have not, and can't gain,
It shall be my contentment to remain
Your faithful servant, till once more I see
My mistress, and with great humility
Do her my service.　And if nothing more
Fall to my lot, I shall at least adore
You as my goddess, wherefore doth arise
From off the altar of my sacrifice
The savour of a burning heart and soul.
And while the waters of the sea do roll
Betwixt us, that you may be of me sure
This diamond I send, as strong and pure
As is your heart; so to my joy and pleasure
I would you make this jewel fitly measure
Your whitest finger.　Wherefore, diamond, say,
A lover sends me here from far away.
In steadfast hope some great renown to gain
Whereby unto your favour he'd attain."

And having read this from beginning to end, she was much astounded at the captain's love, since she had never had any suspicion thereof.　And seeing the beauty of the diamond and the ring of black enamel, she was in great perplexity as to what she should do with it.　But after considering the matter through the whole night, she was very glad not to have any opportunity of giving him an answer, since she thought there was no need to add this trouble of an unfavourable reply to the charges of the King's he had in hand; and so, although she was resolved to refuse him, she left it till his return.　Yet was the diamond a great perplexity to her, for she was not accustomed to adorn herself at the expense of any but her husband.　Wherefore, being of a good understanding, she determined to draw from the jewel some profit to the captain's conscience, and so despatched a servant of hers to his wife, pretending that the letter

she sent by him was written by a nun of Tarrascon. And the
letter was to this intent :

"Mistress, your husband a short while before he embarked
passed by here; and after making confession of his sins and
receiving his Creator like a good Christian, he told me a thing
that was on his conscience—namely, the sorrow he had for that
he had not loved you as he ought. And, at parting, he prayed and
implored me to send you this letter and the diamond, which he
will have you keep for the love of him, assuring you that if God
grant him a safe return from his journey, no wife shall be more
kindly entreated than you; and this stone of steadfastness shall
be security for him. I pray you remember him in your prayers,
since in mine he shall have a place for the remainder of my days."

So, when this letter was finished and signed with the nun's
name, it was sent by the lady to the captain's wife. And when
the good old woman saw the letter and the ring, one need not ask
how she wept with joy and regret at being loved by her husband,
when she could no longer see him. And kissing the ring more
than a thousand times, and watering it with her tears, she
blessed God for that he had brought back to her the love of
her husband, now at the end of her days, when she had thought
it altogether lost to her. And she gave good thanks also to
the nun, who had done so much for her, and made her the best
answer she could. This the serving-man bore back to his
mistress, who was not able to read it, or listen to what he told
her, without much laughter. And so contented was she to have
profitably got rid of the diamond to the reunion of the captain
and his wife, that she would not for a kingdom have done
otherwise.

A short while after there came tidings of the defeat and
death of the poor captain; how he was deserted of them that
should have borne him aid, and his enterprises revealed by the
men of Rhodes, who above all should have kept it secret. All
those who had landed, and they were eighty, were killed;
among them being a gentleman named John, and a Turk who
had the devout lady for his godmother when he was baptised,
and both of whom she had sent on this journey with the
captain. The former of these was killed hardby the captain,
and the Turk, with fifteen arrow wounds, saved himself by
swimming to the French vessels. And by him alone was

learned the truth of the whole affair—namely, that a gentleman, whom the captain had taken for his comrade and familiar
friend, having done him good service with the King and the
nobles of France, as soon as he saw that the captain was
landed, went back with his ships to deep water.   And when the
captain saw that his enterprise was discovered, and that more
than four thousand Turks were at hand, he began to retreat.
But the gentleman in whom he had such trust seeing that, by
his death, he would get the whole charge and profit of this great
armament, called to him all the captains and addressed them to
the effect that it was not right to make hazard of the King's
ships and the brave men in them, for the sake only of eighty
or a hundred; and they, in whom there was no courage held
to this opinion.   And the captain, seeing that the more he
called to them the farther did they go, turned again upon the
Turks, and though he stood in sand up to his knees, so vali-
antly did he do battle, that it seemed as if he was about to
defeat all the host of his enemies, of which his traitorous
comrade had more fear than hope.   At last, despite his valour,
he received so many wounds from those who durst not approach
nearer than bow-shot distance, that he began to lose blood.
Whereupon, seeing the weakness of these true Christian men,
the Turks came upon them with the scimitar; nevertheless, as
God gave them strength, they fought unto the end.   The
captain called the gentleman named John, whom his mistress
had entrusted to him, and the Turk also; and fixing the point
of his sword in the earth, fell on his knees before it, kissing
and embracing the cross, and saying thus: "Lord, take into Thy
hands the soul of one who hath given his life for the exaltation
of Thy name."   The gentleman named John, seeing by these
words that life was failing him, took him and the sword which
he held into his arms, to the intent that he might give him aid;
but a Turk cut through both his thighs from behind, and
crying, with a loud voice: "We go, captain, to Paradise, and
there shall behold Him for whom we died," he became the
captain's comrade in death as he had been in life.   The Turk,
perceiving that he could do no service to the one or the other,
and having fifteen wounds from arrows, turned to the ships and
demanded to be taken on board.   But this, although he alone
was left of eighty, the captain's traitorous companion refused

him; but being an exceeding good swimmer, he went on till he was taken up by a small ship, and after some time was cured of his wounds.   And by means of this poor stranger the truth was made known, altogether to the honour of the dead captain, and to the disgrace of his companion.   And the King and all honourable men, when they heard the report, esteemed his wickedness so great that they thought he deserved death, howsoever a cruel one it might be.   But when he came, he spread abroad so many lying rumours and bribes that not only did he escape punishment, but received the office of him the latchet of whose shoes he was not worthy to unloose.

And when these pitiful tidings were brought to Court, the Regent, who had great liking for the captain, was mighty sorry; so likewise was the King and all of his fellowship. And she whom he loved best of all hearing the strange, pitiful, and Christian manner of his death, changed the chiding she intended to have given him into tears and lamentations, wherein her husband bore her company, for he thereby lost all hope of journeying to Jerusalem.   I would not forget that a maiden who lived in their household and loved the gentleman named John, on the very day on which the two were slain, came to her mistress and told her she had dreamed that her lover, all clad in white apparel, had come to bid her farewell, and that he and the captain were in Paradise.   But when she knew that this dream was the truth, she was in such grief that her mistress had enough to do to console her.   At the end of some time the Court went to Normandy, where the captain had lived, whereupon his widow failed not to come and do her reverence to the Regent.   And to the end that she might lead her into the Presence, the widow addressed herself to the lady whom her husband had loved so much.   And while they were awaiting the appointed hour in a church, the widow began bewailing and praising her husband, saying, among other things: "Alas! madam, mine is the greatest woe that ever befel a wife, for when he was beginning to love me more than he had ever done, God took him from me."   So saying she showed her the ring which, as a sign of his perfect love, she wore on her finger, and all this with many tears.   Thereupon the lady, notwithstanding the grief she felt, was so fain to laugh for the happy issue of her deceit, that she could not bring the widow into the Presence, but entrusted her to some one else, and betook herself to a side-chapel until her laughing fit was over.

"Methinks, ladies, that those to whom like things are given, should use them in like manner, for they will find out that to do good is pleasant. So one should not accuse this lady of deceit, but rather esteem her sense, which turned to good a thing which was worth nothing." "Call you," said Nomerfide, "a rare diamond of two hundred crowns worth nothing? I would have you assured that, if it had fallen into my hands, neither his wife nor his kinsfolk should have got so much as a sight of it. There is nothing which appertaineth more strictly to a body than that which is given. The gentleman was dead, none knew of it, and she would not have made the poor old lady shed so many tears." "In good faith," said Hircan, "you are in the right, for there are certain women who, to show themselves for better than they really are, do good deeds openly against their natural complexion, for we all know that nothing is as covetous as a woman. All the same their vanity oftentimes gets the mastery over their covetousness, and then they are forced to do things which go sorely against the grain. And I believe that she who sent the diamond away was not worthy of wearing it." "Not so fast, prithee," said Oisille, "I suspect I know who she is, wherefore, I entreat you, condemn her not without a hearing." "Mistress," replied Hircan, "I do not condemn her; but if the gentleman was as virtuous as you say, she would be honoured by having such a lover, but perchance one less worthy than he had her so tight by the finger that the ring could not get on." "Verily," said Ennasuitte, "she would have done well to have kept it, since no one was advised thereof." "What," said Geburon, "if only no one is advised thereof, are all things lawful to lovers?" "In good faith," said Saffredent, "there is but one crime I have seen punished, and that is folly; for your murderers, thieves, and adulterers are neither overtaken of justice nor blamed of men, if they be but as crafty as they are wicked. But often their wickedness is so great that it blinds them and they become fools, and as I have said, the fool hangs, while the knave laughs." "Say what you please," said Oisille, "God is this lady's judge, and as for me I consider her deed an honour-

II

able and a virtuous one.   But to make an end on't, I pray you, Parlamente, to give your vote to someone."   "With hearty goodwill," she replied, " I give it to Simontault, as one who, after these two sad novels, will not fail to give us matter for laughter."   "I thank you," said he, "for giving me your vote, and for calling me a Merry Andrew.   So for my vengeance I will declare to you that there are women who make a fair show of chastity to certain men, or at certain times, but the end makes plain of what sort they are, as you shall see by this true relation."

NOVEL XIV.

A very pleasant piece of cozenage done by my lord Bonnivet.

In the Duchy of Milan, while the grand-master of Chaumont was governor, there lived a gentleman named Bonnivet, who afterwards, for his merits, was made Admiral of France. Being mightily beloved by the aforesaid grand-master and all others for the virtues that were in him, he was often found at those assemblies where ladies were gathered together, and was by them more beloved than ever a Frenchman before, as much for his fair speech, his grace, and his beauty as for the renown in which he was held as one of the most brave and excellent warriors of his time.   One day, at a masked ball during the Carnival season, he led out in the dance the prettiest woman in all Milan, and whensoever there fell a pause in the music he failed not to make love to her, which it was confessed he knew as well as any how to do.   But she, who had no reply to his liking, brought him to a halt by saying she neither loved nor would love any but her husband, and, to be short, she would have nothing to say to him.   For all this the gentleman would not hold himself beaten, and plied her vigorously up to Mothering Sunday.   Notwithstanding his resolution, he still found her steadfast in her determination neither to love him nor anyone else, but to this he gave small credit, inasmuch as her husband was ill-favoured and she exceeding beautiful.   So he was resolved, as she had used concealment, himself to use cozenage, and from that time he left off entreating her, and betook himself so well to making inquiries as to her manner of living that he found she loved an Italian gentleman, who was reported both prudent and honourable.

So my lord Bonnivet little by little became of this Italian's fellowship, and so pleasantly and craftily that the Italian did not perceive his intent, but liked him so well that he only came after his mistress. And Bonnivet, to arrest from him his secret, feigned to tell him his own—namely, that he loved a certain lady, of whom in truth he had no thoughts, praying him not to reveal it, so that they might only have one heart and one mind between them. And the poor gentleman, in return for this great love, made a long declaration of that he bore the lady on whom Bonnivet was fain to be avenged; and once in each day they met at a certain place to tell one another what luck they had had with their ladies, one telling lies and the other the truth. And the gentleman confessed to have loved his mistress for three years, without having had anything of her but fair words and assurance of her love towards him. Whereupon my lord Bonnivet showed him the means that might avail to accomplish his end, which he found so much to the purpose that in a few days she was ready to grant him whatsoever he might desire, and all to seek was the way to bring matters to a conclusion, and this, by the help of Bonnivet, was soon found. So one day before supper the gentleman said to him : " Sir, I am more beholden to you than all other men, for by your good counsel I hope to have that to-night which I have desired for so many years." " I pray you then," said Bonnivet, " tell me the manner of it, that I may see whether there is any cozenage or risk, and serve you as a friend." The gentleman told him that his mistress had found means to leave the chief door of the house open, under pretext of an illness of one of her brothers, which made it needful to send to the town on occasions at all hours, and so he might easily enter the court, but was by no means to mount by the great stair, rather making his way by a small one to the right hand, and thence entering into the first gallery he came to where were the rooms of her father-in-law and her brothers-in-law. He was to make for the third door from the top of the stairs, and if softly pushing it he found it shut, he must get him gone and know for certain that her husband was returned, though she expected him not for two days; but if he found it open he was to gently enter, and shutting the door behind him to bolt it hard and fast. And above all he was not to forget to wear felt slippers for fear of making a noise, and to come not earlier than two hours after midnight, since her brother-in-law, being very fond of cards, never went to bed before one. To all this Bonnivet said : " Well done, my friend, may you have good hap and meet with no mischance, and if my fellowship will avail you anything, I will spare nothing in my power." The gentleman gave him his best thanks, but said that in a matter of this sort one could not be too much alone, and went to take order therein.

On his side my lord Bonnivet did by no means sleep, and perceiving that the hour was come for him to be avenged on this cruel lady, he went early to his lodging, and had his beard cut to the length and breadth of the gentleman's, and in like manner his hair, that when she touched him she might not know the difference. Nor did he forget the felt slippers, and, to be short, had all his dress after the fashion of the Italian's. And since he was among the familiar acquaintances of the stepfather he was not afraid of going early to the house, thinking, if he were perceived, to go straight to the good man's chamber on some affair they had together. So at midnight he entered the lady's house, and found much folk both coming and going, but passed among them unknown and got into the gallery. And on touching the two first doors he found them fast, but the third was open. And when he was in the room he bolted the door behind him, and beheld all the room to be hung with white, and the ceiling and the floor after the same manner, and in it there was a bed with a curtain most admirably worked in white. And on the bed was the lady in her nightcap and shift covered with pearls and precious stones; this he saw through a corner of the curtain without her seeing him, for there was in the room a great candle of refined wax, which made it as light as the day. And for fear of being known of her, he first blew out the candle, then doffed his clothes and got into bed beside her. She, believing him to be the man who had loved her so long, made for him the best cheer that she could, but he, knowing it was for another, would not say so much as a single word, and had no thoughts save of putting his vengeance into execution, that is to say, of taking away her honour and chastity without her will and favour. But she

held herself so content with this vengeance of his that she thought
she had made him a full return for all his services, till at last
the clock struck one, and it was time to bid farewell.   Whereupon in as low a voice as he was able he asked her whether
she was as pleased with him as he with her.   She, thinking
him to be her lover, said that not only was she pleased but
mightily astonished at the greatness of his love, which had
prevented him for a whole hour from replying to her.   At this
he burst into a loud laugh, and said to her : "Will you then
indeed refuse me another time, as has been your custom up to
now ?"   She, knowing him by his speech and laughter, was
made so desperate with grief and shame that a thousand times
she called him *villain, traitor, deceiver,* and would have sprung
from the bed to look for a knife that she might kill him, since
it had been her fortune to lose her honour for a man who loved
her not, and who, to make perfect his vengeance, might blaze
abroad the whole matter.   But holding her back with his arms
he spoke to her gently, and assured her that he loved her better
than the Italian, and that he would so conceal her dishonour
that she would take no hurt thereby.   All this the poor fool
believed, and hearing from him how he had found out his
scheme, and the pains he had taken to win her, swore to him
that she loved him better than the man who could not keep
her secret, and that she was now well persuaded that the
common report as touching the French was false, since they
were more wise, secret, and persevering than the Italians.
Wherefore from henceforth she would forget the opinion her
countrymen had of the French, and cleave to him.   But she
entreated him not to be present for some time at any assembly
where she was save it was masked, for she knew well she
should be so ashamed that her face would discover her to all men.
To this he consented, and asked her, when her sweetheart
came at two o'clock, to make good cheer for him also, but
after this little by little to separate herself from him.   At this
she made so great difficulty that, had it not been for the love
she bore him, she would never have granted it.   And in bidding
her farewell, he gave her such good matter of satisfaction that
she heartily wished he could stay longer.

   After he was arisen and had put on his clothes he went from
the room, leaving the door as he had found it.   And since it

was hard on two o'clock, and he feared to meet the Italian on the way, he hid himself near the top of the stair, and soon after saw him pass by and go into the lady's room.   Then he went home to his lodging to rest from his travail, which he did in such sort that nine o'clock in the morning found him still in bed.   And while he was rising the Italian failed not to come and tell him his luck, though it was not of the kind he had hoped for.   He said that when he entered the lady's room he found her out of bed in her dressing-gown and in a high fever, her pulse beating quick and fast, her face afire, and the sweat beginning to run adown it.   In such case was she that she was fain for him straightway to begone, since she had more occasion to think of God than Cupid, telling him she was sorry he had run this risk, since she could not give him what he wanted in a world from which she thought soon to depart.   At all this he was so astounded and grieved that his joyful heat was changed to most mournful ice, and he presently left her.   And while he made this relation so bitterly did he weep that it seemed as if his soul would shortly follow his tears.   Bonnivet, who was as fain to laugh as the other to weep, consoled him as well as might be, telling him that these long-lasting love affairs had always a difficult beginning, and that Love made this delay to the end that the enjoyment of her should be greater, and with this they parted.   As for the lady she kept her bed some days, and when health was restored to her, gave her first lover his dismissal, founding it on her remorse and fear of death.   But she kept in her favour Bonnivet, whose love lasted, as it was wont, as long as the flowers of the field.

"It seems to me, ladies, that the craft of the gentleman was well matched with the hypocrisy of the lady who, after having counterfeited the honest woman, showed herself what she was." "You may say what you will," said Ennasuitte, "but the gentleman did her an evil turn. If a lady loves one man, should another have her by craft?"   "Trust me," answered Geburon, "such commodities, when for sale, are bought in by the best and last bidders. Do not think that lovers take so much trouble for love of their mistresses, for it is only for love of themselves and their own pleasure."   "By my faith," said Longarine, "I believe you, for to speak the plain truth, all the lovers I have ever had made me, my life, my good, my honour,

the first heads of their discourse, but ' finally,' and 'to conclude,'
were themselves, their pleasure, their renown.   Wherefore the
best plan is to put a close to the first part of the sermon, for
when one comes to the second there is not so much honour to
be gained, since it goes without saying that vice is to be met
with a refusal."   "One must needs then," said Ennasuitte,
" refuse a man the moment he opens his mouth without knowing what he would say."   To this replied Parlamente : " This
was not her intent, for we are well assured that at the beginning
a woman ought not to make any sign that she understands
whither the man is going, nor should she seem to be able to
believe him when he tells her, but when it comes to oaths and
the like, I think that it is best for us to leave them on this
brave road, without descending to the valley below." "But ought
we," said Nomerfide, " to believe this of them, that their love
is lust?   Is it not a sin to judge one's neighbour?"   "You
may believe what you please," replied Oisille, " but there is
such strong matter of suspicion that it is so, that when you
perceive the least spark of this fire you should run from it,
since it has burnt up many a heart that thought not of danger
near."   "Truly," said Hircan, " these your laws are too hard,
and scarcely to be borne.   And if women, to whom gentleness
is so befitting, were to follow your advice, we too should make
a change, and for soft entreaty you would have craft and main
force."   "Let each one follow his complexion," said Simontault,
" that seems to me the best; let him love or not love, as he
will, but let there be no deceit."   "Would to God," answered
Saffredent, " that this law of yours would be as much to the
advantage of honour as pleasure."   But Dagoucin could not
refrain from saying : " They who would rather die than make
manifest their hearts could by no means observe your obedience."   " Die !" said Hircan, " is there any such thing as an
honest gentleman who, for a matter of so small account, would
think of death?   But let us no more talk of impossible things,
and rather hear to whom Simontault will give his vote."
" I give it," said he, " to Longarine, for I have been looking at
her a long while, and she is still talking to herself, so I think
that she has some good relation, and it is not her manner to
conceal the truth, be it against man or woman."   "Since you
deem me so truthful," said Longarine, " I will tell you a story

from which, though it be not so much to the praise of women
as I could desire, you shall see that in them there are as bold
hearts as keen wits, and as crafty devisings as in men.   And
if my tale be long, I entreat you bear patiently with me."

NOVEL XV.

A woman will do that for revenge she will not for love.

There lived a gentleman in the Court of King Francis the
First whose name I know well, but will not make mention of
it. He was poor, having an income of only five hundred pounds,
but stood so high in the King's favour that he was enabled
thereby to take to wife a woman so rich that a great lord
would have been well contented with her.   And for that she
was still very young, he entreated one of the most noble of the
Court ladies to have the charge of her, which she did with
hearty goodwill.   Now because this gentleman was of gentle
blood, goodly to look upon, and of an infinite grace, he stood
in excellent case with all the ladies, and notably with one of the
King's mistresses, neither so young nor pretty as his own wife.
And for the great love he bore this woman, he made so small
account of his wife that he hardly slept with her a single night,
and what to her was still more hard to be borne, he never
spoke to her, nor gave her any signs of friendship.   And notwithstanding that he had the enjoyment of her substance, so
little thereof fell to her share that she had not so much as a dress
that was agreeable to her rank and desire.   For all this the lady
with whom his wife lived often reproved him, saying to him
after this sort: "Your wife is pretty, rich, and of an illustrious
house, yet do you make no more account of her than if she
were the opposite of all this.   And being still young she has
borne it hitherto, but I fear lest, when she is come of riper years,
her mirror and one who bears no love for you, will show her that
beauty so little esteemed by you, and she will do that for
vengeance sake which, had she been well entreated, would
never have come into her thoughts."   The gentleman, his
heart being disposed in another quarter, made sport of her, and
for all her warnings continued in his accustomed manner of
living.   But when two or three years were overpast, his wife

began to grow the comeliest woman in all France, insomuch as
it was reported that at the very Court she had no equal. And
the more she perceived that she was worthy of love, the more
she sorrowed that her husband made such small account of her;
in such sort that, had it not been for the consolements of the
lady with whom she lived, she would have fallen into despair.
And having used all means of pleasing her husband that were
in her, she thought that it were impossible he should not love
her, seeing the great love she bore him, if his brain had not
conceived a fantasy for some other woman; and so subtilely did
she search out this, that she discovered the truth, and that he
was so busily engaged every night in another place that he had
forgotten his wife and his conscience.

And when she was surely persuaded of the manner of life
he led, she fell into such a melancholy that she would have no
other gear but black, and would by no means go to any place
where was pleasant entertainment. And although the lady of
the house did all she was able to move her from this sadness,
she could not, and her husband, knowing it well enough, was
readier to make a mock than supply the remedy. You know,
ladies, that a great joy is followed by tears, so bitter sorrow
ends with gladness. So one day it fell out that a great lord,
who ofttimes came to the house, and was near akin to the
mistress of it, hearing the strange fashion of this lady's treatment, had so great pity on her that he was fain to essay somewhat for her consolation, and speaking to her he found her so
comely, so wise, and so virtuous that he became more desirous
to gain her favour than to talk about her husband, save to
show how little cause she had to love him.

The lady, seeing herself abandoned of him who ought to
have loved her, and on the other hand loved and entreated by
so fine a gentleman, held herself exceedingly happy to be in
his favour. And although she was always tender of preserving
her honour, yet she took great delight in speaking to him, and
beholding herself loved and esteemed, for which she, so to say,
hungered and thirsted. And this friendship of theirs lasted a
long while, even until the King perceived it, who for the love he
bore the husband would not willingly suffer any dishonour to
be laid upon him. Wherefore he entreated the prince to put
her out of his thoughts, saying that if he persisted he would be

heartily displeased with him.   So the prince, loving the favour
of the King better than all the ladies in the world, promised for
his love towards him to bring the matter to an end, and that
very evening to bid her farewell. And this as he had promised
so he performed, as soon as he knew her to be gone to her
lodging, where she and her husband had a room above his own.
And her husband, chancing to be at a window, saw the prince
enter his wife's room, and though the prince too saw him, he
went in none the less.   And in bidding farewell to her for
whom his love was hardly begun, he gave for reason the commands of the King.

After their tears and regrets had lasted till an hour after
midnight, the lady made an end by saying: "I praise God, sir,
that he is pleased to deprive you of your love for me, since it is
of such poor and feeble growth that you take it up and lay it
down at the commands of men.   As for me, I neither asked
leave of my mistress, nor my husband, nor my very self to love
you, for this same love, together with your beauty and honour,
has such sway over me that I know no other god or king but
him.   But since your heart is not so filled with this true love
as not to leave a place for fear, you can be no perfect lover,
and I have no wish to love with a perfect love—such as I had
for you—an imperfect lover.   So, sir, I bid you farewell, since
your fear makes you undeserving of a love like mine."
The prince went away in tears, and perceived the husband still
at the window, and that he had seen both his going in and his
coming out.   Wherefore on the morrow he told him wherefore
he had gone to see his wife, and the command the King had
laid on him, at which the gentleman was much pleased, and
thanked the King for it.   But seeing his wife, that she grew
more beautiful day by day, and himself that he was growing old
and losing his comeliness, he began to change his part, and took
to that which he had made his wife play for so long a time, for
he sought her out more than he was wont, and kept watch over
her.   But all the more he did this, the more she avoided him,
wishing to give her husband back in part those sorrows she had
had at being so little beloved of him.   And so as not to lose
all at once the pleasure that love began to give her, she
addressed herself to a young gentleman, so handsome and well
spoken, and of such good grace that he was in favour with all

the ladies of the Court. And making complaint to him of the manner in which she had been treated, she stirred pity for her in his heart in such sort that the young gentleman tried every means for her consolation. And she, to make good the prince she had lost, set herself so well to love the gentleman that she forgot her sorrows overpast, and thought of nothing but the skilful conduct of this love-affair. And this was done by her in such a manner that her mistress perceived nothing of it, for in her presence she took good care not to speak to her gallant, but when she wished to talk with him she went to see certain ladies who were lodged at the Court, amongst whom there was one thought to be her husband's sweetheart.

So, one evening after supper, when it began to grow dark, this aforesaid lady did creep away, and without calling a companion went into the ladies' room, where she found him whom she loved better than herself. Then, sitting close together at a table, they talked with one another, feigning to read from a book. A certain one, whom her husband had set on the watch, came and told him where his wife was, and he, who had some share of wisdom, went thither as quickly as he was able. And on entering the room he saw his wife reading a book, and making as if he saw her not, crossed over to speak to the ladies on the other side. Whereupon his poor wife, seeing herself discovered by her husband with a man to whom before him she had never spoken, was so affrayed that she lost her reason, and not being able to pass along the bench, leapt on the table and fled, as if her husband was following her with a drawn sword, and so sought out her mistress.

And no sooner had she undressed and gone to bed than one of her women came to say that her husband called for her. To this she straightly replied that she would by no means go, since he was of such strange and austere complexion that she was afraid he might do her an evil turn. But at last, for fear of some worse thing, she went as it was commanded of her. Her husband said not one word to her until that they were in bed, and she, who knew not like him how to dissimulate, began to weep. And when he asked her the why and wherefore, she told him that she was afraid he was angry with her, because he had found her reading with a gentleman. To which he replied that he had never forbidden her to speak with men, and that he never had taken such speech in bad part; but she had fled away from his presence, as if she had done something worthy of punishment, and this alone made him think she loved the gentleman. Wherefore he forbade her to hold parley with him in public or in private, assuring her that the first time she did so he would kill her without mercy or compassion. And to this she very willingly agreed, determining within herself not to be such a fool the second time. But since things one wishes for the more they are forbidden all the more they are desired, the poor woman very soon forgot her husband's threats and the promises she had made to him. Nay, the very same evening she, having returned to sleep in another room with some other ladies and their women, sent to the gentleman entreating him to come and see her in the night. But her husband, who was in such torment by reason of his jealousy that he could not sleep, folded his cloak round him, and taking a serving-man went and knocked at his wife's door, for he had heard that her lover was wont to go to her at night. She, expecting none less than him, got up and put on her furred slippers and a robe which came to hand. And seeing the three or four women she had with her that they were asleep, she went forth from the room to the door at which she heard the knocking. And to her question: "Who is that?" they gave for answer the name of her lover, but to be more assured she opened a small wicket, saying: "If you are he whom you say, give me your hand; and shall I not well know it?" And when she touched her husband's hand she was aware of it, and sharply closing the wicket, cried out: "Ah, husband, it is your hand." Her husband in great wrath replied to her: "Why, ay, it is the hand that will fulfil my promise, wherefore fail not to come when I call for you." Saying thus he returned to his lodging, and she to her room, more dead than alive, and in a loud voice cried to her women: "Arise, for you have too long slept, for thinking to deceive you I myself have been deceived." Then all a-swoon she fell into the middle of the chamber. Her women arose at this cry, so much amazed to see their mistress lying on the ground for dead, and to hear the words of her mouth, that they knew not what to do, save to run for remedies to revive her. And when she was able to speak she said to them: "You see before you the most unhappy woman on the face of the earth!" and so fell to relating

her evil case, and praying them to succour her since she held
her life for lost.

And while they were making endeavour to console her,
there came a serving-man to them, who commanded her to
straightway go to her husband. She, embracing two of the
women, began to weep and to wail, praying them not to let her
go since it was surely to her death. But the serving-man told
her it was not so, and that she should suffer no evil, his life for
hers. So, seeing there was no way of resistance, she threw herself into his arms, saying: "Since it must be so, bear this
wretched body to its death!" And, half swooning with
despair, she was carried by the servant to his master's lodging,
at whose feet then fell this poor lady, with these words: "Sir,
I pray you have pity upon me, and I swear to you by my faith
before God that I will tell you the whole truth." Her husband,
as one desperate, replied to her: "By God you shall tell it me,"
and sent away from the room all his people. And since he
had always known his wife for a devout woman, he was well
persuaded that she would not swear falsely upon the cross, so
sent for a brave one, and when they were both alone made her
swear upon it that she would truly answer him all his questions.
But having by this time overcome her first fear of death, she
took courage, being resolved before that she died not to conceal
from him the truth, and also not to say anything that might be
to the hurt of the gentleman her lover. And after that she had
heard all the questions he applied to her, she thus replied to
him: "I have no wish, sir, to justify myself, or to make of less
account before you the love I have borne to the gentleman you
suspect, for after your experience this day you neither could
nor ought to believe it; but I have a great desire to tell you
the causes of my love. Understand, then, that never wife so
loved her husband as I have loved you; and from the time I
was betrothed to you even until now there entered not into my
heart any love but that of you. You know that while I was
yet a child my kinsfolk would have me marry a certain one,
both richer and of a more noble house than you, but from the
hour we spoke together, I could by no means consent to their
will, for against all counsel I was resolved to have you, without
regarding either your poverty or any remonstrances my kinsfolk
might make to me. And you can by no means be ignorant of

the treatment I have received at your hands, and of how you have had for me neither love nor esteem, at which I took such grief that, without the help of the lady with whom you placed me, I should have been in despair.   But at last, seeing myself accounted of great beauty by all save you, I began to have such a lively feeling of your wrong towards me, that my former love was turned to hatred, and my desire of doing your pleasure into a desire of revenge.   And amid this despair a certain prince sought me out ; but he, choosing rather to be obedient to the King than to love, left me, whereas I began to take some comfort in my torment by means of an honourable friendship. And he being gone, I lit upon a man who had to take no pains to seek me out, since his honour, his grace, and his virtues themselves well deserve to be sought out by every woman of understanding.   At my request, and not by his, he has given me his love, and this so virtuous that never yet has he asked anything of me that could not honourably be granted. And though the small love I owe to you might have me excused if I broke with faith and loyalty, the love I owe to God and my honour has well assured me from doing aught of which I should fear to make confession.   I wish not to deny to you that, as often as might be, I have gone to hold parley with him in a closet, making a pretext of saying my prayers, for never, either to man or woman, have I entrusted the conduct of this affair.   Neither will I deny that being in so privy a place I have kissed him with more hearty goodwill than I have kissed you.   But let not God be merciful towards me if aught else hath passed between us, or if he has entreated such from me, or if my heart hath felt of such the desire, for so great was my delight at seeing him that I deemed in the whole world there was no pleasure beside.   And you, sir, who are alone the cause of this annoy, would you take vengeance for a work of which you have for a long time set me the example, save that you have neither honour nor conscience on your side ? For you know well, as I do, that she whom you love doth by no means content herself with what God and reason have enjoined. And though the law of men deem it great dishonour in women who love other than their husbands, yet the law of God metes equal measure for the husbands who love other than their wives.   And if your sin and mine be put into the balance, you

are a man wise and with the experience of age; I, a woman, young
and with no experience of the force and power of love. You
have a wife, who seeks you out, esteems, and loves you more
than her very life; I have a husband who flies me, who hates
me, who despises me more than a serving wench. You love
a woman older, of worse figure, and of worse looks than I; I
love a gentleman younger, handsomer, and more amiable than
you. You love the wife of one of your most familiar friends
and the mistress of your King, doing hurt at the same time to
the friendship you owe the one and the reverence you owe
the other; I love a gentleman who is tied by nothing save by
his love to me. Judge then, without favour, which of the
two is meet to be punished and which excused; you, a man
reputed for prudence and experience, who, without any fault of
mine, have done not only to me but to your King such an
evil turn; or I, young and without experience, despised and
contemptuously entreated by you, who have loved the handsomest and most honourable gentleman in France, and have
loved even him in despair at ever attaining to your love."

The husband, hearing these truthful conclusions, given out
by such a beautiful countenance, and with so well assured
and daring a grace, that she showed herself neither to be in fear
nor desert of punishment, was in such surprise and astonishment that he had nothing to say, except that the honour of a
man and of a woman are not like to one another. But nevertheless, since she had sworn to him that there had been between
her and her lover nothing beside that of which she had made
mention, he was resolved to do her no harm so long as she had
no more talk with him, and that they should neither of them remember any more the things that were past; and this she promised
him, and with this good agreement they went to bed together.

On the morrow an old lady who attended on her, having
been in sore fear for her mistress's life, came to her as she
was getting up and said: "Well, mistress, and how goes it
with you?" She, laughing, answered: "Trust me, there's no
better husband than mine, for he believed me on my oath."
And so passed five or six days, the husband being so tender of
his wife that night and day he kept a spy upon her. But for
all his ward, she still held parley with her lover, and that too in
a dark place and suspicious: natheless, she was so secret in the

matter that no man knew the truth of it. Only there was a
rumour set about by a serving-man that he had found a gentleman with a lady in a stable under the room of the mistress of
the household. At which the husband took so strong a suspicion that he was resolved to put the gentleman to death, and
to this intent gathered together a great number of his kinsfolk
and acquaintance. But the chief among his kinsfolk was so
good a friend of the gentleman's that he sought him out, and
in place of killing him, advertised him of the complot. And
beside this the gentleman was so beloved of all the Court, and
went abroad so well accompanied, that he feared not the power
of his enemy, and, to be short, they never came in his way.
But he went to a church to find his sweetheart's mistress, who
knew nothing of the passages between them, for in her presence
they had not so much as spoken together. And the gentleman told her the suspicions and evil purpose of the husband,
and that, although he was innocent, he was resolved to go on a
long journey to do away with the rumour, which now began
greatly to be raised abroad. The Princess was much astonished
to hear all this, and swore that the husband did great wrong,
insomuch that he suspected an honourable woman whom she
had never known but all virtuousness. But considering the
authority of the husband, and to put an end to this shameful
rumour, the princess counselled him to withdraw himself some
while, assuring him that she gave no credit to these foolish
suspicions. The gentleman, and the lady who was with the
princess, were well content to still possess her favour and good
opinion. And she advised the gentleman before his departure
to have speech with the husband, which advice he followed.
And he found him in a gallery near the Presence Chamber,
where with a steadfast visage, doing him the reverence that pertained unto his rank, he said to him : "Sir, throughout all my
whole life I have been desirous of doing you service, and by
way of reward I hear that this evening you would seek me out
to take my life. I entreat you to have in mind that, though you
have more power and authority than I, yet like you I am a
gentleman, and would not willingly lose my life for nothing. I
beseech you to believe that you have to wife an honourable
woman, and if there be any to say the contrary, I tell him he
lies most villainously. As for me I know of nothing I have

done for which you owe me evil. And, if it please you, I will
remain your servant, or if not, the King's, with which I am
content." The husband, on hearing this, told him that of a
truth he had held him in some suspicion, but that he found
him so honourable a man that he had rather his love than his
hatred; and in bidding him farewell, hat in hand, he embraced
him with great friendship. Conceive, if you can, what was said
of them who, the evening before, had been charged to take the
life of the one, when they saw the other give him such signs of
honourable friendship; but in truth each had his own thoughts
upon the matter. So the gentleman fared forth on his journey;
but since he had a less store of money than comeliness, his
sweetheart sent him a ring of three thousand crowns which her
husband had given her, and he pledged it for fifteen hundred
crowns.

. And some time after this departure, the husband came to
the princess with whom his wife lived, and asked her to take
farewell of her that she might go and live with one of his
sisters. At this the princess marvelled, and so strongly prayed
him to tell her the cause of it that he told her a part, but not
all. And after the young lady had said farewell to her
mistress and the whole Court, without tears or any sign of
sorrow, she went whither her husband wished, being in the
keeping of a gentleman, to whom charge was given that he
should strictly guard her, and above all that she should not
speak on the road with him whom her husband held in suspicion. She, who was aware of these commands, every day gave
them some alarms, mocking them and the care they took of
her. And on one day, as they set out from their lodging, she
found a Grey Friar on horseback. And she riding her nag
talked with him by the way, even from dinner to supper. And
when they were within a quarter of a league of their resting-
place, she said to him: "Holy father, in return for the consolation you have given me this afternoon, I hereby give you
two crowns, the which are in paper, for I am well assured that
otherwise you would by no means touch them. And I pray
you, that when you have departed from me, you will go at a
good rate along the road, and take heed that these men here
see you not. This I say for your good, and for the obligation
I have towards you." The Friar, well pleased with his two

I

crowns, began to gallop away along the road, and when he was
gone some short distance, the lady began to call out to her
servants : "Think you that you are good servants, and careful
in guarding me? Verily he, concerning whom you have had
so many commands that I was not to speak to him, has held
parley with me all this day, and you have not hindered him.
You well deserve that your master, who puts in you so great a
trust, should give you blows in place of wages." When the
gentleman who had her in his keeping heard this, it cut him to
the heart, and he could not answer her a single word, but
putting spurs to his horse and calling two others to his side he
rode so fast that he got up to the Grey Friar. The poor man,
seeing them coming, fled as best he could, but since they were
the better mounted he was taken captive; and not knowing
the wherefore of all this, cried for mercy, and on his throwing
back his hood so as in more lowly sort with bare head to make
his entreaty they knew him not to be the man they sought, and
that their mistress was making a pastime of them. This she
did also when they came back, saying: "Truly it is folk like
you to whom ladies should be entrusted : you who let them
speak to you know not who, and then putting faith in their
words, shamefully entreat the servants of God."

After all this mocking cozenage, she came to the place her
husband had appointed for her, and was subject to her two
sisters-in-law and the husband of one of them. And about
this time her husband heard how her ring was in pledge for
fifteen hundred crowns, at which he was in sore displeasure,
and to save the honour of his wife and to get back the ring, he
told her by his sisters that she should get it back and he would
pay the fifteen hundred crowns. She, caring not at all for the
ring so long as the money stood with her lover, wrote to him
that her husband constrained her to get it back ; and to the
end that he should not think her love was grown less, she sent
him a diamond given to her by her mistress, which she held in
more account than any ring whatsoever. The gentleman sent
the Lombard back his bond with great goodwill, contented
with the crowns and the diamond, and the assurance of his
sweetheart's favour. But while her husband was alive, he
had no means of addressing her, save on paper. And when
her husband was dead, thinking to find her such as she had

promised, he as speedily as he was able sought her in marriage, but found his long absence had given him a fellow better beloved than himself. And for this he had so great grief that, flying from the ladies, he sought places of danger, in which, having as much esteem as a young man can, he ended his days.

"Hereby, ladies, without sparing our sex, I wish to make plain to husbands that women of a great heart are more often overcome by the fire of revenge than by the sweetness of love, the latter of which the woman I have told you of for a long while resisted, but at last was conquered by despair. This is no ensample for an honourable woman, for in howsoever evil a case one may be, it is no excuse for evil-doing. For the greater and the more manifold our temptations, so much the more ought we to show ourselves virtuous, and to overcome evil by good, and not to render evil for evil; since often the ill a body thinks to bring upon another falls upon his own head. Exceeding happy are those women in whom God manifests himself by chastity, gentleness, patience, and long-suffering."
"It seems to me, Longarine," said Hircan, "that the lady of whom you have spoken was more moved by revenge than love, for if the love she bore the gentleman was as great as her pretence thereof, she would not have left him for another; wherefore we may reasonably name her revengeful, obstinate, and inconstant." "You at your ease talk well," said Ennasuitte to him, "but have you ever known how heartbreaking it is when one loves and is not beloved?" "True it is," answered Hircan, "that I have made few trials of this, for let a lady show me ever so small an unkindness, and I have done with the pair of them—love and the lady." "Ay, you," said Parlamente, "who love nothing but your own pleasure; but a virtuous woman cannot have done with her husband in such fashion." "All the same," said Saffredent, "the lady of the story forgot awhile that she was a woman, for a man could not have devised a prettier piece of revenge." "For one devoid of goodness," said Oisille, "we should not esteem all other women to be like to her." "Yet," said Saffredent, "you are all women, and howsoever bravely you may be decked out, he who makes a good search in front beneath your petticoats will still find that you are women."

Nomerfide said to him : " Did we give ear to you the day
would be spent in disputations. But I so greatly desire to
hear another story, that I pray Longarine to give her vote to
someone." Longarine looked at Geburon, and said to him :
" If you know anything as touching a virtuous woman, I
entreat you put it before us now." And Geburon said :
" Since the lot has fallen on me, I will tell you of a thing that
happened in the town of Milan."

NOVEL XVI.

A love persevering and fearless meets with due reward.

In the time of the grand-master of Chaumont there lived in
Milan a lady esteemed one of the most honourable in the town.
She, being the widow of an Italian count, lived in the house of
her brothers-in-law, without any wish of marrying again, and
kept herself so wisely and virtuously that there was in the
duchy neither Frenchman nor Italian who did not hold her in
great repute. One day, on which her brothers-in-law and her
sisters-in-law made entertainment for the grand-master of
Chaumont, although it was not her custom, she was constrained
to be present, and when the Frenchmen saw her they mightily
extolled her beauty and grace, and above all one whose name I tell
not, but it will suffice to know that there was not a Frenchman
in Italy more worthy of love than he, for he was fulfilled with
every brave and knightly grace. And although he saw this lady,
that she was clad in black, and sat apart from the maidens with
old women all around her, yet fearing neither man nor woman
he set himself to talk with her, taking off his mask and leaving
the dances to be in her company. And all the evening he
stirred not from her side, talking to her and the old women
around, which he found more to his liking than if they had
been the youngest and the fairest at Court, in such sort that
when he must needs go, it seemed to him that he had scarcely
sat down. And though he but held with the lady such common
matter of discourse as was fit for the company to hear, yet she
was well persuaded that he was desirous to be of her acquaintance, against which she was determined to guard as well as
might be, and so neither at entertainment nor great assembly

did he see her any more. Having made inquiry of her manner
of living, he discovered that she went often to churches and
convents, and he kept so good watch upon her that let her be as
secret as she would, wherever she went he was there first, and
would stay as long as he was able to see her, and all the while
looking upon her in such a manner that she could not be
ignorant of his love towards her. And for the avoiding of this
she determined for some while to feign sickness and hear mass
in her own house, at which the gentleman was sorely grieved, for
he had lost the only means of seeing her. She, thinking to have
put an end to that habit of his, returned to the churches as before, but love forthwith made it known to the French gentleman,
and he became as devout as ever he was. And for fear lest
she might a second time do something to his hindrance, or lest
he might not have opportunity to make known his mind to her,
one morning, when she thought herself shrewdly hidden away
in a side chapel, he went to the end of the altar at which she
was hearing mass, and seeing that she had no companions, just
as the priest lifted up the Body of the Lord, he turned towards
her, and in a gentle voice and affectionate, said to her :
" Mistress, I will take Him whom the priest holds in his hands
to my damnation if you are not the reason of my death, for
though you deprive me of parley with you, yet you cannot be
ignorant of the truth, since it is manifest in the languishment
of my eyes and my face all amort." The lady, feigning to
understand nothing, replied to him : " Thou shalt not take
God's name in vain, but the poets say the gods laugh at the
oaths and lies of lovers, wherefore ladies of honour should by
no means be credulous or compassionate." Saying thus she
arose and returned to her lodging.

Those who have had experiences like to this will be well
assured that the gentleman was very wrathful. But he, whose
heart never failed him, liked better to have had a bad answer than
to have failed to declare his mind, the which for three years remained steadfast, and all the while he ceased not to pay suit to
her by letters and by all manner of means, losing not so much
as an hour. But during these three years he had no reply from
her, since she fled from him as the hare from the wolf, not out of
hatred, but for fear of her honour and reputation. And the
cause was so plainly manifest to him that never before had he

so vigorously pressed his suit. And after much refusal, pains,
torments, and despair, seeing the greatness and perseverance of
his love, the lady took·pity on him, and granted to him that
which he so much desired and had waited for so long. And when
they had come to an agreement upon the ways and means, the
French gentleman did not fail to risk his life by going to her
house, and the risk was indeed a great one, seeing that all her
kinsfolk were lodged in this same mansion. He, having no less
craft than comeliness, brought it about so well that he got into
her room at the appointed time, and found her lying by herself
on a most rare bed. But as he made haste to doff his clothes
that he might get into bed with her, he heard at the door a
noise of voices speaking low, and the clash of swords as they
touched the wall. His widow lady, with the face of a woman
half dead, said to him: " In good sooth now are your life and
my honour in as great peril as they can ever be, for I plainly
hear my brothers, who seek you out that they may kill you.
Wherefore I pray you hide yourself under the bed, that when
they come and find you not I may reproach them for alarming
me without a cause." The gentleman, who never yet had
known fear, said to her: "And what manner of men are these
your brothers to make an honest man to be afraid? Were all
your kin to be here, I am well assured that they would not
await so much as the fourth blow of my sword, wherefore rest
you in your bed, and leave me to guard the door." And
taking his cloak across his arm with his drawn sword in his
hand, he opened the door to the intent that he might see close
at hand the swords that made such a clashing. And when
it was opened he saw two serving-maids, who, with two swords
in each hand, had caused the tumult, and they said to him:
" Sir, pardon us, since we had commandment from our mistress
to do this, but from us you shall have no further hindrance."
The gentleman, seeing then that they were women, did no
more hurt to them than that, sending them to the devil, he
shut the door in their faces, and got to bed with the lady as
soon as he could, since fear had by no means lessened his love, even
forgetting to ask the reason of all this, and thinking of nothing
but the satisfying his desire. But seeing morning to be near
at hand, he asked her to tell him wherefore she had done him so
many evil turns, both in making him to wait so long and in

this last affair of the swords and serving-maids. She, laughing, replied to him : "It was my fixed resolve never to love, and this I have kept throughout my widowhood ; but your honourable address, from the day you first spoke to me, made me change my resolve and so love you as you have loved me. It is true that honour always guiding me would not allow my love to do that by which my good repute might suffer hurt. But like as the hart, wounded unto death, thinks in moving from one place to another to move from the ill it carries with it, so did I fly from church to church, thinking to escape that which was in my soul, but the proof of your perfect love has made honour come to an agreement with it. Yet to the end that I might be the more assured of placing my heart and my love in a perfect man, I was fain to make this last proof of you by means of my women. And I tell you that if, for the sake of your life or aught else, I had found you fearful enough to get under the bed, I was determined to rise and go into another room, without ever having to do with you. But since I found in you more beauty, grace, virtue, and bravery than I had been advised of, and since fear has no power at all to touch your heart or to chill your love towards me, I am resolved to cleave to you for the rest of my days, for in no better hands could I put my life and my honour than in him who in every way is without a match." And all as if the will of man was unchangeable, they promised and sware what lay not within their power—namely, perpetual love, which cannot arise or dwell in a man's heart. And only those women know this who have tried how long their passion lasts.

"Wherefore, ladies, if you are wise, you will be wary of us, as would the stag, if he had understanding, be wary of the hunter. For our glory, our happiness, and our contentment, is to see you captives, and to take from you that which you hold more dear than life." "What, Geburon," said Hircan, "since when have you turned preacher? Such was not aforetime the manner of your discourse." "It is true," replied Geburon, "that I have just now spoken the very opposite to the deliverances of my whole life ; but since I am grown old and my teeth are too weak to chew the venison, I advise the young deer to beware of the huntsmen, that I may give satisfaction in my old age for the sins of my youth." "We thank

you, Geburon," said Nomerfide, "for that you nave given us
this advice for our profit, but we cannot hold ourselves under
great obligation to you, since such was not the manner of your
discourse to her whom you loved; it is a sign therefore that you
love us not, and do not wish that we should ever be loved.
Yet we deem ourselves to the full as wise and virtuous as those
whom you chased so in your youth, but it is ever the boast of
old men that they were more prudent than those who come
after them." "Yet, Nomerfide," said Geburon, "when the
deceit of one of your lovers hath made you to understand the
wickedness of men; in that hour will you believe that I have
spoken the truth?" Oisille said to Geburon : "It seems to me
that the gentleman whom you praise so much for his courage
ought rather to be praised for the madness of his love, which
is so strong a power that it maketh the most pitiful cowards in
the world undertake things on which the bravest would think
twice." Saffredent said to her : "If it were not that he thought
the Italians a folk better at words than deeds, it seems to me
he had had good occasion of fear." "Ay," said Oisille, "and
if it were not for that fire at his heart that burnt up fear."
"It seems to me," said Hircan, "that since you do not esteem
the courage of him praiseworthy, you doubtless know some
other deed of the same kind more worthy of praise." "It is
true," said Oisille, "that he is praiseworthy, but I know of
one more admirably brave." "I beseech you then," said
Geburon, "to take my place and tell us of him." Oisille
began : "If a man who, for his life and his lady's honour,
showed his courage against the men of Milan, is accounted so
brave, what will you call one, who, for no necessity laid upon
him but from true and inborn courage, did the deed I am about
to tell you?"

NOVEL XVII.

King Francis shows his courage that it is well approved.

There came to Dijon, in the duchy of Burgundy, a German
count named William, of the House of Saxe, which is so near
akin to the House of Savoy that of old they were one. This
count, being esteemed the bravest and most handsome gentleman in Germany, having offered his service to the King of

France, was so well received of him that not only did he accept him as a follower, but kept him close at hand as a servant of the Body. Now my lord de la Tremoille, governor of Burgundy, the same being an ancient knight and loyal servant to the King, was always jealous and fearful of his master, and had spies on all hands, that he might know the counsels of the enemies of the King, and so well did he conduct matters that few things were hid from him. And he was advertised by one of his friends that Count William had received a sum of money, with assurance of more, to the intent that he might in any way cause the King to be murdered. Whereupon my lord de la Tremoille did forthwith advise the King of it, and did not conceal it from his mother, Louise de Savoye, who forgetting that she and this German were akin, implored the King straightway to dismiss him. But the King would have her speak no more of it, saying it was impossible for so good and honourable a gentleman to have undertaken so evil an enterprise. At the end of some time there came a second tidings concerning him to the same intent as the first, at which the governor, burning with love for his master, demanded that he should be sent from his service and banished the realm, or that some manner of order should be taken with him. But the King straightly charged him that he should make no sign, being well persuaded that by some other means he should come to a knowledge of the truth.

And one day, on which he was going a hunting, he took out the best sword that he had, and bade Count William follow hard after him; and after chasing the stag for some time, the King, seeing that all his people were far off, and that the Count alone was with him, turned aside from all the tracks. And when he saw himself alone with the Count in the very depths of the forest, drawing his sword he said to him : " Does this sword seem to you both good to look upon and serviceable withal ?" The Count, handling the point, said he had seen none to overmatch it. " You are in the right," said the King, " and methinks if a man was resolved to kill me, and knew the strength of my arm and the stoutness of my heart, and the goodness of this sword here, he would think twice before having at me; nevertheless, I should hold him for a pitiful scoundrel if we were all alone, without witnesses, and he durst not carry out what he durst conceive." To which Count William, with an astounded countenance, replied : " Sire, the wickedness of such an undertaking would be very great, but the folly of putting it into execution would be no less." The King, with a laugh, put back the sword into the sheath, and hearing the chase hard by, pricked after it as fast as he was able. When he was come up he spoke to no one on the matter, being assured that Count William, though a brave enough gentleman, was not competent for such an enterprise. But the Count, believing that he was found out or at the least suspected, came early on the next morning to Robertet, the King's treasurer, saying that he had considered the privileges and pay the King was willing to give him to stay in his service, and they did not suffice him for the half of a year. And if it was not the King's pleasure to give him double, he should be constrained to depart. And he prayed the said Robertet to ascertain as soon as might be the will of the King, who said that he could do him no better service than go to the King forthwith. And he did this willingly, since he had seen the advices of the governor. So when the King was awake he failed not to tell him what the Count had said, my lord de la Tremoille and Admiral de Bonnivet being present. But they knew not that which the King had done the day before. So with a laugh the King said : " You were desirous of dismissing Count William, and behold he dismisses himself! Wherefore tell him that, since he is not content with the estate to which he agreed when he entered my service, than which estate many a man of a noble house desires nothing better, it is reasonable that he seek his fortune somewhere else. And as for me I will put no let nor hindrance in his way, but shall be glad if he find a place according to his deserts." Robertet was as quick to carry back this reply to the Count as he had been to carry the Count's complaint to the King. And the Count said that, with his good pleasure, he was determined immediately to set forth. And as one whom fear makes to begone, it was not more than twenty-four hours from thence that he took leave of the King, as he was sitting at table, feigning to regret greatly that his poverty forced him away. Likewise he took leave of the mother of the King, who gave him leave as joyful as her welcome, when he came to her as a kinsman and a friend ; and so returned he to his own land. But the King, perceiving his mother and his followers astonished at this sudden parting, told them of the fright he had given him, saying that though he were innocent of what was laid against him, yet his fear was too great for him to stay with a master whose complexion he knew no longer.

" As for me, ladies, I see not what could have moved the heart of the King to make hazard of his life with a man of such repute at arms, except that, leaving the company and the places where Kings find none to give them battle, he wished to meet fairly and equally him whom he suspected for an enemy, in order to make trial of the stoutness of his own heart and the courage of it." " Without doubt," said Parlamente, " he was in the right, for the praises of all men cannot so well satisfy a good heart as the knowledge and experience that it hath indeed virtuousness implanted in it by God," " It is a long while ago," said Geburon, " since the men of old feigned that if any would attain the Temple of Renown, he must first pass through the Temple of Virtue. And I, who know the two persons, of whom you have made us this relation, am well persuaded that the King is one of the bravest men in his realm." " By my faith," said Hircan, " when Count William came to France I should have had more fear of his sword than that of the four shrewdest Italian gentlemen who were at Court." " We know well," said Ennasuitte, " so great is his renown that no praises of ours can equal his merit, and that the day would be too soon gone if each should speak his mind. Where-fore I pray you, mistress, to give your vote to one who will tell us some good of men, if there be any good to be told." Oisille said to Hircan : " Methinks you are so well accustomed to speak ill of women that you will be greatly pleased to tell us of some good story to the praise of men, wherefore to you I give my vote." " That will be an easy task," said Hircan, " for it is so short a time since a story was told me to the praise of a gentleman, his love, firmness, and long-suffering, that I fear not to lose the recollection of it."

NOVEL XVIII.

A notable case of a steadfast lover.

In one of the fair towns of France there lived a nobleman
of an illustrious house, who studied in the schools desiring to
attain the knowledge of the means by which men come to
virtue and honour.   And although he was such a sound
scholar that at the age of seventeen or eighteen years he
seemed to be a teacher and an ensample to all the rest, natheless Love, amid all his learning, made him go likewise to its
lecture-hall.   And for a better hearing and reception, it hid
itself in the face and beautiful eyes of the prettiest maid in all
the countryside, who had come up to town on some matter of
law.   But before that Love had essayed to conquer him by
the beauty of the lady, it had gained her heart by showing to
her the perfections that were in this young lord; for in comeliness, grace, good sense, and pleasant speaking, he had no
rival in any sort or condition of men whatsoever.   You who
know the quick work this fire makes, when it betakes itself to
the extremities of the heart and fantasy, will judge well that,
with two subjects like these, Love never stopped till it had
them at its pleasure, and that it so filled them with its shining
light that their thoughts, words, and wishes were but of this
flame of Love.   Youth, engendering in the gentleman fear,
made him pay his suit as gently as might be; but she, altogether conquered by love, needed no pressing; natheless shame,
which always is companion to a maid, kept her some while
without declaring her mind.   But at the end, the strong-place
of her heart, where honour dwelleth, was in such fashion
brought to the dust, that the poor maid agreed to that on
which in truth they had never disagreed.   Yet, to make trial
of the patience, steadfastness, and love of her servant, she
granted him what he asked on a condition most hard to be
observed, assuring him that if he kept it she would love him
with a perfect love, and if not she would have no more traffic
with him.   And this was her condition: she would be content
to hold parley with him in a bed, the pair of them being clad
alone in their shirts, if he would ask no more of her than
kisses and sweet talk.   And he, thinking no joy was there to

be compared with the joy she promised him, agreed thereto.
And when the evening was come, his promise was kept; in
such sort that for all the good cheer she made him, and for all
the temptations with which he was vexed, he would by no
means depart from his oath. And though he thought his
pains not less than those of purgatory, so strong was his love,
and so assured his hope of the everlasting continuing of this
their love, that he kept watch with patience and rose from
beside her without doing her any wrong. The lady, as I
believe, more astonished than delighted with this good faith,
presently suspected either that his love was not so great as she
had taken it to be, or that he had found her not so sweet as he
had thought; and had no consideration to his honour, long-
suffering, and faithfulness in the keeping of his oath.

This done she determined to make yet another trial of his
love for her before she kept her promise. And to this intent
she asked him to speak with a girl of her household, younger
than herself and mighty pretty, and to hold love discourse
with her, that those who saw him so often come to the house
might think it was for the maid and not for the mistress. The
young lord, well persuaded of being beloved even as he loved,
altogether obeyed her commands, and constrained himself for
love of her to make love to the girl. And she, seeing him of
such pleasant speech and brave address, believed his lie more
than another's truth, and loved him all as if she was verily
beloved of him. And when her mistress saw that things were
thus forward, and that all the same the gentleman ceased not to
remind her of her promise, she granted him to come and see
her an hour after midnight, and told him that she had tried so
well his love and obedience towards her, that it was reasonable
he should be rewarded for his long-suffering. One cannot
doubt of the joy of this faithful lover at hearing of this, and at
the appointed hour he failed not to be present. But the lady,
to try the strength of his love, said to the girl: "I am well
advised of the love a certain lord bears you, and I think your
passion for him is not less. And I have taken such pity on
you two, that I am resolved to give you place and leisure to
parley together at your ease." At this the maid was in such
delight that she could not conceal her desire, saying she would
not fail her. In obedience therefore to the lady she undressed

herself and lay down all alone on a fine bed ; the lady leaving
the door of the room open, and lighting it very brightly, so
that the girl's beauty might the more be manifested.   And
feigning to go away she so shrewdly hid herself near the bed,
that no one might see her.   Her lover, thinking to find her
there according to promise, at the appointed time entered
into the room as softly as he was able ; and after that he had
shut the door and doffed his vesture and fur slippers, he got
into bed thinking to find there what he had desired.   And he
had no sooner stretched out his arms to embrace her whom he
thought his mistress, than the poor girl, believing him entirely
her own, threw her arms round his neck, and spoke to him
with such loving words and with so beautiful a face, that a holy
hermit would have dropped his beads at the sight of her.   But
when as much by hearing as seeing he perceived who she was,
love, which had sent him to bed at such a rate, no less quickly
got him up again, when he found it was not she for whom he
had borne so much.   And wrathful as much with the mistress
as with the maid, he said to her : "Not your folly, nor the
maliciousness of her who has put you there, can make me other
than I am.   But do you labour to become an honest woman,
for, by reason of me, you will never lose your good name."
And thus saying he went forth from the room in a rage, and
for a long time returned not to the place where his mistress
dwelt.   But Love, who is never devoid of hope, gave him
good assurance that the greater the trials the better the
enjoyment.   The lady, having seen and heard the passages
between him and the maid, was so delighted and astonished at
the greatness and steadfastness of his love, that she wearied for
the time of seeing him again, to ask his forgiveness for all the
evils with which she had afflicted him.   And as soon as she
could find him she took such order with him that not only did
he forget his sorrows overpast, but deemed them happy, inasmuch as they were turned to the glory of his steadfastness and
the perfect assurance of his love.   And of this love from that
time forth he tasted the fruition as he had desired, without
hindrance or weariness.

"I entreat you, ladies, find me a woman who has been so
steadfast, so patient, so loyal in love as this man here.   They
who have felt such temptations, find those in the pictures of

St. Anthony small by comparison; for he who can be chaste and patient when he has the opportunity of enjoying a beautiful woman beloved of him, will be virtuous enough to overcome a legion of devils." " 'Tis pity," said Oisille, " that his suit was not done to a woman as good as himself, for then theirs would have been the most perfect and the most honourable love of which I have ever heard." " But, prithee," said Geburon, "which of these two trials is in your mind most difficult to bear?" " It seems to me," said Parlamente, "that the last was the most difficult, for revenge is the strongest of all the temptations." Longarine said she thought the first was the most difficult, for to keep his promise he had to overcome both love and himself. " You talk well at your ease," said Simontault, " but we, who know how much it is worth, should give our opinions. And as for me I deem the man the first time to have been a dolt, and the second an ass; for, trust me, while he kept his promise to his mistress, she was in worse case than he. This oath she only made him take to show herself more virtuous than she was, being assured the while that a love like his could not be bound, by command, oath, or anything else. But she wished to be won by heroical virtues, and so turn dishonour into honour. And the second time he was manifestly an ass for leaving her who loved him better than his mistress, and having also a good excuse in his great displeasure." To this Dagoucin replied that he was of the contrary opinion, and he held him the first time for a man, steadfast, patient, and truthful; and the second time loyal and perfect in his love." " How do we know," said Simontault, " if he were not one of those the Decretals call *frigidi et maleficiatl*. And if Hircan had wished to complete his praise he would have done well to tell us what manner of bedfellow he made when he got that he longed for, and we should be able to judge whether virtue or impotence was at the root of the matter." " You may be well persuaded," said Hircan, " that if I had been told this, I would have concealed it no more than the rest. But since I know the man and his complexion, I esteem him to have been led by the strength of his love, and by no means by impotence or coldness." " If it were as you say," said Simontault, " he ought to have broken his word. For though she, for such a small matter, had been angry, she would have easily been appeased." "Perchance," said Ennasuitte, "she would not have had it so." "And would it not have been an easy matter to have forced her," said Saffredent, "since she herself had offered battle?" "By'r lady," said Nomerfide, "what manner of talk is this? Is that the way to gain the favour of an honourable and virtuous woman?" "It seems to me," said Saffredent, "that one cannot do a woman one courts greater honour than to have her by force; it is but your little miss that desires long prayers and entreaties Others there are to whom one must give many a present before they are won, and still others so foolish that scarcely by any means or craft is it possible to win them; and as to them one has but to think of practical ways and means. But when a body has to do with a woman too wise for cozenage, and too good for words or presents, is it not reasonable to search out every way of gaining the victory over her? And when it comes to your ears that a man has raped a woman, believe that the woman cut him off from every other kind of hope, and think no less of the honest gentleman who for love has risked his life." Geburon, laughing, said: "I have seen places besieged and taken by storm, because it was impossible to bring the garrisons to a parley either by money or threats, and they say a place that is brought to parley is half won." "You believe," said Ennasuitte, "that all the love in the world is bottomed upon these follies; but there have been they who have loved and for a long while continued in their love without a thought of the like." "If you know a history to that intent," said Hircan, "I give you my place for you to tell it." "I both know one," said Ennasuitte, "and most willingly will tell it."

NOVEL XIX.

A pitiful case of two lovers who turn at last monk and nun.

In the time of that Marquis of Mantua, who had for wife the sister of the Duke of Ferrara, there lived in the house of the marchioness a maiden called Pauline. And she was loved in such wise by a gentleman in the service of the marquis that all men were amazed at the greatness of his love, inasmuch as though of poor estate he was handsome, and should, through the love his master bore him, have espoused some lady of wealth. But he, being assured that the greatest treasure in the world was Pauline, trusted to gain her for his own in marriage. The marchioness, wishing that by her countenance Pauline might make a more profitable match, looked with disfavour on the scheme, often charging them not to speak to one another, and warning them that if they were wed they would be in all Italy the poorest couple and the most wretched. But to these counsels the young gentleman paid no heed, and Pauline, though she strove to conceal the love she bore him, yet none the less had him in her thoughts. And this fellowship of theirs lasted for a long while, their only hope being that time would bring them better fortune. But it chanced that war broke out, in which the young gentleman was taken prisoner, together with a Frenchman, whose love for a lady in his own land was as great as the other's love for one in Italy. And these, finding themselves partakers of the same fate, began to tell their secrets one to the other, the Frenchman confessing that his own heart was a fast prisoner, though he told him not the name of its prison-house. But since they were both in the following of the Marquis of Mantua, the Frenchman was well assured of the love his comrade bore to Pauline, and out of the friendship he had for him advised him to banish her from his thoughts. But this, the young Italian swore, lay not within his power, saying that if in recompense of his good service and captivity his lord would not give him the maid to wife, he would presently turn monk, and do suit and service to no master save God. This his comrade could not believe, discerning in him no devotion nor sign of devotion, except it were that which he bore to Pauline. At the end of nine months the French gentleman was enlarged from his captivity, and by his efforts procured likewise the freedom of his friend, using also his good offices with the marquis and marchioness in the matter of the marriage of Pauline. But from this the two lovers gained nothing save warnings of the poverty in which they would both have to live; their parents moreover on both sides were against the match, and forbade him to speak to her any more, to the end that his great love might be overcome by absence and want of opportunity.

And so this man, seeing that he was obliged to obey, prayed

K

of the marchioness to let him take leave of Pauline, and promised that after he had done so he would never speak to her again. This was granted him, and at the appointed time, being come into her presence, he spoke as follows : " Since, Pauline, it seems that heaven and earth are against us, not only in prohibiting us to wed, but what is worse, in disallowing us sight and speech of one another—an order which our lord and lady have laid so strictly upon us that they may truly boast of having broken two hearts with a single word, hereby showing mighty well that they neither have nor have had bowels of love nor compassion—I am well advised that their aim in this is to marry each of us honourably and to advantage, for they know not that contentment is the only true riches; yet with so much misfortune and unhappiness have they affected me, that I can no more heartily do them any service. I know also that if I had never spoken of marriage they would not have been so careful as to forbid us to speak together, but I promise you I would rather die than follow a less honourable love than that with which I have loved you, from whom I have won that which I would defend from all. Since then, if I continued to see you, I could not restrain myself from speech ; and if I saw you not, my heart, unable to remain empty, would be filled with some awful despair ; I have determined, and this for some time, to enter the religious life, for though I know that salvation may be gained by all sorts and conditions of men, yet I would have more leisure in which I may contemplate the Divine Goodness and implore it to have pity upon the sins of my youth, and so to change my heart that it may love spiritual things no less than it has hitherto loved temporal things. And if by grace I obtain grace, my task shall be to pray without ceasing to God for you. And by that strong and loyal love which has been between us, I implore you to remember me in your prayers to our Lord, entreating Him to give me a resolution not to see you, as great as the delight I took in seeing you. Moreover, since throughout my whole life I have hoped to gain from you in marriage that which both honour and conscience allow, and have been satisfied with hope, now, since that is lost to me, and I shall never have from you that which a wife gives to her husband, this one thing I ask, that in bidding me farewell you will treat me as a brother and give me a kiss." Poor Pauline, whose favours had always been few and far between, perceiving the bitterness of his grief, and his honour in making so reasonable a request in all his great despair, without saying another word threw her arms around his neck and wept after such a grievous fashion that words, voice, and strength failed her, and she fell between his arms in a swoon. Whereupon her lover, overcome by pity, love, and grief, must needs do the like, and falling one one way, the other another, they lay for dead till one of Pauline's companions saw them and came to the rescue.

Then Pauline, who had wished to conceal her love, was ashamed, because she had made manifest how strong it was, but yet her pity for the poor gentleman served as a good excuse. For he, not able to endure the saying of that everlasting farewell, went forth from her presence and going unto his own house flung himself upon the bed, and passed the night in such pitiful complaining that his servants thought that he had lost his parents, and his friends, and whatsoever he had on earth. In the morning he commended himself to our Lord, and after he had divided amongst his servants what little worldly gear he possessed, and taken with him a small sum of money, he charged his people not to follow him, and departed by himself to the religious house of the Observance, to demand the cowl, being well determined never to go from that house for the rest of his life. The warden, who had formerly known him, thought at first that he was either being laughed at or that he was in a dream, for in all that land there was none who did less resemble a Grey Friar, since in him was found every honour and every virtue which one could desire in a perfect gentleman. Yet the warden, on hearing of his words, and beholding the streams of tears that flowed (for what cause he knew not) down his face, took him in and entreated him kindly. And soon after, marking his perseverance, he gave him the monastic dress, which having been received by this gentleman with great devotion, the thing was brought to the marquis and marchioness, who, greatly astonished, could scarce believe it possible. Pauline, to hide her love, concealed as well as might be the regret she felt for him, and in such wise that all men said that she had soon forgotten her loyal lover and his devotion for her. And so were passed five or six months, and she gave no sign of the

grief that was in her soul. But it fell out that one day she
was shown by some monks a song which her lover had made a
short while after he had taken the cowl. As to the air 'tis an
Italian one, and ordinary enough, but I have tried to English
the words as nearly as I can, and this is the manner of it: but
first the burthen:

> What will she say, when clad in sober guise
>   Monasticall
> I pass before the eyes
>   That were my all?

> Alas, dear maid, when thou art all alone
>   And tear on tear
> Shall rise for me, and many a bitter moan
>   For our mishap; wise thoughts may lead thee where
> The cloister is a walk for solitude,
> And high built walls shut out all tumult rude.
>   What will she say, &c.

> What will they say, who our love-dream have broken
>   And our estate:
> By whose decree our vows were left unspoken?
>   When by their hate
> They see a love more pure, a flame more holy,
> They shall repent, and kneeling lowly,
>   Bewail with sobs and tears
>   Our saddened years.
>   What will she say, &c.

> But if they come and with a vain endeavour
>   Do ask us to arise,
> And from this holy watch would fain dissever
>   Our hearts and eyes,
> Then shall we say that till our days are ending,
> And to its Lord each soul is wending;
>   These walls that circle round
>   Shall be our bound.
>   What will she say, &c.

> And if they come, and say to us " Go marry
>   And be you blithe and gay,
> Your lives are young, but Time will not long tarry
>   And hasteneth fast away,"
> Then shall we say that all our love and duty
> Are His with whom is perfect beauty.
>   Our marriage is above,
>   For there is Love.
>   What will she say, &c.

O mighty love, O passion and desire
  That bound the cord,
Enflame within my heart a ceaseless fire
  To pray the Lord.
All through the watches, patient without sorrow,
Till Prime doth come of that to-morrow
   Which hath no twilight grey,
   But morn alway.
     What will she say, &c.

Quit wealth, and all contentments of this life,
  Thy're but a chain,
Stronger than steel to forge us fast to strife,
  Our souls to bane.
Quit then the flesh and all its giddy pleasure
Mad without measure.
     What will she say, &c.

Come then and don with me that holiness
  The Lord doth give;
For though the robe 's ash-grey, yet none the less
  We thrive and live;
And like the phœnix shall one day aspire
From out these ashes of our fire.
     What will she say, &c.

And seeing our love showed pure, and had no stain
  To men before;
Much greater praise we doubtless shall attain
  Since we adore
In cloistered walls the Lord of Life and glory,
Till when the end comes to our story
   Love that could never die
   Shall lift our souls on high.
     What will she say, &c.

And when, being by herself in a side-chapel, she had carefully read through these verses, so plentifully did she weep that all the paper was wetted with her tears. And had it not been for the fear she was in of too evidently manifesting her affection, she would straightway have turned hermit, and looked her last on the face of mankind. But the prudence to which her mind was attempered made her for some time conceal her intent, and though she was steadfastly purposed to leave the world behind her, she feigned the very opposite of this, and so joyous was she become in company that she would hardly have been known for her former self. For five or six months she

kept this secret covered in her heart.   But having one day
gone with her mistress to the Church of the Observance to
High Mass, she saw, as the celebrant, deacon, and sub-deacon
came from the sacristy to the high altar, her poor lover, who
had not yet completed the year of his noviciate, preceding them
as server, carrying in his hands the two flagons covered with
silk-cloth, and with eyes bent on to the ground.   When Pauline
saw him in this sad weed, that did but increase his grace and
beauty, she was in such trouble and affray that, simulating a
rheum in the throat, she coughed so as to hide the blushes of
her face.   And her lover, who knew that sound better than
his monastery chimes, turned not his head, but as he passed in
front of her could not restrain his eyes from going the road
they had so often gone before.   But at that most piteous
regard of his he was seized in such wise by the fire he thought
to have extinguished, that striving to conceal it more than he
was able, he fell full length before his mistress.   Yet for the
fear he had of the cause being known, he professed that in the
place where he fell the floor was broken and uneven.   And
Pauline, perceiving that though his dress was changed his
heart was the same as it had been, and likewise that such a
time had gone by since he had become a monk that all men
would deem she had forgotten him, set herself to bring
that to pass which she had desired—namely, to make their
two lives as like one another in dress, estate, and manner of
living as they had been aforetime when they abode in the same
house under the same master and mistress.   And since she had
for more than four months before taken such order as was
necessary previous to becoming a nun, she one morning
entreated leave of the marchioness to hear mass at St. Claire's,
which the marchioness, not knowing what was in her mind,
freely granted.   But as she passed the Grey Friars she asked
the warden to let her see her lover, whom she called her kinsman, and when they had met in a side-chapel by themselves,
Pauline thus spoke to him : " If my honour had allowed me to
put on this dress as soon as you I would presently have done
it, but now, since I have, by not doing so, silenced the slanders
of those who are always more ready to think evil than good, I
am determined to take upon myself this robe, estate, and life of
yours without inquiring of what kind they are.   For if you are

happy, I shall partake in your happiness, and if you are unhappy, in that too I am fain to have my share, for by whatsoever road you fare to Paradise I too would—follow.　For I am assured that He, who alone is worthy to be called the true and perfect Love, has drawn us to his service by a reasonable and honourable friendship which He, by the operation of his Holy Spirit, will turn wholly to himself.　And I beseech you, forgetting this vile and perishable body, to put on that of the true Bride who is Jesus Christ."　Her monkish lover was filled with such delight to hear her holy wishes that, weeping with joy, he strengthened her therein to the utmost of his power, telling her that since the pleasure of hearing her speak was the only one left to him, he deemed himself happy to live in a place where he might always see her; and that they, trusting in the goodness of God, in whose hands no one is suffered to perish, should pass the rest of their lives in a state of holy love.　And with these words, weeping with joy, he made as if to kiss her hands, but she lowered her face to her hands, and in true love they gave to one another the kiss of peace.　So in this joyful wise Pauline departed, and was received into the nunnery of St. Claire, where she took the veil.

But when my lady the marchioness heard all this matter, she was much amazed, and fared on the morrow to the convent, and endeavoured to turn Pauline from her purpose, who replied that she must rest content with having deprived her of her husband in the flesh, that man whom of all men she best loved, and not endeavour to sunder her from that spouse who is immortal and invisible, for it lay not within her power, nor that of any creature upon earth.　Whereupon the marchioness, perceiving her intention was sincere, kissed her, and with a great grief left her.　And for the rest of their days Pauline and her lover lived in such holiness and devotion, each one faithfully obeying the rules of the Order, that we cannot doubt that He whose law is Love said to them at the end of their lives, as to the Magdalen, "Your sins be forgiven you, for you have loved much."

"You cannot deny, ladies, that the love of this man was greater than that of his mistress, nevertheless so well was he recompensed that I would all true lovers were in case like his."

"Then," quoth Hircan, "there would be more foolish men and maids than there are now." "Call you those foolish," said Oisille, "who in their youth love with an honourable love, and end by turning it all to God?" Hircan, with a laugh, replied : "If black choler and despair are worthy of praise, then indeed Pauline and her lover stand beyond compare." "Is it not true," said Geburon, "that God draws us to himself by ways which seem evil at the first, but the end whereof is good?" "Still do I persist in the opinion," said Parlamente, "that no man loveth God who has not loved with a perfect love one of his creatures." "What do you call a perfect love?" said Saffredent. "Do you mean those chilly souls that adore their ladies from afar, without discovering their thoughts?" "I," said Parlamente, "call those men perfect lovers who, when they love seek for some perfection, be it beauty, goodness, or gracious ways ; always striving towards virtuousness, and with hearts of such high aim that death is sweeter by far to them than the doing of a deed of shame. And this because the soul, which was created for nothing but to return to its sovereign good, while it is shut within the body, is ever longing to return thither. But seeing that the senses, through which we obtain our knowledge, can show us nothing nearer perfection than visible things (for through the sin of our first parent they are dull and heavy), the soul pursues these, thinking to find in a visible grace, and in the moral virtues, the ideal beauty, grace, and virtue. But having curiously gone through all these external things, and finding not amongst them that which it really loves, it passes on to others, even after the manner of a child, who, being young, loves dolls and other trifles, the prettiest that it happens to see, thinking a heap of pebbles to be great wealth. But as the child becomes a man he loves dolls that are alive, and veritable riches with which to purchase the goods of this world. So the soul, discovering by hard experience that there is no kind of perfection or happiness in things terrestrial, passes on from these and seeks Him from whom proceeds all perfection and happiness. All the same, did not God grant unto the seeker the eye of faith, it were likely that from being ignorant he should become an atheist ; for it is faith alone that doth enable carnal and sensual man to apprehend the idea of the highest good." "Do you not perceive," said Longarine, "that the uncultivated soil that brings forth everything luxuriously is valued by men because, though what grows thereon is of no profit, they hope that when it has been tilled it will bear good fruit? But that man who hath no love for carnal things will never attain to the love of God by the sowing of his word, since the soil of his heart is barren and will bring forth no fruit of love." "And what is the reason?" said Saffredent. "Is it not because the greater part of our teachers are not spiritual, but lovers of strong drink and nasty serving-maids, not trying what it is to love honourable ladies?" "If I could speak Latin," said Simontault, "I would read you that lesson of St. John's: 'How shall he who loveth not his brother whom he hath seen, love God whom he hath not seen?' For, from the love of visible things, one is drawn to that of the invisible." "But," said Ennasuitte, "*quis est ille* so perfect as you say, *et laudabimus eum.*" "There have been lovers," said Dagoucin, "who have loved with a love so strong and pure, that with them death itself were better than the feeling of the smallest desire against the honour of their ladies, and they do not even wish them to be advised of their love." "Then," said Saffredent, "they have the nature of a chameleon, that feeds on air. For there was never man born of a woman that desired not to declare his love, and to know if he is beloved; and be this love-fever never so hot, if it be not returned, it will presently pass off. And of this I have seen with mine own eyes miraculous proofs." "Prithee," said Ennasuitte, "do you take my place and tell us some story of a lover who was brought from death to life by finding in his mistress the very contrary of that he wished." "All my fear," said Saffredent, "is that I may displease the ladies, whose faithful servant I always have been and always will be, by exposing in my tale their failings; yet I will obey, and conceal nothing of the truth."

NOVEL XX.

My lord de Riant finds his mistress the contrary of what he had desired.

In the country of the Dauphiné there lived a gentleman named my lord de Riant, being of the household of King Francis the First, and as pretty a man as one would wish to see. For a long time he was the lover of a widow lady, for whom he had such a love and reverence, and so great a fear of losing her favour, that he dared not ask for that he most desired. And he, perceiving himself to be a comely man and worthy of love, steadfastly believed that which she often swore to him—namely, that she loved him above all others, and that if she were constrained to do anything for a gentleman, it would be for him alone, who was the most perfect she had seen, praying him to be content with this honourable friendship, and not endeavour to go beyond it. And she assured him that if he was found endeavouring to gain more he would lose her altogether. The poor gentleman was not only content, but deemed himself very happy to have gained the heart of so virtuous a woman. It would be a long story if I were to tell you of their love passages, how oftentimes they were in company with one another, the journeys he made for the sake of seeing her. But to make an end, this poor martyr of so pleasant a fire, that the more it burns the more does one desire to be burned, always kept striving to increase his martyrdom. And one day the fantasy took him of going post haste to see her whom he loved more than himself and all other women in the world. So he, having come to her house, asked where she was, and was told she had hardly come back from evensong, and had gone into the warren to finish the Hours. He got off his horse and went straight to the warren, where he found her women, who told him that she was walking by herself in a long alley. At this his conceit at some great piece of fortune for himself was much increased; and as softly as might be, and not making the least noise, he searched for her every way, hoping above all to find her by herself. But when he was come to an arbour pleached of trees, as pleasant a place as one could wish for, he went into it on a sudden, as being most fain to see her whom he loved. And there, on his entering in, he found her lying upon the grass in the arms of a groom of her household, as ugly, filthy, and infamous a fellow as my lord de Riant was handsome, virtuous, and amiable. I will not undertake to tell you his wrath, but so great was it that it had power in a moment to put out that fire which had outlived so many years. And as full of rage as he had been of love, he said: "Mistress, much good may it do you! To-day, by my knowledge of your wickedness, I am healed and delivered from that continual grief, caused by the goodness I believed of you." And with no more farewell he returned quicker than he had come. The wretched woman made him no other reply than to put her hand before her face, since, though she could not cover her shame, she covered her eyes that they might not behold him, who, notwithstanding her deceit, saw through her quite clearly.

"Wherefore, ladies, I entreat you, if you have not the wish for a perfect love, do not simulate such a love for an honest man, and, for the sake of your vain boasting, do him dishonour; for the hypocrites shall receive due reward, and God loves those whose love is pure." "Truly," said Oisille, "you have kept us a fine piece for the end of the day. But if we had not all sworn to tell the truth, I would not believe that a woman of so high estate could be so wicked in body and soul, leaving an honest gentleman for a filthy groom." "Alas, mistress," said Hircan, "if you knew the difference between a gentleman who all his life has carried armour and been at the wars, and a full-fed servant who has not stirred from the place where he was born, you would find some excuse for this poor widow." "I will not believe, Hircan," said Oisille, "whatever you may say, that you can find any excuse for her." "It has been told to me," said Simontault, "that there are women who like to have hot gospellers to preach them virtue and chastity, and make for them the best cheer they can and the most secret, assuring them that, were it not for conscience and honour, they would grant them their desires. And these poor fools, when in company they speak of their ladies, swear that they can put their fingers into the fire without burning them, maintaining these women to be honourable, since they affirm they have thoroughly assayed their love. So getting honest gentlemen to sing their praises, they show themselves as they really are to those like to them, and chose men who would be afraid to speak of it, and if they spoke would not be believed, by reason of their low and vile estate." "This," said Longarine, "is an opinion I have before heard from jealous and suspicious men; but it is painting a chimera, for if it have so fallen out with one poor wretch, is that reason for our suspecting it of all?" "Verily," said Parlamente, "the more we enter into this discourse the more will my lords hold forth upon Simontault's text, and all at the expense of us women. Wherefore let us to evensong, and not be the cause of so much waiting as we were yesterday."

To this the company agreed, and as they were going Oisille said: "If each one of you should give thanks to God for that on this day he has told the truth, Saffredent should ask His forgiveness for having uttered so shameful a story against the ladies." "By my faith," answered Saffredent, "although I did but hear the tale, yet it is the very truth. But if I were to tell you the things I have seen with my own eyes, I should cause you to make more signs of the cross than are appointed for the consecration of churches." "It is full time for repentance, then," said Geburon, "since confession does but increase your sin." "Since you have such an opinion of women," said Parlamente, "they ought to deprive you of their company and honourable friendship." But he replied: "Certain women have so used your counsel in estranging me and taking away from me things just and honourable, that if I could say worse and do worse to all of them I would do so, and spare not, if haply they would be stirred up to avenge me on her who has done me this great wrong." At these words Parlamente put on her mask, and with the rest came into the church, where, though it was fully evensong-time, they found not so much as a single monk in the choir. And the reason of this was that the monks had heard how the company was wont to assemble in the meadow and there tell tales, and since they loved pleasure better than their prayers, they had all gone likewise to the meadow and hidden themselves in a ditch behind a thick hedge. And so good a listening had they given to the stories that they had not heard the monastery bell, and came in such haste that their breath well-nigh failed them as they began evensong. And when they were asked the reason why their chanting began late, and when it began was out of tune, they confessed the truth. So, seeing that they desired it, it was granted them that henceforth they should assist at these offices seated at their ease behind the hedge. Supper-time was spent merrily in uttering the things they had left unsaid in the meadow, and this lasted all through the evening, until Oisille entreated them to retire, that their wit might be the keener on the morrow after a good sleep, of which she said that an hour before midnight was better than three after. So parted the company, each one to his own room, and so came to an end the second day.

DAY THE THIRD.

ON THE THIRD DAY RELATION IS MADE OF THE LADIES THAT HAVE HAD NO
AIM BUT HONOUR, AND OF THE ABOMINABLE HYPOCRISY OF THE MONKS.

PROLOGUE.

On the morrow they all arose early and came into the hall, but yet found Oisille there before them, she having been for the last half-hour in meditation on the Scripture she was to read. And if on the first and second days she gave them good matter of contentment, she did no less on the third. And had not one of the monks sought them out, that they might hear High Mass, they would not have heard it; for in such wise did they meditate that they made no account of the bell. And when they had with due devotion heard Mass, they dined very soberly, so as not by an excess of meats to prevent each one's memory quitting itself as well as might be. After this they went to their rooms to look at their note-books till the hour was come for going into the meadow, which was no long time. And those who had resolved on telling some merry case had already such pleasant faces that they gave promise of abundant laughter. When they were seated, they asked Saffredent to whom he would give his vote to begin the third day. "It seems to me," said he, "that since the fault I committed yesterday was so great, and you say it is a grievous one, and since I know no tale fit to atone for it, I must give my vote to Parlamente, who with her good sense knows so well how to praise the ladies that she will cover my true story with the cloak of forgetfulness." "I do not undertake," answered Parlamente, "to make atonement for your sins, but only not to follow in your steps. Wherefore, with the truth to which we are sworn and agreed, it is my purpose to show you that there are women who in their love passages always keep honour before their eyes. And since she, of whom I am about to tell you, came of a good house, I will only change the names : and pray you, ladies, believe that love has no power to make alteration in a chaste and honourable heart, the which you shall see by the following relation."

NOVEL XXI.

The steadfast and honourable love of Rolandine, who after many sorrows at last finds happiness.

There was a Queen of France who in her household maintained many maidens of good and illustrious families. Amongst others there was one named Rolandine, who was the Queen's near kinswoman, but for some discontent she had conceived with her father she gave her not over-pleasant entertainment. This girl, not being of the prettiest or the ugliest, was yet so discreet and virtuous that several great personages had asked her in marriage, but met with a cold answer, for her father loved money so well that he made nothing of the advancement of his daughter, and the Queen her mistress, as I have said, held her in such small favour that they who were fain to gain her good grace asked not Rolandine of her. So by her father's neglect and the Queen's misliking the poor girl stayed a long while without being married. And being sad at heart on this account, not so much that she desired to be married as for shame that she was not, she gave herself up wholly to God, leaving behind her all the pomps and vanities of the Court, and her sole delight was in prayer and in the doing of needlework. So in this quiet manner of living her young years were past, and they were as well and virtuously spent as one could desire. Now there was at Court a young gentleman who carried on an exceeding noble coat the bar sinister, though as pleasant a comrade and as honest a man as any, but mighty poor, and for comeliness he had so little that none but she would have chosen him for a lover. For a long while he had lived without a mate, but since one unfortunate seeks out another, he addressed himself to Rolandine, seeing that their fortunes, complexions, and estates were all alike. And while they made complaint to one another of their mischances, they became great friends; and finding themselves to be partakers in the same lot, they sought one another out everywhere, and in this manner was engendered a great and lasting acquaintanceship between them. But those who had beheld Rolandine afore so retired that she spoke to no one, now seeing her incessantly with this gentleman, were mightily scandalised thereat, and told her gouvernante that she should not endure their long talks together. She therefore made remonstrance to Rolandine, telling her that all men took in bad part that she spoke so much to one who was not rich enough for a husband, nor handsome enough for a sweetheart. Rolandine, who had always suffered reproof for her austerity and not her worldliness, said to her gouvernante : " Alas, mother, you see that I cannot have a husband of like estate with myself, and as for those who are young and comely, I have always fled them, lest perchance I fall into the same pit into which others have fallen. And since I find, as you know, this gentleman to be a prudent man and a virtuous, and that his discourse is only on good and honourable things, what wrong have I done in consoling myself in my weariness to those who have spoken to you ?" The poor old woman, who loved her mistress more than herself, said to her : " Mistress, I am well persuaded that you speak the truth, and that the treatment you have had of your father and the Queen is not according to your deserts. Yet, since men handle your honour in this fashion, were he your own brother, you would do well to separate yourself from him." Rolandine, weeping, replied to her : " Mother, I will do according to your counsel, but it is a strange thing not to have any matter of consolation in the world." The gentleman, as was his custom, came to talk with her, but she declared to him all that her gouvernante had said, and with tears implored him that he would be content not to hold parley with her until this rumour was overpast ; and this at her request he did.

But during this estrangement, having both lost their consolation, they began to feel a torment that was new to both of them. She ceased not to pray to God, to go on pilgrimages, and to observe duly the fasts and days of abstinence ; for love, till now unknown to her, made her so unquiet that she had not rest for a single hour. The gentleman was in no less pitiful case ; but he, who had already determined in his heart to love her and endeavour to get her for his wife, thinking both of love and the honour he would have if he succeeded, conceived that he must seek means of speaking with her, and, above all, of winning over the gouvernante. This he did, making remonstrance to her of the misery of her poor mistress, from whom they were fain to take away all

manner of consolation. At this the old woman wept, and
thanked him for the honourable friendship he had for her
mistress. And they took counsel together how he might best
speak with her, and the plan was for Rolandine to often feign
to be sick of the megrims, in which noise is hurtful; and when
her fellows went into the Queen's chamber, they two could
stay by themselves, and then he could talk with her. With
this the gentleman was quite content, and altogether ruled
himself by the advice of the gouvernante in such sort that when
he would he talked with his sweetheart. But this lasted not
for a long while; for the Queen, bearing no great love for her,
asked what Rolandine did in her room. And though one said
it was by reason of her sickness, another would have it she
stayed in her room because parley with the gentleman aforesaid
made the megrims to pass over. The Queen, who esteemed
the venial sins of others in her mortal, made seek her out, and
strictly charged her that she should not speak with this gentleman, unless it were in the presence or in the great hall. The
girl made no sign, but answered : "If I thought he was displeasing to you, I would never have spoken with him." Natheless she resolved within herself to search out some other means
of which the Queen should know nothing, and this she accomplished. For on Wednesdays, Fridays, and Saturdays she
fasted and stayed in her room with her gouvernante, and there
had time, while her fellows supped, for holding parley with
him whom she began to love exceedingly. And the more they
were constrained to cut short their speech, the more affection
was there in it; for they took time by stealth as does a robber
something of great price. But the matter was not kept so
secretly that a servant did not see him go into her room on a
fast day, who told his tale in a quarter where it was not concealed from the Queen. And she was so wroth thereat, that
no more durst the gentleman enter into the maid's room ; but so
as not altogether to lose this blessing of speech, he often made
pretence of going on a journey, returning at eventide to the
castle church in the gear of a Grey Friar or a Jacobin, and so
well disguised that none recognised him; and thither went
Rolandine and her gouvernante. And he, perceiving the great
love she bore him, feared not to say : "You see the risk in
which, for your sake, I put my life, and that the Queen has for-

bidden us to speak together.   And also consider of what sort
is your father, who thinks not in any manner of marrying you.
He has already refused many a good match, in such fashion
that I know not any from far or near who can have you. I know
well that I am poor, and that you cannot marry a gentleman
of my estate; but if love and goodwill were accounted as
great treasure, I should think myself the richest man in the
world.   God has given you riches, and you are in the like-
lihood of having still more, and if I were so happy as to be
chosen by you, I would be your faithful husband, lover, and
follower unto my life's end.   But if you chose one of equal
estate, a thing difficult for you, he would be to you as a master
and would regard your goods more than yourself, and the
beauty of others more than your virtuousness ; and, while he
enjoyed the usufruct of your wealth, he would not treat you as
you deserve.   The desire I have of this contentment, and my
fear lest another possess himself of it, cause me to implore you
that on the same day you make me happy and yourself the
best satisfied and best entreated wife that ever was."   Rolandine
hearing the discourse that she herself had determined to hold
with him, replied with a well-pleased face : "I am glad that
you have made this beginning, for I have for a long time been
resolved to speak with you to this intent, and have thought
upon the matter for the two years in which I have known you,
never ceasing to place before me all manner of conclusions both
for and against.   But since I confess that I wish to enter into
this estate of matrimony, it is now full time that I begin
and chose someone with whom I may live with a contented
mind.   I have not found one, be he rich, comely, or of noble
blood with whom my heart and mind could be in such accord
as with you ; for I know that in marrying you I shall do God
no displeasure, but rather follow his commands.   As for my
father, he has done so little for my good and so much to my
hurt, that the law will have me marry and by no means lose
mine inheritance.   As for the Queen my mistress, I shall not
make it a point of conscience to do her a pleasure and God a
displeasure; since she has done nothing but hinder me from
having any blessing I might have had in my youth. But to the
intent that you may understand that my love is bottomed upon
virtue and honour, you shall promise me that, if I take you in

L

marriage, you will not endeavour the consummation thereof till that my father is dead or I bring him to consent." This promised willingly the gentleman, and they exchanged rings and kissed one another in the church before God, whom they had as witness to their promise; and between them there passed no other familiarity, save kissing.

This small contentment filled with joy the hearts of these two perfect lovers, and they were for some time without seeing but in full security of one another. Now there was no place in which glory might be gained to which the gentleman was not fain to go, since he could not account himself for a poor man, God having given to him so rich a wife; and while he was away she kept their perfect love so in her heart, that all others were as nothing to her. And although there were they who asked her in marriage, they had no answer from her but that, since she had lived such a long while unmarried, she had no wish ever to be married. This answer came to the ears of so many folk that the Queen heard thereof, and asked her wherefore she gave it. And Rolandine said that it was given from obedience to her, who had never desired her to be married to any man who could have made honourable provision for her; and that age and patience had made her resolve to content herself with her present estate. And to all who spoke to her on this manner she gave the same reply. But when the wars were over and the gentleman was returned to Court, she by no means spoke to him before other folk, but would go always to a certain church where, under pretext of confession, she would parley with him; for the Queen had charged both him and her that they should not speak to one another on pain of their lives, except it were in some great assembly. But honourable love, knowing nothing of such charges, was more ready to find means of speech than was the enemy to spy it out; and he, concealing himself under the habit of every order of monks he could think of, they continued in this pleasant fashion till that the King went to his pleasure house near Tours. In that place there was no church to which the ladies could go on foot save only the one pertaining to the castle, and that so badly designed for their purpose that there was no hiding-place or confessional in it in which the confessor could not be clearly recognised. Natheless, if opportunity failed them on one side,

love found them other and easier, for there came to Court a
lady nearly related to the lover of Rolandine.   And she with
the young prince her son were lodged in the King's household,
and the prince's room stood out beyond the rest of the house,
in such a manner that, from his window, it was possible to see
and talk with Rolandine, for the windows were at the angle
where the two parts of the house joined one another.   And in
this room of hers, that stood above the King's Hall, there were
lodged with her all the ladies who were her fellows.   And she,
ofttimes seeing the prince at his window, by her gouvernante
advertised her husband of it; whereupon, after well observing
the place, he feigned to take great delight in the reading of a
book concerning the Knights of the Round Table, which was
in the prince's room.   And when all were gone to dinner he
prayed a body-servant to let him come and read, and to shut
him up in the room, and keep good watch over the door.   The
man, knowing him for a kinsman of his master and one to be
trusted, let him read as much as he would.   On the other hand
Rolandine would come to her window, and that she might the
longer stay there, feigned to have a diseased leg, and dined and
supped so early that she went no more to dinner with the other
ladies.   She likewise set herself to make a quilt of crimson
silk, which she fixed at the window, whereat she was fain to be
alone, and when she saw there was no one at hand she held
parley with her husband, who answered her in such a voice that
could not be heard by others.   And when she saw any folk
she would cough and make some sign to him, so that he might
get him gone in good time.   They that played the spy on
them were persuaded that all love passages were over, for she
never stirred from a room whither of a certainty he could not
come, since he was altogether forbidden to enter it.   But one
day the prince's mother, being in her son's room, placed herself
at the window where was the great book of Romances, and she
had not been there a long while before one of Rolandine's
companions saw her and spoke to her.   The lady asked her how
fared Rolandine, and the girl replied that she could see for
herself if it were her pleasure, and made Rolandine come to the
window in her nightcap.   So, after speaking about her sickness, each went back to her own place.   The lady, looking at
the great book of the Round Table, said to the servant who

had charge of it: "I marvel how young folk can waste their time in the reading of such folly!" The man answered that he marvelled still more that men of age and of repute for wisdom were exceedingly delighted with it; and as a matter for astonishment told her how the gentleman, her kinsman, stayed at the window four or five hours every day to read in this fine book aforesaid. Straightway the reason of it came into the lady's mind, and she charged the servant to hide himself close at hand and take account of what happened. This he did, and found this gentleman's book to be the window whither Rolandine came and spoke to him, and heard many a love-passage they thought to have kept altogether secret. On the morrow he bore this to his mistress, who sent for the gentleman, and after chiding him, forbade him any more to be in that place; and in the evening she spoke to Rolandine, threatening her that, if she continued in this foolish love, she would tell the Queen of all her doings. Rolandine, no whit affrayed, swore that after her mistress's forbidding her she had never spoken to him, let them say what they would, and she called her fellows and servants to witness that such was the truth. And for the matter of the window, she denied to have spoken there to the gentleman; but he, fearing the thing was made known, withdrew himself from the danger, and was a long time without returning to Court, but not without writing to Rolandine in such subtle fashion that, howsoever much the Queen might play the spy, there was not a week in which she did not twice get news of him.

And when a monkish messenger, who was the first he had used, failed him, he sent her a little page, now dressed in one colour and now in another. And he would stop at the doors, through which all the ladies were wont to pass, and give her the letters privily in the press. But one day, the Queen going into the country, a certain one whose charge it was to look after this affair, recognised the page and ran after him; but he, who was of keen wit, suspecting that he would be searched, entered the house of a poor woman who had her pot on the fire, and forthwith burnt up the letters. The gentleman followed him up and stripped him quite naked, and thoroughly searched his vesture, but found nothing, and so let him go. Whereupon the old woman asked the gentleman

why he had searched the boy. He said to her: "To find
certain letters which I thought he had carried." "By no
means could you have found them," said the woman, "so well
were they hidden." "I pray you," said he, "tell me in what
slit they are hidden," having a good hope of getting them
back. But when he understood that the fire was the hiding
place, he knew the page to have been the keener of the two,
and made report of the whole matter to the Queen. And from
henceforth Rolandine's husband could no more avail himself of
the page; so he sent an old servant, who, forgetting the death
that he knew well the Queen threatened against those who inter-
meddled with this matter, undertook to carry letters to Rolandine.
And when he was entered in unto the castle where she was, he
set himself to watch by a door at the foot of the grand staircase
whither all the ladies passed; but a servant who before had
seen him straightway knew him, and told the Queen's master of
the household, who presently came to seek him and clap him
up. But the messenger, prudent and wary, seeing they looked
at him from far off, turned himself to the wall, as if for a
necessary occasion, and tearing up the letter into as small pieces
as he could, threw them behind a door. Forthwith he was
taken and searched in every way; but when they could find
nothing they asked him on his oath if he had not brought
letters, using with him all manner of threats and persuasions to
make him to confess the truth; but promising or threatening,
it was all one, and they none the wiser. Report of this came
to the Queen, and certain of the company were of the opinion
that it would be well to look behind the door near which he
was taken; and this being done they found that they sought—
namely, the pieces of the letter. Then was summoned the
King's confessor, who, after putting the pieces in order on a
table, read the letter at length; and so was brought to light
the truth concerning the concealed marriage, for the gentleman
called Rolandine nothing but *wife*. The Queen, who had no
mind to cover her neighbour's misdeeds, as she ought to have
done, made a great noise of it, and commanded that every way
should be tried to make the poor man confess the truth of the
letter; and when it was shown to him he could not deny it,
but whatever they said or showed to him he would say no
more. Those who had charge of him then led him to the bank

of the river and put him in a sack, saying that he had lied to
God and the Queen against the proven truth. He, who had
rather lose his life than make accusation against his master,
asked of them a confessor, and after easing his conscience as
well as might be, he said to them : " Good sirs, I pray you tell
my lord that I commend to him the life of my wife and
children, for with hearty goodwill I give my life for his service.
Now do your pleasure on me, for no word will I utter against
my master. Thereupon, all the more to affright him, they
threw him bound up in the sack into the river, calling to him :
"Tell the truth and your life shall be spared." But perceiving
that he answered them not a word, they drew him from the
water and brought the report of it to the Queen, who said that
neither the King her husband nor herself had such good
fortune in their servants as a man who had not wherewithal to
pay them. And she would fain have drawn him into her
service, but he would by no means of his own will leave his
master. Natheless, by the leave of the said master, he took
service under the Queen, where he lived in happiness and good
contentment.

And the Queen being acquainted with the truth of the
marriage by the gentleman's letter, made summon Rolandine,
and with a wrathful countenance calling her *wretch* in place of
cousin, laid before her the shame she had done her father's
house, her kinsfolk, and her mistress, in marrying without her
leave or commandment. Rolandine, who for a long while had
known the small love the Queen bore her, gave her as little in
return. And since love was wanting between them neither
had fear any place, and Rolandine thought likewise that this
rebuke before several persons did not proceed so much from
love as from a desire to do her an open shame, the Queen taking
more pleasure in chiding her than grief at seeing her in fault.
So with a face as glad and assured as the Queen's was wrathful
and troubled, she replied : " Mistress, did you not plainly know
your own heart and the manner of it, I would set before you
the ill-will you have for a long time borne against my father
and myself, but this you know so well that it will not appear
marvellous to you that all the world has a suspicion of it; and
as for me, I have felt this intent of yours to my great hurt.
For, if it had been your pleasure to favour me as you do those

who are not so near akin as I, I should now have been married
both to your honour and mine, but you have left me as one
altogether deprived of your grace, so that all the good matches
I might have made are passed away before my eyes, by reason
of my father's neglect and the small account you make of me.
At this I fell into such despair, that if my health allowed of it,
I had entered into the religious life, and so escaped from the
continual sorrows your severity laid upon me.　In this sad case
one sought me out, who would have been of as gentle blood as
myself, if the love of two persons were to be as much esteemed
as the wedding-ring, for you know that his father was before
mine in precedency.　And he for a long while has courted me
and loved me; but you, mistress, who never pardon me any
petty fault, nor praise me for any good deed; although you well
knew that it was not my custom to listen to worldly love
passages, and that I was altogether given up to devotion; have
found it a strange thing that I should speak with a gentleman
as unfortunate as myself, from whom I neither wished nor
sought anything except some matter of consolation.　And when
I saw this consolation taken away from me, I was resolved to
take as much pains to gain it as you took to deprive me of it;
whereupon we promised each other marriage, and confirmed
the promise with a ring.　Methinks, therefore, you do me
great wrong to call me *wicked*, since in this great and perfect
love, in which I found the consolation I longed for, there passed
between us nothing worse than kissing, all else being deferred
by me till, by the grace of God, my father's heart should be
inclined to consent thereto.　Sure am I that I have in no way
offended God nor my conscience, for I waited till the age of
thirty years to see what you and my father would do for me,
having kept my youth so chastely and virtuously that no living
man can cast anything in my teeth.　And using the reason
given to me by God, seeing myself growing old, and despairing
of finding a match according to my estate, I resolved to marry
one according to my wish; not for the satisfaction of the lust
of the flesh, since there has been no carnal consummation; nor
for the lust of the eyes, since you know he is not comely; nor
for the pride of life, he being poor and of small reputation.
But I have taken account alone of the virtue that is in him, the
which all men are constrained to laud and magnify; also of the

great love he bears me, by reason of which I hope to find with
him a life of quiet and good treatment.   And after weighing
duly both the good and the evil that may come of it, I have
fixed on him who seems to me the best, and with whom I have
determined for the last two years to pass the remainder of my
days.   And so steadfast is this my resolve, that not all the
torments I may endure—no, not death itself—can turn me
from it.   Wherefore I pray you to excuse that which in truth
is very excusable, and leave me to live in that peace which I
hope to find with him."

The Queen, seeing her face to be so steadfast and her words
so true, could not answer in reason, but, continuing in wrath
to reproach her, at last fell to weeping, and said: "Wretch
that you are, in place of humbling yourself before me, and
repenting of your great fault, you speak dry-eyed and audaciously, and so make manifest the obstinacy and hardness of
your heart.   But if the King and your father will listen to me,
they will put you in a place where you will be constrained to
talk after another fashion."   "Mistress," answered Rolandine,
"since you accuse me of speaking audaciously, I will be silent,
if it is not your pleasure that I should reply to you."   And
being commanded to speak, she said to the Queen: "It is not
my part to speak audaciously and without due reverence to you
who are my mistress and the greatest princess in Christendom;
and this it was by no means my intent to do, but since I can
call no advocate to speak for me, save the truth that is known
only by me, I am constrained to tell it plainly and without fear,
hoping that when you know it you will not esteem me what it
has been your pleasure to name me.   I am not afraid of any
living creature hearing how I have kept myself in this matter,
since I know that I have thereby offended neither God nor my
honour.   And since I am persuaded that He who sees my heart
is on my side, wherefore should I fear?   And having this Judge
for me, shall I of His subjects be afraid?   And for what cause
should I weep, since neither my conscience nor my heart do
at all reprove me?—nay, so far am I from repentance, that if
I could make a new beginning I would do even as I have done.
But you, indeed, have good cause for weeping, as much for
the wrongs you did me in my youth as for that you now
reproach me before all for a thing which is rather to be imputed

to you than me. If I had justly offended God, the King, you, my kinsfolk, and my conscience, I should be hard of heart if I did not repent with weeping. But for so befitting and holy an agreement, in which no fault can be found save that you have too soon blazed it abroad, showing thereby that you have a greater desire for my dishonour than for preserving the good repute of your house and kinsfolk, I by no means ought to weep; yet, mistress, since such is your pleasure, I will not gainsay you; for whatever pains you lay upon me, I being innocent, will take no less pleasure in the enduring of them than you in the inflicting. Wherefore give what commands you please to my father, and I am well assured that he will not fail you, and as far as my ill is affected he will be altogether your creature; and as obedient to your will he has hitherto neglected my good, so he will be quick to obey you for my evil. But I have a Father in heaven, who, I am assured, will give me patience to bear all your torments, and in Him alone do I put my trust."

At this the Queen was still more wrathful, and commanded that she should be taken out of her sight and put in a room by herself, where she might have speech with no one. But she did not deprive her of her gouvernante, by whose means she let her husband know her case, and that which she thought it was best for him to do. And he, thinking the deeds he had done in the King's service might avail him something, came post haste to Court and found the King a-hunting, and told him the truth of the matter, entreating him to do so much for a poor gentleman as to appease the Queen in such sort that the marriage might be consummated. The King replied nothing save: "Do you assure me that you have taken her to wife?" "Ay, sire," said the gentleman, "by word and gift alone; and if it please you, we'll make an ending to it." The King, lowering his head, and without saying a word more, returned forthwith to his castle, and when he was come thither gave charge to the captain of the guards that he should take the gentleman prisoner. Natheless, one of his acquaintance, who knew the King's intent by his visage, counselled him to get him gone and stay in a house hard-by; and if the King made search for him, as he suspected he would, he would presently let him know so that he might fly the realm; but if things were softened down he would send word for him to come back.

And the gentleman, trusting in his friend, made such good speed that the captain of the guards could not at all find him.

The King and Queen took counsel together what they should do with this poor lady, who had the honour of being akin to them, and by the advice of the Queen it was determined that she should be sent back to her father, who was informed of the whole truth. But before she was sent they made several weighty doctors of the Church and Council hold parley with her, to the intent that since her marriage was a matter only of words, it could easily be dissolved by the agreement of both parties, this being the King's will on the matter, to preserve the honour of his house. Her reply was that in all things she was ready to obey the King save in cases of conscience, but those whom God hath joined together it is lawful for no man to put asunder. So she prayed them to tempt her no more, saying that if love and good-will, founded on the fear of God, are the true and sure bonds of marriage, she was so fast in bonds that neither fire, sword, nor water could burst them, but death alone, to whom and to no other she would give up her ring and her oath, and so entreated them to speak no more on't; for she stood so firm in her resolve that she had rather die and keep faith than live and break it. So these doctors aforesaid carried back to the King her answer; and when the King and Queen saw that there was no way to make her renounce her husband, they sent her back to her father in such mean and pitiful sort that they who beheld her pass by wept to see it. And though she was in fault, so grievous was the punishment and so great her steadfastness, that this fault of hers was commonly accounted as a virtue. And her father, being advised of this her coming, would by no means see her, but made bear her to a castle in a forest, the which he had aforetime built for a reason well worthy to be told. And there he kept her for a long while, saying that if she would renounce her husband he would hold her for his daughter and set her free. All the same she remained firm, and preferred to remain in the bonds both of prison and marriage than to have all the freedom in the world without her husband. And by the manner of her countenance one would have judged her pains to have been most pleasant pastimes, for she bore them for the sake of him whom she loved.

And as to men, what shall I say concerning them? Her husband, so deeply under obligation to her, fled to a country where he had many friends, I would say Germany. And there he showed well by the lightness of his disposition that not so much had he paid court to Rolandine by reason of a true and perfect love, as by reason of his covetousness and ambition. For he became amorous of a German lady, and forgot his letters to her who for his sake had borne so great tribulation. And whereas no ill-fortune, however rigorous, had hindered them from writing to one another, till this foolish and wicked love of his, so grievous was it to Rolandine that she knew no rest. And seeing his letters that they were cold and altogether changed from what they had been, she suspected that some new love separated her husband from her, and had done that which all the torments and pains of her could not effect. But since perfect love bottoms not judgment upon suspicion, she found means to secretly send a servant in whom she trusted, not to write or speak with her husband, but to spy out his ways and discover the truth. And this servant, having returned from his journey, told her that of a surety he had found him paying court to a German lady, and that the common report was that he would endeavour to marry her, since she was very rich. These tidings gave such sorrow to the heart of Rolandine that she fell grievously sick, and they who knew the reason of it told her, on behalf of her father, that after this great wrong done her she would do right to renounce him, and strove to bring her to this opinion. But notwithstanding that she was in very great torment, yet in no way would she change her purpose, and showed in this last temptation the greatness of her love and virtue. For as love grew less on his side, so it grew more on hers, and when she knew that in her heart alone now dwelt the love that formerly was between the two, she was resolved to preserve it until the death of the one or the other. Wherefore the Divine Goodness, which is perfect charity and true love, had pity on her grief and her long-suffering, so that after a few days her husband died while courting another woman. And being well informed of this by those who had seen him laid in the ground, she sent to her father entreating him that he would come and speak to her. The father, who had never spoken to her since she was first put in bonds, went forthwith, and after having heard her just conclusions, in place of reproving her, or as he had often threatened, of killing her, he took her in his arms, and weeping, said: " My daughter, you are more in the right than I; for, if there have been any fault in this matter, it is I that am the chief cause thereof; but since God has so ordered it, I wish to make satisfaction for what has passed." And after that he had brought her to his house, he treated her as his eldest daughter, and she was asked in marriage by a prudent and virtuous gentleman who bore the arms and name of their house. And he held Rolandine, with whom he often talked, in such esteem that he gave her praise where others had but blame for her, since he knew her end and aim to have been virtue. Which marriage, being to the mind of the father, was before long concluded. It is true that a brother of hers, the sole heir of their house, would give her no portion, saying that she had disobeyed her father, and after his death entreated her in such sort that her husband, who was a younger son, and herself, had much ado to live. But God provided for them, since the brother who wished to keep all, by his sudden death, in a single day lost all, both of his and hers. So was she made heiress to a good and rich estate, in which, with her husband's love, she lived piously and honourably. And after having brought up two sons which God gave to them, she joyously rendered her soul to Him in whom she had always placed her trust.

" Now, ladies, let the men who say we are inconstant ever, show me an example of a husband like this wife, and of as good faith and steadfastness. So sure am I that it will be a hard matter for them, that I prefer to hold them quit of it, than put them to the pain of this endeavour. But as to you, ladies, I exhort you, for the better retention of your renown, either not to love at all, or with as perfect a love as was that of Rolandine. And beware lest any say she did wrong to her honour, for by her steadfastness, she worked to the increasing of ours." " Faith, Parlamente," said Oisille, " you have told us the story of a woman with a great and honourable heart ; but that which adds to her glory is the disloyalty of her husband, who could leave her for another." " I think," said Longarine, " that this was the hardest to be borne of all her sorrows, for there is no grief so great but the united love of two cannot easily bear :

but when the one fails in his duty, and leaves all the burden
upon the other, then indeed it becomes unbearable." "You
ought then to have compassion on us," said Geburon, " who carry
the whole weight of love, which you will not so much as touch
with the tips of your fingers." "Ah, Geburon," said Parlamente, "often the burdens of men and women are different.
For the love of a woman, well bottomed upon God and her
honour, is so good and reasonable a thing that he who falls
therefrom is worthy to be accounted poltroon and villain before
God and man. But the love of men for the most part is merely
a matter of pleasure, into which women, ignorant of their evil
intent, cast themselves all too soon; and when God shows
them how vile are the hearts of those they esteem good, they
are well advised to get them gone, with their honour and
reputation, for 'soonest ended best mended.'" "This conclusion of yours is built upon mere fantasy," said Hircan; "if you
would maintain by it that honourable women can with honour
leave the love of men, and not men that of women, as if the
hearts of them in anywise differed, as do their faces and gear.
But as for their inclinations, I hold them to be much alike, save
that the evil which is best hidden is the worst." To this Parlamente, somewhat angry, replied: "I know well that with
you the best women are those whose wickedness is best known."
"Let us leave this talk," said Simontault, "for whether we take
the heart of man or the heart of woman the better of the two is
nothing worth. But to whom will Parlamente give her vote, that
we may hear some brave relation?" "I give it," said she, "to
Geburon." "Since then," said he, "I made a beginning with Grey
Friars, I will not forget the Benedictines, and a small matter
which befel one of them in my time; nevertheless, if I tell you
of a wicked monk, I wish not to hinder the esteem you bear
the good ones. But since the Psalmist says: 'All men are
liars,' and in another place: 'There is none that doeth good,
no, not one,' methinks we must needs think of men as they
really are. For, if there be any good in them, we must set it
down to Him who is the giver of all good, and not to the
creature wherein (by too much giving of praise and glory, or
by believing that there is some good in themselves) most men
are deceived. And to the end that you may believe that, under
great austerity, it is possible for lust as great to be hidden, hear
what happened in the time of King Francis the First."

NOVEL XXII.

How a wicked monk, by reason of his abominable lust, was at last brought to shame.

In the town of Paris there lived a prior of the monastery of St. Martin in the Fields, of whose name I will make no mention for the friendship that I bore him. His life up to the age of fifty years was so austere, that the fame of his holiness was blazed abroad throughout the whole realm, in such wise that there was neither prince nor princess who did him not great honour when he came to see them. And no monastery was put into a state of reformation but that he had a hand in it; wherefore men called him the *father of true monkery.* He was made visitor of the great convent of The Ladies of Fontevrault; and was held by the nuns in such awe that, when he came among them, they all trembled for the fear they had of him. And to the end that they might soften his great severities, they entreated him all as if he had been the King, which at the first he refused; but at last, being hard upon his fifty-fifth year, he began to find the treatment he had at first despised mighty pleasant; and esteeming himself the one support of all monkery, desired to have a better care for his health than had been his custom. Wherefore such good cheer did he make him, that from a very lean monk he became an exceeding fat one; and changing his fare changed also his heart, so that he began henceforth to look upon faces with pleasure, which afore he had but done as matter of duty, and beholding the graces that the veil only made more desirable, began to covet them. So, to satisfy this covetousness, he used such means that at last from shepherd he turned wolf, and if among any of the nuns he found an innocent he failed not to deceive her. But after that he had for a long while continued in this wicked manner of living, the Divine Goodness, taking pity on the poor wandering sheep, would not longer endure the exaltation of this wretch, as you shall shortly see.

One day, as he held a visitation in a convent named Gif, hard-by Paris, it happened that while he confessed all the nuns, there came to him one called Marie Heroet, whose speech was so soft and pleasant that it gave good promise of a heart and countenance to match. So at the very hearing of her voice he conceived a passion for her which surpassed any he had for

other nuns; and while he spoke he lowered his head to look
at her, and saw such cherry lips that he could not restrain himself from raising her veil to see whether her eyes were to match,
as indeed they were.   And at this his heart was filled with a
consuming fire, so that he left off to eat and drink, and the
manner of his countenance was altered, though he was fain to
conceal it.   And when he was returned to his priory he found
there no rest; wherefore his days and nights were spent in
great disquietude, as he sought for means to accomplish his
desire and do to her even as he had done to many others. But this
he feared might be a difficult matter, inasmuch as he had found
her prudent in speech, and of so keen a wit that he could have
no great hopes; and on the other hand, he saw himself that he
was old and ugly, and so was resolved to say nothing to her,
but to strive to win her by fear.   To which intent he soon
afterwards went to the convent of Gif, and showed himself more
austere a man than he had ever done, speaking wrathfully to
all the nuns, and reproving one, that her veil was not low
enough, another that she carried her head too high, and a third
that she did him not reverence in the manner proper to a nun.
In all these small matters so severe was he that they feared him
as if he had been God sitting in assize.   And he, having a
defluction of rheum in the feet, grew so weary in visiting the
usual places, that towards evensong-time, as was his design, he
found himself in the dormitory.   The abbess said to him:
"Reverend Father, it is time to sing evensong."   And he
replied: "Go then, mother, to evensong, for I am so weary
that I will remain here, not for rest, but to speak with Sister
Marie, of whom I have heard a very bad report, for they tell
me that she gossips like a woman of the world."   The abbess,
who was aunt to her mother, prayed him scold her heartily,
and left her all alone with him, save for a young monk he had
in his company.   When he found himself alone with Sister
Marie, he began by lifting her veil, and bade her look at him.
She replied that her rule would not have her look at men.
"'Tis well said, my daughter," said he, "but you must by no
means consider us monks as men."   Wherefore Sister Marie,
fearing to be in fault through disobedience, looked him in the
face, and found him so ugly that it seemed to her more of a
penance than a sin.   The good father, after discoursing some

while on the great friendship he bore her, would fain have put his hand on her breasts, but she, as was her duty, repulsed him. At this enraged, he said to her : " Is it befitting in a nun to know that she has breasts ?" She replied : " I know well that I have breasts, and that neither you nor any other shall lay a hand upon them; for I am not so young and ignorant as not to understand what is sin and what is not." And when he saw that this manner of talk would not win her, he resolved to try another, saying : " Alas ! my daughter, I must declare to you the necessity of my case—namely, that I have a sickness which all the physicians deem incurable, unless I have pleasure of some woman for whom I have a great love. For my part, I would not, to save my life, do mortal sin, but when it comes to that I am well assured that simple fornication is as nothing in comparison with self-murder. Wherefore, if you love my life, you will both do good to your conscience and also to me." She asked him what manner of pleasure he would have of her ; to which he answered that she could give her conscience into his keeping, and that he would do nothing which could be imputed against either of them. And to show her how to begin the pastime he asked of her, he cast his arms around her and essayed to throw her on the bed; but she, perceiving the wickedness of his intent, so well defended herself with arms and voice that he could touch nothing save her clothing. Then, seeing all his plans and endeavours turned to nothing, as a madman not only wanting in conscience but in natural reason, he drove his hand underneath her dress, and so furiously scratched whatever he could touch with his nails, that the poor girl, crying aloud, fell full length on the ground in a dead swoon. At this cry the abbess came into the dormitory, for she, while at evensong, recollected that she had left this nun, her niece's daughter, alone with the good father ; at which her conscience taking some scruple, she left evensong and listened at the door of the dormitory, and hearing her niece's voice, pushed open the door that was held of the young monk. Now when the prior saw the abbess come in, he showed her the nun lying in a swoon, and said : " Without doubt, mother, you did great wrong in that you did not certify me of Sister Marie's complexion; for ignorant of her weakness, I when chiding her made her stand before me, and as you see she has swooned away." And while they were reviving her with vinegar and other medicaments proper to the occasion they found that her head had been hurt by the fall. And the prior, fearing lest she should tell her aunt the reason of it, spoke to her all apart, saying : " My daughter, I charge you, by your obedience and hope of salvation, that you by no means speak to any of what I have done to you, for you must understand that I was constrained by the vehemence of my love. But since I see you have no desire to love, I will speak to you no more on it, but I do assure you that, if you will consent, I will have you chosen abbess of one of the best convents in the kingdom." But her reply to him was to the intent that she would rather die in perpetual imprisonment than have any for lover save Him who died for her on the cross ; affirming that with Him she had rather suffer all the evils that the world could give than be endowed with all its blessings without Him. And she would have no more talk of this kind from him, or else would tell the abbess of it ; but if he kept silence so also would she. So went forth this wicked shepherd ; but that he might show himself to be what he was not, and that he might again look upon her whom he loved, he returned to the abbess, and said to her : " Reverend mother, I pray you make all your nuns sing a *Salve Regina* to the honour of that virgin in whom I place my trust." And while this was being performed, the fox of a prior did nothing but weep, not for devotion but for regret that he had not gained his end. And all the nuns setting this down to his love for the Virgin Mary, esteemed him as an holy man ; but Sister Marie, knowing his wickedness, prayed in her heart that he might be confounded, who held virginity in such contempt.

So went this hypocrite to St. Martin's, where the evil flame that was at the heart of him ceased not to burn day or night, nor to seek for some means of obtaining his desire. And since above all he stood in fear of the abbess, who was a virtuous woman, he sought means to send her away from her convent. Wherefore he betook himself to Madame de Vendosme, then living at La Fère, where she had built and founded a convent of the rule of St. Benedict, calling it *The Mount of Olivet*. And the prior, as the very prince of reformers, giving her to understand that the abbess of the aforesaid Mount Olivet was not fit for the governing of so large a community, the good lady entreated him to find her another whom she could meetly set over it.   And he, asking nothing better, counselled her to take the abbess of Gif as the best that was in France, so Madame de Vendosme forthwith sent for her, and made her abbess of the Convent of Mount Olivet.   And the prior of St. Martin's, who held the whole of monkery in his hands, made choose abbess of Gif a woman to his liking. This done, he went to Gif to try again a second time if, by prayers or gentle persuading, he could gain Sister Marie Heroet. But having no hope of success he returned in despair to his priory of St. Martin, and there, to accomplish his ends and to be avenged on her who had been so cruel to him, he caused the relics that were at the aforesaid convent of Gif secretly to be conveyed away by night, and accused the confessor of the convent, an old and good man, that he had stolen them, and for this cause clapped him up in prison at St. Martin's.   And whilst he held him captive he stirred up two witnesses, who out of ignorance did what the prior ordered them, and they bore witness that they had seen the said confessor and Sister Marie committing a foul and scandalous act in a garden ; and this the prior was fain to make the old man confess for truth.   But he, knowing the failings of the prior, entreated that he might be brought into chapter, where before all the monks he would tell the truth of the matter.   The prior, fearing lest the confessor's justification should be his condemnation, would by no means entertain this request, and finding him not to be moved from his resolve, entreated him so evilly in prison that some said he died there, others that he was constrained to unfrock and quit the realm ; but howsoever this be no man saw him again.

So the prior, thinking to have Sister Marie altogether in his hands, went to the convent, where the abbess, chosen by him to this intent, opposed him in nothing.   Thereupon he began to use his authority as visitor, and made all the nuns, one by one, come before him in a chamber after the manner of visitation.   And when it came to the turn of Sister Marie, who had lost her good aunt, he said to her : "Sister Marie, you are advised of the matter of your accusation, and that for all your cloak of chastity you are well known to be the very contrary thereto."   But Sister Marie, with a steadfast face, replied : "He that accuseth me let him come before me, and you will discover if he persist in his wicked position." He answered: "We have no need of further witness, insomuch as the confessor has been found guilty." "I esteem him too good a man," said she, "to have acknowledged such a lie for truth; but, be it so, and let him come before me that I may prove the contrary to his words." The prior, seeing that in no manner could he affray her, said: "Forasmuch as I am your spiritual father, and desirous that your honour be preserved, I put this before your conscience, and to your words I will give belief. I therefore demand and conjure you, under pain of mortal sin, that you tell me truly whether or no you were a maid when you came hither?" She replied: "My age, father, that was five years, should pass as a safe witness to my maidenhood." "And since that time," said the prior, "have you not lost this flower of your virginity?" She swore she had kept it safe, having had no hindrance thereto but from him. To this he answered that he could not believe it, and that the matter wanted proof. "What proof," said she, "would be to your pleasure?" "The same," said he, "as I use with others; for as I am visitor of souls, so am I of bodies also. Your abbesses and prioresses have all passed through my hands, wherefore fear not for your maidenhood but throw yourself upon the bed and lift your clothes over your face." It was in wrath that Sister Marie replied to him: "You have spoken in such wise of your wicked lust after me, that I am persuaded you wish not to look for, but to take away my virginity; but understand that I will never consent thereto." Then he said he would have her excommunicated, for that she had refused him monastic obedience, and that he would shame her in full chapter by the evil he wot of betwixt her and the confessor. But she, no whit afraid, answered: "He that knoweth the hearts of His servants shall give me as much honour as you before men shall give me shame. And since it has come to this, I had rather you accomplished on me your cruelty than your lust, for I know God, that he is a just judge." Forthwith was gathered together all the chapter, and before them was brought Sister Marie, kneeling on her knees, to whom the prior spoke very dispiteously: "Sister Marie, it is to my displeasure that the good admonitions that I have made to you are found altogether of none effect, and that you are in such case that, contrary to my custom, I am constrained to lay a penance on you. Now your fault is, that your confessor, having been examined as touching certain crimes imputed to him, confesses to have abused your person in the place where the witnesses affirmed they had seen him. Wherefore, since I have placed you in the honourable estate of mistress of the novices, I ordain that not only shall you be the last of all, but, kneeling on the ground, shall eat bread and water before the sisters till your repentance be of a sort to merit pardon." Sister Marie, being advertised by one of her fellows, who knew the whole matter, that if she answered in a fashion displeasing to the prior he would put her *in pace*—that is, in perpetual imprisonment—patiently endured this sentence; raising her eyes to heaven, and praying Him, who had been her resistance against sin, to be her patience against tribulation. Furthermore, the prior of St. Martin's enjoined that, when her mother or her kinsfolk might come to the convent, she should not be suffered to speak with them, nor to write any letter to them, save only such letters as were written in community.

So this wretched man went his way, and returned there no more; and the poor maid was for a long time in the pitiful case you have heard. But her mother, loving her above all her children, and seeing that she no more had any news of her, marvelled thereat, and said to one of her sons, the same being a man of prudence and virtue, that she thought her daughter to be dead, and that the nuns, so as still to have the yearly payment, had concealed it from her. And she prayed him to hit upon some means of seeing his sister, if she were yet alive, whereupon he went forthwith to the convent, and was received with the accustomed excuse—namely, that it was now three years that his sister had not stirred from her bed. But with this he would not be content, and swore if he did not see her that he would climb the walls and take their convent by storm. Thereupon, in much fear, they led his sister to the grate, but with the abbess following so hard on her that Sister Marie could say nothing that was not fit for her ears. But of her prudence she had put in writing all that is set down here, with a thousand other devices of the prior for her deception, of the which I omit relation, because of the length of time thereto required. Yet I will not forget that, when her aunt was abbess, thinking her refusal proceeded from his ugliness, he

had made her to be tempted by a young monk and a handsome;
hoping that, if she obeyed the monk for love, she would do
the same by him for fear. But the poor girl ran from the
garden, where the monk tempted her and used gestures so
shameful that I blush to remember, to the abbess, saying:
"Mother, they who come to visit us are no monks but rather
devils!" Whereupon the prior, fearing to be discovered, said
with a laugh: "Doubtless, reverend mother, Sister Marie is
in the right." And taking Sister Marie by the hand, he said
to her before the abbess: "I had heard that Sister Marie
spoke so well and readily that she was esteemed worldly, and
on this account I constrained myself against the grain to address
her after the fashion that men of the world use with women,
as I had found it in books; for as to experience, I am as naked
of it as the day I was born. And deeming my ugliness and
old age caused her to make such virtuous answers, I charged a
young monk of mine to make love to her, whom you see she
hath likewise virtuously resisted. Wherefore, so good and
prudent do I esteem her, that I command that from henceforth
she be first after you and mistress of novices, to the end that
she may always increase more and more in virtue."

This deed, and many more like to it, did the holy man,
during the three years in which he was amorous of the nun.
And she, as I have said, gave her brother through the grate
the whole matter of this pitiful history. And it having been
borne by him to her mother, she in great despair came to
Paris, where she found the Queen of Navarre, only sister to
the King, to whom she showed the thing, saying to her:
"Madam, put no more trust in these hypocrites; I thought I
had put my daughter hard-by Paradise, or on the way to it,
and lo! it is the road to hell, and she in the hands of worse
than devils, for the devils do but tempt us when it is our pleasure
to be tempted; and these, if love be wanting, are fain to have
us by force." At this the Queen of Navarre was mightily dis-
tressed, for entirely had she put her trust in the prior of St.
Martin's, and had given into his hands the abbesses of Monta-
villiers and Caen, her sisters-in-law. On the other hand the
greatness of the crime was an abomination to her, and filled
her with the desire of avenging the innocence of the poor girl,
in such sort that she made the matter known to the King's

chancellor, the same being also legate, who summoned the prior to appear in his court, and there was found no excuse at all in him, save only that the number of his years was three-score and ten. And to the Queen of Navarre he spoke, praying her, by all the good she had ever wished to do him, and by all he had done for her, and all he had wished to do for her, that she would be pleased to make an end to this case, since he confessed and declared that Sister Marie Heroet was a very pearl of honour and of maidenhood. The Queen of Navarre, hearing this, was so astonished that she knew not what to reply to him, and so without a word left him there; and the poor man returned to his monastery covered with shame, and from henceforth would see no one, and only lived a year after. But Sister Marie Heroet, esteemed according as she deserved for the virtues that God had implanted in her, was removed from Gif, where she had suffered so much tribulation, and made abbess, by the King's mandate, of Giy-juxta-Montargis. This convent she reformed, and lived for the rest of her days as one fulfilled with the Spirit of God, praising him always for that he had been pleased to give back to her both honour and rest.

"Here, ladies, is a relation well according with that Scripture : That God by the weak confounds the strong, and by those of no account in the eyes of men brings to the ground the glory of folk who think themselves to be something, but are in truth nothing. And consider that, without the grace of God, there is no good at all in man, and with this grace no temptation that cannot be overcome, as is manifest by the manner in which he was confounded, to whom was imputed righteousness, and she was exalted whom he would have all men esteem a miserable sinner. In this is fulfilled the saying of Our Lord : ' Whosoever shall exalt himself shall be abased, and he that shall humble himself shall be exalted.' " " Alas," said Oisille, " how many honest folk this prior deceived ! For I have seen men who put more trust in him than God." " I would not have been one of them," said Nomerfide, " for I so hate the very sight of a monk that I could not confess to one ; since indeed I hold them far worse than other men ; and no house do they inhabit but that they sow the tares of shame or strife in it." " There are good ones," said Oisille, " and it were not right that they should be judged alone by the bad ;

but the best are those who are least found in the company of
laymen and women." "You say truth," said Ennasuitte, "for
the less one sees them the less one knows of them, but fami-
.liarity shows what kind of men they are." "Enough of it,"
said Nomerfide, "let us see to whom Geburon will give his
vote." Geburon, to make amends for his fault, if fault it were,
to have manifested the abominable life of a wicked monk, to
the end that they might be on their guard against the cozenage
of men like to him, gave his vote to Oisille, thinking her to be
a gentlewoman as temperate in telling the evil as she was
ready to exalt and publish the good she knew of any one.
"And of this story the intent shall be," said Geburon, "to the
praise of the monks." To this Oisille replied : "So great
oaths have we sworn to tell alone the truth, that I should not
know how to accomplish the telling of such a tale. And in
making your relation you have reminded me of so pitiful a
story that I am constrained to relate it. And by it, ladies, you
shall take warning lest the hypocrisy of those who esteem
themselves more religious than other men do not charm your
understanding in such sort that your faith be turned from the
right way. And beware lest you think to find salvation in any
creature other than Him who willed not to have a fellow in his
work of creation and redemption, and in whom is all power to
save us to life eternal; and in this life temporal to comfort
us and deliver us from all tribulations. And know also that
Satan often doth transform himself into an angel of light, to the
end that the eye of sense, blinded by the outward show of
holiness and devotion, may dwell on those things from which it
ought to flee. Wherefore it seems good to me to tell you this
story, which indeed took place in our own times."

NOVEL XXIII.

How the lust of a Grey Friar made an honest gentleman, his wife, and his
child to perish miserably.

In the country of Perigord there was a gentleman who had
so great a devotion for St. Francis that he regarded all who
wore his dress as holy as the saint himself. And, to his honour,
he had appointed rooms in his house for the lodgment of the

brethren, by whose counsel he ruled all his affairs, even to the smallest, thinking in this manner to make a safe journey through life. And one day it came to pass that his wife, who was both comely, wise, and virtuous, was brought to bed of a fine boy, the which increased much the more the love her husband had for her. And the better to make feast for her, his dear gossip, he had bidden his brother-in-law; and as the hour for supper drew nigh there came to the house a Grey Friar, whose name I will conceal for the honour of the order. At the coming of this his spiritual father, from whom he had no secrets, the gentleman was glad at heart, and, after some talk between his wife, his brother-in-law, and the monk, they set themselves at table for supper. And while they were at supper, the gentleman, looking upon his wife, in whom, indeed, there was enough beauty and grace to make her desired of her husband, began in a loud voice to question the holy father: "Father, is it of a truth a mortal sin in a man to lie with his wife after she has been in childbed?" The father, whose face and words altogether belied his heart, replied with a wrathful countenance: "Without doubt, sir, I esteem such to be one of the greatest sins that can be committed in the estate of marriage. And for what else was the ensample of the Blessed Virgin Mary, who would not enter the temple till the days of her purification were fulfilled, although she stood in no need of purification, but that you should abstain from this small delight? And this you should surely do, seeing that the good Virgin abstained from going to the temple, where was all her joy, to the end that she might obey the law. And besides this, the physicians say that the offspring of such delights stand in great jeopardy." And when the gentleman heard these words he was very sorry, since he had hoped the father would have given him leave; however, he spoke no more on it. The holy man, while he was talking, having had a cup too many, had looked at the dame, thinking within himself that if he was the husband he would not ask the leave of a spiritual father to lie with his wife. And as fire, beginning by little and little, at last sets the whole house aglow, the monk began to burn with such a flame of lust that on a sudden he determined to accomplish that desire he had carried for three years concealed in his heart.

So, supper done, he took the gentleman by the hand, and,

leading him to the bed of his wife, said to him before her:
"Since I see, sir, the great love that is between you and the
dame here, which, conjoined to your youth, doth so much
torment you, I have compassion, and am minded to declare to
you a secret of our holy theology. This is, that the law, which,
by reason of the abuses and indiscretion of husbands, is thus
rigorous, suffers folk of good conscience like you to take some
indulgence. Wherefore, since before your people I uttered
the law in its severity, I will now not fail to show you, being a
prudent man, its softness also. Know, my son, that there are
women and women, just as there are men and men. In the
first place, we must know whether your dame here, it being
now three weeks since she was brought to bed, is freed from
her effluxion of blood?" And the lady replied that she was
so. "Then," said the friar, "I give you leave to lie with her,
and take no scruple for it, but you must promise me two things:
firstly, that you speak to no man of it, but come to her secretly;
secondly, that you come not till two hours after midnight, so that
the dame's digestion suffer no hindrance through your play with
her." All this the gentleman willingly promised, and confirmed
his promise with an oath; and the friar, knowing him to be
rather a fool than a liar, was altogether assured of him. And
after some talk the holy man went to his chamber, giving them
good-night and his blessing; but before going he took the
gentleman by the hand, saying to him: "Come you likewise,
fair sir, and keep not your poor gossip any longer awake."
The gentleman kissed his wife, saying to her: "Sweetheart,
leave me the door of your room open." And this the friar
heard and understood very well, so each one went to his
chamber. But as soon as the father was in bed, he thought
no whit of sleep or rest, since, when all was quiet, about the
appointed hour for saying matins, he crept as softly as he could
to the room where the master of the house was expected, and,
finding the door open, entered in and put out the candle, and
as quickly as he could laid himself down beside her, speaking
not a word. The dame, thinking him to be her husband, said:
"What? sweetheart, you have ill kept the promise you made
our confessor, not to come to me till two o'clock." The friar,
more intent on action than contemplation, and fearful lest he
might be known, thought chiefly of satisfying the wicked desire

that for a long while had corrupted his heart, and made her no reply, at which the lady was much astonished. And when he saw the hour draw near in which the husband was to come, he rose from beside the dame, and returned to his room as speedily as might be.

And in like manner as the rage of concupiscence had taken away from him all sleep, so fear, that always follows an evil deed, would now let him take no rest, so he went to the house-porter, and said to him : "My friend, your master has charged me to go forthwith to our monastery, and there offer certain prayers on his behalf; wherefore, prithee, give me my horse and open me the door, so that no one may be advised of it, for this is a necessary occasion and a secret." The porter, knowing well that to obey the friar was to do his master a service, secretly opened him the door and sent him away. At that hour arose the gentleman, and seeing it was time for him to go to his wife, as the holy father had appointed him, got up in his night-gear and went to her, as was his right by the ordinance of God, without any leave of man. And when she heard his voice speaking to her she marvelled greatly, and knowing not what had been done, said to him : "Is this the promise you made to the good father to have a care of your health and mine? And now not only did you come to me before the appointed hour, but return again. I beseech you think of it." The gentleman was so troubled to hear this that he must needs say : "What means this discourse of yours? I know of a truth that for three weeks I have not touched you, and you reprove me for coming to you too often. If you still persist in this you will make me think my company wearisome to you, and will constrain me against my habit and wish to seek in other quarters the pleasure which, by the law of God, I ought to have of you." The lady thinking he was jesting with her, replied : "Beware lest, thinking to deceive me, you be yourself deceived; for notwithstanding that you did not speak when you were with me the first time, I know well enough that you were here." Then the gentleman perceived that they were both of them cozened, and he swore a great oath that he had never come to her. At this the dame was in such sadness, that with tears and lamentations she besought him to make haste and discover who it could be, for in the house there slept only her brother and the friar. Forthwith the gentleman, struck with suspicion of the friar, hastened to the chamber where he was lodged and found it empty. And to be more assured whether or no he had fled, he sent for the man who kept the gate and asked him if he knew what was become of the friar, and he told him the whole truth. The gentleman, certain of the friar's wickedness, returned to his wife's room, saying : " Of a surety, sweetheart, he who lay with you and played such pretty pranks is our good father confessor !" The dame, who had always loved her honour, was in such despair at this, that forgetting all humanity and womanly nature, she implored him on her knees to avenge her for this great wrong. Wherefore the gentleman forthwith mounted his horse and rode in pursuit of the friar.

The lady remained alone in her bed, having no counsel or consolation with her save her little child that was lately born. And falling to consideration of the dreadful thing that had come upon her, without making excuse for her ignorance, she esteemed herself as the most blameworthy and wretched of women. And then she, who had learned nothing of the friars save a confidence in good works, satisfaction for sin by austerity of life, fasts and discipline, was altogether ignorant of the grace of God given to us through the merits of his Son, the remission of sins through his blood, the reconciliation of the Father to us by his death, the life given to sinners only by his goodness and compassion; and found herself so troubled by the enormity and weight of her sin, and the love she bore her husband and the honour of the line, that she not only turned away from the hope that every christian ought to have in God, but even lost all commonsense. So, overcome by grief, driven by despair beyond all knowledge of her God and herself, like a woman enraged and distempered, she took a rope from the bed and with her own hands strangled herself. And still worse, being in the agony of this cruel death, her body, fighting against itself, made such a struggling that she pressed her foot upon the face of the little child, whose innocence could not save him from following in death his wretched mother. But dying, he cried so loudly that a woman who slept in the room rose in great haste and lighted a candle, and saw her mistress hanging strangled by the bed-cord, and the child choked under her feet. So in great affray she ran to the room where was lodged the brother of the lady, and led him to see this pitiful sight.

The brother, taking at this such grief as would befall a man who loved his sister with his whole heart, asked the serving-woman who had done this. She told him that she knew not, that no one had entered the room but her master, and he had but lately left it. Whereupon going to his brother's room and finding him not, he was assured that he was guilty, and taking his horse, without asking any more questions, chased after him, and met him on the road as he returned from pursuing the friar, in much grief at not having caught him. As soon as the brother saw the husband approaching, he began crying to him: "Villain and poltroon! have a care for yourself, for this day I trust to be avenged on you through God and my good sword." The gentleman, who would have excused himself, found his brother-in-law's sword so near his body that he had enough to do to defend himself without making inquiry as to the matter in debate. And so many and such fierce blows did they give one another that they became feeble through loss of blood, and were constrained to sit down on the ground facing one another. And whilst they were taking their breath, the gentleman asked his brother-in-law: "What cause, my brother, has turned our great friendship into so fierce a fight?" To which the brother replied: "What cause has moved you to murder my sister, as good a woman as ever breathed? And so evilly, under colour of lying with her, to have strangled her with the bed-cord?" The husband hearing this, more dead than alive, went to his brother and, embracing him, said: "Is it possible that you have found your sister in the case you tell me?" And when his brother assured him that it was so, he said: "I pray you, brother, hear the cause for which I went forth from the house." And he told him all the story of the wicked Grey Friar, at which the brother was much astonished, and more grieved that for no reason he had assailed him. "I have done you wrong," he said, "forgive me." The gentleman replied: "If I had done you a wrong I have my punishment, for I am so deeply wounded that I hope not to escape death." So the brother put him on his horse as well as might be, and led him back to his house, where on the morrow he died, declaring and confessing before all the

kin of his brother-in-law that he himself was the cause of his
own death. But his brother, to make satisfaction to justice,
was counselled to go and ask for pardon of King Francis, first
of the name. Wherefore having made honourable burial for
husband, wife, and child, he went on Good Friday to Court to
obtain this pardon, which he got from the hands of Master
Francis Olivier, the Chancellor of Alençon, who afterwards,
for his excellent endowments, was chosen by the King to be
Chancellor of France.

"I believe, ladies, that after having heard this truthful
history you will think twice before you lodge such varlets in
your houses; and know that the better concealed the poison
the more dangerous it is." "Is it not your opinion," said
Hircan, "that this husband was an honest simpleton to bring
such a gallant to sup with his pretty wife?" "I have known
the time," said Geburon, "when there was not a house in the
country but had a room hallowed to the use of these holy
fathers, but now they are so well known that they are dreaded
as common cozeners." "It is my opinion," said Parlamente,
"that when a woman is in bed no priest should enter her room
except it be for the administration of the sacraments of Holy
Church; and when I call one to me, you can judge me to be
in great danger of death." "If all were as austere as you,"
said Ennasuitte, "the poor priests would be worse than excommunicated, being altogether shut out from the sight of women."
"Be not afraid on that account," said Saffredent, "they will
never fail on that score." "And these are they," said Simontault, "that bind us in the bonds of marriage to our wives, and
then strive to burst these bonds by their wickedness, and break
the oath we have taken in their presence." "'Tis pity," said
Oisille, "that those who administer the sacraments should thus
play at tennis with them; they ought to be burned alive."
"More wisely would you honour than insult them, and flatter-
ing them is better than blaming, for these are they who have
power to burn and put to dishonour; wherefore let them be,
and give ear to whomsoever Oisille shall give her vote." This
said Saffredent, and the company found his opinion right, and
leaving the priests alone, entreated Oisille to give her vote to
someone, and so change the matter of discourse. "I give it,"
said she, "to Dagoucin, for I see him to be in such contem-

plation as must be the preparing for some good story." "Since
I dare not say what I would," answered Dagoucin, "at least I
will speak of one to whom cruelty at the first brought hurt,
though afterwards it profited him. For though Love doth esteem
himself so puissant a warrior that he would fain go stark naked,
and can scarce bear to lie concealed, yet ladies, they that obey
his counsels and declare themselves too soon, are often brought
into an evil case. And the thing so fell out with a Castilian
gentleman, whose story you shall hear."

NOVEL XXIV.

The cruelty of a Queen of Castille to one of her lovers, and the profit he took thereby.

In the household of the King and Queen of Castille—the
names of them I know not, for they were not told me—there
was a gentleman so excellently endued with all comeliness of
mind, body, and estate, that there was none equal to him in all
the coasts of Spain. All men admired his virtues, but still
more the strangeness of him, for none could show any lady he
loved or ever had loved. And though there was many a
dame at Court fit to have set ice on fire, not one was there
who could take hold on this gentleman, whose name was
Elisor.

The Queen, who was a woman of much virtuousness, but
not altogether free from that flame which burns the more the
less it is perceived, seeing this gentleman that he loved none
of her ladies, marvelled thereat, and one day asked him if it
were possible that he loved as little as he seemed to do. He
replied that if she could behold his heart as plainly as his face,
she would not ask him that question. She, anxious to discover
his intent, pressed him so hard that he acknowledged to loving
a lady whom he thought the best in Christendom. All her
endeavour, both by prayers and commandments, did she use
that she might know who the lady was, but 'twas of no avail;
whereupon she made pretence of anger, and swore she would
no more speak to him if he did not name her he loved. At
this he was so troubled that he said he would rather die than
be obliged to name her; but seeing that he would lose the
Queen's favour by not telling her a thing so honourable that it

ought not to be taken in bad part by any one, he said to her
in great fear : " Madame, I have not boldness sufficient for the
telling of it, but the first time you go a-hunting I will show
you the lady, and sure am I that you will esteem her to be the
prettiest and the loveliest lady in all the world." For the sake
of this the Queen took good care to go earlier a-hunting than
she would have done, and Elisor being advertised of this made
himself ready, as was his wont, for the attending of her. And
this was the manner of his preparation : he made him a great
mirror of steel after the fashion of a cuirasse, and having put it
on him, covered it well with a cloak of black frieze all welted
with purflew and gold galloon. His mount was a jet-black
horse, caparisoned with a perfect harness, and whatsoever of
this was metal was worked with gold and black enamel after the
fashion of the Moors. His hat was of black silk, and on it
was fixed a cockade which had been devised of a love held
back by force, and all made rich with precious stones. Sword
and dagger were not less fine nor worse devised ; to be short, he
showed most bravely, and rode his horse to admiration, so that
all who saw him left the chase to watch the paces and the leaps
which Elisor made it accomplish. After bringing the Queen
to the place where the toils were set in the fine fashion I have
told you, he got down from his horse and went to help the
Queen dismount her palfrey. And as she stretched out her
arms to him he threw open his cloak, and taking her between
his arms he showed her his mirror cuirasse, saying : " I beseech
you look here." And without waiting any reply he set her
gently on the ground. The chase being ended, the Queen
returned to her castle without speaking with Elisor ; but after
supper she called him to her, saying he was the greatest liar
she had ever seen, for he had promised to show her at the
hunt the lady whom he loved most, and had not done it,
wherefore she was determined to take no more account of him.
Elisor, fearing she had not heard what he had said, replied that
he had by no means failed to fulfil her commandment, for he
had shown her both the woman and the thing he loved more
than all the world. She, feigning not to understand him,
answered that she did not know him to have shown her a
single one of her ladies. " It is true," said Elisor, " but whom
did I show you while I helped you off your horse ?" " Nothing,"

replied the Queen, "but a mirror on your breast." "And
what did you see in that mirror?" "Nothing but myself,"
answered the Queen. "Then," said Elisor, "have I kept
the promise I made to you, for there is no other image within
my breast than that you saw outside it, and that image alone I
am fain to love, worship, and adore, not as a woman, but as my
God on earth, into the hands of whom I commit my life and my
death. And my prayer to you is that this my great and perfect
love, that was my life concealed, may not be my death revealed.
And though I be not worthy that you should look upon me or
accept me as your lover, at least suffer me to live, as I have
been accustomed, in the contentment which I have for that my
heart has dared to bottom its love on so perfect and worthy a
rock, from which love I can have no other delight except that
it is perfect, seeing I must be content to love, though I may
never be loved. And if it be not to your liking, since you
have discovered my great desire, to use me so familiarly as
heretofore, do but continue to me my life, which stands alone
upon my seeing of you. For from you I have now nothing
but what suffices for my extreme necessity, and if I have less
you will have one servant the less, for you will lose the best
and most devoted you have ever had or ever will have." The
Queen, either to show herself other than she was, or to make
long trial of the love he bore her, or because she had another
lover whom she would not leave for the sake of him, or to hold
him as a reserve to take the other's place when he should
commit some fault, said with a countenance nor sad nor glad :
"Elisor, since I know not the strength of love, I will say nothing
to you of your foolishness in aiming at so high and hard a thing
as the love of me; for I know man holds his heart so little at
command, that he is not able to love or hate where he pleases ;
but since you have so well concealed the matter, I wish to know
how long you have been in this case." Elisor, looking at the
beautiful face of her, and seeing that she made enquiry concerning his sickness, hoped that it might be to her liking to
furnish the remedy. But seeing that while she asked him she
still looked gravely and prudently, he was afraid, seeming to
himself to be before a judge, whose sentence he feared would be
against him. But he swore to her that love had taken root in
his heart while he was very young, but he had not felt the pain

till the last seven years, or rather no pain but a sickness, giving
such contentment that to be cured of it would be death. "Since
you have so long and so steadfastly kept the matter secret,"
said the Queen, "I must be as slow to believe as you to tell.
Wherefore, if it is as you say, I am fain to put you to such a
proof as cannot be doubted, which accomplished, I will esteem
you to be towards me even according to your oath, and in like
manner you shall find me such as you desire." Elisor entreated
her to make what proof she pleased of him, since there could
be nothing so difficult as not easily to be borne, if by it she
would believe the love he bore her, and prayed her instantly to
command him according to her pleasure. She therefore said to
him : " Elisor, if you love me even as you say, I am well assured
that to have my favour nothing will be hard for you to endure.
Wherefore I charge you by all the desire you have to win me,
and all the fear you have to lose me, that to-morrow, without
again seeing me, you depart hence and betake yourself to some
place where you shall have no tidings of me, nor I of you till
this day seven years. You, since for seven years you have felt
this love, are well persuaded of it; and I, when I have had
equal experience, shall believe what your word alone cannot
make me to believe nor understand." Elisor, hearing this cruel
command, on one part doubted whether she was not desirous
of estranging herself from him, on the other part hoping that
the proof would speak better than words, accepted it, and said
to her : " Being that I have lived these seven years without any
hope, and keeping this fire concealed; now that it is known of
you, I shall spend these other seven in a better hope and
patience. But if I obey your command, by which I shall be
deprived of all the good I have in the world, what hope do you
give that when they are overpast you will accept me for your
faithful and loyal servant ?" The Queen, drawing a ring from
her finger, said to him : " Behold this ring I give you, let us
cut it into halves, I will keep the one and you the other, to the
end that, if length of time have power to take away my memory
of you, I shall be able to recognise you by this half-ring fitting
with mine." Elisor took the ring and broke it into two, giving
one-half to the Queen and keeping the other himself. And
having taken leave of her, more dead than they who have given
up the ghost, he went to his lodging to take order for his

N

departure. This he did in such sort that, putting all in train at his house, he betook him with but one servant to so solitary a place that none of his kinsfolk or his friends heard tidings of him for seven whole years. As to the life he led during this time, or as to the grief he bore for this absence, none knew of it, but they that loved him could not be ignorant of it. And when the seven years were accomplished, as the Queen went to mass there came to her a hermit with a mighty long beard, who, kissing her hand, gave her a supplication, which she did not forthwith read, though it was her custom to take all supplications given into her hand, however poor might be the petitioner. But about the middle of mass she opened the packet, and found in it the half of the ring she had given Elisor, at which she was astonished and not a little glad. And before the reading of it she commanded her almoner that he should straightway bring before her the hermit-like man who had given her the supplication. So the almoner made search for him on all sides, but could have no tidings of him, save that a certain one affirmed that he had seen him mount his horse, but knew not the road he took. And while that her almoner was gone the Queen read the supplication, the which was indeed a letter written as well as might be. And were it not that I desired you should understand it, I would not have translated it, since, ladies, you must know that the Castilian far better sets forth this passion of love than any other. And this was the manner of it :

> " Time by its power and over-ruling might
> Hath made me love to understand aright.
> Time hath been given me so that by my woe
> She who believed not words might surely know
> The truth of them. My love, the cause of it
> Time hath disclosed ; 'twas beauty and not wit.
> Below this beauty is much cruelty,
> But Time, I once had for mine enemy,
> Hath shown your beauty to be profitless,
> Your cruelty the way to holiness.
> For when you drove me from you, and no more
> I saw the face I did so much adore,
> I saw what was below ; then all my grief
> In exile was converted to relief.
> And there had stayed without a tear or sigh,
> Save that to give my most supreme goodbye

I came to-day.　For Time hath shown how bare
And poor a thing is love; and all my care
Is for the years I lost.　But then above
Time raised mine eyes unto the perfect love,
And made lay by the other : unto this
Is all my worship ; and my service is
Done unto God, not you.　You gave me death
For loving you, but it turned to my breath,
My life, my joy.—I fully hold you quit
Of love for me, I have no need of it,
Not yet of you, but only my dear Lord,
Who changeth not and hath a sure reward.
So I take leave of cruelty and pain,
And say my last to hatred and disdain.
Likewise unto that awful flaming fire
That dwells in you, and stirreth up desire,
As well as beauty.　So to you, 'Goodbye,'
And be assured that never more shall I
Behold your face, nor shall you look on me
Ever again : this hold for certainty."

This letter was not read without much weeping and lamentation, accompanied by a regret passing all belief.　For the losing of a servant, filled with so perfect a love, deserved to be esteemed so great, that no treasure, no, not her very kingdom, could deprive her of her right to be called the poorest and the most wretched woman in the world, since she had lost what all the blessings of the world were not able to recover.　And having heard mass to the end and returned to her chamber, she grieved exceedingly even as her cruelty deserved.　And no mountain, rock, or forest was there, that she did not search for this hermit ; but He who had borne him from her hands had a care he should not fall into them again, and took him to Paradise, before that she could gain tidings of him in this world.

"Learning by this example the lover can hardly say what is for his good and what for his evil.　Still less, ladies, ought you to be thus hard of belief as to demand a proof so difficult that getting your proof you lose your lover."　"Of a truth, Dagoucin," said Geburon, "I had all my life esteemed the lady of your tale the most virtuous in the world, but from henceforth I shall hold her the most cruel."　"Nevertheless," said Parlamente, "it seems to me that she did him no wrong in wishing for seven years to try if he loved her ; for men are so accustomed to lie in like cases that before one trusts them (if trust them one can) one cannot make too long a trial of it."

"The ladies," said Hircan, "are by far wiser than afore, for they are as well assured of a lover in seven days as the others were in seven years." "Yet in this company," said Longarine, "there are they who have been proved to the extremity for more than seven years, and have not yet gained their desire." "You say truth," said Simontault, "but they should be put among the ladies of old time, for in the new age they would not be received." "Yet," said Oisille, "was not the gentleman well treated by the Queen, since by her means he gave his heart altogether to God?" "In a fortunate hour," said Saffredent, "he found God upon the way, for in the grief he was in I marvel he gave himself not to the devil." Ennasuitte asked him: "And when you are evilly entreated of your lady, is it to such a master that you render yourself?" "Thousands and thousands of times have I given myself to him," answered Saffredent; "but the devil, seeing all the torments of hell cannot make me fare worse than does my lady, disdains to take me, knowing himself to be more easily borne than a woman well-beloved and who loves not in return." "If I were like you," said Parlamente to Saffredent, "with such opinions as yours, I would be the servant of no woman." "So great," he replied, "is my love and my foolishness that where I cannot rule I am content to serve, for the ladies' ill-will cannot overcome the love I have for them." "But, prithee, tell me, on your conscience, do you praise the Queen for this her great severity?" "Ay," said Oisille, "for I believe that she neither wished to love nor be beloved." "If this was her intent," said Simontault, "wherefore did she give him any hope after the seven years were overpast?" "I am of your opinion," said Longarine, "for let them who wish not to love give no occasion to the continuance of love." "Perchance," said Nomerfide, "she loved some other who was not to be compared with this honest gentleman, and so for a worse left the better." "Oddsfish!" said Simontault, "I think she held him for future use, to take him when she left her present lover." Oisille, seeing that, under cover of blaming in the Queen of Castille that which in truth is praiseworthy in none, the men let themselves out to speak ill of women, and that the most wise and virtuous fared as badly with them as the mere strumpets, could not endure it any longer, and said: "I am persuaded the more this talk continues the worse shall we come off at the hands of those who like not harsh treatment; wherefore, prithee, Dagoucin, give your vote to some-one." "I give it," said he, "to Longarine, being assured that her tale will be no sad one, and that she will speak the truth, be it against man or woman." "Since you esteem me so truthful," said she, "I will make so bold as to tell you a case that befell a very great prince, who surpasses all others in valourousness. And take heed that lying and cozenage are only to be used in matters of great necessity, seeing that such are abominable and beastly vices, notably in princes and great lords, on whose face truth has a more becoming seat than in any other place. But in this round world there is no prince so great, though he have all the honours and wealth that he can desire, who is not subject to the empire and tyranny of Love. And the more noble and mighty the heart of the prince, the more does Love seem to strive to bring him under his hand. For this god of renown makes no account of common things, and to His Majesty the only delight is a continual working of wonders; as to make weak the strong, to strengthen the weak, to give knowledge unto the simple, to take it away from the learned, to show favour to the passions and to bring reason down to the ground. And as princes are not exempt from love, but are compelled by it to desire to serve, it is permitted them to use lying, cozenage, and deceit, which, according to the teaching of Master Jehan de Mehun, are the means whereby we may overcome our enemies. And since in this estate of love, all these, worthy of blame in others, deserve praise in a prince, I will tell you of the inventions of a young prince, by the which he deceived those who are accustomed to deceive all the world."

NOVEL XXV.

How a young Prince secretly had pleasaunce of the wife of a sergeant-at-law.

There lived in the town of Paris a sergeant-at-law, who stood in greater esteem than any other of like estate, and being sought out by all men, on account of the aptness of his parts, he became the richest of all the brethren of the coif. But having had no children of his first wife, he was minded to see what he could do with a second, and though his body was

decayed, his heart and hopes were as lively as ever. Wherefore he made choice of the prettiest maid in the town, with a
most excellent feature and colouring, and a yet more excellent
taille. Her he loved and entreated as kindly as he was able,
but nevertheless had no more children of her than of his first
wife, at the which she before long grieved greatly. Wherefore
her youth, that would not suffer her to be weary, made her seek
pastime otherwise than at home, and she went to dances and
feasts, but so openly and honourably that her husband could
not take it in bad part, for she was always in the company of
those in whom he had trust.

One day, when she was at a marriage-feast, a very great
Prince was there also, and he, in telling me the story, forbade
me to make mention of his name, but I will tell you this,
that so brave and comely an one there never was in the
realm before, and I think never will be again. So this
Prince, seeing the dame that she was young and pretty, was
overcome with love, and spoke to her in such words and so
graciously that she deemed the discourse to have been well
begun. And she concealed not from him that she had had for
a long time in her heart the love for which he prayed, and
entreated him not to give himself the trouble of persuading her
to what Love at first sight had made her consent. And the
young Prince, having freely received a love well worth a long
service, gave thanks to the god who was favourable to him.
And from that hour he forwarded matters so well, that they
agreed together as to the means of seeing one another, themselves unseen. At the time and place appointed the young
Prince failed not to present himself, and, to preserve the lady's
honour, he went to her in disguise. But not wishing to be
known by the Roaring Boys who coursed the town at night,
he took with him some trusty companions, and at the beginning
of the street where the lady lived he left them, saying: "If
you hear no noise within a quarter of an hour, get you gone to
your houses, and return again to fetch me about three or four
o'clock. This they did, and hearing nothing, returned home.
The young Prince went straight to the lawyer's house, and
found the door open, as had been promised him. But while
he was going up the stair he met the husband with a candle in
his hand, of whom he was seen before he was ware of him.

But love, which in straits of its own bringing about, finds wit and courage also, made the Prince go up to master lawyer and say: "Master sergeant, you are advised of the trust that I and my whole house have always put in you, and that I hold you for one of my best and most loyal servants. It has, therefore, come to my mind to visit you here privily, as much to commend to you my occasions as to pray you to give me to drink, of which I am in great need. And, prithee, tell no one of the matter of my coming, since from here I must go to a quarter where I am not willing to be known." The good sergeant was mighty glad that the Prince did him so great honour as to come thus secretly to his house, and led him to a room whither he bade his wife set forth the best fruits and confections she had, which she did with hearty goodwill, and after the best sort she was able. And notwithstanding that her gear of a kerchief and shawl made her look prettier than she was wont, the young Prince appeared not at all to gaze at her or recognise her, but continued to talk with her husband on his occasions, which for a long while had been in this lawyer's hands. And as the lady served the Prince on her knees, while the sergeant was gone to a side table for drink, she whispered him when he left the room to enter a closet on the right hand, whither she would speedily come and see him. When that he had drunken, the Prince thanked the lawyer, who would have gone with him, but he assured him that in the place whither he was going he had no need for company. And turning to the wife, he said to her: "I would by no means take from you your good husband, who is one of my most ancient servants. So happy are you in the having of him that you have good cause to praise God, and to heartily obey this your husband, and if you do not this you are worthy of all blame." With this virtuous talk the Prince left them, and shutting the door after him so that he might not be followed to the stair, entered into the closet. And when her husband was asleep, my lady came there also, and led him into a small room very bravely decked out, though, to speak truth, there were no pictures in it as fine as he and she, in such gear as it pleased them to put on. And there I doubt not she kept in full all her promises.

From thence he departed at the hour he had advised his

companions, whom he found in waiting at the appointed place.
And since this intercourse lasted a long time, the young Prince
chose a shorter way to go thither, the which passed through a
religious house. And such good interest did he make with the
prior that towards midnight the porter failed not to open the
gate, and in like manner did he at his return. And since the
house of the lawyer was hard-by he took no one with him.
And though he led the life I tell you, yet was this Prince in
the love and fear of God; and though as he went he would
make no stay, yet on his return he never failed to tarry a long
while in prayer in the church; so that the monks, who coming
in and going out still saw him on his knees, had good reason
to think him one of the holiest men in the world.

Now it chanced that this Prince had a sister, who often
went to this monastery, and, loving her brother above the rest
of mankind, was accustomed to commend him to the prayers of
all she knew to be good men. And one day, as she was commending him affectionately to the prior of the monastery, he
said to her: "Alas! who is this you commend to me? You
speak to me of the one man whose prayers I most desire, for if
he is not good and holy I can have no hope of being accounted
for such. For what saith the Scripture: 'Blessed is he who
can do evil, and doeth it not.'" His sister, who was desirous
to know what proof the holy father had of her brother's goodness, asked him so many questions that he told her the secret
after a very solemn fashion. "Is it not a thing worthy of
admiration," said he, "to behold a young Prince and a handsome leave his pleasures and his rest to come and hear our
matins? And he comes not as a Prince, seeking the praise of
men, but like a simple monk he comes all alone and hides himself in one of the side-chapels. In truth, this piety of his so
puts to shame me and my monks that we are not worthy to
be compared with him or to be called 'religious.'" Hearing this,
his sister knew not what to believe, for though her brother were
a worldly man he had great faith and love of God, but as to his
making observances of this sort she had never suspected it of
him. Wherefore she told him the good opinion the monks had
of him, at which he could not restrain himself from laughing in
such wise that she, who knew him as well as her own heart, was
persuaded something was hidden under his devotion, and did

not desist till he had told her the truth. And she has made me put it here in writing, to the end that you, ladies, may understand that neither the keenness of a lawyer nor the craft of monks (the men most accustomed to cozen others) can in a case of necessity hinder them from being deceived by them, whose only experience is that they are deep in love.

"And since Love thus deceives the deceivers, we poor simple folk ought to stand in awe of it. Though," said Geburon, "I have a strong suspicion as to who this young Prince is, I needs must declare that in this matter he was praiseworthy; for one sees few great lords that have a care for the honour of women, or of a public scandal, if only they have their pleasure of them—nay, oftentimes they are well pleased to be thought worse than they are." "Of a truth," said Oisille, "I wish all our young nobles would take this for an ensample, since the scandal is often worse than the sin." "Think you," said Nomerfide, "that the prayers he offered in the monastery were made in good earnest?" "One must not judge," answered Parlamente, "for perchance, as he returned, his repentance was so great that his sin was forgiven him." "It is mighty difficult," said Hircan, "to repent of so pleasant a matter. For my part, many a time have I made confession, but seldom repented." "It would be better," said Oisille, "not to confess at all if there be no repentance." "Nay," answered Hircan, "the sin displeases me, and I am sorry that I have offended against God, but the pleasure always delights me." "You and your fellows," said Parlamente, "would fain have nor God nor law save your own desires." "I confess," replied Hircan, "that I would that God was as pleased with my pleasures as I am, for in that case I would often give to Him matter of contentment." "Yet we cannot make us a new God," said Geburon, "and so must obey the one we have. But let us leave all these matters to the theologians, and let Longarine give her vote to someone." "I give it," said she, "to Saffredent. And, prithee, tell us the best tale you can, and be not so steadfastly purposed to speak evil of women, as not, when there is any good, to tell the truth." "Verily," said Saffredent, "I agree, since I have in my hand the history of a gay woman and likewise of a grave, so take which is most to your pleasure. And understand that, as in the wicked, love works wickedness,

so in a virtuous heart it brings to pass notable good deeds;
for in itself love is a good thing, but the evil that is in the lover
often gives it the surname of loose, light, cruel, or shameful.
And by the history that I will presently relate you, you shall
see that love changeth not the heart, but shows of what sort it
is; light in the light, and prudent in the prudent."

NOVEL XXVI.

The love of an honourable and chaste woman for a young lord, and the manner of her death.

There was in the time of King Lewis the Twelfth a young
lord named d'Avannes, son of my lord Albret, who was brother
to John, King of Navarre, with whom d'Avannes lived for the
most part.   And he at the age of fifteen years was so comely
and graceful that he seemed made for nothing but love and
admiration, which indeed were given by all who saw him, and
notably by a lady living in the town of Pampeluna, in Navarre.
And she being married to a man of great riches lived with
him after such a virtuous fashion that, though she was but
twenty-three years of age, her husband being hard on his
fiftieth year, the manner of her dress was more that of a
widow than a married woman.   And no man ever saw her go
to marriage or feast but that her husband went with her, for
she put his goodness at so high a price, that she preferred it
to the beauty of all other men.   And he on his side, finding
his wife to be thus prudent, was so assured of her that he put
into her hands all the charges of his house.   So it fell out that
on a day the rich man and his wife were bidden to a wedding
among their kinsfolk, and thither also to do honour to the
marriage came my lord d'Avannes, who loved dancing as
was natural in one who therein excelled all the gallants of
his time.   And after dinner, when the dances were beginning,
the rich man prayed d'Avannes to dance, who asked him whom
he would that he should lead out.   He replied to him: " My
lord, if there were a prettier woman, and one more at my command than this wife of mine, I would have you take her, but
since it is not so be pleased to dance with my wife."   This the
young prince did, being still so young that he took more
pleasure in the figures of the dance than in the ladies' beauty.

But his partner, on the contrary, thought more of the grace and comeliness of d'Avannes than the dance, but yet so prudent was she she made no appearance of so doing.   And when supper-time was come, my lord d'Avannes bade farewell to the company and went home to his castle, whither he had for fellow the rich man, riding upon his mule.   And as they fared upon the way the rich man said to him : " My lord, you have this day done such honour to my kinsfolk and myself that it would be great ingratitude in me if I did not put myself altogether at your service.   I know, my lord, that such as you, who have severe and miserly fathers, often need more money than do we plain folk, who by reason of our small household and good economy think of nothing but heaping up riches.   And God, having given me a wife according to my desire, has not willed to make my paradise altogether in this world, since He has not granted to me the joy that a father has in his children.   I know, my lord, that it would not become me to adopt you as a son, but if it were your pleasure to consider me as your servant and declare to me your small occasions, up to the sum of a hundred thousand crowns of my substance, I will not fail to succour you in your necessities."   At this offer d'Avannes was mightily pleased, for his father was all that the other had painted him, and so thanked him, naming him his father by adoption.

From this time the rich man so loved my lord d'Avannes that morning, noon, and night he ceased not to inquire if he needed anything, and concealed not from his wife his devotion to the service of the young lord, for which she did but love him all the more, and henceforth d'Avannes had all things that he desired.   Often did he go and see the rich man, to eat and drink with him, and when he found him not his wife gave him all he asked, and moreover spoke to him so prudently, admonishing him to be wise and virtuous, that he feared and loved her above all other women.   She, having the fear of God always before her eyes, held herself content with sight and speech, wherefrom honourable and virtuous love draws its delight, and in such sort did she that she gave him no cause to judge her love for him other than a sisterly and Christian one.   And while she kept her love fast within her breast, d'Avannes, who by the rich man's aid went always magnificently, came to his seventeenth year, and began to seek out the ladies more than his custom had been. And though he would fain have loved this prudent dame, yet the fear he had lest he might lose her friendship, if he discoursed love-talk with her, made him keep silence and seek his pastime in other quarters.

So he addressed himself to a gentlewoman near Pampeluna, who had a house in the town, and was married to a young man whose sole delight was in horses, hounds, and hawks. And d'Avannes began for love of her to give a thousand entertainments as tournaments, races, masks, banquets, and the rest, at all of which he would have this young lady; but since her husband was a man of fantastic complexion, and her father and mother, knowing her to be both beautiful and gay, were jealous of her honour, they all kept her so straitly that my lord d'Avannes could get no more of her than a word snatched amid the dances. And this, although he knew from the little talk they had had together, that nothing was wanting to the plucking the fruit of their love but a fit time and place. Wherefore he went to his good father the rich man and told him that he had a great desire to go on a pilgrimage to Our Ladye of Montserrat, and prayed him to keep in his house all his retinue, since he was fain to go alone; and all this was granted him. But the wife, who had within her breast love, that great soothsayer, forthwith suspected the truth of the journey, and could not refrain from saying to d'Avannes: "Sir, sir, the Ladye you adore dwells within the walls of this town, so I beseech you above all have a care for your health." He who feared and loved her, blushed so red at this that, without speaking a word, he confessed the truth, and so set forth.

And when he had bought a pair of fine Spanish horses, he dressed himself after the fashion of a groom, and so disguised his face that none would have known him. The gentleman, husband to his gay lady, seeing the two horses and d'Avannes leading them, forthwith would buy them, and after that he had bought them, looking at the groom who led them so well, asked him if he desired to enter his household. My lord d'Avannes told him ay, and that he was but a poor groom who had no craft save the care of horses, but that he could do so well in this that his master would be mightily pleased with him.

Whereat the gentleman was very glad, and gave him authority
over all his horses; and when they were come to the house, he
told his wife he was going to his castle in the country, and that
he commended to her care the horses and the groom.   The
lady, as much because she had no better pastime as to do her
husband a pleasure, went to see the horses, and looked upon
the new groom, who appeared to her somewhat well-favoured,
but she knew him not.   He, perceiving that he was not known,
did her reverence in the Spanish fashion, and in kissing her
hand squeezed it so hard that she knew him; for many a time in
dancing had he played her this trick, and from that moment she
thought of nothing save how she might best be able to speak
with him apart.' And this she accomplished that same evening,
for being bidden with her husband to an entertainment she
feigned to be sick and so unable to go with him.   He, not
wishing to fail his acquaintance, said to her: "Since you will
not come, sweetheart, I pray you have a care to my hounds and
horses, so that they want nothing."   This charge his wife
found mighty pleasant, but, making no sign, she replied that
since he would not employ her in greater matters, she would
let him know by these smaller ones how she desired to do him
pleasure.   Hardly was her husband out of doors before she
went down to the stable, where she found something amiss, and
to take order with it she sent so many of the men one way and
the other, that she remained at last alone with the head groom,
and fearing lest someone should come upon them, said to him :
"Begone to the garden and wait for me there in the summer-
house at the bottom of the alley."   So quick was he to do her
bidding that he had not leisure so much as to thank her.   And
when she had taken such order with the stables she went to the
kennels, where she was so diligent to see that the hounds were
well entreated that she appeared from mistress to have become
maid; and afterwards, having returned to her room, found herself so weary that she lay down on the bed, saying she desired
to rest.   So all her women left her, except one whom she
trusted, to whom she said : "Go to the garden and make come
to me him you shall find at the bottom of the alley."   The
maid went and found there the groom, and led him forthwith
to her mistress, who caused the wench to go outside and keep
watch for her husband's coming.   My lord d'Avannes, seeing

himself alone with his mistress, doffed his groom's gear, took off his false nose and false beard, and not as a fearful groom but as the brave lord he was, without with your leave or by your leave, boldly got to bed with her, and was received as the prettiest man of his time should be received by the fairest and gayest lady in the land.   There he stayed until the master returned, at whose coming, taking again his mask, he left the place he had won by his craftiness and guile.   The gentleman, on entering his courtyard, perceived how diligent his wife had been to obey him, for which he heartily thanked her. "I do nothing but my duty, sweetheart," replied she.   "True it is that if one did not keep watch over the varlets there would not be a hound that had not the mange, or a horse well fed and groomed; but now that I know their idleness and your wishes, you shall be better served than heretofore."   The gentleman, who was fully persuaded he had chosen the best groom in the world, asked how he appeared to her.   "I confess," answered she, "he does his duty as well as any you could find, but he needs our eyes upon him, since he is the sleepiest varlet I have ever seen."

So for some while the husband and wife lived in better agreement than they had before, he losing all his former jealousy, since in like manner as afore she had loved entertainments, dances, and assemblies, so now was she attentive to her household, contenting herself with wearing only a dressing-gown over her shift in place of taking four hours to deck herself out, as had been her custom.   And for this she received praise from her husband and all men, who knew not that the stronger desire had cast out the weaker.   Thus, under the cloak of hypocrisy and virtue, lived this young gentlewoman so voluptuously that reason, conscience, order, or measure found no more any place in her.   But this the youth and delicate complexion of my lord d'Avannes could not bear any longer, insomuch that he grew so pale and thin that without a mask he were well disguised.   Yet the mad love he bore this woman so blinded his senses that he strove to accomplish works too great for Hercules, until at last constrained by sickness, and advised to that intent by the lady, who liked him better sound than sick, he asked leave to return to his kin, which his master gave him with great regret, making him promise that when he was made whole he should come back to his service. And so d'Avannes went his way, and on foot, for he had but to journey the length of a street, and came to the house of the rich man, his father by adoption. And there he found the wife alone, whose virtuous love for him was not at all lessened by the reason of his journey. But when she saw him, that he was so thin and pale, she must needs say to him : " I know not, my lord, how it fares with your conscience, but your body hath not taken much benefit from this pilgrimage; and I strongly suspect that your travail by night hath done you more hurt than your travail by day, for if you had gone to Jerusalem on foot you would have come back more sunburnt, but not so thin and weak. Take good account of this one, and worship no more at such shrines, which, in place of raising the dead to life, bring the living almost to death. I could say more to you ; but if your body has sinned it has been so shrewdly punished that I do not desire to add any new trouble." When d'Avannes heard this he was not less sorry than ashamed, and said to her: " Mistress, I have aforetime heard that repentance follows on sin, and I have well proved it to my sorrow. And I pray you to pardon my youth, that could not be punished save by making trial of the evil it would not before believe."

The dame, changing the matter of the discourse, made him lie down on a fair bed, where he stayed fifteen days, only living on restorative medicaments ; and so well did the husband and wife keep him company that he always had the one or the other with him. And though he had done foolishly, even as you have heard, against the will and counsel of this prudent woman, yet this did not at all lessen the honourable love she bore him, for it was ever her hope that, after passing his youth in these evil ways he would cleanse them and love virtuously, and so should be all her own. And for the fifteen days he was in the house she talked with him to such purpose that he began to abhor the sin he had committed, and looking at this woman, whose beauty surpassed the strumpet's, and knowing more and more the graces and the virtues that were in her, he could contain himself no longer, but one day, as it grew dark, laying aside all fear, thus began : " Mistress, I know no better means of becoming as virtuous as you desire me to be than the being altogether in love with virtue : prithee tell me whether you will give me all the help and favour that lieth in you to this end?" The lady, very glad to hear him speak after this sort, answered him: "I promise you, sir, that if your love for virtue is as great as it ought to be in such a lord, I will help you in your endeavour to attain it unto the utmost of the power that God has given me." "Now, mistress," said d'Avannes, "be mindful of your promise, and understand that God, unknown of men save by faith, hath deigned to take our sinful fleshly nature upon Him, to the end that, in drawing our flesh to the love of His manhood, He might also draw our spirits to the love of His Godhead, and so has willed to use visible means, to make us love by faith the things that are invisible. In like manner, this virtue that I desire to love all my life is an invisible thing and only known by its effects, wherefore it is needful that it should take some bodily form that it may be known among men. And this it has done, clothing itself in your flesh as the most perfect it could find, wherefore I believe and confess that you are not alone virtuous but very virtue, which I, seeing it veiled beneath the most perfect body that ever was, desire to serve and honour all the days of my life, putting behind me all other vain and vicious love." The lady, who was both glad and astonished to hear him talk after this fashion, concealed her delight, and said to him: "My lord, I dare not reply to your theology, but since I am one that is slower to believe good than fear evil I beseech you cease this manner of talk; for if I believed it I should be but lightly esteemed of you. I am well assured that I am a woman, like any other, and imperfect, so that virtue would do a more wondrous thing in transforming me into it than in putting my form upon it, save only that it wished to be unknown in this world, for, under such covering as mine, it would stand in small peril of being revealed. But for all my manifold imperfections I none the less bear you as great an affection as any woman can, and love God and her honour, but this love shall not be manifested to you until your heart receive that patience required of a virtuous lover. And in that hour I shall know well what words to speak, but meanwhile think that you do not so much love your own good, yourself, and your honour, as do I." My lord d'Avannes, fearful, with tears in his eyes, strongly entreated her that, for surety to her words, she would kiss him, but this she refused, saying that for him she would not break the customs of the country. And while they were disputing as to this the husband came in, to whom said d'Avannes: "My father, so great has been the goodness of you and your wife towards me, that I beseech you always account me for your son." To this the good man willingly agreed. "And for a surety of it," said d'Avannes, "grant me to kiss you." This he did. Afterwards he said: "If I were not in fear lest I should transgress the custom of the country, I would ask the same of your wife my mother." At this the husband commanded his wife to kiss him, which she did without any appearance of liking nor yet of misliking. And so the fire which words had kindled in the heart of this poor lord was increased much the more by the kiss as earnestly desired as, on her part, cruelly refused.

Then my lord d'Avannes went to the castle to see the King his brother, to whom he told very brave stories of his journey to Montserrat. And there he heard that the King was minded to go to Oly and Taffares, at which, by reason of the length of the journey, he fell into great sadness, and was resolved to try, before he set out with him, whether his lady bore him no better will than she appeared to do. To this intent he fixed his lodging in a house in the street where she lived, which house was an old wooden one, and in bad repair. And towards midnight he set it afire, the report of which was so noised abroad throughout the town that it came to the rich man, his father by adoption. And he asking from his window where was the fire, was told that it was the house of my lord d'Avannes, whereupon he went forthwith with all his household thither and found the young lord in the street clad only in his shirt. Filled with pity for him he took him in his arms, and, folding him in his robe, led my lord to his house as quickly as he was able, and said to his wife, who was in bed: "Here, sweetheart, is a prisoner for you, treat him as myself." No sooner was he gone than d'Avannes, who would have been mightily pleased to be treated as her husband, leapt lightly into the bed, hoping that the opportunity and the place would make this prudent dame change the manner of her discourse; but he found to the contrary, for as he got in at one side of the bed she got out at the other. And putting on her a loose robe, she sat at the bedside, and said to him: "Was it your thought, my lord,

o

that opportunity could change a chaste heart? Trust me
that as gold is refined in the furnace, so a chaste heart in the
midst of temptation grows more steadfast and virtuous, and the
more it is assailed by the heats of passion the more it is chilled.
Wherefore be assured that, if my mind had been other towards
you than I declared it to be, I should by no means have failed
to find ways and means, of which, since I willed not to use
them, I made no account. But I pray you, if you would have
my affection continue towards you, put away not only the wish
but the thought of ever finding me other than I am." In the
midst of this parley her women came to her, whom she bade
bring all kinds of sweetmeats, but for the time he knew not
hunger nor thirst, in such despair was he at having failed in his
undertaking, and fearing likewise that this manifestation of his
desire towards her might take away all familiarity between
them.

The husband, having taken order with the fire, returned
and entreated d'Avannes to stay for that night in his house.
And in such sort was that night passed of him, that his eyes
were more employed in weeping than in sleeping, and very
early in the morning he gave them farewell while they were in
bed, and in kissing of the lady plainly saw that she took more
pity for the sinner than anger for the sin, and thus was another
coal added to the fire of his love. After dinner he set out with
the King for Taffares, but before departing he went yet another
time to say good-bye to his father and the lady, who, after the
command of her husband, made no more difficulty in kissing
him as her son. But be assured that the more her virtue
hindered her eyes and face from making manifest the flame
within, so much the more did it increase and become unbearable;
in such wise that, not being able to endure the war in her
heart between honour and love, the which she had always
determined never to reveal, and having lost the consolation of
seeing and speaking with him for whom she lived, she fell into
a continuous fever. And the cause of this was a melancholic
humour operating after such a fashion that the extremities of
her body became altogether cold, whilst her inwards were in a
perpetual heat. The physicians (who have not in their hands
the health of men) because of an obstruction which rendered
the extremities cold, began to be grievously afear'd for her, and

spoke to her husband, counselling him to advertise his wife that she was in the hands of God, all as if they that were sound were not.   The husband, loving his wife with a perfect love, was so sad at their words, that for consolation he wrote to d'Avannes, entreating him to come and see him, for he hoped the sick woman would be bettered by the sight of him.   And as soon as he had received the letter, d'Avannes made no long tarrying, but came post haste to the house of his father by adoption, and on entering in thereto found the serving-men and serving-women sorrowing greatly, as was meet for such a mistress.   At this my lord was so astonished that he stayed at the door, being as one who sees a vision, until he saw his father, who, as he embraced him, wept so sore that he was not able to speak so much as a word.   And he led d'Avannes to the room where was the poor sick woman, and she, looking upon him with her languishing eyes, took him by the hand and drew him to her with all her feeble might. And as she kissed him and took him in her arms, she made marvellous lamentation, and said to him: " O, dear my lord, the time has come to put an end to all concealment, and for me to confess what I have taken such toil to hide from you.   And it is this : if your love for me has been great, believe me mine is no less : but my grief has been more grievous than yours, since I have hidden my love against my heart and my desire. For understand that God and my honour would never have me declare it to you, since I feared to increase in you what I was fain to diminish ; but be assured that the *no* I have so often said to you was so dolorous a word to me that it has brought about my death.   And with this I hold myself content, that God hath given me the grace to die before the violency of my love hath done shame to my conscience and good repute, for smaller fires have brought higher houses to the dust.   And again I am content for that before I die I am able to declare to you my love that it is equal to your own, save that the honour of men and the honour of women are not like to one another.   And I entreat you, my lord, henceforth to fear not to address yourself to the most noble and the most virtuous ladies, for in such hearts dwell the strongest passions and   the most wisely governed ; and the grace, comeliness, and virtue that are in you will not let your love be in labour for nothing.   I crave no prayers of yours to God for me, since I know the gates of paradise are not shut to true lovers, and since love is a fire that punishes lovers so well in this life that they are set free from the sharp torment of purgatory.   Farewell, my lord; I commend into your hands my husband, and pray you tell him the truth concerning me, that he may know in what manner I have loved my God and him, and come no more before mine eyes, since henceforth I would fain think of nothing but of gaining those promises given me by God or ever the world was made." Thus speaking, she kissed him, and clung to him as best she could with those feeble arms; and the lord, whose heart was as dead with pity as hers with grief, without power to say a single word, went from her sight to a bed that was in the room, and there several times swooned away.

And after this the lady called her husband, and when they had parleyed one with the other in seemly sort she commended d'Avannes to his care, assuring him that after himself he was the most beloved of her; and, kissing her husband, she bade him farewell.   Then was borne to her the Holy Sacrament of the Altar, after that she had taken extreme unction, both of which she received with the joy of one sure of salvation.   And seeing that her eyes waxed dim, and her strength abated, she said with a loud voice : " *In manus tuas, Domine, commendo spiritum meum.*"   At this cry my lord d'Avannes raised himself from the bed, and, pitifully looking upon her, saw her give back with a gentle sigh her glorious soul to Him from whom it had come.   And when he saw her to have passed, he ran to the dead body, which when living he had approached with fear, and fell to kissing and throwing his arms round it in such wise that hardly could he be drawn away, whereat the husband marvelled greatly, for he had never thought him to have loved her in this manner; and saying to him : " My lord, it is too much," he led him away.   Then after for a long time lamenting her together, d'Avannes told him all the passages of their friendship, and that till she was nigh a-mort she had never shown him any sign save of great severity.   At this the husband grieved all the more for her he had lost, and throughout his whole life did service to my lord d'Avannes.   But he, from this time, being now only eighteen years old, went to Court, where he lived a long while without wishing to see or speak with any woman, for the grief he had for his mistress; and for more than ten years he wore black.

"Behold, ladies, how different is a good woman from a wanton, and how variously love manifests itself in them; for the one died a glorious death, and the other lived all too long known of men as a shameless and wicked strumpet. And as 'precious in the sight of God is the death of his saints,' in like manner is the death of a sinner evil." "Of a truth, Saffredent," said Oisille, "you have told us as fine a tale as could be found, and whosoever knows the people as I do will find it still better, for I have never seen a more honest gentleman, nor one of a better grace, than the aforesaid lord d'Avannes." "Believe me," said Saffredent, "this was a good woman, who, to show herself more virtuous than she was at heart, and to conceal the love reason and nature willed her to have for so brave a gentleman, allowed herself to die rather than take the pleasure she secretly desired." "If she had had such a desire," said Parlament, "she would have found ways and means to show it, but so great was her virtuousness her desire never went beyond reason." "You can paint her," said Hircan, "according to your pleasure, but I know that a worse devil always sends the other out, and that a gentlewoman's pride always inclines her rather to pleasure than to the love and fear of God. And their clothes are so long and so interwoven with deceit that one never knows what is thereunder; for if vice brought them dishonour as little as it does us, you would find that Nature is as complete in them as in us; but since they dare not have the pleasure they desire, they have changed one vice into another and a worse, which they deem more honourable. This is a vain-boasting cruelty, whereby they think to get them an everlasting name, and glorying in their resistance to vice, the law of nature (if indeed anything natural is also vicious), they make themselves like to inhuman and pitiless wild beasts, or rather to devils, in whose pride and crafty malice they have a share." "'Tis pity," answered Nomerfide, "you have a virtuous woman to wife, since not only do you make no account of virtue, but are fain to show that it is vice." "I am well content," said Hircan, "that my wife is not a scandalous woman, nor do I myself wish to be a scandalous husband; but as to chastity of heart, we are children of Adam and Eve, wherefore, when we curiously examine ourselves, we have no need of fig-leaves wherewith to cover our nakedness—nay, rather should we make open confession of our frailty." "I know well," said Parlamente, "that we all stand in need of God's grace, being we are clothed with sin; but yet our temptations are not like to your temptations, for if we sin through pride none takes harm therefrom, nor is there any stain on our hands or our bodies. But your pleasure lies in the dishonouring of women, and your honour is to kill men in battle, these being two things plainly contrary to the law of God." "I confess," said Geburon, "you have ground for your position, yet has God said: 'Whosoever looketh upon a woman to lust after her, hath already committed adultery with her in his heart;' and again, 'Whosoever hateth his neighbour is a murderer.' Do you think, then, that women are more free of these texts than we?" "God who judgeth the heart," said Longarine, "will give sentence on it, but 'tis a great thing that men cannot accuse us of aught, for such is the goodness of God that, if there be none to make accusation against us, He will by no means condemn us; and so well knoweth He the frailty of our hearts, that He will even love us for not putting our evil thoughts into action." "Prithee, now," said Saffredent, "let us leave this disputation, for it savours more of a sermon than a story; and I give my vote to Ennasuitte, and entreat her to make us laugh." "Of a truth," said she, "I have no fear of failing therein, since as I came along I had chosen a very fine relation for this day; but a certain one told me a tale of the two servants of a princess, and so pleasant was it that from mere laughing it made me to forget the sad and pitiful matter I had in hand, the which, therefore, I will put off for the morrow, since now my face would be too joyous for you to relish melancholy."

NOVEL XXVII.

A beastly secretary, and an honest piece of cozenage.

In the town of Amboise there lived a man who served a certain princess as her chamberlain, an honest fellow, and one who willingly entertained the folk who came to his house, and notably such as were servants of the same mistress. And no long while ago there lodged with him for ten days a fellow-servant, a secretary, and so ugly a man was he that he was rather like to a king of cannibals than a Christian. And notwithstanding that his host treated him as a friend and a brother, and after as honourable a sort as was within his power, nevertheless this man behaved himself towards him as one who not only forgets all honour but who has never had it in his heart. For he pursued with a dishonourable and unlawful love the wife of his host, she having nothing in her inciting to lust but rather the opposite, natheless a good woman, and none better in the town where she lived. And she, knowing the evil intent of the man, chose rather by cozenage to manifest his vice than by a peremptory refusal to cover it up, and so feigned to receive his proposals in good part. Wherefore he, thinking the place was won, having no regard to her fifty years, nor her ugliness, nor the good repute she had for an honest woman and one that loved her husband, incessantly pestered her.

One day, when her husband was in the house, and they by themselves in a large room, she told him he had but to find a safe place and he might hold what parley with her he liked. Forthwith he replied that they would climb up to the garret, and she accordingly rose and prayed him go first and she would follow after. He, with as sweet a smile as a jackanapes when he makes feast for his acquaintance, stepped lightly up the ladder; and expecting his desire to be fulfilled, burning with no clear fire, as does the juniper, but rather with that of a black coal in the furnace, listened whether she came after him. But in place of footsteps he heard her voice saying to him: "Master secretary, master secretary, do but wait awhile, and I will learn of my husband whether it is his pleasure that I follow you." Conceive, ladies, how he showed weeping, who laughing was so mighty ugly; but he presently came down again with tears in his eyes, praying her by the love of God not to break up by her words the friendship between him and his fellow. She replied: "I am assured so great love do you bear him that you would not say anything to me that he may not hear. Wherefore I go tell him." And let him entreat or threaten as he would, she did according to her word, and he fled the place covered with shame. And when he heard how he had been confounded, the husband was well content with the honest cozenage his wife had used, and so much did her virtue please him that he made no account of his fellow's vice, holding him enough punished by the shame he had thought to bring upon that house being turned upon his own head.

"Methinks honest men should learn by this tale to take care lest they have about them folk whose heart, conscience, and understanding are alike ignorant of God, honour, and true love.'

"Though your tale be brief," said Oisille, "yet I have heard none more pleasant, and it is to the honour of a good woman."

"Oddsfish," said Simontault, "'tis no great honour in a woman to refuse so beastly a fellow as you make this secretary; but if he had been comely and a brave man she would then have shown some virtue. And since I suspect I know his name, I could tell you a tale of him as pleasant as this, if it were my turn."

"Let not that hinder you," said Ennasuitte, "for I give you my vote." So Simontault began: "They that are wont to live at Court or in fine towns deem themselves so knowing that they think all other men are as nothing compared with them; but the truth is that, in all sorts and conditions of men, there are always to be found crafty and deceitful folk. But because of their pride, who esteem themselves so shrewd, the jest is much the better when they are deceived, as I would fain show by this relation of a case that fell out no long while ago."

NOVEL XXVIII.

A notable pasty, and what was found therein.

It fell out that when King Francis, first of the name, was in the town of Paris, and with him his sister the Queen of Navarre, that she had a secretary named John, who was by no means in the number of those who let a crumb fall to the ground without picking it up. So greedy a fellow was he, that there was nor president, nor counsellor, nor merchant, nor wealthy man that he did not often visit. And about that time there came to the said town of Paris a merchant of Bayonne, named Bernard du Ha, as much for his occasions as for the advice and help therein of the high sheriff, who was a countryman of his. The Queen of Navarre's secretary often went to see this officer, as one who was a good servant to his master and mistress, and going there on a saint's day he found neither the master nor his wife, but very plainly heard Bernard du Ha, who with some kind of a viol was teaching the serving-maids to dance the Gascon fling. And when the secretary saw him he would have him believe that he was committing a great offence, and that if the mistress of the house and her husband were advised of it they would take it in very bad part. And after setting the fear of this well before his eyes, the Gascon at last prayed him not to speak of it. Whereupon the secretary asked him: "What will you give me if I keep silence?" Bernard du Ha, whose fear was by no means as great as his pretence, for he perceived the other was minded to cozen him, promised to give him a pasty of the best Basque ham he had ever tasted. The secretary, well pleased at this, asked that he might have the pasty the following Sunday, after dinner, which was promised him. And trusting to this promise he went to see a lady of Paris, whom above all things he desired to have to wife, and said to her: "Fair mistress, if it be your pleasure I will sup with you on Sunday, and have you no care save to provide good bread and good wine, for I have so deceived a blockhead from Bayonne that the remainder of the feast will be at his charges, and by my deceit you shall eat as fine a Basque ham as ever was in Paris." The lady, believing him, called together two or three of the neighbouring gentlewomen whom she loved, and gave them assurance of tasting a dish altogether new to them.

When the Sunday was come, the secretary, looking for his merchant, at last found him on the Pont-au-Change, and graciously accosting him, said: "Begone a twenty devil way for the toil you have given me to find you." Bernard du Ha replied that many a man had taken more pains than he, who at last had not such a dainty dish for his reward. So saying he showed the pasty, which he carried under his cloak, huge enough to feed an army. So joyous thereat was the secretary that, though his mouth was of a monstrous size, he made it so small that one would not have thought he could have chewed the ham with it. So forthwith taking it, without bringing the merchant with him, he carried it to the lady, who was mighty curious to know whether the provaunt of Gascony equalled that of Paris. And when soup had been brought in and they were eating it, the secretary said to them: "Leave

that mawkish fare, and let us taste this lovely whet for wine."
So saying he opened the great pasty, and thinking to find the
ham found it so hard that he could not set his knife into it, and
after striving to do this several times he was advertised of the
cozenage, and discovered his ham to be a wooden shoe, such as
they wear in Gascony, with a firebrand for knuckle, and all
powdered with iron-rust and sweet-smelling spices. Who then
was chapfallen but master secretary, as much for that he was
deceived of him he thought to deceive, as that he had deceived
her to whom he wished most of all to speak the truth; and,
beside all this, a supper of soup was by no means to his liking.
The ladies, well-nigh as angry as he, would have accused him
of the fact had they not been well assured, by the manner of his
countenance, that he was more wrath than they. So after this
light refection the secretary went away in a great rage, and
seeing that Bernard du Ha had broken his promise, he was
determined to cry quits with him, and betook himself to the
sheriff's house, resolved to say the worst he could of the aforesaid Bernard. But he came not there so soon as the merchant,
who had opened to his countryman the whole matter, and he
mocked the secretary, telling him that he had cozened a
Gascon to his cost, and this was the only consolation he got
from him.

" Such misadventures befall many who, thinking themselves
exceeding crafty, are overmatched in craftiness; wherefore let
us do unto others as we would they should do unto us." " I
do assure you," said Geburon, "that I have often known like
cases have like issues, and seen men esteemed simple country
folk deceive your brave city wit; for there is no greater fool
than he that thinks himself wise, nor any wiser than he who
knows his nothingness." " Certainly," said Parlamente, " he
something knows who knows he nothing knows." " Now,"
said Simontault," " for fear lest time be wanting to us to complete the tale, I give my vote to Nomerfide, for sure am I that
her tricks of rhetoric will keep us no long time." " And I will
give you," said she, " that which you hope for of me. It is
no matter of wonderment to me, ladies, that love gives a prince
means to save himself from peril, for he has been brought up
among such a knowing sort of people that I should be mightily
astonished if he were found wanting in such cases. But it is

in lovers of dull wit that love manifests its power of invention, and to that intent I will relate you a pretty matter done by a priest with love alone to help him; for of all else he was so ignorant that he could scarce read his missal."

NOVEL XXIX.

A parson's ready wit.

In the county of Maine there lived at a village named Carrelles a rich farmer, who in his old age had taken to wife a pretty wench, and had of her no children. And she, to console herself, was exceeding friendly with many gentlemen, and when they failed her she returned to her last resource, I would say the church, and took for companion in her sin him who was able to absolve her of it—that is, her spiritual shepherd, who often came to visit his sheep. Her husband, old and stupid, had no suspicion of her, but since he was a harsh man and a sturdy, his wife played her mystery as privily as might be, fearing lest, if he was advertised of it, he would kill her. And on one day, when he was gone out, his wife, thinking he would not soon return, sent for master parson to come and confess her. And while they played together her husband came, and so suddenly that the parson had no time to retreat from the house; but looking whither he might hide himself, he climbed, by the woman's advice, up into the granary, and covered the trap-door with a winnowing fan. Thereupon the husband came into the room, and fearing he might have some suspicion, she made him eat and drink at dinner in such wise that, being afore weary with his toil in the fields, he fell asleep sitting in his chair beside the hearth. The parson, thinking he had spent enough time in the granary, came to the trap-door, and stretching out his neck as much as he was able, perceived the good man to be asleep. But while he was looking at him he leant by mischance so weightily upon the winnowing fan, that both fan and man came down upon the sleeper, who at this awoke. And the parson rising before the other had seen him, said: " Friend, here is your fan, and many thanks for it." Thus saying he fled home. The poor farmer, all astounded, asked his wife : " What is this ?" She replied ! " 'Tis but the fan,

sweetheart, the parson has borrowed, and now returns to you."
And he, grumbling mightily, said: "'Tis a very rude fashion
of returning what one has borrowed, for I thought the house
was about my ears." In this way did the parson save himself
at the expense of the good man, who found no fault at all in
him save the roughness he had used in returning him his
winnowing-fan.

"His master the devil was keeping him, ladies, to the end
that he might have him in his hands and torment him for a longer
while." "Think not," said Geburon, "that simple folk and
men of low estate are less crafty than we; nay, they are the
much more cunning. For prithee, consider thieves, murderers,
sorcerers, utterers of false coin, and all this sort of people, whose
wit is never at rest, they are all poor and apprenticed to some
mere mechanical craft." "It is no matter of surprise to me,"
said Parlamente, "that they excel us in craft, but that love
should torment them amid their manifold labours, and that so
gentle a passion can hold assize in a churlish heart." "Mistress," said Saffredent, "you know the words of Master Jehan
de Mehun:

> " Love doth no less
> Dwell in such folk as have a homespun dress
> Than where are silk and plush for comeliness."

And as to the love in the tale it is not of a sort to make one
carry harness; for since the poorer sort of people have not
our riches or honours, they have in place the natural things
more to their pleasure than we. Their meats are not so dainty,
but their appetite is keener, and they live better on coarse bread
than we on pheasant. Not so brave and fine their beds as
ours, but their sleep is sweeter and their rest more calm. No
ladies have they prinked and painted like the goddesses of our
idolatry, but they enjoy their pleasures of this kind more often
than we without fear of tell-tale tongues, save it be of the
beasts and birds that see them. In what we have, they are
wanting; and where we have not they have abundance."
"Prithee," said Nomerfide, "have done with this peasant and
his wife, and let us finish our day before the bells are ringing
unto evensong. And let Hircan bring it to a close." "Truly,"
said he, "I have as strange and as pitiful a case to tell as you

have ever heard.　And though it is not to my humour to tell
a tale which brings shame to the ladies, since I know that men
are so evil-minded that for the fault of one they blame you all,
yet the matter is so strange an one that it must needs be told.
Perchance, too, the foolish ignorance of one being brought to
light will make the rest more prudent.　And so, nothing fearful, I will tell you my tale."

NOVEL XXX.

A man takes to wife one who is his own sister and daughter.

In the time of King Lewis the Twelfth, and while a lord of
the house of Amboise, nephew to Georges the legate of France,
was legate of Avignon, there lived in the land of Languedoc a
gentlewoman of better than four thousand ducats a-year, whose
name I will conceal for the love I bear her family.　And she,
when the mother of an only son, became a widow very early,
and, as much for the sake of her husband as her son, determined
never to marry again.　And to fly the occasion of so doing, she
would thenceforth only see devout folk, thinking that the
opportunity makes the sin, though the truth is that the sin will
find an opportunity.　So this young widow gave herself entirely
to the service of God, fleeing all worldly assemblies, in such
sort that it was only as matter of duty that she would be present at weddings, or hear the organs playing in church.　And
when her son was come to the age of seven years she chose a
man of holy life for his schoolmaster, so that by him he might
be disciplined in all piety and devotion.　But when her son's
years were fourteen or fifteen, Nature, who keeps a school in
the heart, finding him full-fed and exceeding idle, taught him
lessons somewhat different to his tutor's, so that he began
to look upon and lust after the things he thought fair, and
among the rest a wench who slept in his mother's chamber.
But of this they had no suspicion, for they held him but as a
child, and in that house was heard nothing but godly talk.　The
young gallant began to pester the girl in privity, and she told
her mistress of it, who loved and esteemed her son so much
that she thought the girl told it to make her hate him; but so
strongly did she affirm the truth to the gentlewoman, that at last

she said : "If I find him to be as you say, he shall by no means
lack chastisement ; but if this accusation of yours is no true
one, have a care to yourself." And that she might by experience know the truth of the matter she commanded the wench
to fix him a time and place to go to bed to her—namely, midnight, in the room of her mistress, where she slept all alone in
a bed by the door. The girl obeyed this command, and when
the evening drew nigh the gentlewoman lay down in the servant's
bed, determined, if she spoke the truth, to take such order
with her son that he would never again lie with a woman
without having it in remembrance.

And while she pondered wrathfully over this, her son came
to bed to her, and she, for all that she saw him come, would not
believe that he had in his mind to do any shameful deed, and
so delayed speaking to him till that she had for certain some
sign of his evil intent. For she would not be convinced by
small things that his was a criminal desire, but so great was her
long-suffering, and so frail her nature, that her anger was converted into an abominable delight, and she forgot that she was
his mother. And even as water that has been kept back by
force rushes the more vehemently when it is let go, so was her
boasting in the constraint she put on her body turned unto her
shame, for when she had descended the first step to dishonour
she found herself on a sudden at the bottom of the ladder.
And in that night she was made great with child by him whom
she would have kept from fouling others. No sooner was this
sin accomplished than the tooth of conscience began to gnaw
her with such remorse that her whole life was one repentance,
and so sharp was it at the first that, rising from beside her son,
who always thought he had had the wench, she went into her
closet, and there calling to mind the goodness of her design and
the wickedness of her act, passed all the night in weeping and
lamentation. But in place of humbling herself and considering
the frailty of our carnal nature, which without the help of God
doeth nothing that is not sin, she endeavoured by her own tears
and by her own power to make satisfaction for the past, and
by her orethought to avoid all evils in the future. So she
always made the occasion an excuse for her sin, and made no
account of her own wickedness, for which God's grace was the
sole relief, and thought so to order herself as never to sin any

more after that fashion. And as if there were but one sin that could bring to pass her damnation, she put out all her strength to flee from that alone. But the pride that was rooted in her heart, which the conviction of her sin should have plucked out, increased more and more, so that in avoiding one pitfall she fell into many others. And on the morrow, very early, as soon as it was light, she sent for her son's tutor, and said to him: "My son is near that age when it is no longer fit for him to be at home. I have a kinsman, named Captain Monteson, who is with my lord the grand-master of Chaumont across the mountains, and he will be well content to take him into his company. To which end take him thither this very hour, and so that I may not sorrow the more have a care that he come not to me to say farewell." So saying she gave him the monies necessary for the journey, and the young man set out that very morning, for, after enjoying his sweetheart, he desired nothing else than to go to the wars.

For a long while the gentlewoman continued to be very sad and melancholic, and, were it not for the fear of God, she would many a time have desired the unhappy fruit that was in her womb to perish. She made a pretence of sickness, to the end that she might go in a cloak, and thereby conceal that she had sinned. And when the time drew near for her to be delivered, she pondered within herself that there was none in the world whom she so trusted as her bastard brother, to whom she had given much of her substance, and she told him her ill-hap, but named not her son as the author of it. So she prayed this brother to give her his aid, and a few days before her time he would have her take a change of air, saying that she would get back her health in his house sooner than in any other place. Thither she went, and with a mighty small following, and found there a midwife come as if for her brother's wife, who knew her not, and one night delivered her of a fine maid child, whom the gentleman gave to a nurse under the name of being his own. And when his sister had stayed with him a month, she returned whole to her house, and there lived in stricter sort than before, keeping fasts and austere observances. But her son having come to manhood, there being no longer any war in Italy, sent to his mother entreating her to permit him to come back to his own home. She, fearing to fall again into

the same ditch, was fain not to grant him leave, but at last so
strongly did he press her that she, having no reason to assign
against his coming, gave way. Yet she would by no means
have him appear before her till that he had taken to wife one
he heartily loved, telling him to take no thought for her substance so long as she came of gentle blood. During this time
the bastard brother, seeing the girl that was in his charge
growing up into a perfect beauty, thought fit to put her in
some house a long way off, where she should be unknown, and,
using his mother's counsel, he gave her to Catherine Queen of
Navarre. And the girl, being now twelve or thirteen years
old, was so comely and good withal, that the Queen of Navarre
had a great liking for her, and was very desirous that she
should be honourably married to one of high estate. But, by
reason of her poverty, she had many lovers, but no husband.
It fell out that one day the gentleman who was her unknown
father, having journeyed across the mountains, came to the
house of the Queen of Navarre, where, as soon as he saw his
daughter, he loved her. And since he had leave from his
mother to marry whomsoever he would, he made no inquiries
concerning her, save as to whether she was of gentle blood, and
being told that it was so, he asked her in marriage of the
Queen, who gladly gave him her, since she knew the gentleman
that he was rich and also handsome, and of a noble house.

And when the marriage was consummated, he wrote to
his mother, saying that henceforth she could not deny him
her house, seeing that he would bring with him as pretty
a daughter-in-law for her as one would wish to see. The
gentlewoman, having inquired with whom he had allied himself,
found it was the very daughter of herself and him, and fell
thereby into such grievous despair that she was like forthwith to
have died, since the more she put hindrances in the path of her
sin the further it journeyed onwards. And, knowing not what
else to do, she went to the legate at Avignon, and to him confessed the greatness of her sin, and asked counsel as to the
manner in which she should order herself. The legate, to
satisfy her conscience, sent to several weighty doctors of the
schools, to whom he opened the affair, without naming the
persons. And their counsel was that the gentlewoman should
never say a word of it to her children, for as to them, since

they were in ignorance, they had done no sin, but as to herself all her life should be spent in penance. So the poor woman went back to her house, and soon her son and daughter-in-law arrived there. And so great was their love towards one another that never were there husband and wife who loved one another better, or were more nearly allied; for she was his daughter, his sister, and his wife; and he was her father, her brother, and her husband. And this love of theirs always continued, so that the poor gentlewoman, of her great repentance, could not see them so much as kiss without going apart to weep.

"See, ladies, how it fares with them who, trusting in their own strength and their own virtuousness, think to overcome love and nature, and all the powers God hath implanted in them. But the better way would be, knowing one's frailty, not to play at jousts with such enemies, rather betaking oneself to Him who is true love, and saying with the Psalmist, 'I am afflicted very much: quicken me, O Lord, according unto Thy word.'" "It is not possible," said Oisille, "to hear a stranger case than this. And methinks every man and woman ought to humble themselves in the fear of God, seeing that by one whose mind was to do well, so much ill was brought about." "Be persuaded," said Parlamente, "that the first step taken by a man trusting in himself is likewise the first step from God." "He is wise," said Geburon, "who knows himself for his chiefest enemy, and who holds in suspicion his own will and inclinations." "Howsoever great," said Longarine, "was the appearance of goodness and holiness, there is no appearance of such sort as to make it right in a woman to lie beside a man, near akin though they be, since tow hard-by to fire is in no safe keeping." "Without any manner of doubt," said Ennasuitte, "she was a vain-boasting fool, who by the dreams of the Grey Friars believed herself so holy that she was not able to do any sin. But many of those same Friars would have us believe that we of ourselves can be sinless, the which is a monstrous error." "Is it possible, Longarine," said Oisille, "that there are any foolish enough to believe this?" "Ay, and much more," answered Longarine, "for they maintain that one should accustom oneself to chastity; and to make trial of their strength they parley with the prettiest women they can find, and the ones they like the best, and so by kisses and touching of them they

P

try whether the carnal nature is altogether dead within. And when they feel themselves stirred by these toyings they get them gone, and betake them to fasting and mortification. And when they have so far brought the flesh that kissing or talking are as nothing to them, they make trial of a strong temptation—I would say lying together and embracing one another—without any evil concupiscence. But for one pair who have come off scot free there have been so many fallen into scandal, that the Archbishop of Milan, in whose see this devotional exercise is common, was constrained to separate the monks and nuns, and put the men in a monastery and the women in a nunnery." "Truly," said Geburon, "'tis the extremity of folly to endeavour to render themselves sinless by seeking out all the occasions of sin." "There are others," answered Saffredent, "who do the contrary to this; for they fly all occasions, but yet does concupiscence follow hard upon them. And the holy St. Jerome, after scourging himself and hiding him in the wilderness, confesses that he could not escape this fire that burnt up his inwards. Wherefore we must commend us to God, for if he uphold us not with his arm, we shall fall very low—ay, and take delight in so falling." "But," said Hircan, "do you not see that while we were telling our stories the monks behind the hedge did not hear the bell for evensong, and when we began to talk about God they vanished, and are even now ringing the second bell." "We shall do well in following them," said Oisille, "and in praising God for that we have so joyously passed this day, even to admiration." So saying they arose and went to the church, where they heard evensong with due devotion. And afterwards they fell to supper, discoursing on the matters that were overpast, and calling to mind many another case, so as to see which were the most worthy of relation. And when the evening had been gaily spent they betook themselves to sweet rest, hoping on the morrow to continue this undertaking that was so much to their contentment. And so the third day came to an end.

DAY THE FOURTH.

ON THE FOURTH DAY RELATION IS MADE FOR THE MOST PART OF THE VIRTUOUS PATIENCE AND LONG-SUFFERING OF WOMEN TO WIN THEIR HUSBANDS; AND OF THE PRUDENCE USED OF MEN TOWARDS THEIR WIVES FOR THE PRESERVING OF THE HONOUR OF THEIR HOUSES AND LINEAGE.

PROLOGUE.

Oisille, according to her good custom, rose on the morrow a long while before the rest, and meditating on the Holy Scripture, awaited the company, who one by one assembled together. And the slug-a-beds excused thenselves in the words of the Parable, saying: "I have a wife, and therefore I could not come." So Hircan and his wife found the lesson well begun. But Oisille had the wit to search out that place of Scripture reproving them that are negligent to hear the word, and not only read it but made such a goodly and fructifying discourse thereon that it was impossible to weary at the listening to it. The lesson ended, Parlamente said to her : "I was sorry, when I came, to have been so lazy, but since my fault has been the occasion of your speaking to me to such good purpose, my laziness hath profited me double, for I have both given rest to my body and keenness to my mind, the better to hear your godly conversation." "Then for penance," said Oisille, "let us go to mass and pray Our Lord to give us the will and the means to keep His law; and then let Him command us according to His pleasure." As they said these words they came into the church and heard mass with due devotion ; and afterwards, when they were at table, Hircan did not forget to laugh at his wife and her laziness. When dinner was finished they went to rest and to study their parts, and at the appointed hour they found themselves at the accustomed place. Oisille asked Hircan to whom he would give his vote to begin the day. "If my wife," said he, "had not begun yesterday's entertainment, I would have given her my vote; for though I have always thought she loved me above all other men, this morning she plainly manifested her love for me that it was greater than that she had for God and his word, inasmuch as she despised your good lesson to the end that she might keep

me company. So, since I cannot give my vote to the wisest of
the whole company, I will give it to the wisest among us men,
who is Geburon. But I pray you show the monks no mercy."
"It skills not praying," said he, "for they are set so fast in my
head that I cannot forget them. And no long while ago I
heard a tale told by my lord de St. Vincent, ambassador from
the Emperor, which by no means deserves forgetfulness, and
therefore I will tell it again."

NOVEL XXXI.

**The horrid and abominable lust and murder of a Grey Friar, by reason of which his
monastery and the monks in it were burned with fire.**

In one of the lands subject to the Emperor Maximilian of
Austria there stood a monastery of Grey Friars, the which was
in great esteem. And hard-by it was the house of a gentleman,
who bore the monks such goodwill that he shared with them
all his goods, so as to have a part in the benefit of their fasts
and austerities. And among them there was a tall and comely
friar whom this gentleman had chosen for his confessor, and
such power had he to give commands in the house as had the
master of it. Now this friar, seeing the gentleman's wife that
she was fair, and likewise a good and prudent woman, became
so amorous of her that he lost not only his appetite for food and
drink, but his very reason. And one day, thinking to bring the
matter to a conclusion, he went all alone to the house, and finding
not the master, asked the dame whither he had gone. She told
him he was gone to a place where he must needs stay three or
four days, but that if he had need of him she would send an
express messenger. He answered no, and began to come and
go about the house, as a man who has some urgent matter in
his brain, and when he was gone out of her room, she said to
one of her two women, for she had no more : " Go after the
good father and discover what it is he desires, for his face is
the face of one who is not well pleased." The serving-maid
went to the courtyard where he was, and asked if he needed
anything, whereupon he answered that he did, and drawing her
into a corner took a dagger he had in his sleeve and drove it
through her throat. No sooner was this done than there came
into the yard a serving-man on horseback, who had gone to get

the rent of a farm. And when he stood on the ground the friar saluted him, and as he put his arms round him stabbed him in the back of the throat with the dagger, and shut the castle gate. The lady, seeing her maid did not return, was astonished she stayed so long with the friar, and said to the other : "Go see what hinders your fellow that she does not come." Straightway she went, and as soon as the monk saw her he took her apart and did to her as he had done to her fellow. And perceiving himself to be alone in the house he went to the dame and told her that for a long while he had lusted after her, and that the hour was come in which she needs must do his will. She, who would never have suspected him, said : "I am assured, father, that if I had so wicked an inclination you would cast the first stone on me." The monk replied : "Come hither and you shall see what I have done." And when she beheld her two women and the serving-man lying dead, she was in such affright that she stood as a statue without uttering a word. Then this evil man, who did not wish to have her only for an hour, would not take her by force, but said : "Mistress, be not afraid, you are in the hands of the man who of all the world loves you best." So saying he doffed his habit, having under it a small one, the which he gave to the dame, telling her if she would not put it on he would lay her among them she saw dead before her eyes.

She, already more dead than alive, resolved that she would feign to obey him, both to save her life and because she would gain time wherein she hoped her husband might return. And, the friar so charging her, she began as slowly as she was able to take off her headdress, and when it was done he, not regarding the beauty of her hair, hastily cut it off. Next he made her take off all her clothes save her shift, and clothed her in the small habit, putting on him again the large one he was accustomed to wear; then as soon as might be he set forth from the house, leading with him the little friar he had so long lusted after. But God, who has compassion on the innocent in tribulation, regarded the tears of this poor dame in such sort that her husband, having accomplished his affairs sooner than he thought to have done, returned to his house by the same road as went his wife. But when the friar saw him afar off he said to her : "Behold, I see your husband drawing near.

I know that if you look upon him he will take you from my hands, wherefore walk on before me, and by no means turn your head towards him, for if you make but a single sign I will have my dagger in your throat before he can deliver you from me." While he said this the gentleman drew near and asked whence he came. He replied: "From your house, where I have left the dame in good case, and waiting for you."

The gentleman passed by and saw not his wife, but a servant he had with him, who was always wont to talk with the friar's companion, who was called Brother John, began calling to his mistress, thinking her to be his friend. The poor woman, who dared not turn her eyes on her husband, answered him not a word, but the servant crossing the road to see her face to face, the lady, without saying anything, made him a sign with her eyes that were full of tears. So the man followed after his master and said to him: "Sir, I crossed the road and saw the friar's companion, who is by no means Brother John, but altogether is like to the dame your wife, and her eyes are most pitiful and full of tears." The gentleman told him he dreamed, and made no account of it, but the servant persisting, asked leave of him to go back and see if matters were as he thought, whilst his master waited for him on the road. The gentleman gave him leave, and waited for whatsoever news he might bring him. But when the friar heard the servant behind him calling out Brother John, he suspected the lady was known, and came to meet him with a great club of iron which he carried, and gave the servant with it such a blow that he fell from his horse to the ground, and leaping upon his body the monk forthwith cut his throat. The gentleman, seeing his servant fall from afar off, thought it to be from some mischance, and ran back to succour him. And as soon as the monk saw him he smote him with his club in like manner as he had smitten the servant, and threw him to the earth, and leapt upon him. But the gentleman being strong and powerful, threw his arms round the friar in such sort that not only did he get no hurt but forced the dagger from his fist, which his wife took and gave to her husband, and with all her might held the friar by his hood. And the gentleman gave him several blows with the dagger, till at last he entreated forgiveness and confessed the evil he had done. But the gentleman having no mind to kill him, prayed his wife go to the house and fetch his people and a cart wherein to put the friar. This she did, taking off her monkish dress and running to the house with her shaven head in her shift alone. Presently came all the servants to the aid of their master, and to lead away the wolf he had taken prisoner, and finding him in the road where he had been captured they bound him and clapped him up in the house. And the gentleman, after some time, made take him to the Emperor in Flanders, where he was lawfully tried, and confessed his wickedness. And by his confession, and proof made by commissioners on the spot, it was found that a great number of women of gentle blood and comely wenches had been borne to that monastery by the same means as the monk had used with the dame, and in this he had had good success but for the grace of Our Lord, who always succours them that put their trust in Him. And the goods in the monastery that were stolen, and the comely women that were therein, were taken out of it, and the monks having been shut up were burned together with it, for a perpetual memory of this evil deed. And by this we may learn that there is nothing more dangerous than love when it is bottomed upon vice, as in like manner there is nothing more kindly and praiseworthy than it when it has its habitation in a virtuous heart.

"I am heartily sorry, ladies, that truth does not find us tales to the advantage of the Grey Friars, as it does to their disadvantage. For it would be a great delight to me, who have a liking for their order, to find some tale wherewith I could sing their praise; but we have so sworn to speak the truth, that after the witness of so many trustworthy men I could not conceal this matter from you. But I do assure you that, when the monks shall do some notable and glorious deed, I will take much the more praise to relate it of them than I have taken to tell you this true history." "In good faith, Geburon," said Oisille, "this was a love well deserving to be called cruelty." "I wonder," said Simontault, "how he had the patience, seeing her in her shift, and in a place where he had the lordship over her, not to take her by force." "He was no dainty man," answered Saffredent, "but a glutton; for since he was minded to have his fill of her every day, he wished not to amuse himself by a mere taste." "'Tis not that," said Parlamente, "but you must understand that the wicked are always fearful, and the fear of him, lest he should be surprised and robbed of his prey, made him bear away his lamb to devour it at his ease, as a wolf doth with a sheep." "Natheless," said Dagoucin, "I cannot believe he loved her, or that in so vile a heart the virtuous god of love could have a dwelling place." "Be that as it may," said Oisille, " he had a punishment even as he deserved; and I pray God that like deeds may have a like success. But to whom do you give your vote?" "Unto you," said Geburon, "who will not fail to tell us some good story." "Since it has come to my turn," said Oisille, "I will tell you a thing that fell out in my time, and under the eyes of him that told it me. I am assured you know that death puts a close to our misfortunes, but since it does this let us rather call it our happiness and our rest. The chief misfortune then that can befall a man is to desire death and not to have it; wherefore the greatest punishment one can give to an evil-doer is not death but perpetual torment, thus great that it makes him long for death, and thus small that it brings death no nearer. And in this sort did a gentleman use his wife, as you shall hear."

NOVEL XXXII.

The notable manner in which a gentleman punished his wife whom he had taken in adultery.

King Charles, the Eighth of his name, sent into Germany a gentleman named Bernage, lord of Sivray, near Amboise, who to make good speed spared not to journey by day nor night, and so one evening came very late to a house and asked there for lodging. At this great difficulty was made, but when the master understood how great a king he served, he entreated him not to take in bad part the churlishness of his servants, since, by reason of certain kinsfolk of his wife, who were fain to do him a hurt, it was necessary that the house should be under strict ward. Then the aforesaid Bernage told him the reason of his embassage, which the gentleman offered to forward with all his might, and led him into his house, where he honourably lodged and entertained him.

It was now supper-time, and the gentleman brought him into a large room, bravely hung with tapestry work. And as the meats were set upon the table there came a woman from behind the tapestry, of a most surpassing beauty, but her head was shorn and the rest of her body was clothed in black gear of the German fashion. After that the gentleman had washed his hands with Bernage, water was borne to the lady, who when she had washed her hands sat herself down at the bottom of the table, without a word from her or to her. My lord de Bernage looked at her very attentively, and she seemed one of the comeliest women he ever had beheld, save that the manner of her countenance was pale and melancholic. And when she had eaten a little she asked for drink, and this was brought her by a servant in a most marvellous vessel, I would say a death's-head with the eyes closed up with silver, and so from this she drank three or four times. And her supper having come to an end she washed her hands, and with a reverence to the lord of the house she returned behind the tapestry without a word to anyone. Bernage was so astonished to see so strange a case that he fell into a thoughtful melancholy, which being perceived of the gentleman, he said to him : "I know well that you marvel within yourself at what you have seen done at this table ; and for that I judge you to be an honourable man, I will not conceal the affair from you, to the intent that you may not think there is so great cruelty in me without a weighty cause. The lady you have seen is my wife, whom I loved as man never loved before, so much indeed that to wed her I forgot all fear and brought her here by force against the will of her kinsfolk. And she in like manner gave me so many evident proofs of her love that I would have risked ten thousand lives to bring her here as I did, to the delight of the pair of us, and we lived awhile in such quietness and contentment that I esteemed myself the most fortunate gentleman in all Christendom. But while I was away on a journey made for the sake of my honour, she so far forgot her virtuousness, her conscience, and the love she had for me, that she fell in love with a young gentleman whom I had brought up in my house, and this I perceived upon my coming home. Yet I loved her so well that I was not able to distrust her till experience gave belief unto my eyes, and with them I saw what I feared more than death. Then was my love turned to madness and my trust to despair ; and so well did I play the spy upon her that

one day, feigning to go out, I hid myself in the room which is
now her dwelling-place.   And very soon after she saw me go,
she went away and made the young man come to her, and him
I beheld handling her in such fashion as belonged to me alone.
But when I saw him get upon the bed beside her, I came forth
from my hiding-place, and, taking him between her very arms,
there put him to death.   And since the offence of my wife
seemed to me so great that death would not suffice for her
punishment, I appointed one that I deem is much more bitter
than death to her: namely, to shut her up in the room where she
had her greatest pleasures of him she loved more than me, where
I have set all the bones of her lover in an aumbry, as a precious
thing and worthy of safe keeping.   And to the end that in
eating and drinking she may not lose the memory of him, I have
made serve her at table, with the head of that villain in place of
a cup, and this in my presence, so that she may see living him
whom she has made through her sin a mortal enemy, and dead
for love of her him whom she preferred before me.   And so at
dinner and supper she beholds the two things which should most
make her to despair; the living enemy and the dead lover; and
all through her own sin.   For the rest, I treat her as myself,
save that she goes shorn, for an array of hair doth not belong
to a woman taken in adultery, nor the veil to an harlot.   Wherefore her hair is cut, showing that she has lost the honour of
virginity and purity.   And if it be your pleasure to see her, I
will take you there."

To this Bernage willingly agreed; and they went down the
stair and found her in a fine room, sitting alone before a fire.
Then the gentleman drew a curtain that was before a high
aumbry, and in it were hanging all the bones of the dead man.
Bernage had a great desire to speak with the lady, but for fear
of the husband durst not do it.   He perceiving this, said to
him : "An it please you to say anything to her, you shall see
how admirably she talks."   Forthwith Bernage said : "Mistress,
your long-suffering and your torment are alike great.   I hold
you for the most wretched of all women."   The lady, with tears
in her eyes, graciously yet most humbly answered him : "Sir,
I confess my sin to be so great that all the ills the lord of this
place (for I am not worthy that I should call him husband) can
bestow upon me, are as nothing compared with my sorrow that
I have done him a displeasure."   So saying she fell to weeping

bitterly; and the gentleman took Bernage by the arm and led him away. And very early on the morrow he went on to execute the charge given him of the King. But, in bidding the gentleman farewell, he could not refrain from saying to him: "Sir, the love I bear you, and the honour and privity you have used towards me in this your house, constrains me to tell you that, in my opinion, seeing the repentance of your poor wife, you should have compassion on her. Furthermore, you being still young have no children, and it would be a great pity that such a brave line as yours should come to an end, and they for whom, perchance, you have no great love, should be your heirs." The gentleman, who had resolved never again to speak to his wife, thought for a long while on what my lord de Bernage had said to him, and finding him to be in the right, promised that if she continued in her humble repentance he would one day have compassion on her. And so Bernage went forth on his embassage. And when he was returned to the King his master, he told him the whole matter, which the prince, having made inquiry, found to be as he had said. And among other things, Bernage having spoken of the lady's beauty, the King sent his painter, John of Paris, thither, that he might draw her to the life. This he did, and with the consent thereto of the husband, who, beholding her long repentance, and having a great desire for children, took pity on his wife, who with such humbleness had borne her punishment, and, taking her back to him, had of her many brave children.

"If all, ladies, in like case, drank out of like vessels, I am afraid that many a golden cup would be turned into a death's-head. God preserve us from the like, for if His goodness do not keep us, there is not one of us that may not fare worse. But having confidence in Him, He will have a care to them that confess they are not able to have a care to themselves; and they that trust in their own strength stand in jeopardy of being so tempted as to be constrained to confess their frailty. The high-minded I have often seen to stumble and to fall, whilst they that were of less reputation went safe and sound. To this intent is the old saw: *What God keeps is well kept*." "Her punishment," said Parlamente, "I deem mighty reasonable, for, when the crime is worse than death, so also should be the punishment." But Ennasuitte said: "I am by no means of your opinion, for I would rather look upon the bones of my

lover all the days of my life than die for his sake, since there is
nothing ill-done that cannot be àmended, but when one is ended
one cannot be amended."   "How then would you mend
shame?" said Longarine, "for you know that when a woman
has done a deed of this kind her honour can by no means be
repaired, do she what she may."   "Prithee, then," answered
Ennasuitte, "tell me whether the Magdalen has not now more
honour among men than her sister, who was a maid."   "I
confess," said Longarine, "that she is praised of us for the
great love she bore to Jesus Christ, and for her repentance;
yet the name of *Sinner* abides with her always."   "I care not,"
said Longarine, "how men call me, for if I be forgiven of God,
and likewise of my husband, there is nothing for which I am
fain to die."   "If this dame loved her husband as she ought,"
said Dagoucin, "I marvel how it was she did not die of grief
as she looked upon the bones of him whom, by her sin, she had
sent to death."   "What! Dagoucin," said Simontault, "have
you yet to learn that in women dwells neither love nor regret?"
"I have yet to learn it," answered Dagoucin, "for I have never
yet made trial of their love, lest haply I find it less than I
desire."   "You live then on faith and hope," said Nomerfide,
"as the plover does on wind?   Truly you are easy to be fed."
"I hold myself content," said he, "with the love that I know
is in me, and with the hope that it is in my lady's heart likewise.   But if I was assured that as I hope so it is, I should be
in such delight that I could not bear it and live."   "Be wary
lest you die of the plague," said Geburon, "for as to that
sickness you name, I will assure you of it.   But I would know
to whom Oisille will give her vote."   "I give it," said she,
"to Simontault, who I am persuaded will spare no one."
"Does not that," said he, "say, in so many words, that I am
somewhat of an evil-speaker?   But in the tale I shall tell you
you shall see that the evil-speakers spoke the truth.   I am
assured, ladies, that you are not so foolish as to believe whatever men tell you, be they ever so pious in appearance, if the
proof of what they say is not so great as to put an end to all
doubt.   And even under the form of miracles there are many
abuses done, wherefore I desire to tell you of a miracle, which
shall be no less to the praise of a faithful prince than to the
shame of a wicked minister of the church."

NOVEL XXXIII.

The hypocrisy of a parson, who having got his sister with child concealed it under the cloak of holiness.

When the Count Charles of Angoulême, father to King Francis, and a faithful prince and a God-fearing, was at Cognac, it was told him that in a village hard-by Cherves there lived a maid so austerely that it was matter of admiration, and yet for all that she was big with child. Of this she made no concealment, assuring all people that she had never known a man, and that she knew not how she came to be in such case, save it were the work of the Holy Ghost. And the people readily believed this thing, and among them she was accounted for a second Virgin Mary, since all knew that from her youth up she had been so good and prudent that there never had been displayed in her so much as a sign of worldly lust. Not only did she fast on the days appointed by the Church, but many other days in the week from her own devotion. Whenever there was any service at the church she would never stir from it; wherefore her life was in such repute among the common folk that men came as to a miracle to behold her, and happy was he that could touch her garment. The parson of the parish was her brother, a man in years, and very austere, loved and esteemed by his parishioners as an holy man. And he used such rigorous treatment with his aforesaid sister, that he clapped her up in a house and kept her there, and this was taken of all the people in very bad part, and so great was the noise of it that, as I have told you, it came to the ears of the Count. He, seeing the people to be blinded by some error, and desiring to enlighten them, sent a Master of Requests and an almoner, two exceeding honest men, that they might make discovery of the truth. And they went to the place and informed themselves of the matter with their utmost diligence, addressing themselves to the parson, who, so weary was he of it, prayed them to be with him when he made out the truth, and this he hoped to do on the morrow.

And early in the morning the parson sang mass, his sister being present on her knees, and to say truth mighty big. And at the end of mass, the parson took the *Corpus Domini*, and before all said to his sister : "Wretch that thou art, behold Him who suffered for thee his Death and Passion, before whom I adjure thee, tell me if thou art a maid, the which thou hast oftentimes assured me." She answered boldly that she was. "How then can this thing be, that thou art great with child and still a maid ?" She answered him : "I can give no reason, save it be the grace of the Holy Ghost, who doeth in me according to his pleasure ; but I cannot deny the grace of God given to me, whereby I am still a maid, and never have I wished to be married." Then her brother said to her : "I give thee the precious Body of Jesus Christ, the which thou wilt take to thy damnation if the truth is other than thou hast said. And of this they who are here present on behalf of my lord and Count are witnesses." The girl, who was nearly thirteen years of age, swore with this oath : "I take the Body of Our Lord here present to my damnation, before you, sirs, and you, my brother, if ever a man has touched me any more than you." So saying she received the Body of Our Lord. The Master of Requests and the almoner, beholding this, went away in confusion, believing that under such an oath there could not be deceit. And they made report of the matter to the Count, being fain that he should believe even as they believed. But he who was a wise man, after having well thought on the matter, made them tell him the very words of the oath. Thereupon he said : "She spoke the truth and so deceived you ; for she said that never man had touched her any more than her brother, and I am persuaded that it is her brother that has got the child, and would fain cover his wickedness under this monstrous deceit. But we, believing one Jesus Christ to have come, wait not for another. Wherefore get you gone and clap the parson in gaol, and I am assured he will confess the truth." And the thing was done even as he had commanded, not without remonstrance from many, for that they put that good man to open shame. But so soon as the parson was taken he made confession of his wickedness, and of how he had counselled his sister to talk in the manner she had done, so as to cover the life they had led together, not only because the excuse was an easy one, but that thereby they might have honour of all men. And when his wickedness was laid before him, in that he had taken the very Body of Our Lord for her to swear upon, he replied that he

had not been so bold, but had taken an unconsecrated and un-
blessed wafer.   The report of this being brought to the Count
of Angoulême, he commanded that justice be done upon them
after the accustomed manner.   So they waited till the girl was
brought to bed, and after that she was delivered of a boy the
brother and sister were burned alive together, whereat all the
people marvelled greatly, who had seen under the cloak of
holiness so monstrous a deed, and under so pious and praiseworthy a life a most hateful crime.

   " Behold, ladies, the faith of the good Count, that it was
not overcome by signs nor wonders, since he knew well that
we have but one Saviour, who when he said : *Consummatum
est*, made plain to us that He left no place for a successor who
should accomplish our salvation." " I promise you," said Oisille,
" this was the extreme of audacious hypocrisy, to cover under
the cloak of God and true Christianity so monstrous a sin." " I
have heard," said Hircan, " that they who, on pretext of a commission from the King, do cruel deeds and tyrannous, receive a
double punishment, for that they have used the kingly justice as a
cloak for their own injustice.   So the hypocrites, though for a
while, beneath the cloak of God and holiness, all goes well with
them, yet when the Lord God raises the cloak they are discovered and sent naked away.   And in that hour their filthy
and abominable nakedness is esteemed more vile, because the
covering was so honourable."   " There is nothing more pleasant," said Nomerfide, " than to speak out the thoughts of
one's heart." " It causes merriment," answered Longarine, " so
I suppose you give your opinion from your own habit."   " I
tell you," said Nomerfide, " that I see fools, unless they die
violently, live longer than the wise and prudent, and there can
be but one reason, that they do not hide their passion.   If they
be wrathful they deal out blows, and if they be merry they
laugh ; but they that deem themselves to be wise so conceal
their imperfections that their hearts are all corrupted thereby."
" Methinks," said Geburon, " you say well, and that hypocrisy,
be it towards God, men, or Nature, is the cause of all evil."
" This would be a brave thing," said Parlamente, " if our
hearts were so fulfilled of Him who is all virtuousness and all
gladness, that we could freely show them to the whole world."
" That will be on the day when there is no longer any flesh on

our bones," said Hircan. "Yet," said Oisille, "the Spirit of God, who is stronger than death, can so mortify our heart within us, without change or decay of the body." "Mistress," said Saffredent, "you speak of a gift of God, scarcely partaken of by men." "'Tis partaken of," said she, "by them that have faith, but since it skills not to speak on this matter to such as are fast bound in carnal bondage, let us know to whom Simontault gives his vote." "I give it," said he, "to Nomerfide, "for as her heart is glad, her words will not be sad." "Truly," said Nomerfide, "since you desire to laugh I will take the occasion. And that you may know how hurtful are fear and ignorance, and that not to understand a word is often a cause of evil, I will tell you of a case that befel two Grey Friars at Nyort, who, through not understanding the words of a butcher, were in fear of death."

NOVEL XXXIV.

A very merry case of two Grey Friars who lodged in the house of a butcher.

There is a village betwixt Nyort and Fors named Grip, the which appertains to the manor of Fors. And it fell out that one day two Grey Friars, journeying from Nyort, came very late to this place Grip and lodged in the house of a butcher. And since between their room and that of their host there were but boards badly joined, they became desirous of hearing the discourse of the husband and wife in bed together, setting their ears to the boards that were nearest to the bed. And the husband having no suspicion of his guests talked with his wife upon the privy concernments of their household. "Sweetheart," said he, "I must needs rise early on the morrow that I may go see our Grey Friars, for one of them is a mighty fat fellow. Him we will kill, and if we salt him forthwith he will greatly profit us." And though his discourse was on his pigs, which he called *Grey Friars*, yet the two poor brethren, who heard this awful doom, were well persuaded that it was for them, and in fear and trembling waited the dawn of day. Now the one of them was exceeding fat, and the other somewhat lean. And the fat friar was fain to make his confession to his fellow, for, as he said, the rogue butcher, having ceased to walk in the fear and love of God, would make no more ado of slaughtering them than an ox or any other animal. And seeing that they were shut up in their room, and were not able to get out unless they passed through that of their host, they should hold themselves as dead men, and commend their souls to God. But the young friar, who was not so overcome with fear as was his fellow, said that since the door was shut on them, they must essay a passage through the window, and at the worst they could meet with nothing more grievous than death. To this the fat friar agreed. The young one opened the window, and seeing that it was not too far from the ground, leapt down and fled away without so much as waiting for his companion. And he likewise essayed this hazardous jump, but in place of leaping fell so heavily, by reason of his weight, that he was sorely hurt in one of his legs and could not stir from the ground.

And seeing himself to be abandoned by his fellow, and not able to follow him, he looked all around for a hiding place, and saw nothing better than the pigstye, whither he crawled as well as might be. And as he opened the door to hide himself within, out rushed two monstrous pigs, in whose place the poor friar bestowed himself, hoping that, when he heard the noise of folk passing by, he could call out and be succoured. But so soon as the morning was come the butcher made ready his mightiest knives, and would have his wife bear him company while he went to kill his fat pig. And when he came to the stye, where the friar had hidden himself, he began to bellow at the top of his voice as he opened the little door: "Come out! come out! master Grey Friar, for it is my fixed intent this very day to taste your chitterlings!" The poor friar, not being able to stand on his legs, crawled out of the stye on his hands and knees, crying as loud as he was able for mercy. But if the friar was in great terror, the butcher and his wife were in no less, for they thought that St. Francis was wrathful with them because they called a beast a *Grey Friar*, and so fell on their knees before the poor man, asking forgiveness of St. Francis and all his whole order. So on one side was the friar imploring mercy of the butcher, and on the other the butcher craving forgiveness of the friar, in such sort that it was a full quarter of an hour before they were assured of one another At last the good father, understanding the butcher wished him no harm, declared wherefore he had hidden himself in the stye, at which their fear was forthwith converted to laughter, save for the poor Grey Friar, whose leg was too sore to let him make merry. But the butcher took him into his house and entreated him mighty well. As to his fellow, who had left him in his necessity, he had run all night and about the hour of prime came to the manor-house of the lord of Fors. Here he made complaint of the butcher, whom he suspected had killed his companion, since he had not followed after him. The lord of Fors sent forthwith to Grips to know the truth of the matter, which being found out was by no means judged an occasion for weeping. And the lord of Fors told it to his mistress, the Duchess of Angoulême, mother of King Francis I.

"So, ladies, 'tis not a good thing to listen to other folk's secrets, lest haply one hear ill of oneself." "Did I not know," said Simontault, "that Nomerfide would give us no reason to weep, but rather to laugh? And this I think we all of us have done to admiration." "And what is the cause of it," said Oisille, "that we are always more inclined to laugh at idle folly than true wit?" "For that," said Hircan, "it is more pleasant and more like our own nature, which of itself is never wise; and like always is attached to like—fools to folly, and wise men to wit. Yet I am persuaded that any, be he fool or wise man, could not refrain from laughing at this tale." "There are men," said Geburon, "whose heart is so possessed by a love of wisdom, that for all the tales they may hear they will never laugh; for they have a gladness of the soul and a well-moderated contentment that nothing can move." "What folk are these?" said Hircan. "The philosophers of old days," said Geburon, "by whom nor joy nor sorrow were at all experienced, or, at the least, they showed them not; so great glory did they think it to conquer themselves and their passions. And I esteem it a good thing to do as they did, and conquer a vicious passion, but as to a natural desire leading to no evil this seems a profitless victory. But yet they esteemed it a great virtue." "It is not said," answered Saffredent, "that they were all wise men; and haply there was more appearance of sense and virtue in them than reality." "Natheless," said Geburon, "you will see that they rebuked all evil; and Diogenes himself trod on the bed of Plato, it being too rare and curious for his liking, to show that he despised and would fain put under his feet Plato his vainglory and covetousness. 'I trample upon and despise,' said he, 'the pride of Plato.'" "But you tell not the whole," said Saffredent, "for Plato answered that his trampling was but pride of another kind." "In truth," said Parlamente, "'tis not possible that this conquest over ourselves can be accomplished by ourselves, save with a monstrous pride especially to be avoided, since it engenders the death and destruction of all the other virtues." "Did I not read to you this morning," said Oisille, "how that they who trusted themselves to be more wise than other men, and who by the light of reason came to know a God, a creator of all things, yet fixing this glory on themselves, and not on Him whence it came, thinking by their own toil they had come to this knowledge, were made not only more ignorant and void of reason than other men, but even than fourfooted beasts? For since they had erred in their minds, attributing to themselves that is God's alone, they showed their errors by bodily disorders, forgetting and perverting their sex as St. Paul to-day declared to us in the Epistle to the Romans." "There is not one of us," said Parlamente, "that will not confess that sin is the fruit of inward evil; which the more it is concealed by an outward show of virtue, the more it is hard to be plucked out." "We men," said Hircan, "are nearer to salvation than you; for since we conceal not our fruits the tree is easily known; but you who dare not show the fruits, and do such brave outward works, are hardly able to discover that great tree of pride, which, well concealed, grows fast." "I confess," replied Longarine, "that if the word of God doth not show us by faith the leprosy of infidelity that is hidden in our hearts, God does us good service when we fall into some open sin, by the which the secret plague becomes clearly manifest. And happy are they whom faith has so humbled that they have no need of making trial of their sinful nature by its outward effects." "But consider," said Simontault, "how we are going on, for setting out from a most foolish tale we are now deep in theology and philosophy. Let us leave these matters to them that are more fit for such musings, and ask to whom Nomerfide gives her vote." "I give it," said she, "to Hircan, commending to him the honour of the ladies." "It is safe in my hands," answered he, "but yet we must needs confess that the nature of woman and man is of itself inclined to vice, if it be not preserved therefrom by Him to whom belongeth the honour of every victory. So to abate your pride, when your honour is lauded by anyone, I will tell you this most truthful story."

NOVEL XXXV.

Of a rare case of spiritual love, and a good cure for temptation.

In the town of Pampeluna there lived a fair and virtuous lady, as chaste and devout as any in the land. So well did she love and obey her husband that he entirely put his trust in her : at divine service and at hearing of sermons she was always to be found, and would persuade her husband and children to go there with her. And on a certain Ash-Wednesday, she having come to the age of thirty years, when ladies are content to put by the name of fair for that of discreet, she went to church to take the ashes which are for a memorial of death. And the preacher was a Grey Friar, a man held by all the people as holy on account of the great goodness and austerity of his life, which, though it had made him to be thin and pale, yet hindered him not from being as comely a man as one could desire to see. The lady listened to his sermon, with eyes fixed upon his venerable person, and eyes and mind ready to hear what he said. And the sweetness of his words passed through her ears even unto her soul; and the comeliness and grace of his body passed through her eyes and smote her so at heart, that she was as one in a dream. When the sermon was finished she was careful to look at what altar the preacher was to say mass, and there she presented herself to take the ashes from his hand that was as fine and white as any lady's. And to this hand the devout woman paid more attention than to the ashes it gave to her. So being assured that this manner of spiritual love and certain pleasures she felt therein could do her conscience no harm, she failed not to go every day and hear the sermon, taking her husband; and so great praise did both of them give the preacher that at table or elsewhere they spoke of nought else. Then did this fire named spiritual become so carnal that it burnt up first the heart and next the whole body of this poor lady; and as she was slow to feel it, so swift was it to spread, and, before she knew she was in love, she felt all love's delights. And as

one altogether surprised by Love her enemy, she resisted none
of his commands; but it was sore grief to her that the physician
for all her sickness was not so much as ware of it. Wherefore,
setting aside all fear of showing her foolishness to a man of
wisdom, and her wickedness and vice to a man of virtue and
goodness, she set down as softly as she could the love she bore
him in a letter, and gave it to a little page, telling him what he
had to do, and above all enjoining him to have a care lest her
husband should see him going to the Grey Friars. The page,
seeking for the shortest way, passed through a street where
was his master sitting in a shop; whereupon the gentleman,
seeing him go by, came out to discover whither he was going,
and when the page saw him, much affrighted, he hid himself in
a house. At this his master followed him, and taking him by
the arm asked whither he went, and finding no sense or
meaning in his excuses, and the face of him terrified, he
threatened to beat him shrewdly if he would not say whither
he was going. The poor page said to him: "Alas, sir, if I
tell you the dame will kill me;" so the gentleman, suspecting
that his wife was treating for some commodity in which he
should have no share, assured the page that if he told the truth
he should have no evil but rather all good, but if he lied he
should be put in gaol for life. The little page, so as to have
the good and avoid the evil, told him the whole matter, and
showed him the letter his mistress had written to the preacher,
which gave the husband as much astonishment as anger, since
he had altogether trusted his whole life in his wife's faithfulness,
and had never found in her any fault. But being a prudent
man, he concealed his wrath, and entirely to discover what his
wife was minded to do, he counterfeited a reply as if the
preacher had written it, thanking her for her goodwill towards
him, and declaring that on his side there was no less. The
page, having sworn to conduct the matter discreetly, carried to
his mistress the counterfeited letter; and so great gladness did
it give her that her husband plainly perceived the manner of
her countenance to be altered, since in place of being thin, as is
fitting in the Lenten Fast, she was fairer and more ruddy than
in the Carnival.

And now it was Mothering Sunday, yet did she not cease to
send the preacher by letters her mad ravings, nor for the matter

of that during Passion and Holy Week. For it seemed to her,
when he turned his eyes to that part of the church where she was,
or spoke of the love of God, that love of her was at the bottom
of it; and as far as her eyes could tell him her mind, she did
not spare them. And to all these her letters the husband failed
not to reply after the same sort, and after Easter he wrote to
her in the preacher's name praying her to devise some means
of speaking with him privily. She, who for this hour waxed
weary, counselled her husband to go see some lands he had in
the country, to which he agreed, and went and hid himself in
the house of one of his acquaintance. The lady failed not to
write to the preacher that the time was come for him to see
her, since her husband was in the country; and the gentleman,
willing to sound his wife's heart to the very bottom, went to
the preacher, praying him for the love of God to lend him
his habit. But the monk, who was a good man and an honest,
told him his rule forbade him, and by no means would he lend
it for masquerading in; yet the gentleman, assuring him that
he would make no ill use of it, and that it was necessary to his
wellbeing, the friar, who knew him for a good and devout man,
lent it him. And putting the habit on him, and drawing the
hood over his face so that his eyes could not be seen, the
gentleman got him a false beard and a false nose like to the
friar's, and with cork in his shoes made himself of the fitting
height. In this gear he betook himself, when evening was
come, to his wife's room, where she awaited him with much
devotion. And the poor fool stayed not for him to come to
her, but, as a woman out of her wits, rushed to throw her arms
around him. He, with his face lowered, so as not to be known,
began to draw away from her, making the sign of the cross,
and saying the while only one word: "Temptation! temptation!" The lady said: "Alas, father, you are in the right, for
there is none stronger than what comes from love. But since
you have promised to be the cure, I pray you now we have
time and leisure to have compassion upon me." So saying she
strove by force to throw her arms around him, but he, flying
round the room, making great signs of the cross, cried all the
while: "Temptation! temptation!" But when he saw she
pressed him hard, he took a stout stick he had under his habit,
and so entreated her with it that her temptation was overcome,

and he not known of her. This done he forthwith gave back
the habit to the preacher, assuring him he had done him a
great kindness.

And on the morrow, making a pretence of returning from
afar, he came to his house and found there his wife in bed, and,
as if he knew it not, asked what ailed her, and she replied that
it was a rheum, and, moreover, that she could not stir hand nor
foot. The husband, though exceeding desirous to laugh,
feigned to be much grieved; and, as a matter of consolation,
told her he had bidden the good preacher to sup with them
that very evening. But to this she instantly answered : " Be
it far from you, sweetheart, to ask such folk hither, for they
work ill in every house they enter." " Why, sweetheart, how
is this?" said the husband ; " you have always mightily praised
this man. I, for my part, think that if there be a holy man on
this earth it is he." The lady replied : " They are good at the
altar and in the pulpit, but in houses they are Anti-Christ.
Prithee, sweetheart, let me not see him, for with this my sickness it would be the very death of me." The husband said :
" Since you wish it not you shall not see him, but for all that
he must sup with me." " Do as you will," said she, " so long
as I do not see him, for I hate the monks like the devil." The
husband, having given the good monk his supper, said to him
as follows: " Father, I esteem you so beloved of God that He
will not refuse you anything you ask Him, wherefore I entreat
you have compassion on my poor wife, who these eight days
hath been possessed of an evil spirit, in such sort that she
endeavours to bite and scratch whomsoever she sees. Of cross
or holy water she makes no account, but I firmly believe that
if you put your hand on her the devil would come out; and
this I pray you to do." The good father said : " My son, to a
believer all things are possible. Do you steadfastly believe that
the goodness of God refuses no grace to him who asks it faithfully?" "I do believe it, father," answered the gentleman. " Be
then also assured, my son," said the friar, " that God is able to
do what He wills, and is as all-mighty as He is good. Let us go,
then, strengthened by faith, to resist this roaring lion, and snatch
from him his prey, that God hath won for Himself by the blood
of His dear Son, Jesus Christ." So the husband led the good
man to the room where his wife lay on a small bed ; and she,

thinking she saw him who had beaten her, fell into great astonishment and wrath; but for that her husband was also present,
lowered her eyes and was dumb.   Then said the husband to
the holy man : " While I am with her the devil no longer tor-
menteth her, but as soon as I am gone forth, do you cast holy
water upon her, and you will see the evil spirit do his work."
So saying he left the friar alone with his wife, but stayed by
the door, so as to observe the fashion of their discourse.   And
when she saw herself alone with the friar, she began as one
mad, to cry out at him, calling him wretch, villain, murderer,
deceiver.   The good father, thinking that of a very truth she
was possessed of an evil spirit, would have taken her by the head
to say his exorcisements over it, but she scratched and bit him
in such wise that he was fain to parley with the devil from
afar ; and while he cast the holy water on her very plentifully, said many a devout orison.   And the husband, thinking
him to have done his duty, entered the room and thanked him
for the pains he had taken, and as he came in his wife ceased
her cursing and abuse, and for her fear of her husband, kissed
the cross with much meekness.   But the holy friar, who had
seen her before so furiously enraged, firmly believed that by his
prayer to Our Lord the devil had come out of her, and went
his way praising God for this mighty work.   The husband,
seeing his wife to have been well chastised for her brainsick
folly, would not declare to her what he had done; for he was
content to have conquered her desire by his wisdom, and to
have taken such order with her that she mortally hated what
aforetime she had loved, and so gave herself up more than before
to her husband and her household.

   " Herein, ladies, you can discover the good sense of a husband, and the frailty of a woman of fair repute ; and I think
that, when you have well looked in this glass, in place of
trusting in your own strength, you will learn to return to Him
who holds your honour in the hollow of his hands."   " I am
well pleased," said Parlamente, " that you are become preacher
to the ladies, but still better would it be if you made these fine
sermons for all the ladies to whom you speak."   " Always when
you hear me," said Hircan, " you shall have discourse no less
virtuous."   " The intent of that is," said Simontault, " that
when you are not by he will speak after another sort."   " He

must talk as he pleases," said Parlamente, "but I am fain to believe, for my content, that he talks always so. But at the least the example he has given will stand them in good stead who believe that this spiritual love is not dangerous, for me-thinks it is of all kinds the worst." "Yet it appears to me," said Oisille, "that to love a good man and a virtuous, and a fearer of God, is no matter of contempt, but rather of edifica-tion." "Mistress," answered Parlamente, "I pray you believe that nothing is more foolish nor more easy to deceive than a woman who has never loved. For in itself love is a passion that takes hold on the heart before one is ware of it; and 'tis such a pleasant thing that if it can borrow the cloak of virtue hardly can it be discovered before some harm come of it." "What harm can come," said Oisille, "of loving a good, honest gentleman?" "Mistress," replied Parlamente, "many a man is esteemed good, but to be good with respect to ladies, to have a care for their honour and conscience—I am well assured that up to this time no such man hath ever been found. And those women who put their trust in men, and believe otherwise, will find themselves at last to have been deceived; and, entering on this manner of friendship with God beside them, will go out of it with the devil for their fellow. For I have seen many women begin under pretext of speaking about God, and when at last they wish to make an end they cannot, for that the cloak is so honourable a one. Now a vicious love fails by reason of its own imperfection, and cannot long endure in a chaste heart, but what they call a virtuous one hath such dainty silken chains, that we are taken before we see them." "So then," said Ennasuitte, "you would have a woman take no man for her lover? But your law is so harsh that it cannot be long kept." "I know it well," answered Parlamente, "but for all that I cannot but desire that every wife would be content with her husband, as I am with mine." Ennasuitte, who felt herself pricked by this, changed colour, and said: "You ought to think the hearts of other wives no worse than your own; or are you of opinion than you are more perfect than all others?" "Well," said Parlamente, "lest we dispute together, I would fain know to whom Hircan will give the vote." "I give it," said he, "to Ennasuitte, so that she may cry quits with my wife." "If, then, it has come to my turn," said she, "I will spare nor man nor woman, and in this manner treat all alike, and you shall see that it will be a hard thing for you to confess the virtue and goodness of men. So I shall answer the last story by one like unto it."

NOVEL XXXVI.

How the president of Grenoble came to make his wife a salad.

There lived in the town of Grenoble a president, whose name I will not tell you; I say only that he was no Frenchman. He had a mighty pretty wife with whom he lived in great love and contentment. But she, finding her husband grow old, took for her lover a young clerk named Nicolas; and when he would go in the morning to the Justice Hall, the aforesaid Nicolas came into his room and took his place. And this was perceived by a servant of the president, the same having been in his household for thirty years, and from the loyalty he bore his master he could not refrain from advertising him of it. The president, for that he was a wise man, would not lightly believe this thing, telling the man he was desirous of putting contention between him and his wife, and that if the truth were as he said, he could easily show it to be so, but if he did not evidently prove it, he should be esteemed as one who had contrived a lying tale to put enmity betwixt him and his wife. The man assured him that he should see it to be true with his own eyes; and one morning as soon as the president was gone to court, and Nicolas was in the room, this servant sent one of his fellows to tell his master to come quickly, while he himself kept watch upon the door lest Nicolas should sally out. And as soon as the president saw one of his servants making signs at him, feigning sickness, he left the bench and came hastily to his house, where he found his old follower at the door of the room, who strongly affirmed to him that Nicolas was within, having scarce entered. And his lord said to him: "Stir not from this door, for you know well that there is none other incoming or outgoing to the room, save only a small closet, and I alone have the key of it." Then he entered the room and found his wife and Nicolas in bed together, of whom the clerk in his shirt, throwing himself on his knees before him, asked forgiveness, and his wife on the other hand fell to weep-

ing.   Then said the president: "Though the deed you have
done is such as you yourself can judge it to be, yet I am not
willing that on your account my house be dishonoured and the
daughters I have had of you brought to shame.   Wherefore I
charge you weep no more, and hear what I shall do; and do
you, Nicolas, hide yourself in my closet and make no sound."
When it was thus done he opened the door and calling his old
serving-man, said to him: "Didst thou not assure me that thou
wouldst show me Nicolas and my wife together, and on thy
word I am come hither in danger of putting this poor wife of
mine to death, and have found nothing of what thou didst tell
me?   I have searched through this room as I will make plain
to thee," and so saying he made the man look under the beds
and in every quarter.   And when he found nothing, all astonished
he said to his master: "Needs must be that the devil has
carried him away, for I saw him come in, and though he went
not out at the door, I am persuaded he is not here."   Then
said his lord to him: "Thou art a very wicked servant who
wouldst fain put enmity between me and my wife; wherefore
I bid thee begone, and for all that thou hast done for me, I pay
thee what I owe thee, and more also, but go quickly, and beware
that I see thee not in the town after this day."   And the president gave him payment for five or six years in advance, and
knowing that he had been a faithful servant, hoped to advantage him in more.   But when the man had gone out weeping,
the president made Nicolas come forth from the closet, and
having opened his mind to him and his wife on the wickedness
they had wrought together, he forbade them to let any know of
it.   To his wife he gave command to array herself more bravely
than she had been accustomed, and to go frequently to assemblies, dances, and entertainments.   And he would have Nicolas
live more merrily than he had afore, but that as soon as he
should whisper in his ear, *Begone!* he should beware of being
found in the town three hours after.   And thereupon he
returned to the Justice Hall and made no sign, but for two
weeks and a day, against his custom, set himself to make feast
for his neighbours and acquaintance.   And after the feast he
would have music for the ladies to dance thereto.   And on the
fifteenth day, seeing that his wife danced not at all he commanded Nicolas to lead her out, which he, thinking his past

sins to have been forgotten, did most joyously. But when the
dance was finished, the president, making pretence of giving
him some charge as to his household concernments, whispered
in his ear : "Begone, and return no more !" So went Nicolas,
sorry enough to lose his mistress, but yet most glad to have
saved himself alive. And when the president had set firmly in
the heads of his kinsfolk and his acquaintance, and all the
country side, the great love he bore his wife, one fine May-
day he went into his garden and gathered herbs and made a
salad therefrom. And such herbs were they that his wife did
not live more than twenty-four hours after the eating of them ;
whereat he made such an appearance of grief that none suspected him to have been the occasion of her death ; so he
avenged him on his enemy and preserved the honour of his
house.

"I do not wish, ladies, to praise the president, but only to
show you the folly of a woman and the great prudence and
patience of a man, and I entreat you be not angry at the truth
which may sometimes go against us as well as men. For to
men and women virtue and vice are common." "If all the
women who love their servants," said Parlamente, "were constrained to eat of such salads, I do not suppose they would
take such delight in their gardens, but rather would pluck out
certain herbs to avoid that which preserves the honour of the
line at the expense of the wanton mother's life." Hircan, who
guessed for whom this was spoken, said in wrath : "A good
woman should by no means suspect that in another she would
not do herself." Parlamente replied : "Knowledge is not
foolish suspicion ; and this poor woman suffered the penalty
many an other deserves. And I think her husband, though he
desired vengeance, governed himself with an admirable prudence
and wisdom." "And likewise with a great hatred and a cruel
vengeance," said Longarine, "that well showed him not to
have his God or his conscience before his eyes." "What
would you have him do then," said Hircan, "to be avenged
for the greatest wrong a wife can work her husband?" "I
would have him," said she, "kill her in his wrath, for the
divines say such sin is pardonable, since the first motions of a
man are not in his power, and on this account forgiveness may
be granted him." "Ay," said Geburon, "but his daughters

and his line would always have borne the stain of it." "He should not have slain her at all," said Longarine, "for since his hot anger was overpast she would have lived with him as an honest wife, and there would have been no talk about it." "Think you," said Saffredent, "that his anger was appeased because he concealed it? As for me I think that on that last day when he gathered herbs for the salad, he was as wrathful as on the first; for there are men whose passions rest not till they have put them into action, and I am mightily pleased that the school-authors esteem such sins pardonable, for such is my opinion." "One must take heed to one's words," said Parlamente, "before such dangerous folk as you, for I spoke of passion when it is so strong that it takes hold on all the senses, and reason can find no place." "So," said Saffredent, "I understand your words, and conclude from them that a man deeply in love can do no sin save a venial one, do he what he may; for I am persuaded that if love hold him fast bound, reason can get no hearing from his heart or from his understanding. And, to speak truth, there is not one amongst us but has been thus brainsick; and the sins done by one thus affected I deem not only to gain an easy pardon, but I believe also that God will not be wrath thereat, since love is a ladder to climb unto his perfect love, to which none shall attain who hath not trod the steps of this world's love. For St. John saith: 'How shall a man love God whom he hath not seen, if he love not his brother whom he hath seen.'" "There is no place of Scripture too good for you to twist to your own use," said Oisille. "But beware lest like the spider you turn wholesome meat into poison. And consider that it is a perilous thing to quote the Scripture nor advisedly nor of necessity." "Do you say," said Saffredent, "that to speak the truth is to speak nor advisedly nor of necessity? You would then also say that when in speaking to you incredulous women we call God to witness, we take his name in vain; but if these be sins, you alone ought to bear the punishment, for your unbelief makes us search out every oath our brains can conceive. And even then we cannot kindle the flame of love in your hearts of ice." "'Tis a sure proof," said Longarine, "that you are all liars, for if truth were in your words, so strong is it that it would make us to believe. But there is danger lest the daughters of Eve give ear too soon

unto the serpent." "I am persuaded, Parlamente," said Saffredent, "that the women are not to be overcome by us men,
wherefore I will be silent, and hear to whom Ennasuitte will
give her vote." "I give it," said she, "to Dagoucin, for I
think he will never speak against the ladies." "Would to
God," said he, "that I got from them as good as I give. But
to show you how I have set myself to honour virtuous gentlemen, by studying the deeds they have done well, I will tell
you of one. And I do not deny that the patience of the
gentleman of Pampeluna and of the president of Grenoble was
great, but so also was their vengeance. And when one praises
a man for that he is virtuous, one must not take account of one
virtue only, for it may be but a cloak to cover as great a vice;
but to do a virtuous deed, and this only from the love of virtue,
is praiseworthy. And the manner of this I desire to show you
by my relation of the patient virtue of a lady, who in all her
good deeds had no other end than God's honour, and her
husband's salvation."

NOVEL XXXVII.

How a good and prudent wife saved her husband from the love of a nasty serving-maid.

There was once a lady of the house of Loué, so prudent
and virtuous that she was loved and esteemed of all her neighbours. Her husband trusted her, as he ought, in all his affairs,
and so wisely did she direct them, that his house, by her means,
grew to be one of the richest and best furnished of any in all
Anjou and Touraine. In this manner she lived a long while
with her husband, and bore him several fine children, till her
happiness, which is always followed by its opposite, began to
diminish, for that her husband, finding honest rest hard to be
borne, set himself to look for travail and weariness. And his
manner was, as soon as his wife slept to rise from beside her
and not to return until it was near morning. Now the lady of
Loué took this custom of his in very bad part, and fell into a
great melancholy, which, though she was fain to conceal it,
made her to forget the affairs of the house, her person, and her
family, as one who deemed herself to have lost the fruit of her
toils, I would say her husband's love, to gain which there was

no pain she would not have willingly endured. But having, as
she thought, lost this, she became so neglectful of all other
household matters, that the loss of her soon made itself evident;
since her husband, on the one hand, spending his substance at
random, and she no longer having a hand in the management,
at last matters grew to such a pass that their timber began to
be felled and their estates to be mortgaged. So one of her
kinsfolk, who knew her ailment, made remonstrance with her
for her fault, and told her that if, for the love of her husband,
she would take no care to the advantage of his house, at the
least she should consider her poor children. And her pity for
them gave her back her wit, and she strove by all means to win
again her husband's love. And one night she played the spy
on him, and when he arose she did the like, and having had
her bed made, put on her dressing-gown, and while she awaited
his return read her Book of Hours. But when he came in she
went to him and kissed him, and brought him a bason of water for
him to wash his hands. He, astonished at this new thing, said he
came but from the privy, and needed not to wash himself; but
she replied that, though it was a small matter, yet it was a good
thing to wash one's hands when one came from so beastly and
dirty a place, desiring in this manner to make him to know
and abominate his wicked manner of living. But for all that
he mended not his way, and his wife continued to serve him
with water every night for a whole year. And when she saw
that it was of no avail, one night, waiting for her husband, who
stayed longer than he was wont, she became desirous of going
in search of him. And passing from room to room at last she
found him in a closet at the back of the house, in bed and
asleep with the ugliest and most beastly serving-maid they had.
Then, thinking in what manner she should reprove him for
leaving his good wife for such a filthy slut, she took some
straw and set it afire in the middle of the room, but when she
saw the smoke would kill her husband before it awoke him,
she took him by the arm, crying out " Fire! fire!" And if he
was grieved and ashamed to be found by so good a wife with
such a nasty strumpet, he had good occasion both for grief and
shame. Then she said to him: " Sir, I have tried for a whole
year, by gentleness and patience, to take this stumbling-block
out of your way, and to show you that making clean the out-

side you should cleanse also that is within ; but when I saw all my endeavour was of no avail, I called that element, which shall bring all things to an end, to my help ; and I assure you that, if this does not make you to amend, I am by no means certain whether a second time I will rescue you from the danger as I have now done." The husband, well pleased to have escaped so cheaply, promised that he would give her no longer any occasion to sorrow on account of him, and this she readily believed, and, with her husband's consent, drove away the strumpet who had done her so much hurt. And from this time they lived together in so great love, that even the faults that were overpast, by being compared with their present ease, served as matter to increase their contentment.

"I pray you, ladies, if God gives you such husbands, not to despair until you have for a long while tried all means to reform them, since in every day there are twenty-four hours, and in any one of these a man may change his mind; and a wife should deem herself more happy by patience and long-suffering to have won back such a husband than if luck and her kinsfolk had given her one more perfect." "Behold," said Oisille, "an example well worthy to be followed by all married women." "Who will, let her take pattern by it," said Parlamente, "but I, for my part, think it would not be possible to have so long a patience, which, though in all estates of life it be a brave virtue, yet I believe in marriage would cause at least enmity. For when suffering injury from one's fellow, it is necessary to separate oneself from him to one's utmost, and from this estrangement cometh a contempt for the fault of him, and in this contempt love, little by little, waxeth weak, for as we value a thing so do we love it." "But," said Ennasuitte, "the impatient wife would be in jeopardy of finding a furious husband, who would not give her patience in return but grief." "And what could such a husband do," said Parlamente, "worse than he did in the story that has been told to us?" "What?" said Ennasuitte ; "why, beat his wife, and make her lie in the servant's bed, and the servant in the bed of state." "I believe," answered Parlamente, "that an honest woman would not be so grieved at being beaten in anger as at being despised by one not her equal ; and after a woman's love for her husband has been taken from her, he can do nothing else for which she take any care. And so says the tale; that the trouble she took to regain him was for the love she bore her children, and this I can well believe." "Do you deem it great long-suffering in her," said Nomerfide, "to light a fire hard-by the bed where her husband slept?" "Ay," said Longarine, "for when she saw the smoke she aroused him, and this, perchance, was her only fault, for the cinders of such a husband would have been good for making lye." "You are cruel, Longarine," said Oisille; "surely you would not live so with your husband?" "No," answered she, "for, praised be God, he gave me occasion to lament him, and not to complain of him, for all my life." "But had he been of such kind," said Nomerfide, "what would you have done?" "So well loved I him," said Longarine, "that I believe I should have first killed him, and then myself, for to die after such vengeance would have been sweeter to me than to live faithfully with one who was faithless." "In my poor judgment," said Hircan, "you only love your husbands for your own sake. If they do according to your desire, you love them; but if on Saturday they make the least slip, they lose the toil of the whole week. So, I suppose, you would fain see the wife the master; and as for me, I would agree to this if all other husbands would do the like." "'Tis in reason," said Parlamente, "that the man should rule us as our head, but not that he should abandon or ill-treat us." "God has taken such order," said Oisille, "with husband and wife, that if it be not abused, I hold marriage to be the surest and best estate in the world; and so I am persuaded all of you here present believe, whatever face you may put upon it. And since the man calls himself the more prudent member, the fault, if it come from his side, will be more worthy of blame. But having brought the matter thus far, to whom will Dagoucin give his vote?" "I give it," said he, "to Longarine." "You do me great pleasure," said she, "for I have a tale worthy to follow yours, and since we are set on praising the virtuous patience of ladies, I will manifest to you a more notorious example thereof than the lady of Loué, and so much the more since she is a city dame, and in cities the upbringing is not accustomed to be so virtuous as elsewhere."

NOVEL XXXVIII.

How a woman returned good for evil, and so won back her husband.

There lived at Tours a good and pretty townswoman, who for her virtues was not only loved but feared and esteemed of her husband. But yet, following the custom of men who grow weary at the eating of the fine white bread, he became amorous of a certain farmer's wife, and often he would set out from Tours and go to the farm, where he would stay two or three days, and when he came back to Tours was so weary and ailing that his wife had enough to do to cure him. And so soon as he was whole he failed not to return to the place, and there amidst his pleasures forgot all his sickness. But his wife, who above all had a care for his health, seeing him constantly return in such bad case, went herself to the farm, where she found the young woman whom her husband loved. And not wrathfully but with a most gracious address she spoke to her, saying that she was advised that her husband came thither often to see her, but she was ill content that he was so evilly entertained of her, in such wise that he came home weary and with great loss of his radical heat and moisture. The poor farmer's wife, as much from reverence to her mistress as from the force of truth, did not deny the fact, but entreated pardon for it. And the lady would fain see the room and the bed in which her husband slept, and found them so chilly, dirty, and disorderly, that she took pity on him. So forthwith she made fetch a fine bed, appointed with blankets and curtains and quilt according to her husband's liking; then she made deck out the room with hangings and tapestries, gave the woman a brave cup and platter for his meat and drink, a pipe of good wine, sweetmeats and confections; and bade her no more send back her husband in such evil case. The husband waited no long while before he went, as was his custom, to see the farmer's wife, and marvelled greatly to find the poor lodging in such brave order, much more when she served him with drink in a silver cup; and at last asked her whence came all these good things. The woman said, weeping, that it was his wife, who had taken such compassion on his bad treatment at the farm, that she had furnished the house in this manner, and com-

mended his health to her.   He, seeing the great goodness of
his wife, who for all his evil had rendered him good, esteemed
his fault as great as her kindness ; and giving money to the
farmer's wife he counselled her to live henceforth as an honest
woman.   Then he returned to his wife and made confession of
all his sins, telling her that without her great gentleness and
goodness he would never have left his wicked manner of living:
And from that time he lived with her in peace and affection,
and an entire amendment of his former life.

" Trust me, ladies, there are few husbands whom the long-
suffering and love of their wives will not gain at the last ; for
though they be harder than rocks, yet these doth soft dropping
water in time make hollow."   Then said Parlamente : "She
was a woman without heart, or gall, or liver."   "She did
according to the commands of God," said Longarine, "namely,
returned good for evil.   What more would you have her do ?"
" I believe," said Hircan, "that she was in love with some
friar, who gave her the penance of having her husband well-
treated in the country, so that while he was away she might
have leisure to give the friar good treatment in the town."
"There," said Oisille, "you make manifest the evil in your
heart, passing a bad judgment on a good deed.   But I rather
believe her so to have mortified her carnal affections with the
love of God, that her care was but for her husband's soul."
" Methinks," said Simontault, "that he had more occasion to
return to his wife when he was badly entreated at the farm-
house than when it was so bravely decked out."   " By that, I
presume," said Saffredent, "that you are not of the same
humour as a certain rich man of Paris who, while he lay with
his wife, could not put off any of his dress but that he took
a rheum.   But when he went to see his serving-maid in the
cellar, he would go in the depth of winter without cap or slippers, and would take no hurt ; and his wife was as pretty as
the wench was ugly."   "Have you not heard," said Geburon,
" that God always has a care for fools, lovers, and drunken folk ;
perchance this rich man of Paris was all three together."
" Would you draw from that," said Parlamente, "that God
has no care for the prudent, the pure in heart, and the sober ?
They that can help themselves have no need of help.   For He
who said He came for the sick and not for the whole, came

through pity to succour our infirmities, arresting the severity of His condemnation. And he that believeth himself wise is foolish in the sight of God. But to bring an end to our sermon, to whom does Longarine give her vote?" "I give it," said she, "to Saffredent." "I hope then," said Saffredent, "to make plain by example that God shows no favour unto lovers. And although it has been said that vice is common to men and women, yet a crafty device shall be found more quickly and after a more subtile fashion by a woman than by a man. And this I tell you for an example of it."

NOVEL XXXIX.

In what manner my lord of Grignaulx exorcised an evil spirit.

A certain lord of Grignaulx, Esquire of the Body to Anne Duchess of Brittany and Queen of France, returning to his house, from which he had been absent more than two years, found his wife at another demesne hard-by. And when he would know the reason of this, she told him there was a ghost in their house that tormented them so much that none could live in it. My lord de Grignaulx, who put no belief in such fantasies, told her that he feared it not, were it the very devil, and so brought his wife to the house. And at night-time he made light many candles to see the ghost more clearly, and after watching a long while to no purpose, fell asleep. But on a sudden he was wakened by a mighty buffet on the cheek, and he heard a voice crying aloud: *Brenigue, Brenigue,* and this was the name of his grandmother. Then he called his wife who lay beside him to light a candle, the which were all put out, but she durst not rise from the bed. Straightway he felt the quilt pulled from off him, and heard a great noise of tables, trestles, and stools falling all about the room; and it ceased not all through the night. And he was more troubled in that he had lost his rest than for fear of the ghost, for he by no means believed it to have been such, and the next night he determined to take Master Goblin a prisoner. So a little after he was come to bed he made a great pretence of snoring loudly, and put his hand open near his face. And while he waited he knew that something was approaching him, and so snored all the more.   At this the ghost, taking heart, gave him a mighty buffet, whereupon my lord de Grignaulx took his hand from his face and seized it, crying to his wife : " I have the ghost." And she rose and lighted a candle, and they found it was the maid that slept in their room, who falling on her knees entreated forgiveness, and promised to tell the truth.   And this was that she had for a long while loved a serving-man of the house, and so had undertaken this brave mystery, thereby to drive from the house the master and mistress, so that they, who would have had all the care of it, should have means of entertaining one another, which indeed when they were all alone they by no means failed to do.   My lord de Grignaulx, who was a somewhat surly man, commanded that they should be beaten in such sort that they would never forget the ghost, and this having been done, they were driven away.   And thus was the house freed from the ghostly torments that had plagued it throughout two whole years.

" 'Tis a wondrous thing, ladies, to think what this mighty god of love can do.   From women it takes away all fear, and makes them to torment men so that they may gain their desire. But in like measure, as the serving-maid is to be blamed, so is the master to be praised for his good sense, that knew the spirit returneth not from the place whither it has gone." " Of a truth," said Geburon, " Love showed small favour to the maid and the man, and I confess their master's good sense stood him in good stead."   " Yet," said Ennasuitte, " the wench, by reason of her craftiness, lived a long while at her ease." " 'Tis a pitiful kind of ease," said Oisille, " bottomed upon sin, and ending in punishment and shame."   " That is true," answered Ennasuitte, " but many folk have sorrow and suffering while they live righteously, not having the wit all their days to take their portion of pleasure as did these two."   " Yet I am steadfast in my opinion," said Oisille, " that no pleasure can be perfect, save the conscience is at rest."   " Are you advised of this ?" said Simontault ; " the Italian author would maintain that the greater the sin the greater the pleasure." " Of a truth," said Oisille, " he that said so is himself the very devil. Wherefore enough of him, and let us know to whom Saffredent will give his vote."   " To whom ?" said he.   " None but Parlamente remains, but if there were a hundred I would still give

my vote to her, since thereby we shall learn something."
"Since, then, I am to bring the day to an end," said Parlamente, "and since I promised yesterday to tell you for what
reason the father of Rolandine made build the castle where he
kept her so long captive, I will even do so."

NOVEL XL.

Wherein is given the cause wherefore Rolandine s father made build the castle in the forest.

The father of Rolandine, who was entitled the Count of
Jossebelin, had several sisters, of whom some were married to
exceeding rich men, and the rest were nuns, save one who lived in
his house unmarried, though beyond compare she was prettier
than all the others. And so well was she beloved of her brother
that he preferred before her nor wife nor children. And she
was asked in marriage by many of good estate; but her brother,
for fear of the separation, and loving too well his money, would
not listen to them. So she passed some time without being
wed, living virtuously in her brother's house. Now there lived
there also a young and comely gentleman, who having been
brought up by the Count from his childhood, so grew in comely
stature and virtuousness of living, that he bore a peaceful rule
over his master, in such sort that when he had any charges for
his sister, it was ever the young gentleman that gave them.
And with such familiarity did the Count use him that evening
and morning would he send him to his sister, so that by this
frequent converse together a great love was engendered
between them. But since he feared for his life if he should
haply offend his master, and she had no less fear for her honour,
they had in this love of theirs none other contentment save
words only. And the lord of Jossebelin would often say to
his sister that he wished the gentleman was richer, and of as
good a house as she, for he knew no man he would have liked
better for his brother-in-law. So many times did he say this,
that the lovers, having taken counsel together, judged that if
they were to wed he would readily pardon them. And Love,
that easily believes what it wishes, made them to suppose that
nothing but good could come of it; and so on this hope their

marriage was solemnised and consummated, and none knew thereof but a priest and certain women.

And after that they had lived for some years in the delight that a married pair can have together, as one of the bravest in all Christendom, and bound by the greatest and most perfect love, Fortune, that hated to see two persons so much at their ease, stirred up an enemy against them, who spying out the lady, perceived her great happiness in her husband, but yet knew not that they were married. And this man came to the lord of Jossebelin, saying that the gentleman in whom he had so great trust went too much into his sister's room, and at hours in the night when it was not meet for men to enter therein. And this the Count at the first would not believe, for the trust he had in his sister and the gentleman; but the enemy, as one who loved the honour of his house, so many times repeated it, that at last a watch was put, and so shrewd a one that the poor folk, suspecting nothing, were surprised. For one evening the lord of Jossebelin was advertised that the gentleman was in his sister's room, and presently going thither he found them, blinded by their love, in bed together. Wrath took away speech, and drawing his sword he ran at the gentleman. But he, being agile in body, fled from him in his shirt, and not able to escape by the door let himself down by a window into the garden. The poor lady threw herself on her knees before her brother, and said to him: "O sir, save my husband's life, for indeed I have wed him, and if there be any fault punish me alone, for he married me at my desire." Her brother, beside himself with wrath, only replied to her: "If he be a hundred times your husband, yet will I punish him as a wicked servant who hath deceived me." So saying he set himself at the window and cried with a loud voice to kill him, and so it was done straightway by his command and before the eyes of him and his sister. But she, beholding this piteous sight, and knowing that prayers were of no avail, spoke to her brother as a mad woman, saying: "Brother, I have nor father nor mother, and am come to an age at which I can marry according to my pleasure, and so chose one whom oftentimes you have said you were fain had been my husband. And for that I did by your counsel a thing I could by the law have done without your consent, you have made kill the man for whom you had a great liking. And since no prayers of mine could prevent his death, I entreat you by all your love towards me to make me in this hour a fellow with him in death, as I have been in all his other chances. And so you will both satisfy your cruel and unjust anger, and give rest to the body and soul of her who nor can nor will live without him." Her brother, though he was in such a rage as almost took away his reason, yet had such pity on his sister that, without granting or refusing her prayer, he left her. And after that he had well considered the deed he had done, and understood that the gentleman had married his sister, he would have been heartily glad not to have committed such a crime. But for the fear he had lest his sister should demand vengeance and justice on him, he made build for her a castle in the midst of a forest, whither he placed her, and forbade any to speak with her.

And after some time, to satisfy his conscience, he essayed to win her back to him, and made some talk about marriage; but she sent word to him that he had given her so ill a breakfast that she wished not to sup off the same meat, and that she had a good hope to live in such wise that he would have no second husband of hers to put to death, and that she hardly thought he would forgive another, since he had used so evilly the man for whom he had such a liking. And though she was weak, and had not the power to avenge herself on him, yet she trusted in Him who is the true judge and suffers no evil deed to go unpunished. And with His love alone she intended to pass the remainder of her days in her retreat. This she did, and stirred not from the place till her death, living in such patience and austerity that men came from all parts to her sepulchre as to that of a saint. And from the time she died her brother's house came to such a ruinous condition that of six sons he had not one that was left alive, for they all perished miserably; and at last the heritage passed, as you have heard in another tale, to his daughter Rolandine, who was kept in the prison that was made for her aunt.

" I pray God, ladies, that this ensample be so profitable to you that none amongst you shall have any desire to be married for her own pleasure without the consent of them to whom obedience is due; for matrimony is so long-lasting an estate that one ought not lightly to enter upon it, nor without the advice of our best friends and kinsfolk. And do as well as you may, there will be no less pain in it than pleasure." "In good faith," said Oisille, "were there no God nor law to teach maids to be prudent, this example would suffice to make them take more heed to their kin and not marry at their own pleasure." "Yet," said Nomerfide, "she who has one good day in the year is not unhappy all her life. She had the pleasure of seeing and speaking for a long while with him whom she loved better than herself, nay more, she enjoyed him as her husband without scruple or stain on her conscience. So great do I esteem this contentment that I believe it surpassed all the sorrow that she bore." "You will have it, then," said Saffredent, "that women have more pleasure to lie with a man than pain to see him killed before their eyes?" "Not so," answered Nomerfide, "for then I should speak against the experience I have had of women; but I mean that an unwonted pleasure, such as to marry the man we love best of all, should be greater than the pain of losing him by death, for death is a thing common enough." "Ay," said Geburon, "natural death; but this was over cruel. And it seems to me a strange matter, for he was neither her father nor her husband, but only her brother, and she was of an age lawfully to marry whom she would. How then durst he do this cruel deed?" "I find it no strange matter," said Hircan, "for his sister, whom he loved and who was beyond his power, he did not kill, but only the gentleman whom he had brought up as his son and loved as his brother, and after having given him honour and wealth in his service, he took his sister in marriage, the which by no means did appertain to him." "Likewise," said Nomerfide, "'twas no common nor wonted pleasure for a lady of a noble house to marry one of her gentleman servants for love. If the death was strange, so also was the delight, since it had against it the opinion of all wise men, and for it the contentment of a heart full of love, and a restful soul, since God was by no means offended at it. And as to the death which you call cruel, methinks, since we must all die, the shortest death is the sweetest, for we know that it is a way we all must go. And I deem happy them that stay no long while before the gates thereof, and who from that we call *happiness* in this world, fly without delay to the true happiness that endureth for ever." "What call you the gates of death?" said

Simontault. "They that are troubled in spirit," answered Nomerfide; "they that are for a long while sick, and from the extremity of suffering in mind and body, find death come too slowly; these, I say, tarry at the gates of death and shall tell you the resting-places, where is less rest than lamentation. This lady must have lost her husband by death, but, through the wrath of her brother, she was saved from seeing him a long time sick or weary of life. And she, converting the joy she had with him to the service of our Lord, could well count herself happy." "Is this nothing," said Longarine, "that she was shamefully imprisoned?" "I suppose," said Nomerfide, "that one who loves with a perfect love and in obedience to God's commandment knows not shame nor dishonour, save when it lessens or diminishes the perfection of her love. For the glory of true love knows no shame; and as to the imprisoning of her body, I believe that since her heart was at large, joined to God and her husband, she made no account of it; but thought her loneliness great freedom. For inasmuch as she saw not what she loved she could have nought better than to think upon these without ceasing, and stone walls are not too narrow, when thought can pass through them at its pleasure." "The words of Nomerfide are true altogether," said Simontault, "but he who did this thing in his madness would well be called unhappy, insomuch as he offended God, love, and honour." "In good faith," said Geburon, "I marvel that the love of woman is so various a thing, and plainly see that the more virtuousness the more love, but those who have less love, wishing to appear virtuous, simulate it." "It is true," said Parlamente, "that a heart, honouring God and man, loves more than one that is vicious, and fears not to be seen to the very bottom." "I have ever heard," said Simontault, "that men are not to be reproved for seeking the love of women, since God hath put into their hearts the love and boldness to ask; and in the hearts of women He hath put the fear and the chastity to refuse. So if a man use the powers given him and be punished, a wrong hath been done him." "But this was a hard matter," said Longarine, "that he had a long time praised him to his sister. Methinks his brainsick cruelty is like unto a man that kept a fountain, and praised the beauty of the water to one who while he looked on it fainted with thirst. But when the thirsty

soul would fain have tasted the water, the keeper killed him."
"Truly," said Parlamente, "by the sweetness of his words he
kindled a flame that he should by no means have put out with
the sword." "I marvel," said Simontault, "that it was taken
ill for a simple gentleman, using no force or pretence, to take
to wife a woman of a noble house, since the philosophers consider the least of men to be more worth than the mightiest
and most virtuous woman in the world." "To the intent that
the Commonwealth should be ordered peacefully," said Dagoucin; "for this reason, they take account alone of the rank of
the families, the age of the parties, and the ordinances of the
laws, without weighing the love or the virtue of men, and all
this lest things be turned upside down. Whence it comes that
in marriages made between equals, according to the judgment
of kinsfolk and all men, m n and wife are often so diverse in
heart, complexion, and disposition, that in place of entering upon
an estate leading to salvation, they journey to the by-ways that
are about Hell." "Also," said Geburon, "it has come to
pass that they who married for love, without regard to rank or
lineage, having like hearts, complexions, and dispositions, have
nevertheless repented then of their folly. For a great love
that knows no reason turns often to brainsick jealousy." "It
seems to me," said Parlamente, "that neither the one way nor
the other is praiseworthy; but that folk should submit themselves to the will of God without regard to rank, or riches, or
pleasure; but loving with a virtuous love, and with the goodwill of their kinsfolk, they should desire to live in the estate of
marriage as God and nature have ordained. And though in
this life there be no estate but has its tribulation, yet have I
seen these last spend their days without regret; and we married
folk here present are not so unhappy that some of us are not
in this number." Forthwith Hircan, Geburon, Simontault, and
Saffredent swore that they had married after this sort, and had
never repented thereof; and whatsoever of truth there was in
it, their wives were so content thereat, that thinking they could
hear nothing more to their taste, they went to the church to
give thanks to God on that account, and found there the monks
ready to sing evensong. Service ended, they went to supper,
not without much talk of their marriages, the which lasted all
the evening, as they told the changes and chances that befel

them while they courted their wives. But though these stories were no less pleasant than those in the meadow, they cannot be set down at length, insomuch as one would break into the speech of another. So great delight did they take therein that bedtime came before they were ware of it. Mistress Oisille made the company separate, and so joyously did they go to bed, that I believe the married folk slept no longer than the rest, telling again of their loves that were overpast, and giving evident proof to one another of their present affection. And in such pleasant sort was passed the night, even until the morning.

DAY THE FIFTH.

On the Fifth Day relation is made of the virtuousness of such maids and wives of whom honour hath been preferred before pleasure; of them likewise who have done the contrary thereto; and of the simpleness of certain others.

PROLOGUE.

When the morning was come Oisille had made ready for them a spiritual breakfast of such good savour, that it was sufficient both for body and soul; and at the hearing of it the whole company was mighty attentive, and it seemed to them that they had never heard a sermon to such profit before. And when they heard the last bell ring for mass, they went into the church to meditate on the godly discourse they had heard. After mass was heard, and they had sauntered about for a while, they set themselves at table, promising one another that the present day should be as brave as any that went before. And Saffredent said that he would the bridge was another month a-building, for the delight he had in their entertainment; but my lord abbot made the workmen use great diligence, since it was by no means to his pleasure to live among so many honest folk into whose presence he could not bring his accustomed female pilgrims. And when they had rested some while after dinner they returned to the meadow, where, each having taken his seat, they asked Parlamente to whom she would give her vote. "Methinks," said she, "Saffredent would do well to begin the day, for by his face I judge him to have no desire to make us weep." "Then," said he, "you will be

very cruel if you do not weep for pity of a friar, whose story I
am minded to tell you.   And you may think from the tales
that some of us have told about the friars, that they entreat
poor ladies in this fashion, because the easiness of the matter
takes away all fear.   But to the end that you may know that
it is their brainsick concupiscence that carries from them all
fear and prudence, I will tell you of a case that fell out in
Flanders."

NOVEL XLI.

A new and very pleasant penance imposed on a maid by a Grey Friar.

When Margaret of Austria came to Cambray to treat on
behalf of the Emperor her nephew with the Most Christian
King, he on his part sent his mother Louise of Savoy, and with
her was Margaret Countess of Aiquemont, who bore the fame
of being the comeliest of all the ladies of Flanders.   And when
this great gathering was dispersed, the Countess of Aiquemont
returned to her house; and Advent being come, she sent to a
monastery of Grey Friars asking for a skilled preacher and a good
man, not only that he might preach, but also confess her and
her whole house.   So the warden sought out the most worthy
he could find for this office, since the brethren had received
much benefit both from the house of Aiquemont and that of
Fiennes, to which the Countess belonged.   So the Grey Friars,
who more than the other orders desire the good esteem and
liking of great houses, sent the best preacher in the monastery,
and throughout Advent he did his duty well, and the Countess
was satisfied with him.   And on Christmas Night the
Countess, intending to receive the Holy Sacrament, made the
confessor come to her, and having confessed in a chapel well
shut up, so that it might be more secretly performed, she gave
place to her Maid of Honour, who having confessed, sent for
her daughter, that she too might pass through the hands of the
good priest.   And after the girl had opened all her mind to him,
he knew somewhat of her secrets that gave him the desire and
the courage to lay on her an unwonted penance.   For he said to
her: "My daughter, your sins are so grievous that I give you
as penance my cord, to wear it on your naked flesh."   She, not
willing to disobey him, answered: "Give it me, father, and

I will not fail to wear it." "My daughter," said he, " it will avail nothing put on by your hands; but these hands of mine, that shall give you absolution, must first have girded the cord round you: then shall you be absolved of all your sins." The girl, weeping, said she would not suffer it. "What," said the ghostly man, " are you a heretick, that you refuse the penance that God and our Holy Mother the Church have enjoined?" "I use confession as the Church commands," replied she, " and am fain to have absolution and do penance, but I will not have you put your hands on my naked flesh, and I refuse this your penance." "Then," said the confessor, " I will give you no absolution." The girl got up from beside him with a troubled conscience, for she was so young that she feared she had not done well in refusing in such sort her ghostly father; and when mass was sung and the Countess of Aiquemont had received the *Corpus Domini*, her Maid of Honour, wishing to go after her, asked her daughter if she were ready. The girl, weeping, said she had not confessed. "What then have you done all the while with the preacher?" said her mother. "Nothing," she answered, " for since I refused the penance he gave me he refused his absolution." The mother made prudent inquiry, and discovered the strange penance the holy father had given her daughter, and so having caused her to confess to another priest they received together the Body of Our Lord. But when the Countess was returned from the church the Maid of Honour made complaint to her of the preacher, at which she was as astonished as wrathful, seeing that she had had a good opinion of him. But for all her wrath she laughed most heartily at this new kind of penance, yet this did not hinder her from having the friar taken and shrewdly striped in the kitchen, where at the point of the rod he confessed his fault. And afterwards the Countess sent him back bound hand and foot to the warden, praying him another time that he would intrust the preaching to a better man.

"Consider, ladies, if they are not afraid to show their wickedness in so honourable a house, what they must do in the poor cottages where they are accustomed to go their rounds, and where opportunities are so readily given them that it is a miracle when they escape without scandal. And this makes me pray you to convert your poor esteem of the friars into compassion for the women, for the devil that blinds the one will by no means spare the other if he find them fit for his purpose." "Truly," said Oisille, "this was a very wicked friar; monk, priest, and preacher, and yet to work such ungodliness on Christmas Day, in a church, and under the cloak of confession, all the which are circumstances that aggravate his sin." "Did you think, then," said Hircan, "that the friars were angels, or better than other men? You have heard so many examples that you should rather think them worse; and methinks the man had many excuses, that he was alone, at night time, shut up with a pretty maid." "Ay," said Oisille, "but it was Christmas Night." "That does but better his excuse," said Simontault, "for taking Joseph's place with a pretty virgin, he was fain to try make a child, to play the Mystery of the Nativity to the life." "Truly," said Parlamente, "if Joseph and the Virgin Mary had been in his mind, he had not had so wicked a desire. But it was an arrant knave and a daring to undertake such an enterprise with such poor hopes of success." "The Countess, methinks," said Oisille, "punished him so well that his fellows would take warning by him." "But it may be questioned," said Nomerfide, "whether she did well in this manner to put her neighbour to open shame, and whether she had not done better to have gently remonstrated with him on his sin than thus to have blazed it abroad." "Ay," said Geburon, "that would have been the better way, for we are commanded to reprove our neighbour secretly before we tell his sin to any man or proclaim it in the congregation. And after a man has been put to open shame, he will never mend his doings; for the fear of this shame keeps as many from sin as conscience." "I think," said Parlamente, "that this counsel of the Gospel should be used towards all men, save them that preach the word and do it not; for one need not fear of shaming them that are a shame to the whole world. And I esteem it a good deed to make them appear such as they really are, so that we take not glass for a fine ruby. But to whom will Saffredent give his vote?" "Since you ask, I will give it you," said Saffredent, "to whom no man of understanding would refuse it." "If you will have it so," said she, "I will tell you of a case to which I myself can bear witness. And I have always heard that virtuousness

abiding in a weak and feeble vessel, but assailed by mighty and all
powerful vice, is much to be praised, and to be held at its best:
for if the strong withstands the strong, 'tis no great matter for
admiration; but when the weak fights with the strong and
prevails, 'tis a very glorious and notable affair.   And since I
know the folk of whom I am fain to tell you, methinks I should
do a wrong to that virtuousness I have seen going in such poor
raiment that no account was made of it, if I did not speak of
her who did such honourable deeds.   Wherefore I will make
you the relation."

NOVEL XLII.

How the virtuousness of a maid endured against all manner of temptation.

In one of the fairest towns in Touraine there lived a lord
of an illustrious house who had been brought up there from
his earliest youth.   Of his perfections, graces, comeliness, and
great virtues, I say nothing; but know that in his time he had
no match.   Being at the age of fifteen years, he took more
pleasure in hunting than looking at the ladies; but one day
while he was in church he saw a young girl, the same having
been when she was a child brought up in the castle where he
lived.   And after the death of her mother, her father married
again, wherefore she went to Poitou with her brother.   And
she, whose name was Frances, had a bastard sister, whom her
father loved greatly, and married to the prince's chief butler,
and he kept her in as good estate as any of the family.   And
when her father died he left Frances as her heritage the lands
he had near the said town, on which account she came to live
hard by her demesne.   But for that she had yet to marry, and
was under sixteen years, she was unwilling to live alone in her
house, and so went to lodge with her sister, the butler's wife.
And the young prince seeing this girl that for a light brunette
she was pretty, and of a grace that passed her condition of life,
for she more resembled a gentlewoman or great lady than a
townswoman, looked for a long while at her, and never before
having been in love, felt an unwonted pleasure in his heart.
And when he was returned to his castle, he made inquiry
about the girl he had seen at church, and remembered that in
her youth she came to play at dolls with his sister, whom he

reminded of her. And his sister sent for her and entreated her kindly, praying her to come often to the castle, which she did when there was a marriage feast or great assembly, and with such goodwill did the young prince behold her, that he knew he was deep in love. And perceiving her poor and mean estate, he hoped easily to gain his desire, but having no means of speaking with her, he sent a gentleman of the bed-chamber to her to do his business for him. And she who was a good woman, fearing God, told the gentleman that she did not believe his master, so brave and good a prince, would divert himself by looking upon so poor a thing as herself, since in his castle there were fair ladies enow without seeking for them in the town, and she professed not to doubt that he had spoken of his own authority without his master's commandments. And when the young prince heard this reply, love that strives the more where it is strongly opposed, set him more hotly on this enterprise than before, so he wrote a letter praying Frances to believe entirely what the gentleman had said to her. She, knowing well how to read and write, read his letter through, but let the gentleman entreat her as he would, made never any reply to it, saying that it pertained not to one of such low degree to write to such a prince, and asked him not to think her so foolish as to believe his master had such love for her. And she said that if he hoped, by reason of her poor estate, to have her for his pleasure, he deceived himself, for she had a heart no less honourable than the greatest princess in Christendom, and esteemed all the treasures of the world as nothing compared with her honour and her conscience, entreating him not to hinder her in the keeping of them safe, since she would rather die than change her mind. This answer the young prince found by no means to his taste, natheless he still loved her, and failed not to place his seat by hers at the church where she went to hear mass, and during the service fixed his eyes on her alone. And when she perceived this she changed her place and went into another chapel, not to fly the sight of him, for she had not been a reasonable creature if she loathed to look at him, but because she feared his seeing her, and did not esteem herself worthy of being loved honourably and for marriage, and would not, on the other hand, be loved wantonly for his pleasure. And when she saw that, in whatsoever part

s

of the church she sat herself, the prince made sing mass at an altar hard by, she would no longer go to this church, but went always to one as far off as she was able.   And when there was feasting at the castle, she would no more go there, though the prince's sister often sent for her, but she excused herself for that she was sick.   The prince, seeing that he was not able to speak with her, took counsel with his butler, and assured him of great gain if he would help him in this matter, which the butler promised willingly as much to do his master a pleasure as for the hope of a reward.   And, day by day, he told the prince what she said and did, but that above all she fled every occasion of seeing him.   So the great desire he had of speaking with her at his ease made him light upon another device.   That was, that one day he took his great horses, of which he began well to understand the management, into the town square in front of his butler's house, where lived Frances.   And after making his paces and leaps where she could easily see them, he let himself fall from his horse into the mud, and so softly that he did himself no hurt, but yet made enough complaint, and asked if there were no house where he might change his raiment.   Each one offered his house, but a certain man said that the nearest and the best was his own butler's, which was forthwith chosen.   He found the room bravely decked out with tapestry, and there stripped himself to his shirt, for all his clothes were fouled with the mud, and so lay down in a bed. And when he saw that all his people, save the gentleman of the bedchamber, were gone to get him fresh clothes, he called his host and hostess, and asked them where was Frances.   And they had enough to do to find her, for so soon as she saw the young prince come into the house she went and hid herself in the most secret place that was in it.   Natheless, her sister found her, and bade her fear not to parley with so good and virtuous a prince.   "What, sister," said Frances, "do you, whom I hold as my mother, wish me to go speak with a young lord, of whose intent toward me I am, as you know, by no means ignorant?"   But her sister made so many remonstrances with her, and promised so often not to leave her alone with him, that she went with her, with so pale and sad a face, that she was more fit to move compassion than concupiscence.   And when the young prince saw her near his bed, he took her by her cold

and trembling hand and said: "Do you think me to be so
villanous a man, Frances, and so cruel a fantastic, that I eat
the women I look upon? You know that in whatsoever place
it was possible I have sought out to see and speak to you, and
have had therein but poor success. And to do me a greater
wrong you have fled the churches where I was wont to see you
at mass, to the end that I might have no more delight from
sight than from speech. But all that you have done hath
availed you nothing, for I ceased not till I came here in
the manner you saw, and have risked my neck, in tumbling of
my own will off my horse, so as to have the delight of speaking
to you at my ease. Wherefore, prithee, Frances, since with
so great toil I have won this opportunity, let it not be for
nought, but by the greatness of my love let me win yours."
And when for a long while he had awaited her reply, and saw
that her eyes were full of tears and fixed on the ground, he
drew her as near to him as he could and would have thrown
his arms about her and kissed her; but she said to him: "No,
my lord, that which you seek for you can never have, for though
compared with you I am but a poor worm, yet so dear do I
hold my honour that I would rather die than see it diminished
for any pleasure this world can give me. And the fear I have
of them who have seen you come here, lest they suspect the
truth, has made me thus to tremble and to be afraid. And
since it has been your pleasure to do me the honour of speaking
to me, you will pardon me if I speak also to you in the manner
my honour requires of me. I am not so foolish nor so blind,
my lord, that I do not see the beauties and the graces that God
hath given you, and her who shall possess the body and the
love of such a prince I deem the happiest in the world. But
what is all this to me? for not to me nor to my estate does it
pertain, and the very desire thereof would be the utmost folly.
And what reason can I give for your addressing yourself to
me, save that the ladies of your household (whom you love, if
beauty and grace be beloved of you) are so virtuous that you
dare not ask nor hope that of them which the smallness of my
condition makes you hope to have of me? And sure am I
that if from a woman like to myself you got that you asked, it
would serve as good matter of entertainment for two hours and
more with your mistress, to tell her the conquests you achieved

over one who is of the weakest.　Wherefore be pleased, since
God hath not made me a princess, to be your wife, nor of an
estate to be your mistress and sweetheart, not to put me in the
number of the poor unfortunates, since I think you are and
desire you may always be one of the happiest princes in all
Christendom.　And if you are fain to have women of my condition for your pastime, you will find enough in this very town,
beyond compare prettier than I, who will not give you the
trouble of so long a wooing.　Be content, then, with them that
will gladly sell their honour to you, and trouble no more her
that loves you better than herself.　For if God this day
required either your life or mine, I should hold myself happy
to offer up mine to save yours; since it is no want of love that
makes me fly your presence, but rather too great a love for
your conscience and mine, for I love my honour better than my
life.　I desire to remain, my lord, if it please you, in your good
grace, and all my life I will pray God for your health and
wealth; and true it is that the honour you have done me will
make me to be more esteemed among my own sort of people;
for what man of my own rank would I look upon after I have
talked with you?　So my heart shall be at large, save that it
shall always pray God for you, and no other service can you
have of me."　The young prince, hearing this honest answer,
was by no means pleased thereat, but yet was not able to
esteem her less good than she was.　He did all that was in his
power to make her believe he would never love any other
woman, but so wise was she that such an unreasonable thing
could have no place in her understanding.　And whilst they
were thus talking together, though it was often told him that
his clothes were come from the castle, in such delight and ease
was he that he bade answer he slept; even till it was supper-
time, at which he durst not fail his mother, who was one of the
most prudent and most severe dames in the world.　So the
young prince went his way, esteeming more than ever the
virtue of the maid.　And he often spoke concerning her to
the gentleman of his bedchamber, who, thinking gold would
avail more than love, counselled him to offer the maid a good
sum for doing him a kindness.　The young prince, whose
treasurer was his mother, had not much money for his privy
pleasures, and so borrowed, making up altogether five hundred

crowns, and sent them to the girl, praying her to change her mind. But when she saw the gift, she said to the gentleman: "I pray you tell my lord that I have a heart so virtuous that if by any means I could be compelled to obey his desires, the beauty and the grace that are in him would have ere this made a conquest of me; but since against my honour they are as nothing, all the gold in the world is much less. Wherefore take it back to him, for I prefer honest poverty to all the substance in the world." The gentleman, hearing this stiff reply, thought she might be won by severity, and threatened her with the authority and might of his master. But she, laughing a good deal, answered him : "Make a dreadful thing of him to the maids that know him not, for I am well assured that he is too good and virtuous for such discourse to come from him, and I am persuaded he will deny it altogether when you tell it him. But though he were the man you say, no death nor torment could move me, for, as I have told you, since love has not turned my heart, not all the ills nor all the goods you can give me can stir me one step from my position." The gentleman, who had promised that he would gain her, carried back these tidings in a wondrous rage, and would have his master pursue her in every possible manner, telling him it would be a blot on his honour to have failed in winning a woman of her estate. The young prince, not willing to use any dishonourable means, and fearing also lest the affair should be commonly reported, and so should come to his mother's ears, who would be very wrathful with him, durst undertake nothing, till the gentleman showed him so easy a way, that he thought to have her at last. And to put it into execution he spoke to his butler, who, determined to do his master any fashion of service, asked his wife and his sister-in-law to come and see their vintages in a house he had near the forest, to which they agreed. And when the appointed day was come he advertised the young prince of it, who was resolved to go all alone with the gentleman, and made hold his mule ready for them to set out when the time should draw near. But it was God's will that on that day his mother was decking a most admirable cabinet, and for her help she had all her children with her, and so the young prince diverted himself with her till the hour was passed. But the butler had made his wife feign sickness in

such sort that when he and his sister-in-law were on horseback,
she on the crupper behind him, his wife came to tell him she
could not come.   And when he saw that the hour in which
the prince should have come was gone by, he said to his sister-
in-law : "I do suppose we can return to the town."   "And
what stops us?" said Frances.   "Why," said the butler, " 'tis
my lord, for whom I am waiting, since he promised me he would
come."   When his sister heard his wickedness, she said : "Wait
not for him, brother, for I am assured he will not come to-day,"
so her brother believed her and took her home.   And when
they got to the house she showed her great anger, telling him
he was the devil's servant, and did more than his master bade
him, for she knew the scheme was invented by the gentleman
and himself and not by the young prince, whose money he had
rather gain by aiding him in his follies than do the duty of a
good servant, but since she knew him for such an one she would
no longer tarry in his house.   Thereupon she sent for her
brother to take her to his own country, and straightway left the
house of her sister.   The butler, having failed in his undertaking, went to the castle to hear on what account the prince
had not come, and he had not gone far before he met him on
his mule with the gentleman in whom he trusted.   And he
asked the butler : "Is she still there?" who told him all that
had been done.   The young prince was very sorry to have failed
in this last and extreme means of gaining her, but, seeing no
cure for it, sought her out in such wise that he met her in an
assembly whence she could not fly from him, and spoke bitterly
to her for that she had been so cruel towards him, and was now
leaving her brother's house.   But she answered that she could
live in no worse house nor one more perilous for her, and told
him he was fortunate in his butler, insomuch as he served him
not only with his body and his substance, but also with his soul
and his conscience.   And when the prince saw he could do
nothing more, he determined to pester her no longer, and
esteemed her greatly all his days.   And a servant of the prince,
seeing the goodness of the maid, was fain to have her to wife,
but she would by no means consent without the leave and
command of the prince, in whom she had placed all her affection, and this she made report to him.   So by his goodwill
the marriage was concluded, and she lived all her life in great
repute, the prince doing her many a good turn.

" What shall we say to this, ladies? Are our hearts so mean that we will make our servants the masters; for this woman was not to be overcome by any force of love. I pray you let us take pattern by her and make a conquest of ourselves, for than this there is no victory more worthy of praise." " One thing alone appears to me wrong," said Oisille, " namely, that she did not act thus virtuously in the days of the old historians, for they that have extolled so greatly their Lucreece, would have left her the end of their pens to set down at length the virtues of this maid." " And so great are these virtues of hers," said Hircan, " that were it not for the oath we have sworn to speak the truth, I could not have believed her to be such as you say. For you have seen many a sickly man leave good and wholesome meats, and devour that which is bad and hurtful. So perchance this girl had some meaner lover that made her set all nobility at nought." But to this Parlamente replied that the whole life of her showed she had never loved any living man save him she loved more than her life, but not more than her honour. " Away with such notions from your brain !" said Saffredent, " and hear how this word *honour* came into such repute among the women, for haply they that talk most of it know not whence it proceeded. Know then that in the beginning, when men were not so crafty, nor was there so much evil in their hearts, love was so simple and yet so strong, that it was made no matter of concealment. And he who loved with the most perfect love was deemed worthy of most praise. But when covetousness and sin took hold on man's heart, they drove thence God and love, and took to them in place thereof, love of self, hypocrisy, and deceit. And the women, seeing that the name of *hypocrisy* was hateful to men, gave it instead the name of *honour;* so that they who had in them no perfect love, might be able to declare that *honour* forbade them. And this in their cruelty they made a law for all, so that even they that have the true love conceal it, thinking virtue to be vice; but they that are of a good understanding and sound judgment, fall not into such heresy, knowing the diversity betwixt light and darkness, and that true honour is to show the purity of their heart, which ought to live on love alone, and do no service to the vice of concealment." " Yet," said Dagoucin, " men say that the love that is most secret is most worthy of praise." "Ay, secret," said Simontault, "from the eyes of them that would judge evilly of it, but clear and manifest to the two persons to whom it especially pertains." "Such is my opinion," said Dagoucin, "and I think it would be better even for one of the two to be ignorant of it, than that a third should be advised thereof; and I believe the love of Frances was all the stronger for that she kept it in her heart." "Howsoever that be," said Longarine, "this virtue of over-coming one's own heart must be esteemed the greatest of all. And seeing the occasions that this maid had of forgetting her conscience and her honour, and the virtue she had to overcome her heart, and her will, and him she loved better than herself, with all the temptations that were put in her path, I say she is to be accounted a brave woman." "Since you make the mortification of self the measure of virtue," said Saffredent, "I affirm the prince to be more worthy of praise than she; if you will but consider the greatness of his love, his power, and his opportunities. And with all these, yet he would not offend the laws of true love, which makes earl and churl equal, but would only use the means that honour allowed him." "There is many an one," said Hircan, "who would not have done so." "All the more is he to be esteemed," said Longarine, "in that he overcame the evil common to all men; for he who can do evil and does it not, may well be accounted blessed." "By this talk," said Geburon, "you make me call to mind the case of a woman who had more fear of offending man than God, honour, or love." "Prithee tell us the tale," said Parlamente, "for I give you my vote." "There are folk," said Geburon, "who have no God, or if they do believe in one, it is as being so far from them that He cannot see nor hear their evil deeds, or even if He sees them they deem Him so careless that He will not punish them, thinking of Him as one who has no care at all for this world below. Of this opinion was a lady, whose name I will alter for the sake of her family, and I will call her Jambicque. She often would say that the woman whose only concern was with God, was lucky, if for the rest she could keep her honour unspotted before men. But you shall see, ladies, that her prudence and hypocrisy could not hinder her secret from being revealed; and I will tell you all the manner of it, save that the names of people and places have been changed."

NOVEL XLIII.

Of a woman who was willing to be thought virtuous, but yet had secret pleasure
with a man.

In a mighty fine castle there dwelt a great princess, and
one possessed of much authority, and she had a lady in her
household named Jambicque, the same being very haughty.
And this lady had used her mistress in such sort, that she did
nothing without taking her counsel on the matter, since she
held her for the most prudent and virtuous lady that she
knew.   And so wrath was this Jambicque against light love,
that when she saw any gentleman amorous of one of her
fellows, she would reprove them sharply, and give such an
account of them to her mistress, that they often were publicly
rebuked, wherefore in that household she had a larger share of
fear than love.   For herself, she spoke to no man, save
haughtily and in a loud voice, and in such wise that she was
reputed as a mortal enemy to all love, though her secret
inclinations were altogether very amorous.   For there was a
gentleman in the household of her mistress for whom she had
so great a desire that she could scarce bear it, but yet her love
for her honour and repute made her quite to conceal her liking
for him.   And when she had endured this passion for a good
year, not willing to ease herself, as other lovers do, with looks
and words, it kindled such a flame in the heart of her, that she
was fain to seek for the last cure for love-sickness, thinking she
would do better to satisfy her lust and have God only for a
witness, than tell it to any one who might reveal it to all.

And having resolved upon this it fell out that she was in a
room that looked upon a terrace, and saw walking thereon him
she loved so well, and after gazing on him so long that the day
drew to an end and it became dusk, she called to her a little
page, and showing him the gentleman, said: "Mark well that
man yonder with the doublet of crimson satin and the cloak of
lynx-fur.   Go tell him that one of his acquaintance would
speak with him in the garden gallery."   And so soon as the
page was gone, she went through the closet of her mistress
and came to the gallery, having put on her low hood and her
half-mask, and when the gentleman had come, she straightway

shut the two doors by which they might be taken unawares.
And without taking off her mask she threw her arms round
him, and spoke as low as she could, saying : "For a long time,
sweetheart, my love towards you hath made me desire to find
time and place for seeing you, but fear for my honour has been
so great that it has constrained me, against my will, to conceal
for awhile my passion. But at last the strength of love has
overcome fear, and by the knowledge I have of your honour,
if you will promise me to love me and to speak of me to no
one, nor to inquire who I am, I give you good assurance that I
will be your true and faithful mistress, and will never love any
other but you. But I had rather die than you should know
who I am." The gentleman promised all she asked him, and
this easily made her be as civil, that is, not to refuse anything
he was fain to take. The hour was between five and six in
the winter, so he had no sight at all of her, but touching her
dress he found it was of velvet, that in those days was not worn
every day, save by ladies of noble and illustrious houses. And
as for her underclothing, as far as he could judge by feeling it,
all was in good case, neat, and well cared for. So he took
pains to give her the best entertainment he was able, and she
on her side did no less. And one thing the gentleman perceived very plainly, that she was a married woman.

She would have returned forthwith to the place from
whence she came, but he said to her : "I greatly esteem the
kindness you have done to me who deserve it not, but still
more shall I esteem that I am about to ask of you. So satisfied
am I with the favours I have had that I pray you conceive that
I hope for a continuance thereof; but in what manner shall I
obtain this, since I know not who you are ?" "Trouble not
yourself," said the lady, "but be assured every evening I will
send word to you, but take heed that you be on the terrace
where you were before. And if it is told you to be mindful
of your promise, understand by that that I am waiting in the
gallery, but if the talk is of going to meat, either begone or
come into our mistress's room. And above all I desire you
never to seek to know me, save you wish our friendship to be
broken in twain." So with this the lady and gentleman parted,
each on his several way. And for a long time their love passages endured, and he knew not who she was, whereat he fell

into great pensiveness, musing within himself on the matter, for
he surely thought there was no woman in the round world who
would not fain be seen as well as loved.   And he feared she
was an evil spirit, having heard of some senseless preacher that
no one can look the devil in the face and love him; and by
reason of this fear he resolved to ascertain who it was that
entreated him so kindly, and one time she sent for him he took
in his hand a piece of chalk, with which, while he threw his
arms round her, he made a mark on her back by the shoulder
without her perceiving him.   No sooner was she departed
than the gentleman ran round to the chamber of his mistress
and set himself at the door, to look at the shoulders of the
ladies who came in.   Among the rest he saw Jambicque
enter the room, gazing so proudly about her, that he was afraid
to look at her like the rest, being quite persuaded that she was
not his mistress.   But as she turned he saw on her shoulder
the mark of his white chalk, whereat he was so astonished that
he could scarce trust his eyes.   Yet having well regarded her
figure, he found it none other than the one he had touched,
and in like manner with the face of her, and so of a surety he
knew that she it was.   And at this he took no small contentment to think that a woman who was reputed never to have
had a lover, but rather had refused many an honest gentleman,
should have chosen him.   But love, that never continueth in
one stay, would not let him live thus restfully any longer, and
put in him such vain-boasting and idle hope, that he was resolved to make his love known to her, thinking that when she
was discovered, her love for him should be all the more
increased.   And so one day, when the princess was walking in
the garden, and Jambicque in an alley by herself, he seeing her
alone went up to talk with her, feigning to do so for the first
time.   "Mistress," said he, "'tis a long while since I have
carried my affection for you in my heart, fearing to make it
manifest lest it should do you a displeasure; and am come
thereby to such a pass that I can keep my pain a secret no
longer and still live; for I truly believe man never loved you
as do I."   Jambicque would not suffer him finish his discourse,
but broke in mighty wrathfully: "Have your seeing or hearing
ever told you that I had sweetheart or lover!   Marry!   I think
not, and I marvel you dare talk in this fashion to an honest

woman like me, since this house has held you long enough for
you to know that I love my husband and none other, wherefore have done or beware for yourself." The gentleman at
this piece of deceit could not refrain from laughing, and said
to her: "You are not always so cruel as now, and what
profits it to use this concealment? Is not perfect love
better than imperfect?" Jambicque replied: "I have no love
for you, perfect nor imperfect, save as one of my mistress's
servants; but if you cease not this manner of talk, I shall
surely have such a hatred for you as will be to your mischief."
But the gentleman persisted in his discourse, and said: "And
where is the good cheer you make me when I cannot see you?
Wherefore do you deprive me of it now when the noonday
shows me your beauty and your perfect grace?" Jambicque,
with a great sign of the cross, replied to him: "Either you
have lost your reason, or you are the greatest of all liars, for
never in my life to my knowledge have I made you better or
worse cheer than I do now, so prithee tell me what is your
intent." Then the poor gentleman, thinking to have the
vantage over her, told the place where they had met, and the
mark of chalk whereby he knew her; and at this so hot was
her anger that she told him he was an evil man, and had contrived this abominable lie against her, for which she would
labour to bring him to repentance. He, knowing how well
she stood with her mistress, would have appeased her, but to
no purpose, for furiously leaving him she went up to the princess, who left all others to talk to Jambicque, since she loved
her as herself. And finding her to be so wrathful, she asked
the cause of it, which Jambicque, by no means willing to conceal,
told, and all the talk of the gentleman, and so little to his
advantage that the princess bade him that very evening begone
to his house, without speaking to any one, and to stay there
till that she sent for him. And this he did in great haste, for
fear lest some worse thing should befall him. And so long as
Jambicque dwelt with the princess, the gentleman did not
return to court, and never heard any more tidings of his mistress, who had so well kept her promise that in the hour in
which he sought to find her he should lose her.

"Whereby, ladies, you see how a woman that preferred
the glory of the world to her conscience, lost the one and the

other, for this day is known of all men that she would fain
conceal from her lover, and flying the mockery of one, she is
mocked of all. Nor can she be excused for that her love proceeded from the simplicity of her heart, the which would be
deserving of pity, but she is condemned because she concealed
her wickedness under the cloak of honour and glory, and would
have God and man esteem her as other than she was. But He
that giveth not his glory to another, uncloaked her and gave
double shame."   "Verily," said Oisille, "her wickedness is
beyond excuse. For who shall speak for her, when God,
honour, and even love are against her?"   "Why," said Hircan,
"pleasure and wantonness, the attorneys-general to the ladies."
"If we had no other attorneys beside those of yours," said
Parlamente, "our cause would be poorly defended, but women
who are overcome of pleasure ought no more to be called
women but rather men, whose honour takes no hurt by rage
and concupiscence. For a man that avenges him on his enemy
and puts him to the sword, because he hath given him the lie,
is accounted the braver gallant for it; and in like manner when
he loves a dozen women over and above his wife. But our
honour stands on another bottom, namely, on gentleness, long-
suffering, and chastity."   "You are speaking only of good
women," said Hircan.   "Ay," replied Parlamente, "since of
the rest I take no note."   "If there were no foolish women,"
said Nomerfide, "they that are fain to be believed of all men
would very often be found liars."   "I give you my vote,
Nomerfide," said Geburon, "and, prithee, forget you are a
woman, that we may learn what it is that men accounted
truthful tell of the folly of your sex."   "Since virtue will have
it so, and you give me your vote, I will tell you what I know.
I have heard none here, be it man or woman, that has spared
to speak evil of the friars, and for the compassion I have for
them, I am resolved to speak well of them."

NOVEL XLIV.

How a Grey Friar for telling the truth receives two pigs in place of one.

There came a Grey Friar to my lady of Sedan, who was
of the house and lineage of Crouy, asking of her a pig, which
every year she gave them for an alms. My lord of Sedan, who

was a wise man and of a pleasant speech, made the good father
to eat at their table, and amongst other talk said to him, to put
him in the lists : " You do well, father, to ask for alms, while
you are yet unknown; for I greatly fear, when once your
hypocrisy is discovered, you will eat no longer the bread of the
poor children that the sweat of the father's brow hath gained
them." The friar was in no wise taken aback by this, but
replied : " My lord, our Order is on such a sure foundation,
that while the world remains it will endure; for this foundation
will never fail while man and woman inhabit the earth." My
lord of Sedan was very desirous to know what was this foundation, and earnestly prayed the friar to tell him, who after
many excuses at last said : " Since you are pleased to command
me to tell you, you shall know that our Order is bottomed upon
the foolishness of women, and as long as the world hold a silly
woman or a foolish, we shall not die of hunger." My lady of
Sedan, being of a choleric complexion, at the hearing of this
grew so wrath, that had her husband not been there, she would
have done the friar a hurt, and swore a great oath that he
should not have the pig she had promised him; but my lord of
Sedan, for that the friar had not concealed the truth, swore he
should have two pigs, and made take them to his monastery.

" So it was, ladies, that the friar, being sure the benefits of
the ladies would never fail him, found means by concealing
nothing of the truth, to have the favour and the alms of men ;
if he had been a flatterer and dissembler he would have been
more agreeable to the ladies, but not so profitable to himself
and his brethren." The novel was not brought to an end
without much laughter from all the company, and most of all
from them that knew the lord and lady of Sedan. And Hircan
said : " The friars then should by no means endeavour by their
preaching to make the women wise, seeing that their foolishness doth so much profit them." And Parlamente said :
" They do not by their preaching endeavour to make women
wise, but to make them think themselves wise; for they that
are altogether foolish and worldly give them no great alms, but
they who for that they often go to the monastery church, and
carry with them paternosters marked with deathsheads, and
wear their hoods lower than other women, think to be esteemed
wise, but are in truth foolish. For they ground their salvation

on the confidence they have in these sons of iniquity, whom for their outward appearance they think to be well nigh gods." "But how shall we not believe on them," said Ennasuitte, "being that they are ordained of our prelates to preach the Gospel to us, and to reprove us of our vices?" "Because," said Parlamente, "we have discovered their hypocrisy, and know the diversity between the teaching of God and the teaching of the devil." "Jesus!" said Ennasuitte, "do you think that they would dare to preach bad doctrine?" "Think, say you?" said Parlamente, "nay, I am assured that they believe nothing less than the Gospel; I speak of the bad amongst them, for I have known many an honest friar who preached the word in all purity and simplicity, and lived without scandal, ambition, or covetousness, and with a pure and chaste heart, neither feigned nor constrained. But with such good stones as these the streets are not paved—nay, rather for the most part with the contrary thereto ; and the good tree beareth good fruit." "I thought of a surety," said Ennasuitte, "that we were bound, under pain of mortal sin, to believe whatsoever they told us sitting in the chair of truth; that is, when they preached only what is in the Scripture, or in the comments of the holy doctors of the Church." "For my part," said Parlamente, "I cannot be ignorant that there have been amongst them men of very bad faith, and notably one Colimant, a brother of the Order, and a doctor in theology, and a preacher of great repute, was fain to persuade some of the brethren that the Gospel is not more worthy of belief than Cæsar his Commentaries, or any other authentic history, and from that hour I have not placed my trust in the words of any of their preachers, if I found it not conformable to the word of God, which is the true touchstone whereby we can know truth from lies." "Be assured," said Oisille, "that they who often humbly read therein will never be deceived by fables devised of men, for he that hath a mind filled with all truth can by no means receive a lie." "Yet," said Simontault, "methinks one of simple mind is more easy to be cozened than another." "Ay," said Longarine, "if you account foolishness simplicity." "I tell you," replied Simontault, "that a good woman, mild and simple, is more easy to be cozened than a crafty and malicious." "I am persuaded," said Nomerfide, "that you know a woman too full of this same goodness, wherefore I give you my vote that you may tell of her." "Since you have guessed so well," said Simontault, "I will relate the matter to you, but so that you promise me not to weep thereat. They that declare, ladies, that your craftiness is greater than men's, would have much ado to bring forward my tale to support their position; since in it I will tell you of the great cunning of a husband, and also of the simpleness and goodness of his wife."

[In place of the preceding novel, Claude Gruget published in his edition of 1559 what follows.]

How two lovers, after secretly having pleasure of one another, were happily married.

In the town of Paris there lived two citizens of ordinary condition, one of whom was in the employ of the state, and the other a silk mercer. And these two were ancient friends and affectionate, so that they would often go to one another's houses, whereby the son of the former, named Jaques, a young man of a good address, was enabled frequently to go to the mercer's, and the cause of his going was the great love he bore to Frances, the mercer's daughter. And so well did he do his suit to her that he found her to be no less loving than beloved; but in the midst of these passages the army was sent into Provence against Charles of Austria, and Jaques being called out was compelled to go with it. And at the very beginning of the campaign his father departed this life, the tidings whereof gave him double sorrow, both for the loss of his father and for the difficulty he should have to see his well-beloved on his coming home. Natheless, as time went on the one sorrow was forgotten and the other increased, since death is but a natural thing, for the most part falling to the father before the children, and so the sadness for it little by little glides away. But love, in place of bringing us death, brings us life by the procreation of offspring which in a manner make us to live for ever, and this it is that causeth our desires to grow and increase. So that Jaques, when he was come back to Paris, thought of nothing else but in what manner he might frequently go to the mercer's, and there, under pretext of mere friendship, traffic in his dearest commodity. And on the other hand, while he was away, Frances had been eagerly sought in other quarters, as much for her comeliness as her ready wit; but though she was a long while since marriageable, yet her father would not do his part in the matter, either for his covetousness or for his great desire of putting her in a good estate in life, as his only daughter. And this was by no means of advantage to her honour, for now-a-days men do take occasion of scandal a long while before it is given, notably in anything that concerns the virtue of a comely wench or a woman. And her father was nor blind nor deaf to the gossip that was commonly noised abroad, not wishing to be like them that, in place of reproving the faults of their wives and daughters, do rather seem to incite them thereto; for he kept Frances so straitly that even they who would see her as to marriage had but few opportunities, and always her mother was present with them. It skills not asking whether this was hard to be borne by Jaques or no, and he fell into a hesitancy between jealousy and love, not being able to believe that they would keep her so straitly without some grave cause. But at last he was determined to know the reason of it, be the hazard as it might; but in the first place, that he might discover whether her affection was unchanged towards him, he took such order that one morning he heard mass kneeling beside her, and perceived by the manner of her countenance that she was not less glad to see him than he to see her. So, knowing her mother to be less severe than her father, he plucked up courage to accost them as they went from their lodging to the church, familiarly and as a friend might. And in appearance it was altogether a chance meeting, but in truth done by him of express design and so as to reach his ends. To be short, as the year of mourning for his father drew to an end, he resolved, when he put off his blacks, to go more like himself and be an honour to his forefathers. This he told his mother, who found his intent a good one, and much wished to see him well married, since she had only one child beside him, a daughter already honourably bestowed in wedlock. And so, like the good dame she was, she stirred up still more a love of virtue in him, by an infinity of examples drawn from the young men of his own age who were advancing themselves in life, or at least showed themselves worthy of the houses whence they came. Nothing remained but to consult

T

where they should get their gear.   But his mother said: " I
am of opinion, Jaques, that we should go to old Pierre's (now
he was the father of Frances), for since he is of our acquaintance
he will not cozen us."   His mother tickled him in the place he
itched, natheless he withstood her, saying : " We will go where
we can get the best gear at the lowest cost.   But since we
know old Pierre, I am content that we go there first."   So one
morning mother and son went to see Pierre, who gave them a
hearty welcome, as you know a merchant will do when profit
seems at hand.   Then they made him bring forth great piles
of silk of all sorts, and chose therefrom what they wanted.
But as to the price they could not agree, for Jaques of design
beat the merchant down, because he did not see his sweetheart's
mother; and so at last they went elsewhere to see if the merchandise was better and of a lower price.   Yet could Jaques
find no silk so brave as that where Frances lived, and thither,
having returned some time after, they found the dame, who likewise welcomed them very heartily.   And after the things
having been said and done which are accustomed to be done in
such shops, Jaques said to the wife, who drove a harder bargain
than her husband : " Verily, mistress, you are very severe with
us, but since we have lost the father we are known of none."
So saying, he made pretence to weep and wipe his eyes at the
remembrance of his father, but it was for the better accom-
plishing of his designs.   His good mother, taking his speech
in good faith, said likewise : "Since his death we are no more
visited than if we had never been known.   In such account are
poor widows held !"   Then they made new engagements of
friendship, and promised to visit one another more often than
ever; and while they were amid these passages there came in
other merchants, whom the master himself took to the back of
his shop.   And the young man, perceiving his time was come,
said to his mother : "I have often seen the good lady here go
on feast days to visit the holy places hard-by our quarter; if
sometimes she would deign in passing to take a cup of wine
with us she would do us pleasure and honour."   The merchant's
wife, who in this saw no harm, answered that for the last fortnight or more it had been her intent to go to their quarter;
and if it were fine on the next Sunday she would go thither,
and not fail to revisit them on her way.   This business brought

to an end, so also was that of the silk, since for a little money
it would not profit to let so brave an opportunity go by. So
the agreement made, and the merchandise carried away, Jaques
knowing that he could not all alone bring to an end this undertaking, was constrained to declare it to a faithful friend named
Olivier, and they took such counsel together that it only
remained to put the design into execution. And when the
Sunday was come the mercer's wife and his daughter failed not,
as they returned from service, to enter the widow's house, where
they found her talking with a neighbour in a gallery overlooking
the garden, and her daughter walking beneath with Jaques and
Olivier. And as soon as Jaques saw his sweetheart he so
ordered himself that he met her and her mother without any
change in the manner of his countenance; and since the old
are wont to seek out the old, the three dames sat together on
a bench with their backs to the garden, into which by steps at
a time the two lovers entered, walking to the place where were
the two others. And after some pleasant things had passed
between them they fell again to walking, and so well did the
young man declare his pitiful case to Frances that she durst
not grant and could not refuse what her lover asked of her, in
such sort that he knew she likewise was sore touched at heart.
But I would have you understand that while they talked they
continually passed and repassed in front of the arbour where
the good dames were seated, speaking the while on ordinary
matters so as to take away all suspicion, and now and again
running in sport hither and thither about the garden. And
when in the space of half an hour the dames were well accustomed to all this, Jaques made the appointed sign to Olivier,
who so disposed his person in front of the girl he had with him
that she did not perceive the two lovers going into a cherry-
close shut in by a hedge of rose trees and tall gooseberry
bushes ; thither they made pretence of going to gather almonds
from a tree in the corner of the close, but their intent was to
gather plums. So Jaques, instead of giving his sweetheart a
green gown gave her a red one, so that the colour came to her
face at being thus taken unawares a little before she had
expected. And since these plums of theirs were ripe, so quick
were they to gather them that Olivier himself would scarce
have believed the thing done, had he not seen the girl hanging

down her head and showing a shame-faced countenance. And
this made him to know the truth, since before she had carried
her head aloft, as one who fears not lest the vein in the eye
(which should be red in maids) had taken a blue colour. But
when Jaques perceived this he brought her back by remonstrances proper to the occasion to her accustomed address.
Natheless, as they took two or three turns round the garden,
the girl ceased not to sigh and weep, and to say ofttimes :
" Alas! and was it for this that you loved me ?   O my God,
what shall I do ?   For the rest of my days I am as one that is
lost !   In what esteem henceforth will you have me ?   I am
assured that you will no more make any account of me, at least
if you are amongst them that love only for their pleasure.
Alas! would that I had been dead before I fell into this sin !"
Now all this was not without much weeping, but such good
matter of consolation did Jaques give her, with so many oaths
and promises, that when they had accomplished three more
turns of the garden, Jaques again gave the signal to his comrade, and they again entered the close by another path.
Whereupon, do what she would, she found her second red
gown still more to her pleasure than the first ; and from this time
so well did she like them that they took counsel together as to
how they should see one another more often and more at
their ease, until her father was minded to give his consent.
And in the gaining of this a young woman, neighbour to old
Pierre and very far akin to Jaques, and a great friend of Frances,
was of notable aid to them.   And so they continued without
open shame (or so it was told me) till the consummation of
the marriage, when for a mercer's daughter she was found to
be very rich.   True it is that Jaques waited for the better part
of his worldly gear till the decease of the father, for so grasping
was he that it seemed to him that the one hand would rob him
of what he held in the other.

"Consider, ladies, a love affair well begun, better carried
on, and best of all finished ; for though 'tis common amongst
you men to despise a girl or woman after she has freely given
you that you seek most from her ; yet this young man, filled
with a good and sincere love, and having found in his sweetheart what every husband desires in his wife ; and knowing her
to be of good family and prudent, save as to the sin which he

himself had made her to commit, would not be an adulterer or
make an evil marriage with some other woman; wherefore I
deem him worthy of all praise." "Yet," said Oisille, "they
were both to blame, and the third also, who aided, or at the
least, consented to the rape." "Do you call that a *rape*,"
said Saffredent, "when the two parties were agreed together?
Or does any more perfect marriage than this come of such
light love? Wherefore we say in the proverb that marriages
are made in heaven. But surely not forced marriages, nor
bought marriages, nor those that are held as well approved
when the father and mother have given their consent." "Say
what you will," said Oisille, "it is necessary that we should
allow obedience to be due to father and mother, and in default
of these, to other kinsfolk. For if every lad and lass might
marry at pleasure, what a multitude of cuckolds there would
be! Can one suppose that a young man and a girl of
twelve or fifteen years know what is meet and right for them?
He who shall consider well the estate of matrimony shall find
that at the least as many marriages made for love have had an
evil issue as those made by compulsion; and this because
young folk, who know not what is fitting for them, take the
first mate that offers and think no more on't, but little by little
they find out their mistakes and thereupon make bad still worse.
On the contrary, such couples as have been wed forcibly, were
wed by them that had seen more and had a better judgment
than the parties themselves; who when they come to perceive
the good they knew not of, embrace and cling to it all the
more and with much greater affection." "But, mistress," said
Hircan, "you do not remember that this girl was of full age,
fit to be married, and with a full knowledge of her father's
iniquity, who let a rust grow on her maidenhead for fear of
rubbing it off his broad pieces. And you must consider that
Dame Nature is an arrant slut. She loved, she was beloved,
she found matters ready to her hand, and may haply have
remembered the old saying: 'She that refuseth, after museth.'
All this, together with the short work her lover made with her,
gave her no time to resist. Likewise you have heard that there
was seen in her face afterwards a great change. 'Twas perchance for regret at the short time she had given her to consider whether the thing were good or bad; for it needed no

long whispering in her ear to make her give it a second trial."
" For my part," said Longarine, " I should find no excuse at all
in the matter, save for the good faith kept by the young man,
who ruling himself in all honesty, did not abandon her, but
kept her as he had made her. For which, methinks, he is
worthy of great praise, seeing that our youth are now become
exceeding corrupt. But for all that I do not excuse him of his
rape of the girl and subornation of the mother." " Not so,
not so," said Dagoucin, " there was neither rape nor subornation; all was done by mere consent. As to the mothers,
though they were deceived, they hindered it not, and as to the
daughter she found it altogether to her liking, and so made no
complaint on the matter." " It all fell out," said Parlamente,
" through the great goodness and simpleness of the merchant's
wife, who in all faith led her lamb, without thinking of it, to
the slaughter-house." " Rather to the marriage feast," said
Simontault, " in such sort that this simpleness was no less profitable to the girl than hurtful to one who let herself be easily
cozened by her husband." " Since you know such a story,"
said Nomerfide, " I give you my vote to tell it us." " And
this I will by all means do," said he, " but so that you promise
me not to weep thereat. They that declare, ladies, that your
craftiness is greater than men's, would have much ado to bring
forward my tale to support their position ; since in it I will tell
you of the great cunning of a husband, and also the simpleness
and goodness of his wife."

NOVEL XLV.

How a tapestry-maker gave a wench the Innocents, and his pleasant device for deceiving a neighbour who saw it done.

In the town of Tours there lived a man of very subtile
and keen wit, who was tapestry-maker to the late Duke of
Orleans, son of King Francis the First. And though he by
the hap of sickness was become deaf, yet was his understanding
not diminished, for in his trade he had no match for keenness,
and so in other matters, and you shall see how good a care he
could have for himself. He had to wife an honest woman with
whom he lived in great peace and quietness, fearing much to do

her a displeasure, whilst she for her part only sought to be obedient to him in all things.   But notwithstanding the great love
he bore her, so charitable was he, that he would often give to
neighbouring women what belonged only to his wife, and this
as secretly as he was able.   Now they had in their household
a serving wench of a very pretty figure, of whom this tapestry-
maker became amorous.   Yet, fearing lest his wife might come
to know of it, he often made pretence of chiding and rebuking
her, saying she was the idlest wench he had ever seen, and that
he marvelled not at it, since her mistress never beat her.   And
one day when they were talking about giving the Innocents,
the tapestry-maker said to his wife : " It were mere charity to
give them to that idle wench of yours, but it must not be from
your hand, for it is too feeble, and your heart too pitiful ; but
if I made use of mine, we should perchance be better served
than we are now."   His poor wife, suspecting nothing, prayed
him to do execution on her, confessing she had neither heart
nor strength for the business ; so the husband, who accepted
the charge with mighty goodwill, playing the stern executioner,
made buy the sharpest rods that could be found, and, to show
his great desire not to spare her, put them in pickle, so that his
wife had more pity for the wench than suspicion of her husband.
So Innocents Day being come, master tapestry-maker rose very
early in the morning, and went up on high to the room
where the wench slept all alone, and there gave her the Innocents, but in a different fashion from that he had spoken of
with his wife.   The wench fell amain to weeping, but it availed
her nothing ; natheless, for fear lest his wife should come up he
began striking the rods which he held in his hand against the
bedstead, till he had got the bark off them and had broken
them ; and thus broken he carried them down to his wife,
saying : "I believe, sweetheart, that your maid will have some
remembrance of the Innocents."   And when the master was
gone from the house the poor wench came and threw herself
on her knees before her mistress, and told her that he had done
her the greatest wrong that a man might do a maid.   But the
mistress, thinking that this was on account of the beating he
had given her, would not let her finish her discourse, but said :
" My husband has done well, for it is more than a month I
prayed him to do so ; and if he pressed hard on you I am well

content thereat. But whatever he did set it down to none but me, and even as it is he has not done as much as he ought to have done." The wench, seeing her mistress approve of the affair, thought it could not be the great sin she had conceived, since so good a woman had been the occasion of it, and henceforth durst say no more on the matter. But the master, seeing his wife as content to be deceived as he was to deceive, determined to give her often matter for contentment, and took such order with the wench that she wept no more at having the Innocents. For a long while he continued this manner of living, without his wife perceiving anything of it, till there was a great fall of snow; and just as he had given her the Innocents in his garden on the grass, so he wished to give her them upon the snow. And one morning, before any in the house were awake, he took her in her shift to make the sign of the crucifix upon the snow, and there they pelted one another, but did by no means forget the game of the Innocents. And this was seen by a neighbour of theirs, who had set herself at a window looking straight upon the garden, to see what weather it was; but seeing this wickedness she waxed so wrathful that she resolved to tell her good gossip, to the end that she might no longer be deceived by such a bad husband, nor served by such a wicked wench. The tapestry-maker, after these brave diversions, looked all around him to discover if any saw them, and perceived his neighbour at the window, at which he was sore troubled. But he, knowing how to colour tapestry of any device, thought he would so colour this matter that their neighbour would be as much deceived as his wife. And as soon as he had got back to bed, he made his wife rise in her shift, and took her to the garden as he had taken the wench, and played a long while with her in the snow as he had done with the other, and gave her the Innocents just as he had given them to the other; and afterwards they both went to bed together. When this good wife was going to mass, her neighbour and dear gossip did not fail to seek her out, and with great zeal but without saying any more entreated her to send away her serving-maid, for that she was a very bad and dangerous wench. But she would not do this before she knew wherefore her neighbour held her in such ill-fame, and at last she told her how she had seen the wench that morning in the garden with her husband. The good woman fell to laughing heartily, and said : " Why, dear gossip, 'twas myself" " What, gossip? She was in her shift; at five o'clock in the morning." The good woman replied : " Faith, gossip, 'twas myself." The other continued her discourse : " They pelted one another with snow, maybe on the breasts, maybe on certain still more privy parts." The good woman said : " Why, dear gossip, 'twas myself." " But gossip, I saw them afterwards doing on the snow a thing that was not pretty nor seemly." " Gossip," said the good woman, "I have told you, and I tell you again, 'twas myself and none other who did all you mention, for my good husband and myself do use to play thus privily. Prithee, then, be not scandalized thereat, for you know we are bound to do our husband's pleasure." So her neighbour went her way, more desirous of having such a husband than she had been before wishful of exposing him to her good gossip. And when the tapestry-maker returned home his wife told him the whole story. " Consider then, sweetheart," replied he, " that if you had not been an honest woman and of a good under-standing, we should a long while ago have been divided the one from the other; but I hope God will keep us in this love of ours to His glory and our contentment." " Amen, sweet-heart," said the good woman, " and I hope that on my side you will never find any fault."

" He would be slow of belief, ladies, who, after hearing this true story, would still maintain that your craft is greater than men's ; though, without doing wrong to anyone, if we are to praise this man and his wife, we must, to speak truth, allow that neither was of much account." " The man," said Par-lamente, " was wondrous wicked, for on one side he deceived the wench, and on the other his wife." " You have not well understood the story," said Hircan, " for it is said he contented the pair of them in one morning, and this I count a mighty deed of valour both of the flesh and of the spirit, to say and do things to make two opposites content." " Therein," said Parlamente, " he is doubly bad, to satisfy the simplicity of the one with a lie, and the wickedness of the other with a wicked deed. But I am assured that when such sins come before such judges they get an easy pardon." " Yet," answered Hircan, " you may likewise be persuaded that I shall never undertake so great and hard a task, for if I satisfy you I shall have done no bad day's work." "If mutual love contenteth not the heart," said Parlamente, "no other can content it." "Truly," said Simontault, "I believe there is no greater anguish in the world than to love and not to be beloved." "To be loved," said Parlamente, "you should turn to them that love. But oftentimes they that are beloved, and will not love, are beloved the most, and they that are the least beloved, love the most." "You bring to remembrance," said Oisille, "a tale I was not minded to tell amidst good ones." "Prithee tell it us," said Simontault. "That will I do willingly," answered Oisille.

NOVEL XLVI.

How a friar cured a maid of slothfulness.

In the town of Angoulême, where Count Charles, father of King Francis, often resorted, there lived a friar named De Vale, accounted for a learned man and a great preacher. So it fell out that one Advent season he preached in the town before the Count, and got such fame thereby that all who knew him were fain to have him dine with them. And amongst these was the Judge of Exemptions for the county, he having to wife a good and pretty woman, whom the friar loved better than his life, but had not the boldness to tell her, which she perceiving made a mock of him. After that he had shown several appearances of the folly in his brain, he one day saw her mounting all alone to her granary, and, thinking to take her unawares, began to climb up after her; but she, hearing the noise, turned round and asked him whither he was going. "I am coming," said he, "to tell you a certain secret matter." "Then by no means come, good father," answered she, "for it is not my mind to talk with such folk as you in secret, and if you mount higher up this ladder it will repent you of it." He, perceiving that she was alone, made no account of her words, but hasted to climb up, but she, being of good courage, seeing him at the top of the ladder, gave him a kick in the belly, and saying, "Down, down," threw him from the top to the bottom. At this the good father was so ashamed that he forgot his bodily hurts, and fled hotfoot from the town, for he was well assured she would not conceal the thing from her husband, as indeed she did not, and told it likewise to the Count and Countess, for which cause the friar durst no more appear before them. And to fill up the measure of his iniquity he went to live with a dame that loved the friars above all other folk, and after that he had preached a sermon or two before her he perceived her daughter that she was very fair. And this daughter he often rebuked for not getting up in the morning to hear the sermon, in the presence of her mother, who said to him: "Would to God, father, she had a taste of the discipline you monks give one another." The friar swore that if she continued thus idle he would give it her, which the mother earnestly entreated him to do. After a few days the good father entered the lady's room, and asked where was her daughter. The lady answered: "She fears you so little that she is still a-bed." "Without doubt," said the friar, "'tis a very bad thing for young maids to be idle. Few people make any account of the sin of slothfulness; but as for me, I esteem it as one of the most deadly both to body and soul; wherefore you would do well to chastise her, and if you will give the charge to me I will have a care that she be no longer in bed at the hour in which she should be praising God." The poor dame, thinking he was an honest man, prayed him to be pleased to chastise her, which he did straightway, and, mounting by a small wooden stair, found the maid all alone asleep in bed, and there while she slept he took her by force. The poor girl, waking up, and not knowing whether it were man or devil, fell to crying out as loudly as she could, and called her mother to the rescue; but her mother, standing at the bottom of the stair, said to the friar: "Have no compassion on her, father; give it her a second time, and chastise this wicked wench." And when the friar had accomplished his evil intent, he came down the stair to the dame, and said with a face all a-fire: "I believe, mistress, your daughter will remember my discipline." The mother, after giving him great thanks, went up to her daughter and found her in such grief as becomes an honest woman that has fallen into so evil a case. And when she knew the truth she made seek for the friar on every side, but he was already afar off, and was no more found in the realm of France.

"You see, ladies, with what security such charges are given

to them that are not fit. The chastisement of men pertains to
men, and the chastisement of women to women; for women
would be as pitiful in the chastising of men as men are cruel in
the chastising of women." "Jesus!" said Parlamente, "what
a wicked and abominable friar!" "Say rather," said Hircan,
"what a silly and foolish mother, who, cozened by their deceit,
used so familiarly them that should only be seen in church."
"Truly," said Parlamente, "I confess she was one of the most
foolish mothers that have ever lived, and if she had been like
to the judge's wife she would sooner have sent him down the
stair than up it. But this devil that is half an angel is the
most dangerous of all, for he knows so well how to transform
himself into an angel of light that one is half afraid of suspecting
him to be what he really is, and methinks a woman that is not
suspicious is in some sort worthy of praise." "Natheless,"
said Oisille, "the evil that is to be avoided ought to be
suspected, notably of them that are in charge of others,
for it is better to suspect an evil that is not than to fall
through foolish belief into an evil that is. And never have I
seen a woman deceived for that she was slow to believe the
words of men, but many have I seen deceived for too easily
putting faith in a lie; wherefore I say that the evil that may
come cannot be too much suspected, and especially of them that
bear rule over men, women, towns, or states, for howsoever
good the watch, so strong are wickedness and treachery that
the shepherd that is not careful will always be deceived by the
craftiness of the wolf." "Yet," said Dagoucin, "a suspicious
man is not able to be a perfect friend, and many through suspicion are divided one from the other." "If you know an
example thereof," said Oisille, "I will give you my vote for
the telling of it." "So true a tale will I tell you," said
Dagoucin, "that you will take pleasure to hear it. I will tell
you, ladies, how a brave friendship was broken in twain, I
would say when the surety thereof began to give place to suspicion. For as to believe and trust in a friend is the greatest
honour you can do him, so to distrust him is the greatest dishonour, for in that way one esteems him other than he should
be, and so many a fine friendship is broken up and friends
become enemies, as you shall see by the relation I am about to
make you."

[The forty-sixth novel was suppressed by Claude Gruget and the following published in its place.]

The order taken by the same friar between husband and wife.

In the town of Angoulême, where Count Charles, father of Francis the First, often resorted, there lived a Grey Friar named De Valles, a learned man and so fine a preacher that he was chosen to preach the Advent sermons before the Count, whereby his fame grew still greater. And it fell out that one Advent season a young rattle-pate of the town took to wife a comely lass, but yet continued to run his courses among other women, and this more than the bachelors. And his wife being advertised thereof could not keep silence, speaking to her husband in such a manner that he paid her for it in a fashion not at all to her liking; natheless she for all that would not forego her lamentations and railing, whereat the young man grew wroth and beat her even to bruises and blood-letting. But the women who were her neighbours, knowing the cause of her complaints, could not more be silent than the wife, crying aloud at the corners of the streets : "Woe, woe, on such husbands, to the devil with them !" By good hap the friar De Valles passing by, heard the noise and the reason of it, and determined to touch upon the matter in his sermon on the morrow, and failed not to do so. For drawing his discourse to matrimony, and the love to be observed therein, he greatly magnified it, blaming the infringers of the same, and comparing conjugal love with parental. And amongst other things he said it were a more dangerous thing, and more grievously punished, for a man to beat his wife than to beat his father or mother. "For," said he, "if you do the latter they will send you by way of penance to Rome; but if you beat your wife, she and all her gossips will send you to the devil, whose home is hell. Consider then how diverse are these two penances, for from Rome it is common for men to return, but from hell, alas ! no one returns any more, *nulla est redemptio.*" Now after this homily he was advised that the women fortified themselves on the strength of it, in such wise that their husbands could take no order with them, wherefore he resolved to do them a kindness as he had before done their wives. So in one of his

sermons he likened women to devils, calling these two the
greatest of man's enemies, that ceased not to tempt him, and of
whom, but notably women, he could by no means rid himself.
" For," said he, " with respect to the devils, when the cross is
shown them, they fly from before it; but contrariwise women are
tamed by this very cross, by reason of it they fetch and carry, and
give their husbands an infinity of torments. Know, then, good
folk, what you must do to them. When you find your wives
cease not to trouble you, as is their manner, take the handle off
the cross, and with it press them hard a good while; you will
not have tried this cure three or four times before you take
some benefit therefrom; and in like manner as the devil is
warded off by the virtue of the cross, so will you ward off your
wives and put them to silence by the virtue of the handle
alone."

   " This, ladies, was one of the homilies of Father De Valles,
of whose life I will tell you nothing more, and for a good cause;
but be assured (for I knew him) that, howsoever good a face he
put upon it, he was by much the more inclined to the side of
the women than the men." " Yet, mistress," said Parlamente,
" he showed but little of his inclinations in his last sermon
wherein he teaches men to evilly entreat their wives." " You
understand not his device," said Hircan, " since you are not
used to warfare, its wiles and stratagems; of which the greatest
is to sow discord in the camp of the enemy, for that when he
is divided against himself he is mighty easy to be conquered.
So master monk knew well that wrath and hatred between a
husband and his wife do very often cause the woman to give
rein to her honour, which honour, being freed from the guard
of virtue, finds itself in the wolf's teeth before it thought to
have strayed away." " Howsoever that may be," said Parlamente, " I could bear no love for him that had put discord
between my husband and myself, so that we came to blows, for
these same blows are altogether the death of love. Natheless, as it hath been told me, so craftily do they go to work,
when they would gain an advantage over a woman, and use
such pleasant discourse, that I am persuaded it were more
perilous to listen to them in secret than publicly to be beaten
of a husband, who for the rest might be a good one." " In
truth," said Dagoucin, " they have made their ways so mani-

fest, that it is not without cause that one fears them, though methinks the woman who is not suspicious is in some sort worthy of praise."

[For the remainder of the discussion see the epilogue to the forty-sixth novel.]

NOVEL XLVII.

How a man who was jealous without a cause thereby separated himself from his familiar friend, and made him to be his bitterest enemy.

Hard by the land of Perche there lived two gentlemen, who from childhood had dwelt together in so great and perfect friendship, that the two had but one heart, one bed, one table, and one purse. Thus for a long while they continued, always one in thought and word, and were it not for the diversity of their bodies it might be said that they lived not as two brothers but as one man. But one of the two took unto himself a wife, natheless, he left not for that account their companionship, but still dwelt, as he had been accustomed, in perfect friendship with his fellow. And when they were straitened for lodging, he made him lie with his wife and himself, though, 'tis true, he slept in the middle. So they had all things in common, and neither marriage nor anything that might fall out could diminish their love for one another. But after some time this world's happiness, which by nature is changeful and various, could no more endure in that too fortunate house; for the husband, without any occasion, forgot the surety he had with his friend and his wife, and could not conceal his thoughts, but spoke shamefully to her. At this she marvelled greatly, for he had charged her, save in one thing only, to make as good cheer for his friend as for himself; and now forbade her to speak to him, except it were in some great assembly. And she advertised her husband's friend of this command, who believed it not, since he knew he had never been minded to do anything which should be a great cause of anger for his comrade, and also that there had never been any concealment at all betwixt them. He therefore told him what he had heard, and prayed him not to hide the truth, since he was not willing for that or aught else to be the means of breaking up the friendship they

had so long continued to use with one another. The married
gentleman assured him that the matter had never been in his
thoughts, and that they who had set the report about had lied
most damnably. His friend thereupon said to him: "I know
well that jealousy is a passion as hard to bear as love, and were
you jealous, be it of myself, I would not impute it to you as a
wrong, for you could not help yourself. But if you should do
what it is in your power to avoid, namely, conceal your sickness
from me, I should have just cause for complaint, since you have
never yet concealed any of your thoughts or passions from me.
So on my side; if I were amorous of your wife, you should
not impute this to me for wickedness, for love is too hot a coal
to be held in the hand and dealt with at one's pleasure : but if
I were to conceal it from you and seek to reveal it to your
wife, I should be the wickedest friend that ever was. But I
do assure you, though she is a good woman and a virtuous,
that she is the last of all women, save inasmuch as she is your
wife, on whom my fancy would fix itself. And, though you
have no ground for suspicion, I do require of you that if you
have the very least notion of it, you advise me of the same, to
the intent that I may take order therewith, and our so ancient
friendship shall not be broken up by reason of a woman. For
if I loved her more than all the things that are, yet would I
never speak to her, since I esteem your honour above all
else." The husband swore to him, using the most binding
oaths he was able, that he had never thought on the matter,
and prayed him continue in his house after his custom. The
other replied to him: "I will so continue, but I warn you
that after this if you have a suspicion of me, and conceal it,
thinking evilly of me, I will no longer abide in your fellowship or company." For some while they lived together after
their former fashion, but the married gentleman fell again into
a worse jealousy than before, and charged his wife no more to
show his friend a pleasant face, and this she told him, herself
praying him no more to speak to her since she was forbidden
to speak to him. The gentleman, perceiving by her words
and by certain mouths he saw his friend making, that he had
broken his promise, said to him mighty wrathfully · "If you
are jealous, 'tis natural and no fault of yours; but after the
oaths you swore to me, I am displeased that you have con-

cealed this thing, for I always thought that betwixt your heart and mine there was no gulf or separation. But now, to my great sorrow, and without any fault of mine, I see to the contrary, not only because you are jealous of my wife and myself, but because you would fain conceal it from me, to the end that your sickness endure so long that it turn all into hatred, and thus our friendship, that was the most perfect these days had seen, shall be converted into the most mortal enmity. What I was able I have done to avoid this mishap, but since you suspect me thus wicked and thus contrary to what I have always been towards you, I swear to you by my faith that I will be such a man as you esteem me. And I will never cease till I have won that from your wife you thought I was endeavouring to gain, so henceforth beware of me, for as suspicion hath cut me off from your fellowship, so vengeance shall cut you off from mine." And though the husband would fain have him believe that he in nowise suspected him, yet he would trust him no more, and took his moiety of the goods and furniture that had been in common between them. So from this time their hearts were as far apart as they had been near together; in such sort that the bachelor rested not till he had made his friend a cuckold, as he had promised him.

"And may they that think evilly of their wives without a cause meet with like hap. And many a husband, by suspecting his wife, makes her what he suspects her to be, for an honest woman is more easily to be overcome by despair than by all earthly pleasures. And if you say that jealousy is love, I deny it, 'tis not so, for like as ashes proceed from fire and yet quench it, so jealousy, proceeding from love, brings love to a close."

"I suppose," said Hircan, "that there can be no greater annoy to man or woman than to be suspected without a cause, and as for me, there is nothing that breaks up fellowship between my friends and myself more than this same jealousy." "Yet there was no reasonable excuse," said Oisille, "for her to take vengeance for her husband's jealousy by her own shame; 'tis rather like to one who, not being able to kill his enemy, gives himself a sword thrust across the body; or not being able to scratch him, bites his own fingers. She would have done better no more to have spoken to the man, thereby showing to her husband the wrong he had done her, and time would have made them at one." "'Natheless 'twas done like a woman with a bold heart," said Ennasuitte, " and if more wives were of the same mind, their husbands would be less outrageous than they are now." "Howsoever that may be," said Longarine, "long suffering giveth a woman at last the victory, and chastity makes her worthy of praise, and that is enough." " All the same," answered Ennasuitte, " a woman can lose her chastity, and yet do no sin." " What mean you by this," said Oisille, " when she takes another man for her husband?" " But what woman is so foolish," said Parlamente, " and who knows not the difference between her husband and another man, in whatever guise he be?" " There have been, and there will be a few," said Ennasuitte, " who have been thus deceived, and so are innocent and remain without sin." " If you know of an example," said Dagoucin, " I give you my vote to tell it; for I find this a strange thing that innocence and sin can abide together." " Listen, then," said Ennasuitte, " and though by the tales that have been already told you perceive how dangerous a thing it is to have in your houses them that are wont to call us *worldlings,* and think themselves holier and better than we, I am minded to give you yet another example whereby you may know that they are not only of like passions with other men, but that there is a somewhat devilish in them that surpasseth the common wickedness of men. And this you shall see by my history."

NOVEL XLVIII.

How a friar played his part in a marriage feast, and the manner of his punishment.

In a certain village of Perigord a marriage feast was made at the inn, and there all the friends and kinsfolk of the bride and bridegroom made good cheer together. And on the day of the wedding there came thither two friars, to whom supper was given in their own room, since it was not meet for men of their condition to be present at the feast. But the chief of the two friars, he having the greater authority and subtilty, resolved within himself that, since they kept him from the board, he would have a share in the bed, and show them one of his craft secrets. So when the evening was come, and the dancing begun, the friar looked for a long while through a

window on the bride and found her mighty pretty and altogether to his taste. And having made careful inquiry of the
serving-maids as to the room where she was to lie, he found to
his great contentment that it was hard-by his own; and the
better to gain his ends, kept such good watch that he saw the
old women leading her after their custom away from the hall.
Now since it was very early the husband would not leave the
dance, persisting in it so long that it seemed as if he had forgotten his wife, the which the friar had by no means done,
for as soon as he heard the bride was a-bed, he doffed his grey
habit and went and took the husband's place. But for fear of
being found there he stayed but a short while, and walked to
the end of a passage where stood his fellow keeping guard for
him, who made a sign that the husband was still dancing. So
the friar, who had not yet satisfied his wicked concupiscence,
went again to lie with the bride, till that his fellow warned him
it was time to get him gone. Then came the bridegroom to
bed, and his wife, who had been so entreated by the friar that
she craved nothing but rest, could not refrain from saying :
" Is it your purpose to take no sleep, and to never cease from
troubling me ?" The poor man, having hardly come, was
much astonished, and asked what trouble he had given her,
since he had but now left the dance. " A very brave dance,"
answered the poor girl, " inasmuch as this is the third time you
have lain with me ; methinks you would do better to go to
sleep." Hearing these words he marvelled still more, and
forgot all else to know the truth of the matter, and when she
had told him her tale, he suspected the friars who were lodged
in the house. So he arose forthwith and entered their room,
which was hard-by his own. And perceiving they were not
there he fell to calling help so loudly that he got together all
his friends, and they, having been advised of what had been
done, came to his aid with torches, lanterns, and all the dogs
that were in the village, and so made inquisition for the friars.
And finding them not indoors, they made such good speed
that they caught them in the vineyards, and there entreated
them as they had deserved ; for after that they had well beaten
them they cut off their arms and legs, and left them amidst
the vines to the care of Bacchus and Venus, whom they followed rather than St. Francis.

"Be not astonished, ladies, if such folk, separated from our common manner of living, do things that would shame a freelance. Marvel rather that they do not still worse, when God takes his favour from them; for the cowl is so far from making the monk that it often, through pride, unmakes him. And for me the 'religion' of St. James is good enough: 'Pure religion and undefiled before God and the Father is this, To visit the fatherless and widows in their affliction, and to keep himself unspotted from the world.' " "Shall we never," said Oisille, "have done with these tales of the wicked friars?" Ennasuitte replied: "If princes, ladies, and gentlemen, be not spared, methinks we honour the friars mightily by deigning to speak of them; for so useless are they that, if they had not done evil deeds worthy of remembrance, there would be nothing to tell concerning them, and it is said that one had better do evil than do nothing. And our posy shall be the finer for having in it flowers of all sorts." "If you would promise," said Hircan, "not to be wrath with me, I will tell you of a great lady so wicked, that you will have the poor friar excused, who supplied his needs where he was able, since the lady of my story, though she had enough to eat, was so shamefully dainty." "As we are sworn to tell the truth," said Oisille, "so are we sworn to hear it. Wherefore speak freely, for the evil we say of men and women is not to do them peculiar shame, but to take away all confidence in the creature, by showing the mischances into which men fall. And thereby to fix our hope on Him who alone is perfect, and without whom man is but imperfection." "Then freely and without fear," said Hircan, "I will tell you the history."

NOVEL XLIX.

A pleasant case of a gentlewoman that had three lovers at once, and made each to believe himself the only one.

In the days of King Charles—I say not which, for the sake of her of whom I am about to speak, and whose name I will not give you—there came to Court a Countess of a very illustrious house, but a foreigner. And because whatsoever is new is pleasant, this lady, at her coming, as much for the novelty of her dress as for its great richness, was looked upon by all;

and though she was none of the prettiest, yet she had such a daring grace and such a weighty manner of speaking that none durst approach her save the King, who loved her exceedingly. And that he might parley with her the more privily, he gave certain charges to the Count her husband, the which kept him a long while away, and during this time the King and his wife entertained one another right merrily. So several gentlemen about the Court, knowing their master to have had good treatment at her hands, made bold to speak to her, among others one Astillon, a hardy man and of a brave address. And in the beginning she held herself gravely towards him, threatening to tell the King his master, whereby she thought to make him afraid; but he, who was not accustomed to dread the threats of great warriors, made but small account of hers, and pressed her so hard, that she granted him to parley with her alone, showing him the manner wherein he should come to her room. In this he failed her not, yet to the end that the King might have no suspicion, he prayed leave of him to go on a journey, and set out from Court, but on the first day left all his people, and returned by night to obtain the promises made to him by the Countess. She discharged them in full, and so satisfied was he thereat, that he was well pleased to stay five or six days shut up in a closet without going forth from it, and his meat there was only strengthening medicaments. But during the eight days he was clapped up in this closet there came one of his companions, whose name was Durassier, to make love to the Countess, who received him in the same manner as she did the first: in the beginning with stern and haughty discourse, that grew softer every day, and when the time came for her to set free her prisoner she put another in place of him. And while Durassier was there, another courtier named Valnebon did in like manner as his fellows had done, and after this two or three others had a share in the pleasant prison.

And this fashion of living lasted a long while, and so subtilely was it ordered, that none of them suspected his fellow, for though each knew of the other's love, yet each thought that he alone got what he asked, and mocked his fellow for that he had failed in so rare a quest. But one day, as the aforesaid gentlemen were feasting and making merry together, they fell to talking of the chances of war, and the prisons they had been in. And Valnebon, who had hardly been able to conceal from his fellows his great good fortune, began to say : "I know nothing of your prisons, but for my part I, for the love I bear one in which I have been, will speak well of it all my days, and of others also for the sake of it; for I esteem no delight in the world equal to that of being a prisoner." Astillon, who had been the first prisoner, suspected what prison it was, and said to him : "Valnebon, what gaoler or gaoleress was it that entreated you so kindly, and whose prison-house is it that you love so well?" Valnebon replied : "Whosoever the gaoler might be, so pleasant was my captivity that I would it had lasted longer, for never was I better treated or more content." Durassier, a man of few words, knowing very well that the talk was of the prison which he had shared with the rest, said to Valnebon : "On what meats were you fed in this prison you praise so much?" "On what meats?" said Valnebon. "His Sacred Majesty hath not better nor more invigorant." "But still I am fain to know," said Durassier, "if your gaoler made you work well for your bread?" Valnebon, suspecting he was understood, could not refrain from saying : "Gadsfish! had I then fellows where I thought to have been alone?" Astillon, seeing plainly how he had shared his fortune with the rest, said with a laugh : "We have all been under one master and in one fellowship from our youth, wherefore if we have been fellows in good luck, we ought to rejoice thereat. But to know if the matter be as I deem it is, I pray you give me leave to interrogate and do you confess the truth, for if it have fallen out as you suppose, it will be as pleasant a case as was ever written and imprinted in a book." They all swore to tell the truth, if his questions were such as they could not deny. He said : "I will tell you my hap, and do you answer yea or nay whether yours was like unto it." They all agreed, and so he began : "I prayed leave of the King to go on a journey." All made answer : "So we." "When I was distant two leagues from Court, I left my people and rendered myself prisoner." All made answer : "So we." "I abode there seven or eight days, and lay in a closet, where I was fed but on restorative medicaments, and the most opiparous fare I have ever eaten; and at the end of the eighth day they that kept the prison enlarged me, weaker by far than when I came." "My captivity," said Astillon, "began and ended on such and such a day." "Mine," said Durassier, "began on the very day that yours came to an end, and lasted to such a day." Valnebon, losing all patience, began to swear and to say : "'Sblood! from what I hear I was the third, while I thought to have been the first and the only captive, for I went in and came out on such and such a day." The other three who were at the board swore to the due order of their several captivities. "Since this is as it is," said Astillon, "I will make interrogation as to the estate of our gaoleress : is she married and her husband in a far country?" All answered that this was she. "Well," said Astillon, "to put us quite out of our pain, I, who was the first on the roll, will be likewise the first to name her; 'tis the fair Countess, who was so haughty that when I won her love, I was as if I had overcome Cæsar. To the devil with the strumpet that made us win her with such toil, and deem ourselves happy in that we had gained her! Sure there never was the like of her; for, whilst she had one in her closet, she was fooling another, so as never to be without pastime. I had rather die than see her get off scot free. All asked as to what manner of punishment she should receive, and affirmed themselves ready to give it her, and one would have the King, who accounted her a goddess, advertised of the affair. "By no means," said Astillon; "we have power sufficient to avenge us on her, without calling in the King our master. Let us find out to-morrow when she goes to mass, and let each carry an iron chain around his neck, and when she goes into the church we will give her a befitting salutation."

This counsel was found good by all, and each one got for himself an iron chain. And when morning was come, all clothed in black, with their chains about their necks in place of collars, they went and made search for the Countess as she went to church. And so soon as she saw them thus mournfully arrayed, she fell to laughing, and said to them : "Whitherwards go ye, most dolorous folk ?" "Mistress," said Astillon, "we come to accompany you as your prisoner, bound to do your service." The Countess, feigning to understand nothing of this, answered : "You are none of my prisoners, and I know not wherefore you are bound to do my service more than other men." Then Valnebon came forward and said : "Since we have so long time eaten your bread, we should be mighty ungrateful if we did not your service." She put on an appearance of not understanding aught of this, supposing that thereby she would dumbfounder them, but they pursued her with their discourse in such wise that she knew that the whole matter was discovered. And straightway did she find means to cozen them afresh, for having quite lost her honour and conscience, she, despite their endeavour, refused to be at all shamefaced; but as one who had rather pleasure than all the honour the world can give, received them none the worse nor changed her countenance towards them, and so astonished were they at this that the confusion with which they would have covered her was turned upon their own heads.

"If, ladies, by this tale you are not persuaded that women are as bad as men, I will seek out others for your satisfaction on the matter; natheless I think this should suffice to show you that a woman who has lost all shame is a hundred times more hardy to do evil than is a man." No woman was there in the company who, in the telling of this tale, did not make as many signs of the cross as if she saw all the devils in hell before her eyes. But Oisille said to them: "Let us humble ourselves, ladies, at the hearing of this dreadful case; since she who is left of God is made conformable with him to whom she is joined: for as they that are joined to God have His Spirit with them, so is it with them who are joined to the devil; and one that hath not the Spirit of God is like unto the brutes." "Howsoever this poor woman may have sinned," said Ennasuitte, "I cannot praise them that boasted of their prison-house." "I believe," said Longarine, "that a man has no less trouble to conceal his good luck than to obtain it, for every hunter blows his horn over his quarry and every lover over his conquest." "That is a position," said Simontault, "I would maintain for heretical before the Inquisitors of the Holy Office itself; for more men are secret than women, and I know well that some there are who would rather not gain their desires at all than that any should be advertised of the same. Wherefore the Church, like a good mother, hath ordained men to be confessors and not women, since they can keep nothing secret." "'Tis not so," said Oisille, "but because women are so great enemies to wickedness that they would not as easily grant

absolution as men; and would be too severe in their penances."
"If they were as severe therein," said Dagoucin, "as in their
answers, they would rather drive sinners to despair than lead
them along the way to salvation, and so the Church has ordained
well altogether. But for all that, I would by no means excuse
the gentlemen who thus made a boast of their prison-house, for
a man of honour speaks no ill of women." "Since the lot
was common to all," said Hircan, "methinks they did well to
console one another." "But," answered Geburon, "for their
own honour's sake they should never have made confession.
For it is written in the books of the Round Table that 'tis no
honour for a good knight to overcome one who is of no
account." "I marvel," said Longarine, "that this poor wretch
did not die of shame in the presence of her captives." "They
that have lost all shame," said Oisille, "do hardly get it back,
save strong love caused them to lose it. Of such I have seen
many an one return." "I do suppose," said Hircan, "you
have seen just so many return as you have seen go; by that
way at least, for strong love in a woman is a thing mighty hard
to find." "I hold not to your opinion," said Longarine, "for
I believe that many a woman hath loved unto death." "So
much do I desire to hear of this new thing," said Hircan, "that
I give you my vote that we may know somewhat concerning
that love in women which I never thought to have existence."
"Then hear and believe," said Longarine, "that there is
nothing stronger than this same passion of love. And all as it
doth make men to undertake impossible things, to gain some
of this life's contentments, so more than aught else doth it
bring to despair him or her that has lost hope of good success,
as you shall see by this history."

NOVEL L.

*The pitiful end of two lovers, wherein is shown that it is possible to love even
unto death.*

In the town of Cremona no long while ago there lived a
gentleman named Messire Giovanni Pietro, who for some time
had loved a lady dwelling hard-by to his house, but for all his
pursuit of her he could not get the answer he desired, and this
although she loved him with all her heart. Whereat the poor

gentleman became so wearied and oppressed, that he kept himself in his lodging, resolved no more vainly to endeavour a thing the desire for which was wearing his life away. And the better to drive this fantasy from his brain he went several days without seeing her, and in this manner grew so melancholical that the fashion of his countenance was altered and hardly to be known. Wherefore his kinsfolk made summon the physicians, who, seeing the face of him that it was yellow, thought there was an obstruction in the liver, and would have him blooded. His mistress, who had so long played the prude, being persuaded that this sickness of his came but from her refusals, sent to him an old woman in whom she trusted, and told him that since she perceived his love was true and not feigned, she was determined to grant him all that she had till now refused, and she had found means to go forth from her lodging to a place where she might privily entertain him. The gentleman, who in the morning had been blooded in the arm, found himself better cured by these words than by any medicament or cupping-glasses, and sent word that he would not fail her at the time and place she had appointed, and that she had worked an evident miracle, for with one word she had cured a man of a sickness for which all the physicians could find no remedy. And when the evening was come so much desired of him, the gentleman went to the place agreed upon, and so great was his joy that not being able to grow more, it needs must grow less and come to an end. And he had waited but a short time when she he loved more than his life came and sought him out. No long discourse did he make for her diversion, since the fire that burned within made him haste to obtain that which he could scarcely believe was in his power. Then filled with love and pleasure as with strong drink, and thinking he had found wherewithal he might lengthen his days, in place thereof he cut them short, for having in his sweetheart altogether forgotten himself, he perceived not that the bandages on his arm were loosened, and the wound, bursting forth afresh, gushed out with so much blood that this poor man was quite bathed in it. But, thinking his weariness came from excess in love dalliance, he was minded to return to his house. Then did love, that had brought them into such close communion, act in such wise that as he departed from his mistress the soul departed from his body, and, by reason of the great pouring forth of his blood, he fell dead at the lady's feet. And she stood still as one beside herself with dreadful astonishment, considering the loss of so perfect a lover, of whose death she alone was the cause. And also she thought on the shame that would abide with her if his dead body were found in the house; so that the thing might not be known, she and a serving-maid in whom she trusted carried the body into the street. But there she determined not to leave him alone, and, taking the dead man's sword, she pierced through and through her heart, the cause of all the evil, and the dead body of her fell on that of her lover. And her father and mother, going forth on the morrow from the house, saw there that pitiful sight, and, after sorrowing with a great sorrow, buried them both together.

"So, ladies, a great love brought about a great mischance." "This is a case that pleases me mightily," said Simontault, "when love is so equally divided that one dying, the other will not live. And if by God's grace I had found such a mistress, I believe no man would have loved her with a more perfect love." "Yet I am of opinion," said Parlamente, "that love would not have so blinded you that you would not have bound up your arm better than did this poor man, for the time when men forgot their lives for their ladies is overpast." "But," said Simontault, "the time is not overpast for women to forget their lovers' lives by reason of their own pleasures." "I believe," said Ennasuitte, "that there is no woman in the world that takes pleasure in the death of a man, though he be her enemy. Natheless, if men will kill themselves, we women cannot save them." "Yet," said Simontault, "he that refuseth a morsel of bread to a poor man dying of hunger is accounted as a murderer." "If your demands," said Oisille, "were as reasonable as those of the poor, who ask but for their necessity, the women would be cruel above measure did they refuse you; but, thanks be to God! this sickness kills but those that are appointed to die within the year." "I know not, mistress," said Simontault, "how any necessity can be greater than that which makes all others to be forgotten; for when love is strong a body thinks of no meat nor bread save the looks and the words of her he loves." "If you were left thus to fast," replied Oisille, "and no other victuals given you save these, you would soon change your story." "I confess," answered he, "that the flesh might fail me, but never the heart nor the mind." "Then," said Parlamente, "God hath been very mindful of you, in that He hath made you to do your suit and service to so unthankful a mistress, that you are of necessity forced to console yourself with victuals and drink, wherein you quit you so manfully, that you shall praise the Lord for so merciful a severity." "In such manner," answered he, "have I fed on torment, that I well-nigh give thanks for the ills whereat others mourn." "It may be," said Longarine, "that your lamentations shut you out from her presence, where if you rejoiced you would be welcome, for there is nothing more wearisome than an importunate lover." "Save only," answered Simontault, "a cruel lady." "I plainly see," said Oisille, "that if we heard Simontault his conclusions to the end, it would be compline and not evensong time, for he has the matter at heart. Wherefore let us begone to praise God that this day has been spent with no more grievous quarrel." So she arose, and all the rest followed her; but Simontault and Longarine ceased not their quarrel, and yet so gently was it ordered that Simontault, without drawing his sword, came off the conqueror, convincing her that the strongest passion was the greatest necessity. Thereupon they came into the quire, where the monks awaited them, and, having heard evensong, made their supper as much off words as meat. For their talk lasted the whole while they were at board and far into the evening, till that Oisille said they would do well to give rest to their imaginations, and that the five days overpast were filled with such fine tales that she was in great fear lest the sixth should not equal them, since it were not possible, even should they invent them, to tell better tales than they had already recounted. But Geburon said that, as long as the world lasted, things would be done worthy to be had in remembrance. "For the wickedness of the wicked is always as it has been, and also the goodness of the good. So long as evil and good reign upon the earth they will ever accomplish new deeds, although it is written there is nothing new under the sun. But we, inasmuch as we are not called to the privy counsels of God, and therefore know not the causes of things, find all things new the more admirable that we ourselves cannot or will not do them, so be not afraid lest the days that are to come be worse than they that went before; and do you, for your part, endeavour to do your duty." Oisille said she commended herself to God, and in His name bade them good-night. So all the company departed, and the fifth day was brought to a close.

DAY THE SIXTH.

On the Sixth Day relation is made of the deceits between man and woman, through covetousness, vengeance, and craftiness.

PROLOGUE.

On the morrow earlier than she was wont, Oisille went into the hall to make ready her lesson; and the company being advertised of this, for the desire they had to hear her wholesome exhortations, made such speed to dress themselves that she had no long time to wait. And perceiving their spirits to be stirred up, and having before expounded to them the Epistle of St. Paul to the Romans, she on this day read to them the Epistle of St. John the Divine, the which is full of all love. So pleasant was this refection to them that were present that, although they had been there a full half-hour over and above the accustomed time, yet the whole seemed not more than a quarter of an hour. From thence they passed to the adoration of the Blessed Sacrament, commending themselves to the Holy Ghost that what they had heard on that day might be profitable unto them. And after they had broken their fast and rested for a while, they went to the meadow for their wonted pastime. And Oisille asked who should make a beginning to the day. Longarine answered and said: "I give my vote to Mistress Oisille: for so good a lesson hath she given us this morning, that she will doubtless tell us some story worthy of the same." "I am sorry," said Oisille, "that I cannot speak to you this afternoon as profitably as in the morning; natheless, the intent of my history shall not be at variance with that place of Holy Scripture where it is written: 'O, put not your trust in princes, nor in any child of man; for there is no help in them.' And to the end that this Scripture may not fall into forgetfulness for want of an example, I will give you a true one, and so fresh is it in men's memory that the tears are scarce wiped away from the eyes of them that saw this pitiful sight."

NOVEL LI.

The cruel and treacherous vengeance of an Italian nobleman upon a woman that
had done him a displeasure.

The Duke of Urbino, named the Prefect, the same that
took to wife the sister of the first Duke of Mantua, had a son
of the age of eighteen or twenty years, who was in love with
the daughter of a good and honourable house, and having the
Abbot of Farse for her brother. And since, as the custom of
the country is, he was not free to speak with her as he would,
he used the help of a gentleman of his following, who was
amorous of a young gentlewoman in the service of his mother,
mighty pretty and virtuous, and by her the son of the Duke
made known to his sweetheart the great affection he had for
her. And this the girl thought no shame, taking pleasure in
doing him a kindness, and esteeming his intent so good and
honourable that she could do no harm by declaring it to his
sweetheart. But the Duke, who cared more for the advantage
of his house than for honest love, was greatly afraid lest these
passages should bring his son into marriage with his mistress,
and so kept a shrewd watch. And it was told him that this
poor gentlewoman was mixed up in the complot and had given
certain letters from his son to her he loved, whereat he was so
wrathful, that he determined to take effectual order in the
matter. Yet he could not disguise his anger so that the girl
should not be advertised of it, and she knowing the craftiness
of the Duke that it was great, and his conscience but small,
fell into marvellous alarm, and came to the Duchess praying
leave to get her gone to some place removed from his sight
till his fury was overpast. Her mistress told her that she must
first know her husband's will before she gave her leave: all
the same she soon understood the Duke's mind towards her,
and knowing his complexion, she not only gave her leave, but
counselled her to enter a monastery till this storm was blown
over. This she did as privily as she was able, but yet the
Duke was advised of it, and putting on a feigned gladness,
asked his wife where was the gentlewoman, and she, thinking
he knew the truth well, confessed it to him, at which he made
a pretence of grief, saying she had no need of so doing, and
that for his part he wished her no ill, and since the rumour of

such things was hurtful, she would do well to come back. His wife replied that if the poor girl were so unhappy as to want his favours, it were better that for some time she should not appear in his presence, but he would give ear to none of her reasons, and bade make her return. The Duchess failed not to declare to her the will of the Duke, but she could in no wise assure herself thereof, entreating her mistress not to make her thus tempt fortune, and saying she was persuaded that the Duke was not so ready to grant forgiveness as he feigned to be. Natheless the Duchess declared that she should take no hurt, and pledged her honour for her life. And the girl, knowing that her mistress loved her, and would not wantonly deceive her, put trust in her promise, thinking that the Duke would by no means break such a pledge wherein was engaged the honour of his wife, and so returned to the Duchess. But so soon as the Duke was ware of it, he forthwith came into his wife's room, and when he saw the girl said to his wife: "And so such an one is returned?" Then went he back to his gentlemen bidding them take her and clap her up in prison. At this the poor Duchess, who on her word had drawn her from the liberties of the monastery, became desperate, throwing herself on her knees before her husband, and entreating him for the love of her and her house not to do such a deed, since in obedience to him she had enticed her from the place where she was in safety. Yet no prayers that she could make availed at all to soften his hard heart, nor to overcome his fixed resolve to take vengeance on her, so, not replying to his wife, he went quickly from her, and without form of justice, forgetting alike his God and the honour of his house, he cruelly made hang the poor gentlewoman. I will not endeavour to tell you of the sorrow of the Duchess, for it was that which should befall an honourable lady and a kind-hearted, who against the pledge given of her, saw one die whom she was fain to have saved. Still less can be told the bitter grief of the poor gentleman her lover, who failed not to endeavour to the utmost to save his sweetheart's life, offering to die in her stead. But no manner of pity or compassion could touch this Duke, who knew none other happiness than to be avenged on his enemy. So was this innocent gentlewoman put to death by the cruel Duke against all law and honour, and to the great sorrow of them that knew her.

"Consider, ladies, what cometh of malice when it is joined to power." "I have heard," said Longarine, "that the Italians are subject to three vices in particular, but I never thought their cruel vengeance would have gone thus far, as for so small an occasion to send a woman to a shameful death." Saffredent, laughing, said to her: "Longarine, you have truly told us one of the three vices, but I would know as to the two others." "If you knew not," answered she, "I would tell you, but sure am I that you know them all." "Do you then esteem me," said Saffredent, "so exceeding vicious?" "Not so," answered Longarine, "but that you know so well the foulness of vice, that better than any other you can avoid it." "Marvel not," said Simontault, "at this piece of cruelty, for they that have been in Italy tell of such deeds that this is a mere peccadillo by comparison." "Truly," said Geburon, "when Rivolte was taken by the French, an Italian captain, accounted a brave soldier, seeing dead one who was only his enemy in that he was of an opposite faction, tore out his heart, and hastily roasting it, ate it. And he replied to certain that asked how it tasted, that he had never eaten so dainty a dish or one so savoury, and not content with this he killed the wife of the dead man, and snatching from her womb the fruit thereof, dashed it against a wall. Then he filled the two bodies of husband and wife with oats, and made his horses eat from them. Think you this man would not surely have put a girl to death, whom he suspected to have done him a wrong?" "It must be confessed," said Ennasuitte, "that the Duke had a greater fear lest his son should make a poor marriage, than desire to give him a wife according to his taste." "I suppose one cannot doubt," said Simontault, "that the habit of the Italians is to love more than nature things merely created for the service of the same." "Nay, and worse than this," said Hircan, "for they make a god of things that are against nature." "These be the sins I would tell you of," said Longarine, "for 'tis well known that to love money, beyond our honest necessities, is to commit idolatry." Parlamente said that St. Paul had not forgotten the vices proper to the Italians and to all them who thought to pass and overcome other men in honour, prudence, and earthly reason, on which so strongly do they bottom themselves that they give not to God the glory that belongs to Him. Where-

fore the Almighty, who is a jealous God, maketh them that
esteem themselves to be of keener wit than other men
more witless than the beasts of the field, causing them to
manifest by their unnatural deeds that there is no health in
them. Longarine broke in amidst her words, saying that this
was the third sin that was in her mind. "By my faith," said
Nomerfide, "this talk is mighty pleasant to me. For since
those spirits esteemed the noblest and highest are so punished
that they become more foolish than the beasts, needs must be
that the small and humble and they of no reputation, like
myself, are filled with the wisdom of angels." "I do assure
you," said Oisille, "that I am not far from your opinion, for
none is more ignorant than he who thinks he knows." "I
have never seen," said Geburon, "the mocker who was not
mocked, the cozener that was not cozened, nor the vain-boaster
that was not humbled." "You call to remembrance," said
Simontault, "a piece of cozenage that, if it were seemly, I
would willingly have told you." "Since then we are here to
tell the truth," said Oisille, "be it as it may, I give you my
vote." "That being so," said he, "I will tell you the story."

NOVEL LII.

How an apothecary's prentice gave two gentlemen their breakfast.

Hard-by the town of Alençon there lived a gentleman named
my lord de la Tireliere, who came one morning from his house
to the town on foot, as much because it was no long distance
as for that it was freezing hard enough to split the stones, on
which account he had not left at home his great cloak lined
with fox-skin. And when he had done his business, he lit
upon a lawyer named Antony Bacheré, who was of his
acquaintance, and after some talk of his affairs, said to him
that he was desirous of finding a good breakfast, but it must
be at another's charges. And while they spoke to this effect
they sat them down before an apothecary's shop, where the
apprentice heard their discourse, and resolved forthwith to
provide them with a breakfast. So he went out from his shop
to a certain street in the town, where all men performed their
occasions, and found there a mighty lump of ordure, frozen so

hard that it was like to a small loaf of refined sugar; straight-way he wrapped it in brave white paper, as he was accustomed to do with his drugs that they might be an admiration to men, and hid it in his sleeve. And as he passed before the gentle-man and the lawyer he let this fine sugar-loaf fall near them as if by mischance, and entered into a house whither he feigned to be carrying it. My lord de la Tireliere, thinking it was a sugar-loaf, hasted to pick it up, and so soon as he had done so the knave of an apprentice returned searching and asking for his sugar on every side. The gentleman, who conceived he had admirably cozened him, went quickly with his fellow to a tavern, saying: "The charges of our breakfast are provided for by master apprentice." When he was in the inn he called for good bread, good meat, and good drink, being persuaded that he had wherewithal to pay; but when as they ate they began to grow warm, the sugar-loaf began to thaw and filled the room with its own peculiar stink. Whereat he that bore it in his bosom began to chide the serving-maid, saying: "You of this town are the beastliest folk I ever have seen, for either you or your children have strown all the floor with filth." The serving-maid answered: "By St. Peter, but there is no filth in this house, unless you have brought it in with you." On this they arose for the great stink that was in their nostrils, and stood hard-by the fire, where the gentleman, drawing a hand-kerchief from his breast, found it all besmeared with the melted sugar. And when he opened his great-cloak lined with fox-skin, it was altogether spoilt, and he had nought to say to his fellow but: "The rogue we thought to deceive hath paid us well for it!" And having discharged their reckoning they went out as sad as they had come in glad, thinking to have cozened the knave of an apprentice.

"We often find, ladies, a like hap befall them that take delight in like cozenage. If the gentleman had not wished to eat at the expense of another he would not have drunken so filthy a brew at his own. It is true, ladies, my tale is not as clean as might be; but you gave me leave to tell the truth, which I have done, to show you how when the cozener is cozened no one is sorry." "Men say," says Hircan, "that words do not stink, but they that utter them are not so easily quit of them as not to give forth some stench." "It is true

that words of this kind," said Oisille, "do not stink; but
others there are called *smutty*, that give forth such an evil odour
that the soul takes more heart at the hearing of them than the
body at the smelling of a sugar-loaf like that in the story."
"I pray you," said Hircan, "tell me what words you esteem
so foul as to do hurt to the soul and mind of an honest woman."
It would be a brave thing, truly," said Oisille, "were I to say
to you the very words I counsel no woman to say." "Thereby,"
said Saffredent, "I understand well what these words be.
Women who desire to be of good reputation do not commonly
use them, but I would know of the company here present why
it is that, though they dare not use them, they are so easily
moved to laughter when they are uttered in their presence."
Parlamente answered: "We do not laugh to hear these brave
words, but true it is that all men are inclined to laugh when a
slip is made, or one word said for another, the which happens
to the most discreet and ready speakers. But when a man
talks smuttily without any ignorance but with evil intent, I
know no honest woman to whom such talk is not an abomination, and who would not only turn a deaf ear to men of this
fashion, but would also separate herself from their company."
"You say truly," said Geburon, "for I have seen women make
the sign of the cross at the hearing of these words." "But
how often," asked Simontault, "doth a woman put on her
mask so that she may secretly laugh and openly rebuke?"
"It were better to do thus," said Parlamente, "than to let it
be known that one took pleasure in such talk." "You praise,
then," said Dagoucin, "hypocrisy in ladies equally with virtue?"
"Virtue would be better by far," answered Longarine, "but
when it fails us we must call hypocrisy to our aid, as we use
high-heeled shoes to conceal our littleness. It is no small thing
if we have imperfections to be able to hide them." "By my
faith," said Hircan, "it would sometimes be better for you to
show a small failing than to cover up all so closely under the
cloak of virtue." "It is true," said Ennasuitte, "that the
borrowed cloak when it is snatched away doth do her as much
dishonour as it was before honourable; and there was once a
woman who by too much concealing of a small fault fell into a
greater. "I suspect," said Hircan, "I know her of whom you
speak, but, at least, do not give her name." "And I," said

Geburon, "do give you my vote, if after you have told the
story you will tell us the names, the which we will swear never
to reveal." "I promise you," said Ennasuitte, "for there is
nothing that cannot be told in a seemly fashion."

NOVEL LIII.

How a lady by too close concealment was put to shame.

Once upon a time King Francis the First was at a fine
castle whither he had gone with a small following for the sake
of hunting, and also to get some rest from affairs of state. In
his following was one called the Prince of Belhoste, as honourable, virtuous, and prudent a man as any at Court, and married
to a wife of somewhat low condition. Yet he loved her and
treated her as well as any husband could treat his wife, and
altogether trusted her, and when he fell into love with any
other woman he concealed it not from her, knowing she thought
only as he did. Now this prince conceived a great affection
for a widow lady named Madam de Neufchâtel, who passed
for as pretty a woman as was to be seen: and if the Prince of
Belhoste loved her well, his wife did the like, often bidding her
to dinner, and found her to be so discreet and virtuous, that in
place of being wrathful with her husband, she rather rejoiced
to see him do his suit in so good and honourable a quarter.
This friendship lasted a long while, and was of such sort that
in all the affairs of Madam de Neufchâtel the prince employed
himself as if they had been his own ; and his wife did no less.
But by reason of her beauty her favour was earnestly sought by
many great lords and gentlemen ; some craving love alone, and
others the wedding ring also, for beside her comeliness she had
much riches. Among the rest there was one young gentleman
called my lord des Cheriots, who pressed her so hard, that he
failed not to be at her levee and couchee, and as far as was in
his power he kept by her side all the whole day. Now this
was not pleasing to the Prince of Belhoste, since he thought a
man of his small estate and mean address did not deserve so
good and kindly a reception: wherefore he often made remonstrance with the lady. But she, being a true daughter of Eve,
excused herself, saying she held parley with all men, and their

love would be the more concealed that she spoke to one as
much as to another.   But at the end of some time my lord des
Cheriots pressed his suit so well that, more for his importunity
than for any love she bore him, she promised marriage, praying
him not to make her declare the same till that her daughters
were wed.   Henceforth, without fear or scruple, the gentleman
went to her room at all hours as he was minded, and only a
bedchamber woman and gentleman were privy to the matter.
The prince, seeing the gentleman grow more and more familiar
in the house of her he loved, took it in so bad part that he
could not refrain from saying to the lady: "I have always
prized your honour, even as that of mine own sister, and you
know the honourable passages that have been between us, and
the contentment I have had in the loving of a lady as discreet
and virtuous as you are : but if I conceived that another, who
deserves it not, had gained by his importunity that which I
would not crave from you against your inclination, this would
be a grievous weight for me to bear, and to you a great dishonour.   I dare tell you this because you are young and comely,
and hitherto have been in good repute: and now you begin to
be in ill-fame, for though he be no match for you in house, nor
substance, far less in authority, wit, and address, yet it would
have been better for you to have married him than to have
made all men suspicious.   Wherefore, prithee tell me whether
or no you are resolved to have him for a lover, since I will be
no fellow of his, and will leave him to you altogether, and rid
myself of the goodwill I have borne you."   The poor lady
fell to weeping, for fear lest she should lose his friendship, and
swore to him she had rather die than wed the gentleman of
whom he spoke ; but so importunate was he that she could not
keep him out of her room when all other folk entered it.   "Of
that," said the prince, "I do not speak, for I can come there
then as well as he, and all can see what you do ; but it is
reported to me that he goes to you after your couchee, the
which I esteem so indiscreet, that if you continue this manner
of living and do not declare him for your husband, you will be
esteemed the most scandalous of all women."   She swore to
him that she held him neither as a lover nor a husband, but the
most importunate gentleman that ever was.   "Since it is so,
and he wearies you," said the prince. "be assured that I will

rid you of him." "What!" said she, "would you then kill him?" "Not so, not so," answered the prince, "but I will make him understand that the house of His Most Sacred Majesty is not the place to bring shame upon ladies : and I swear by the love I bear you, that if after my words he will not cleanse his ways I will cleanse them for him in such wise that others shall take example by him." Thereupon he went out, and failed not at the door to light upon my lord des Cheriots, to whom he spoke after the same sort, assuring him that the first time he found him there after the accustomed hour for gentlemen to speak with ladies, he would give him such a fright as he would never forget, and that her kinsfolk were too noble for him to play with her in this fashion. The gentleman swore he had never been in the room except with others, and gave him leave, if he found him there, to entreat him as evilly as he was able. But some time after, believing the prince to have forgotten the matter, he went to see his lady in the evening and stayed with her somewhat late. And the prince told his wife that Madam de Neufchâtel had a grievous rheum, wherefore she prayed him to go see her for the two, and to make her excuses for not going, since she was kept to her room by a necessary occasion. So the prince waited until after the King's couchee, and then went to see the lady ; but, as he began to mount the stair, a servant came down, who when he asked how his mistress did, replied that she was a-bed and asleep. The prince went down the stair thinking that he lied to him, wherefore he looked behind him and saw the servant returning at great speed whither he came. The prince then sauntered in the courtyard by the door to see if the servant would come back or no, and a quarter of an hour after he saw him coming down the stair again, and looking all around to see who was in the courtyard. From this he suspected that my lord des Cheriots was in the room with the lady, and durst not come down for fear of him, which made him persist to walk about the courtyard. But he called to mind that in the lady's room there was a window, not over high and looking on a garden, and thinking of the saw : *He who is not able to pass through the door may leap through the window,* instantly beckoned to a servant he had with him and said : " Go into the garden behind the house, and if you see a gentleman come down from a

window, as soon as he shall put foot to earth, draw your
sword and clash it against the wall, and cry aloud: "*Slay, slay!
But beware you touch him not at all.*" So the servant did as
his master had bidden him, and the prince walked in the courtyard till it was about three hours after midnight. But when
my lord des Cheriots heard that the prince was still in the
courtyard, he determined to get away by the window, and after
having first thrown out his cloak, with the aid of his good friends
he leapt into the garden. And so soon as the servant saw him
he failed not to clash his sword, and cried aloud: "*Slay, slay!*"
at which the poor gentleman, taking him for his master, was so
grievously afeared that, without a thought of his cloak, he fled
away as speedily as he could. And he lit upon the bowmen
of the watch, who were mightily astonished to see him thus
running, but he durst not tell them anything, and only prayed
them to open him the gate, or to lodge him with them till the
morrow: and this they did, for as to the gate they had not the
keys of it. In that hour the prince came to bed, and finding
his wife asleep he awoke her, saying: "Guess what hour it
is." She replied: "Since I went to bed I have not heard one
stroke of the clock." He said: "It is three hours past midnight." "Where then," said his wife, "have you been? I fear
greatly your health will suffer for it." "Sweetheart," answered
the prince, "waking will never hurt me, when thereby I keep
them that would deceive me from sleeping." So saying he fell
to laughing heartily, and his wife asked him the cause wherefore
he did it, which he told her, and showed her the wolfskin cloak
that his servant had brought. And after they had made merry
at the expense of the poor couple they fell into a pleasant sleep,
while the two others passed the night in fear and trembling
lest their passages should be revealed to all. But the gentleman, knowing he could not hide the matter from the prince,
came on the morrow to his levee, entreating him not to make it
manifest, and to give him back his cloak. The prince made
pretence of his being ignorant of the whole affair, and kept so
well his countenance that the gentleman was altogether at a
loss. But at last he talked to him after another fashion than
he had looked for, telling him that if he went again to the lady's
room he would tell the King, and make him to be banished
from the Court.

"I pray you consider, ladies, if this poor woman had not
done better to have spoken freely to him who so honoured her
by his love and esteem, than by deceit to have forced him to
make so shameful a proof of her." "She knew," said Geburon,
"that if she confessed the truth, she would altogether lose his
favour, the which she was not at all minded to do." "Methinks," said Longarine, "since she had chosen a husband to
her liking, she had no need to fear to lose the friendship of all
other men." "I do believe," said Parlamente, "that if she
durst have declared her marriage she would have satisfied herself with her husband, but since she wished to conceal it till
that her daughters were wed, she would not lose so honourable
a cloak." "'Twas not on that account," said Saffredent, "but
for the ambition that is so great in all women, that they will
not content themselves with one alone. And I have heard that
the more discreet will have three, nor more nor less—namely,
one for honour, one for profit, one for pleasure; and each of
these three deems himself the best beloved, but the two first
are as slaves to the last." "The women of whom you speak,"
said Oisille, "have nor love nor honour." "Mistress," answered
he, "the ladies I speak of are honourable ladies, ay, and
esteemed the most virtuous in the land." "Trust me," said
Hircan, "a crafty woman will gain her bread when all the rest
die of hunger." "Yet," said Longarine, "when their craft is
known, it is the death of them." "Not so, but rather their
life," answered Simontault, "for they account it no small glory
to be reputed crafty of their fellows. And this reputation for
craftiness doth more avail to bring them lovers than beauty.
For the greatest pleasure of two lovers is to order their passages
with cunning." "You speak," said Ennasuitte, "of unlawful
love, for honest love doth stand in no need of concealment."
"I entreat you," said Dagoucin, "to get quit of that opinion,
since the more precious the drug the less it should feel the air,
and because of the malice of them that only judge by outward
signs. Wherefore love, be it virtuous or the contrary, should
always be hidden from such folk as cannot believe that a man
ever loves a woman honourably, for they think, since they are
subject to lust, so are all others. But if we were all of good
faith, looks and words need not be concealed, at least from
them that had rather die than think evilly of their brethren."

" I assure you, Dagoucin," said Hircan, "you have so high a philosophy that there is not a man here understands or believes it, for you would have us believe that men are angels, or stones, or devils." "I know well," said Dagoucin, "that men are men, and subject to all manner of passions, yet there have been lovers who would die rather than have their ladies do for their pleasure aught against conscience." "Rather die is a great deal," said Geburon; "I would not believe this did it come from the mouth of the austerest monk in the world." " But I believe," said Hircan, "there is not one that does not believe the very contrary thereto. Natheless, they say the grapes are sour when they grow too high to be plucked." "I do suppose," said Nomerfide, "that the prince's wife was mighty glad when her husband found out what women are like." " Not so," answered Ennasuitte, "but sorry, for she loved this lady." "I like her also," said Saffredent, "who laughed when her husband kissed the serving maid." "Of a truth," said Ennasuitte, "you shall tell us the tale; I give you my vote." "Though my tale be short," said Saffredent, "I will it you, for I had rather make you laugh than talk for a long time."

NOVEL LIV.

A curious and notable case of shadows on a wall.

Between the Pyrenees and the Alps there lived a gentleman, having a wife and children, a mighty fine house, and so many blessings and contentments, that he had good reason for happiness. But with all this he was subject to a dreadful pain at the roots of his hair, for which cause the physicians advised him to lie apart from his wife, to which she consented very willingly, having no care but for the health and strength of her husband. So she made set another bed for her in a corner of the room opposite to that of her husband's, and in so straight a line with it that when they put their heads outside the curtain they could plainly see one another. This dame kept two serving-maids, and ofttimes, when she and her lord were a-bed, each would take a book to read for pastime, and the maids held the candle for them; that is to say, the young one for the master and the other for his wife. And seeing the maid to be younger

and prettier than his wife, the gentleman took such pleasure to
look upon her that he would break off his reading and they would
parley together.   And the wife heard them very plainly, and
found it a good thing that the serving-men and serving-women
should entertain their master, not thinking that he loved any
beside herself.   But one evening when they had read a longer
while than was their custom, the lady, looking towards her
husband's bed, where was the maid with the candle, saw only
the back of her; and of her husband she saw nothing, save
by means of the chimney that jutted out into the room, for the
wall of it was white, and shining with the light of the candle.
And upon the aforesaid wall she plainly beheld the likeness of
her husband's face, and the likeness of the maid's ; if they drew
near, if they went apart, or if they smiled, she was as plainly
advertised of it as if she had seen them.   The gentleman, being
sure that his wife could not by any means perceive them, took
no care, and kissed the maid, the which for the first time his wife
bore without saying a word, but when she saw the shadows
often thus communed with one another, she was afraid lest
beneath them there might be some solid substance, and therefore burst into a loud laugh, in such sort that the shadows grew
afraid and went apart.   And the gentleman asked her wherefore she laughed so loudly, and would have her make him a
partaker in her merriment.   She replied : "I am such a fool,
husband, that I laugh at my shadow."   And never, inquire
of her as he might, would she say anything else ; but for all
that this shadowy communion was seen no more.

   " And this is how the tale was brought to my remembrance
when you spoke of the dame that loved her husband's sweetheart."   " Faith," said Ennasuitte, "if my woman had used me
thus I had arisen and broken the candle on her nose."   " You
are mighty terrible," said Hircan ; " but how would it have fared
with you if your husband and the woman had banded together and
beaten you heartily?   And it skills not to make such an outcry
on a mere question of kissing ; wherefore the wife would have
done still better had she not said a word and left him to a
pastime which might lighten his sickness."   " But," said Parlamente, " she was afraid lest this pastime should make his sickness more grievous."   " She was not amongst those," said
Oisille, " against whom our Lord speaks : ' We have piped

unto you, and ye have not danced; we have mourned to you, and ye have not wept,' for when her husband was sick she mourned with him, and when he was merry she laughed. So ought all good wives to have the half of their husband's good and evil, sorrow and gladness, and to love, serve, and obey them as the Church does Christ." "Our husbands, then," said Parlamente, "should be to us as Christ is to the Church." "So we are," answered Saffredent; "and, if it be possible, more also; for Christ died but once for his Church, and we die for our wives day by day." "Die?" said Longarine; "methinks you and the others that are here present are with more pounds since you are married than pence before." "And I am well advised of the reason thereof," said Saffredent; "'tis that our valour is so often tried, but yet our shoulders feel the weight of the cuirass very grievous." "If you were constrained," said Ennasuitte, "to wear harness for a month and to sleep on the hard ground, you would be mighty desirous to come back to the bed of your good wife, and carry the cuirass of which you now complain. But it is well said that one can bear all things save ease, and one knows not what rest is till it is lost. And this fine dame who laughed when her husband was merry could take her rest whatever fell out." "I suppose," said Longarine, "that she loved rest more than her husband, insomuch as she took nothing to heart, let him do what he might." "She took one thing to heart," said Parlamente, "namely, that he might do harm to his health and his conscience, but for so small a matter she was unwilling to take any great annoy." "When you talk about conscience," said Simontault, "you make me laugh, for 'tis a thing I would have no woman trouble herself with." "Your desert would be," said Nomerfide, "to have a wife like that one who showed, after her husband's death, that she had a far greater love for his monies than his conscience." "I pray you," said Saffredent, "tell us the tale, and I will give you my vote." "I had determined," said she, "not to tell so short a story, but since it comes to hand I will do so."

NOVEL LV.

How a widow sold a horse for a ducat and a cat for ninety and nine.

In the town of Sarragossa there lived a rich merchant, who
seeing his death draw nigh, and that he could no longer keep
what perchance he had gathered together by evil means, thought
that if he made God a small present, it would be in some sort
a satisfaction for his sins; as if God would sell his grace for
money.   And when he had set his house in order, he said that
he devised his fine Spanish horse to be sold at the highest price
that could be got, and the money given to the poor; praying
his wife not to fail, so soon as he was dead, to sell the horse
and distribute the money according to his desire.   And when
the burial of him was at an end, and the first tears had fallen,
the wife, who was no more of a fool than other women of
Spain, went to a servant who had likewise heard his master's
pleasure, and said to him: "It seems to me that the loss of the
husband I loved so well is enough for me to bear, without also
losing his substance.   Yet I would in nowise disobey his will,
but rather do it after a more perfect manner, for the poor man,
misled of the covetous priests, thought to do God a great service by giving, after his death, these monies, of which in his life
he would not have given a single ducat in a case of extreme
necessity, as you well know.   Wherefore I am of opinion that
we do what he charged us at his death, and after a better
fashion than he would have done himself had he lived five days
longer; but not a single soul must be privy to the matter."
And when she had the servant's promise to keep it secret she
said to him: "You shall go sell the horse, and to them that
ask how much, you shall answer a ducat; but I have a mighty
serviceable cat which I am minded to put into the market, and
you must sell it together with the horse for ninety-nine ducats,
and so the cat and the horse will bring the hundred ducats
that my husband would have taken for the horse alone."   The
servant forthwith did as he was commanded of his mistress, and
as he led the horse through the market place, holding the cat
under his arm, a gentleman who had afore seen the horse and
desired to have it, asked the price thereof.   The servant replied
a ducat.   The gentleman said: "Prithee do not mock me."

"I do assure you," said the man, "it will cost you but a single ducat. It is true you must buy the cat along with it, of which the price is ninety-nine ducats." Straightway the gentleman, thinking it was a reasonable bargain, paid him one ducat for the horse, and ninety and nine for the cat, as it was asked of him, and bore away his commodities. The servant, on the other hand, took the money to his mistress, which she received right merrily, and failed not to give the one ducat that was the price of the horse to the poor beggars, as her husband had enjoined, and kept the ninety and nine for herself and her children.

"What think you? Was she not wiser than her husband, and was not her care for her conscience small in comparison with her care for his money?" "I think," said Parlamente, "that she loved her husband well, but since men for the most part wander when they are near to death, she, knowing his intent, interpreted his words to the profit of her children; wherefore I esteem her to have done prudently." "What!" said Geburon, "do you not esteem it a great sin to make the will of the departed of none effect?" "I do so esteem it," answered Parlamente, "being the deviser is of sound mind and not wandering." "Call you it wandering to give of one's substance to the Church and to the poor?" "By no means," said Parlamente, "when a man distributes to the poor what God hath put in his hands, but to make alms of another's goods I esteem no great wisdom. For you commonly see the worst usurers build the bravest and most admirable chapels, thinking to appease God for a hundred thousand ducats of robbery with ten thousand ducats of building, as if God could not keep account." "Truly," said Oisille, "I have often marvelled how they think to do God a pleasure with the selfsame things that he reproved when on earth, such as buildings adorned with gold and painting. But if they would attend to what God hath said in one place where he asks of us not sacrifice but a humble and contrite heart, and in another where St. Paul tells us we are the temples in the which God would dwell; they would labour to adorn their souls while they are alive, and not wait for the hour when men can do nor good nor evil, laying a charge on them that remain to do alms to the poor whom, while they are alive, they deign not so much as to look upon. But He that knoweth the heart of man is not deceived, and will judge them not only for their works but also for the faith and love they have had for Him." "How comes it then," said Geburon, "that the Grey Friars and Mendicants at our death talk of nothing but of making benefactions to their monasteries, assuring us that they will send us forthwith to paradise, whether we will or no?" "What! Geburon," said Hircan, "have you forgotten the craft of the friars that you yourself have told us of, that you ask how it is possible for them to lie? I declare to you that I deem them the greatest liars in the world, and though they that speak on behalf of the whole community are not worthy of reproof, yet there are certain of them that forget their vow of poverty to satisfy their covetousness." "Me-thinks, Hircan," said Nomerfide, "you know of some tale to the purpose. I pray you, if it be worthy of this company here present, to tell it." "I will do so," said Hircan, "though it wearies me to talk of these folk, for it seems to me that they are in the number of them of whom Virgil says to Dante : 'Pass on, and heed them not.' Natheless, to show you that they leave not their worldly passions with their worldly habits, I will tell you how the case fell out."

NOVEL LVI.

Of a cozening device of an old friar.

It was told to a French lady in Padua that in the bishop's prison there was a friar, and seeing that all men made a jest of him, she asked the reason of it. And she was told that this friar, an old man, was confessor to an honourable and devout lady who for some time had been a widow, and had one only daughter whom she loved so much that her care was but to heap up riches for her and to find her a good match. And perceiving her daughter to be growing of age, she incessantly troubled herself to find her a husband who could live with them in peace and quietness; that is to say, she would have a man with a good and honest conscience. And since she had heard a foolish preacher declare that it is better to do wrong by the counsel of the doctors of the Church than do right by the inspiration of the Holy Ghost, she addressed herself to her confessor, a man then stricken in years, a doctor in theology, esteemed of good life by all the town, assuring herself that with his counsel and prayers she would not fail to gain peace and quietness for herself and her daughter.   And on her earnestly entreating him to choose a husband for her daughter, and such a man as he knew would be befitting for a maid that loved God and her conscience, he replied that first of all he must implore the grace of the Holy Ghost with prayer and fasting, and then, God confirming his understanding, he would hope to find what she wanted.   So the friar went apart to ponder the matter, and hearing from the lady that she had got together five hundred ducats to give her daughter's husband, and would feed, lodge, and clothe the pair, he bethought him that there was a young friar of his acquaintance, of a good figure and pleasant countenance, to whom he would give the maid, the house, and an assured maintenance, and keep the five hundred ducats as an easement for his unspeakable covetousness.   And having spoken to the young friar he agreed with him, and returned to the lady, saying: "I steadfastly believe that God hath sent me his angel Raphael, as he did to Tobit, to find a perfect husband for your daughter, for I do assure you I have in my house the bravest gentleman in all Italy, who, having several times seen your daughter, is mightily pleased with her, and this very day, while I prayed, God sent him to me, and he declared the desire he had for this marriage; and I, knowing his house and lineage, and that he comes of a very notable stock, promised him to speak with you on the matter.   It is true that one thing, and one only, is not as it should be with him; that is, that, wishing to save a friend whom another would have killed, he drew his sword for to part them; but it fell out that his friend killed the other, and so he, though he struck no blow, is fled from his town, since he was present to the murder and drew his sword.   And, by the counsel of his kinsfolk, he has hidden himself in this town in the habit of a scholar, and remains here unknown till his friends have brought the matter to a conclusion, which he hopes will be no long time.   Wherefore the marriage must be done secretly, and you must be content for him to go during the day to the public lecture, and sup and lie here every night."   To this the good woman answered: "I deem your words, father, to be spoken greatly to my advantage, for at the least I shall have by me that I desire most of all things." Then the friar brought in his fellow, clad in a crimson satin doublet, and altogether very brave, so that as soon as he was come the betrothal was performed, and on the last stroke of midnight mass was sung and they were married. Then they went to lie together, but at the dawn of day the bridegroom said to his wife that he must begone to the college if he would remain unknown, and, taking his doublet and his long robe, together with his coif of black silk, he bade farewell to his wife, who was still in bed, and promised to take his supper with her every evening, but she must not look for him at dinner. So he went his way and left his wife, she esteeming herself the most fortunate of women, in that she had met with such a good match. But the young married friar returned to the old father confessor, and gave him the five hundred ducats according to their agreement, and in the evening supped with her who took him for her husband, and in such wise did he obtain her love and that of her mother-in-law that they would not have changed him for the greatest prince in the world.

This manner of living endured for some time, but since God has compassion on them that are deceived through no fault of their own, he put it into the hearts of the mother and daughter to go to hear mass at the Grey Friars' Church of St. Francis, where likewise they would see their good confessor who had provided the one with so dutiful a son-in-law, and the other with so brave a husband. And it chanced that, not being able to find the confessor, or any other of their acquaintance, they were pleased to wait his coming, and in the meanwhile to hear high mass, which was then beginning. And as the daughter gazed with attentive eyes on the holy mysteries being performed at the altar, when the priest turned him to the people to say the *Dominus vobiscum*, she was struck with a great astonishment, for it seemed to her that the priest was either her husband or the express image of him. But she said not a word, and waited till he should turn a second time, looking upon him more carefully, and doubted not that he was the man. Wherefore she touched her mother, who was in a devout contemplation of the mysteries, and said to her: "Alas! alas! mother, who is that I see?" Her mother asked her who it was. "'Tis my husband that is now singing mass, or the one man in the world who is altogether like to him." Her mother, who had not carefully looked upon him, said: "I entreat you, daughter, let no such imaginations enter your brain, for 'tis a thing plainly impossible that these holy men should devise such a cozening device, and you will sin grievously against God if you put faith in this fantasy." Natheless the mother did not omit to look upon him, and when he turned him at the *Ite missa est* she clearly perceived that never were twin brothers more like to one another than this priest to her son-in-law. Yet so simple was she that she would fain have said: "Save me, O God, from believing mine own eyes!" But since it touched her daughter she would not leave the matter thus in darkness, and resolved to know the truth of it. And when the time was come in the evening for the husband to return, the mother said to her daughter: "Now, if you are willing, we can know the truth concerning your husband, for as soon as he is bedded I will come in, and do you snatch off his coif from behind so that he perceive you not, and we shall see if he has a tonsure like him who sang mass." As it was resolved, so it was done, for when that evil husband was in bed the old dame came in, and while she took him by the hands, as if in jest, her daughter snatched off his coif and left him with his fine tonsure, whereat the two women were mightily astounded. But forthwith they called the servants that were in the house, and made them take him and keep him fast in bonds till the morning, and no excuse or talking at all availed him. And on the morrow the lady sent for her confessor, feigning to have some great secret for his ear, so he came in great haste, and she made take him like the young friar, reproaching him with the deceit he had used toward her. And after this they were haled before the judges, and these, if they were honest folk, would by no means let them escape unpunished.

"By this, ladies, you perceive that they who are vowed to poverty are not freed from the temptation of covetousness, which is the cause of many evils." "Nay, but rather many blessings," said Saffredent, "for the monk made good cheer on the five hundred ducats the old woman would have stored up, and the poor maid, who was in such earnest expectation of a husband, was enabled thereby to have two if she had a mind, and knew better how to speak the truth of all hierarchies."

Y

"Your positions," said Oisille, "are always of the falsest, for you think that every woman is of the same complexion as yourself." "With your good favour, mistress," said Saffredent, "I maintain no such thing, for I would that women were as easy to satisfy as we are." "That was an evil speech," said Oisille, "for there is not one present that knoweth not to the contrary. And to prove the truth thereof, doth not the story that was but now told show the simpleness of poor womenfolk, and the craft of those we consider far better than other men; for neither mother nor daughter wished to do according to their own will, but submitted themselves unto ghostly counsel." "And some women," said Longarine, "are so hard to please that they think they ought to have angels for husbands." "For which cause," said Simontault, "they often light upon devils; and chiefly they that, putting no trust in God, deem by their own good sense, or that of another, to find that happiness in this world which is given alone of God." "What! Simontault," said Oisille, "I knew not there was so much of good in you." "Mistress," answered Simontault, "'tis pity I have had no trial, for by reason of your not knowing me, you have already passed a bad judgment on me; but since a friar hath intromitted with my craft, why should not I practise the craft of a friar?" "This, then, you call your craft," said Parlamente, "to deceive women? Out of your own mouth you are condemned." "When I shall have deceived a hundred thousand," said Simontault, "even then I shall not be avenged for the torments that one hath made to suffer." "I know," answered Parlamente, "how often you make complaint of the ladies, and all the while we see you so stout and joyous that it is not to be believed that you have suffered all the ills you say. But as *La Belle Dame Sans Merci* replies, *you do well to talk thus since you draw some comfort from it.*" "You bring in a notable doctor," said Simontault, "who not only is wearisome himself, but makes all who read him and follow his teaching wearisome likewise." "Yet," replied Parlamente, "his teaching is as profitable to maids as any I know of." "If it were thus," said Simontault, "and the ladies were without compassion, we could give our horses a rest, and let our armour rust till the next war, and think of nought else but the household. And, prithee, tell me whether it is a brave thing for a lady to have the name of being without pity, without charity, without love, and without compassion?" "Let her not be," answered Parlamente, "without charity and love; but this word *compassion* hath such an ill sound in a woman's ears, that we cannot use it without doing a hurt to our honour; for compassion is to grant some favour which is asked, and we know what favour a man would ask." "With your good pleasure, mistress," said Simontault, "some there be so reasonable that they ask but a word." "You make me to remember," said Parlamente, "him who was content with a glove." "We must know," said Hircan, "who was this easy lover, wherefore I give you my vote." "And I will willingly tell the tale," said Parlamente, "for it is full of honourable passages."

NOVEL LVII.

The great oblectation taken by an English lord in a very small matter.

It chanced that King Lewis the Eleventh sent my lord de Montmorency into England as his ambassador, who was so welcomed that the King and all the lords loved and esteemed him exceedingly, and did so much as tell him their secret occasions that they might have his advice thereon. One day, as he sat at a feast the King made for him, he had by him at the board a lord of a great house, who had a small lady's glove fixed on to his doublet by golden hooks, and where the fingers joined it was so adorned with diamonds, rubies, amethysts, and pearls, that it was assuredly a glove of great price. My lord de Montmorency looked at it so often that he who wore it perceived he would fain ask wherefore it was so magnificent, and esteeming that the tale would be altogether to his advantage, he began: "I plainly perceive that you find it a strange thing for me to have thus gorgeously arrayed a poor glove, and I still more desire to tell you the reason, for I esteem you for an honest gentleman and one who knows what manner of passion is love, and if I have done well therein you shall praise me for it, and if not, you will make excuse for me, inasmuch as this same love bears rule in every honourable heart. Know then that all my life I have loved one lady, whom I love now, and shall love after her death. But though my heart was so bold as to address itself in a high quarter, yet my tongue could not take courage to speak, and for seven years I tarried without a sign, fearing lest, if she was ware of it, I should lose the means I had of often seeing her, the which I feared more than death. But one day, as we were in a meadow, while I looked upon her, so violently did my heart beat, that I lost all colour and the manner of my countenance was changed. And she perceiving this, and asking what ailed me, I answered that it was a heartache hardly to be borne, and she, thinking it was a sickness in which love had no share, showed pity on me. Wherefore I entreated her to put her hand upon my heart to see how grievously it was beating, and this she did, but more out of kindness than love, and as I held her hand upon my heart, it fell to beating in such wise, that she perceived I had spoken nought but the truth. And then holding her hand upon my breast I said to her : 'Alas ! mistress, take this poor heart of mine, that would fain break through my breast and lie in the hand of you from whom I crave favour, and life, and pity ; wherefore I must now tell you of the love I have so long concealed, since neither I nor my heart can overcome this almighty deity.' And when she heard this discourse of mine, finding it mighty strange, she would have drawn back her hand, but I kept it so that this glove was left to me in the place of her cruel hand. And since I have never since had any commerce with her, I have fixed the glove upon my heart as the best emplaster for it, and have adorned it with all my fairest jewels, though I hold the glove itself as more excellent a thing than this whole realm of England, nor do I esteem any of the world's goods equal to having it upon my breast." My lord de Montmorency, who would have rather had the hand than the glove of a lady, extolled him for his honourable dealing, saying he was the most perfect lover he had ever seen and worthy of kinder treatment, since of so small a thing he had made so much. Though perchance, if he had more than the glove, he would die from mere excess of pleasure. To all this the English lord agreed, not perceiving that the other was making a mock of him.

"If all men were thus honourable, the ladies might well trust them, since the cost would be but a glove." "I was of the acquaintance of my lord de Montmorency," said Geburon, "and I am sure he would not have desired to love after the fashion of this Englishman; for had he contented himself with so little he would not have had his notable successes in love affairs, as the old song says: ' Faint heart ne'er won fair lady.' "

"Trust me," said Saffredent, "the poor lady drew back her hand pretty speedily when she felt how the heart of him was beating; for she thought he might die, and they say there is nothing more hateful to a woman than to touch a dead man."

"If you had resorted to the hospitals as much as to the taverns," said Ennasuitte, " you would not talk after this sort, for you would there see women making the dead ready for burial, when men, brave as they may be, dare not touch them."

"It is true," said Saffredent, " that any woman, when a penance is laid upon her, will do that most contrary to her inclinations, as was apparent in a lady of a good house who was found at four of the clock one morning kissing the dead body of a gentleman who had been killed the day before, and with whom she had not been at all particular. And this was done by way of satisfaction for past delights, and the pleasure she had taken to kiss a man she loved." "Since every good work done of a woman," said Oisille, "is taken in bad part by man, I am of opinion that, dead or living, there should be no kissing if it be not in accordance with the commandment of God." " As for me," said Hircan, " I care so little for kissing women, save only my wife, that I will agree to whatsoever may be ordained in the matter; but I pity the young folk from whom you would take away this small contentment, thereby making the commandment of St. Paul, who will have us kiss *in osculo sancto*, of none effect." "If St. Paul had been like unto you," said Nomerfide, " we should have required most evident signs of the Spirit of God speaking in him." " To the last," said Geburon, "you will rather doubt Holy Writ than forsake one of your petty observances." " May God guard us," said Oisille, "from doubting Holy Writ, so long as we put small trust in your lies; for there is no woman who knows not what her belief should be, namely to have no doubt in the word of God, and no faith in the word of man." " Yet do I believe," said Simontault, " that there are more men deceived of women than women deceived of men. For they loving us but a little, put no trust in the truth we tell them; whilst we, loving them greatly, believe their lies in such sort that we are deceived before we suspect that it is possible." " Methinks," said Parlamente, " you have heard the complaint of a fool deceived of a wanton, for your conclusion is of so little weight, that it stands in great need of an example to confirm it. Wherefore, if you are advised of such, I give you my place to tell it. But I do not say that we are obliged to believe what you tell us, and if you speak evil of us our ears will not burn, since we know what is true and what false." " Insomuch as I have leave to speak," said Dagoucin, " I will tell you the story."

NOVEL LVIII.

The pleasant revenge of a lady on her lover.

At the Court of King Francis the First there was a lady of a mighty keen wit, who for her graciousness, honour, and pleasant manner of speaking had won the heart of many lovers; keeping her virtue safe all the while, and so ordering her passages with them that they knew not on what to lay hold, for the most assured would presently despair, and the most desperate pluck up courage. Natheless, though for the most part she made a mock of them, yet she loved exceedingly one she called her cousin, the which name was a pretext for a somewhat close commerce. And since no thing continueth in one stay, often was their love turned to anger, and from anger converted to love, in such sort that the whole Court knew of it. One day this lady, as much to cause it to be known that she had no deep affection for anything as to give pain to him on account of whom she had borne much annoy, showed him a kinder face than she had ever done before. Wherefore the gentleman, who lacked not courage neither in love nor war, began to seek in a very lively fashion that he had ofttimes craved of her, and she, feigning to be overcome by compassion, granted him his request, and told him that to compass the matter she would go to her room, which was in the loft, and there she was persuaded they would find no one, charging him so soon as he saw her go out to follow her, since she would be alone. Believing her words the gentleman was so content with her goodwill towards him that he fell to playing with the other ladies till the time came to follow her out. And she, who was in no wise lacking in woman's craftiness, went to Lady Margaret, daughter of the King, and to the Duchess of Montpensier, and said to them: "If it be your pleasure I will show you as brave a jest as you have ever seen." They being not at all melancholical, prayed her tell them what was the manner of it. "You know," said she, "such an one, that he is as honest and daring a gentleman as may be. You know likewise how many bad turns he has done me, and how, when I loved him most, he set passages on foot with other women, at which I took more annoy than I made evident. And now God hath delivered him into my hands, for as I go to my room in the loft, if it please you to keep good watch, you will see him presently follow me, and when he shall have passed through the galleries and is about to mount the stair, I pray you both go to the window and help me to cry thief. You shall behold his rage at it, and I think he will carry it with no bad grace, and if he do not rail at me aloud, he will assuredly do so in his heart." The enterprise was agreed upon, and not without laughter, for there was no gentleman that did wage such war with the ladies as this one, and he was so beloved and esteemed of them all that they would not for anything have made themselves a jest for him; and it seemed good to the two ladies to have a part in the glory which one alone might have gained for herself. Wherefore, as soon as they saw her who was the principal in the undertaking go out, they kept watch on the gentleman's face, who waited no long time, and when he had passed the door, the ladies went into the gallery so as to lose sight of him. And he, suspecting nothing, folded his cloak around his neck to hide his visage, and went down the stair into the courtyard, but finding one there whom he wished not for a witness, he crossed the yard, and returned by another way. All this was seen of the ladies unknown to him, and when he came to the stair whence he might go in safety to the room of his mistress, they forthwith set themselves at the window where they saw her up above, who began to cry thief at the top of her voice, the two ladies below answering so loudly that they were heard all through the castle. I leave you to imagine how wrathfully the gentleman fled to his lodging, not so secretly as not to be known of them that were of the mystery, who often mocked him with it, as did she that did him this bad turn, telling him she was well avenged. But he had his replies and excuses so pat, that he half made them believe he suspected somewhat all the while, and had agreed to see the lady only to make a jest of her, since for the love of her he would not have taken the trouble, inasmuch as for a long while she had been out of his thoughts. But the ladies not receiving this for truth, the affair is still matter of disputation, natheless it is probable that he believed his mistress, for so discreet and brave a man was he that in his time he had few to match and none to oversmatch him, as was evident to all by his glorious and knightly death.

"Methinks we must confess, therefore, that the love of honest men is so great that, for putting too much belief in their ladies, they are ofttimes deceived." "In good faith," said Ennasuitte, "I praise the lady for the wrong she did him ; for when a man is beloved and leaves his mistress for another, there is no revenge too bitter." "Ay," said Parlamente, "if she is beloved of him, but there are women who love without sufficient assurance of their love being returned, and when they find out that the men are courting elsewhere, they call them fickle. Wherefore such women as are discreet are never deceived by idle talk, since they give no belief to them that speak the truth, for fear they may be perchance liars, insomuch as truth and falsehood use the same language." "If all were of your opinion," said Simontault, "the men might put their prayers into their coffers ; but whatsoever you and they like unto you may say, we will never allow that women are as slow to believe as they are pretty. So we shall live as content in this persuasion as you, by your conclusions, would make us to be afraid." "Of a truth," said Longarine, "knowing who it was that handled the gentleman in this fashion, I could believe anything of her, since she who spares not her husband will not spare her lover." "Her husband, say you?" said Simontault ; "you know more than I ; so I hereby give you my place to tell us the story." "Since you will have it so I will tell it you," said Longarine.

NOVEL LIX.

How a lady practised upon her husband, and caused him to take her to Court.

This lady aforesaid was married to a rich gentleman of an ancient and honourable house, and they were wed alone for the great love there was between them. She, being mighty fair and open in her speech, did not conceal from her husband that she had lovers, of whom she made a mock and a pastime, and he at first was content, but at last he grew a-weary of it, on the one hand misliking that she should so much entertain folk that were none of his friends nor kinsfolk, and on the other vexing for the great charges she put on him for the maintenance of a splendid appearance, and in following of the Court. Wherefore as many weeks as he could he spent at his country house, whither came so much company that his expenses were diminished by but a little; for his wife, wheresoever she might be, always found means to pass the time in dancing, games, and such-like contentments as may be used of young maids without dishonour. And when her husband would laugh and say to her that their disbursements were too heavy, she would reply to him that he might be assured she would never make him *coqu* (which we call cuckold), but only *coquin,* that is, a beggar. For she loved rich gear so well that she must go drest as bravely as any lady of the Court, whither her husband took her as seldom as he could, and whither she did all in her power to go, and on this account made herself so pleasant to her husband that he could hardly refuse her anything she asked.

And when all her invention availed nothing to persuade him to make this journey to Court, one day she perceived that he was vastly civil to one of her bedchamber women, the which she hoped to turn to her own advantage. So taking the girl apart, she sifted her, part by promises and part by threatenings, in such wise, that she confessed that from the time she came into the house there was not a day that her master did not importune and solicit her; but she would rather die than do this thing against God and her virtue, let alone the honour that had been done her by being taken into the household, and so if she had consented she would be doubly wicked. The lady, hearing of the unfaithfulness of her husband, was smitten with joy and grief; with grief, since her husband, while he made so much pretence of loving her, was seeking to do her shame in her own household; and she also upheld herself for a prettier and more graceful than the woman he preferred before her. But her joy was for that she hoped to take her husband in such a fault that he would no more be enabled to rail at her lovers, and keep her away from Court; and to that intent she prayed the girl to grant little by little her husband's requests, upon certain conditions she told her of. The wench made some difficulty over this, but being assured by her mistress of her honour and her life, she agreed to do her pleasure in the matter.

And the next time the gentleman solicited the girl he found her countenance altogether changed towards him, so he pressed her harder thán he was wont. But she, having well learnt her part, made remonstrance to him of her poverty, and said that if she obeyed him she would be dismissed from the service of her mistress, from whom she had good expectancy of getting a husband. To this he soon replied that she need take no care for aught of this, since he would marry her to more advantage than her mistress was able to do, and that he would order the affair so secretly that no one would know of it. Thereupon it was concluded between them; and on considering what place was most fit for their exercitations, she said there was none better nor less obnoxious to suspicion than a small house in the park, wherein was a room and a bed entirely to the purpose. The gentleman, to whom no place would have been amiss, agreed thereto, and he wearied for the day and the hour to draw nigh. The girl observed her promise to his wife, and told her all the whole matter, and how it was to be performed on the morrow after dinner, and that she would make a sign when the time came. Now on the morrow, after that they had dined, the gentleman was more kindly observant of his wife than he had ever been, which was not taken of her in very good part, but yet she dissembled so well that he perceived nothing. After dinner she asked him what should be their pastime, and he replied that he knew of none more pleasant than piquet, so forthwith they set them to the game, but she would not play, feigning to have as much delight in the looking on at it. And as the gentleman sat down he failed not to charge the girl to remember her promise; and she, while he was playing, passed out of the hall, and made a sign to her mistress of the journey she was about to perform, which was plainly perceived of her, but not at all of her husband. Natheless, at the end of an hour, one of his servants signed to him from afar, and he said to his wife that he had a trifling rheum in the head, and was constrained to go rest himself and take the air. She, very well knowing the manner of his sickness, asked if she should take his cards; and he answered ay, and that he should soon return. But his wife assured him that she could take his place for two hours, and not weary of the game; so the gentleman went his way to his room, and from thence by an alley into the park. The lady, who was advised of another and a shorter path, waited a little while, and suddenly made pretence of having a colick, giving her cards to another; and so soon as she was out of the hall she doffed her high-heeled boots and ran very speedily to the place where she was not willing that the dance should be without her. And in such good time did she come that she entered by one way as her husband entered by the other, and, hiding herself behind the door, she listened to the fair and honest discourse of him with the servant. But when she saw him approaching very near to the criminal point she took him by the back of his dress, saying: "I am too near for you to have another." It skills not asking whether the gentleman was enraged or no; as much because the delight he hoped to have received was taken from him, as for his wife to know more than he would have had her, whose love he was in great fear of losing for ever. But thinking the crossbite was of the girl's devising, without a word to his wife, he rushed at her so furiously that he would have killed her had not the lady taken her from his hands. And he swore she was the most wicked wench he had ever seen, and that if his wife had waited to the end she would have known it was but a jest, for in place of doing what she thought he would have striped her with rods. But his wife, understanding what coin he was fain to pass upon her, would not take it for good, and made such remonstrance with him that he was mightily afraid she was minded to forsake him. So he promised her whatsoever she might ask of him, and confessed that he had been in the wrong to take offence at her lovers; insomuch as an

honest woman is none the less honest for that she is loved, so
that she neither do nor say anything dishonourable; but a man
who, against his wife and his conscience, solicits the love of a
wench who cares not for him, is deserving of a shrewd punishment.   Wherefore he promised never to put any hindrance in
her going to Court, nor to take it in bad part that she had
lovers, since he was persuaded she parleyed with them more
for jest than for affection's sake.   All this was by no means
displeasing to the lady, and she thought she had gained a great
point; but yet her speech was contrariwise, feigning to mislike
the going to Court, since she no longer had his love, without
which all companies were a weariness to her.   And she professed that a wife, loving her husband, and in like manner being
beloved of him, carried a safe-conduct to speak with all men
and to be reproached of none.   The poor gentleman so laboured
to assure her of his love that they went forth from thence good
friends, but so as to fall no more into such mishaps he prayed
her send the girl, who had been the occasion of so much
trouble, away from her service.   This she did, but 'twas but to
marry her to a good honest man, and at her husband's charges.
And so that his wife might altogether forget his folly, he erelong brought her to Court in such magnificent array that she
had good reason for contentment.

"And this it was, ladies, that made me say I marvelled not
at what she had done to one of her lovers, since I knew of this
affair with her husband."   "You have shown us," said Hircan,
"a crafty wife and a foolish husband; for since he had gone
thus far, wherefore did he halt on so fair a road?"   "What
should he have done, then?" said Longarine.   "That he had
undertaken," answered Hircan; "for his wife was as angry with
him for his evil intent as if he had put it into execution, and
perchance she would have had more liking for him as a brisker
gallant."   "But where," said Ennasuitte, "shall you find a
man who can overcome two women at once?   For the wife
would have defended her rights and the girl her maidenhead."
"Be it so," said Hircan, "but a strong man and a daring need
have no fear to assail two weak women, and would certainly
gain his end."   "I know," said Ennasuitte, "that if he had
drawn his sword he could have killed the pair of them, but
otherwise I see no way out.   Wherefore prithee tell us what

you would have done?" "I would have thrown my arms round my wife," said Hircan, "and borne her out, and then I would have had my pleasure of the girl by love or by force." "Hircan," said Parlamente, "it suffices that you know how to do evil." "Sure am I, Parlamente," said Hircan, "that I do not scandalise the innocent before whom I speak, and I would by no means sustain an evil deed. As for the undertaking, I wonder at it and consider it a worthless one; and for the undertaker I have no praise, since it was more for fear than love of his wife that he did not bring it to a close. I praise indeed a man that loves his wife according to the commandment of God, but when he loves her not I think no better of him for fearing her." "In truth," said Parlamente, "were you not through love a good husband, I should not make much account of what you might do through fear." "You need have no care, Parlamente," said Hircan, "for the love I have for you doth cause me to be more obedient than the fear of death and hell." "You may speak according to your liking," said Parlamente, "but I have reason for contentment in what I have seen and known of you; and as for that I know not, I wish neither to know nor to make inquiry concerning it." "I hold it great foolishness," said Nomerfide, "for wives to be curiously inquisitive as to their husbands, and in like manner husbands as to their wives. For sufficient for the day is the evil thereof, without need to take thought for the morrow." "Yet," said Oisille, "it is sometimes needful to inquire on matters that touch the honour of a house, but this only that order may be taken therewith, and not for the ill-judging of persons, since there is none without fault." "Many an one," said Geburon, "hath fallen into mischance, for want of a curious inquiry into his wife's fault." "I pray you," said Longarine, "if you know of an example thereof, hide it not from us." "One is well known to me," answered Geburon, "and since it is your pleasure I will tell it."

NOVEL LX.

How a man, for putting too great trust in his wife, fell into much misery.

In the town of Paris there lived so good-natured a man, that he would have thought it a sin to believe one was lying with his wife, though he had seen it with his eyes. And he was married to a very wicked woman, whose wickedness he never perceived, but treated her as if she was as good as any in the world. But one day, when King Lewis the Twelfth was in Paris, his wife left him for one of the songmen of the aforesaid prince; and when the King went away and she could see her lover no more she determined to forsake her husband and follow him. To this the songman agreed, and took her to a house he had at Blois, where they lived a long while together. The poor husband, finding his wife to have wandered away, sought for her on every side, and at last it was told him that she was with the songman; and willing to recover his lost sheep, that he had so badly guarded, he wrote her many letters, praying her to return, and saying he would take her back again if she would from henceforth live virtuously. But his wife, who had such delight in the singing of her songman that she had forgotten her husband's voice, made no account of all his kindness, but mocked him; wherefore he grew angry and let her know that he would get her by the laws ecclesiastical, since in no other way she would return to him. And she, fearing lest if the law should deliver her into his hands, she and her songman would fare badly, devised a plot well worthy of her. And, dissembling sickness, she sent to certain honourable women of the town asking them to visit her, and this they did gladly, hoping through sickness to draw her from her wicked life, and to this intent each one did make unto her most seemly remonstrances. Then she, feigning to be grievously sick, wept and bewailed her sins in such sort that all present had compassion on her, steadfastly believing that she spoke from the bottom of her heart. And seeing her thus redeemed and repentant, they set them to console her, saying that God was not so terrible as the preachers for the most part declared, and that he would never refuse his pity. Thereupon they sent for a good and discreet man to hear her confession; and on the morrow came the parson to administer the Holy Sacrament, the which she received so devoutly that all the honourable women of the town who were present wept to see her, praising God that of His goodness He had pity on this poor soul. Afterwards, feigning she could eat no more, the parson gave her extreme unction, which she received with pious signs, since scarcely now could she speak ; for such was her pretence. So she remained a long time, seeming little by little to lose sight, and hearing, and all the other senses, whereat all present fell to crying aloud *Jesus !* And since night was near at hand, and the ladies lived afar off, they all left her, and while they were going from the house it was told them she was gone, and saying a *De Profundis* for her, they returned each one to her own house. The parson inquired of the songman where he would that she should be buried, who answered that she had charged him to bury her in the cemetery, whither it would be good to carry her at night. So the poor wretch was made ready for burial by a servant that took care to do her no hurt, and then with brave torches she was borne to the grave the songman had made. But when the corpse passed before the houses of those women who had been present at the giving of extreme unction, they all came out and followed her to the grave, and soon both priests and women left her with the songman, who, so soon as he saw the company at some little distance, together with the servant took out of the grave his sweetheart more alive than ever, and brought her privily to his house, where he kept her a long while in hiding.

Her husband, who pursued after her, came to Blois and craved justice, and there he found that she was dead and buried in the estimation of all the ladies of the town, who told him the manner of her end. At this the honest man was very glad ; that her soul was in paradise, and he was quit of her wicked body. In this contentment he went back to Paris, where he took to wife a young and pretty woman of good repute and a notable housewife, of whom he had several children ; and they lived together for fourteen years and upwards ; but at last Fame, that can keep nothing hid, advertised him his wife was not dead, but alive and with the wicked songman. And the poor man concealed this so long as he was able, dissembling that he knew of it, and desiring to believe it was a lie. But the affair was told to his wife, a discreet woman, and she was so anguished thereat, that she was like to die of grief; and had it been possible for her, with a safe conscience, to hide this mischance, she would willingly have done it, but it was not so, for the bishop's court presently took order with them, and in the first place put them asunder till the whole truth should be known. So was this poor man constrained to eschew the good and ensue the evil, and came to Blois, a little after the coronation of King Francis the First. And there he found Queen Claude and the Regent, before whom he made his plaint, asking her that he would have fain not received; but needs must he take her, wherefore he was mightily pitied of all the company. And when his wife was brought before him, for a long time she stiffly maintained she was not his wife, the which he would have gladly believed if he could. She, more sad than sorry or ashamed, told him she had rather die than return to him, and this was good news for her poor husband. But the ladies, before whom she made her wicked pleadings, condemned her to return, and used such threats with the songman, that he was forced to tell his mistress, and indeed she was an ugly woman enough, to go back to her husband, since he would have no more commerce with her. So, since she was obliged, the poor wretch returned to her husband, and was more kindly entreated of him than she had deserved.

"Wherefore I say, ladies, that if this poor man had been more watchful of his wife, he had not lost her, for well-kept is hardly lost, and the occasion makes the thief." "'Tis a strange thing," said Hircan, "how strong is love when it appears least bottomed on reason." "It hath been told me," said Simontault, "that it were easier to break two marriages, than to sow enmity between a priest and his wench." "I do believe it," said Ennasuitte, "for they that bind others in wedlock, know so well how to tie the knot, that only death can loosen it. Furthermore the doctors maintain spiritual discourse to be above all other, when it follows that spiritual love is the greatest of all." "This thing," said Dagoucin, "I cannot pardon in a lady, to leave a good husband or a sweetheart for a parson, be he never so comely a man." "Prithee, Dagoucin," said Hircan, "intermeddle not with our holy mother the Church, but believe that it is a great delight for poor secret fearful women to sin

with men who can absolve them, for there are some who are
more ashamed to confess their sins than to commit them."
"You speak," said Oisille, "of them that have no knowledge
of God, and who do not bethink them that what is done in
secret shall one day be made manifest before the heavenly host.
But I do not believe that, for the sake of confession, they intro-
mit with confessors, but rather that they are so blinded of the
devil that they have more care for secresy and a virtuous cloak
than for absolution of sins of which they do not repent." "Repent,
say you," answered Saffredent, "nay, but they esteem themselves holier than other women, and I am sure that some take
honour for that they are constant to their lovers." "You speak
in such sort," said Oisille to Saffredent, "that methinks you
know of some story to the purpose. Wherefore I pray you on
the morrow, to begin the day, you will tell us what you know.
But I hear the last bell ringing for evensong, since the monks
went when they had heard our tenth story, and left us to bring
our dispute to a close." Thereupon the company arose, and
came to the church, where they found the monks waiting for
them. And when they had heard evensong, they took supper
together, telling many a pleasant tale. Then after supper and
their accustomed divertisement in the meadow they went to
rest, so as to have the clearer brains for the morrow.

DAY THE SEVENTH.

ON THE SEVENTH DAY RELATION IS MADE OF THEM THAT HAVE DONE WHAT
THEY LEAST DESIRED.

PROLOGUE.

On the morrow Mistress Oisille failed not to administer to
them their wholesome refection, reading from St. Luke concerning the acts and deeds of the glorious knights and apostles
of Jesus Christ. And she told them that this relation should
suffice to make them desire to see such a time, and to bring
tears for this degenerate age. And when she had read and
sufficiently expounded the beginning of this holy Gospel, she
entreated them to go to the church, where they should unite
their prayers as did the apostles, asking of God his grace, which

z

was never refused to them that craved it faithfully. And as they came into the church the mass of the Holy Ghost was beginning, and this seeming much to the purpose, they heard the service with great devotion. Afterwards they went to dinner, calling again to mind the life apostolical, and took such pleasure therein that their tales were well-nigh forgotten. This Nomerfide, who was the youngest, perceived, and said to them : " Mistress Oisille hath so filled us with devotion that we let the time go by, in the which we are wont to go apart, to make us ready for the telling of our novels." These words made all the company to arise, and after they had stayed some while in their rooms they went forth into the meadow as they had done on the precedent day, and when they were seated at their ease Oisille said to Saffredent : " Though I be assured that you will say nothing to the advantage of women, yet I must require you to tell the novel that yesterday evening was in your mouth." " I except, mistress," answered Saffredent, " to acquiring the fame of an evil speaker for telling the truth ; nor should I lose the favour of such ladies as are virtuous for recounting the deeds of wantons, for I know what it is to lack the sight of them, and if I was put out of their favour also I could no longer live." So saying he turned his eyes towards her who was the occasion of his weal and woe ; but chancing to look on Enna-suitte, he made her to blush, all as if she had been the one to whom his discourse was addressed, yet none the less was it understood of her to whom it was spoken. And Oisille assured him he could tell the truth freely, let who would bear the blame. Then began Saffredent, and said :

NOVEL LXI.

Of the shamelessness and impudency of a certain woman who forsook her husband's house to live with a canon.

Hard-by the town of Autun there dwelt a lady, tall, fair, and of as goodly a feature as I have ever seen. And she was wed to an honest gentleman somewhat younger than herself, who loved and entreated her so well that she had good reason to be satisfied with him. Some space of time after they were married he brought her with him to Autun where he had some business, and while he pleaded in the court his wife went to

church to pray to God for him.   And she resorted so much to
this holy place that a rich canon grew amorous on her, and paid
his suit to such purpose that the poor wretch submitted to him,
of which her husband had no suspicion, taking more thought
for his substance than for his wife.   But when she must needs
depart thence and return to her home, seven long leagues from
Autun, she grieved sore, though the canon promised he would
often come and see her.   This he did, feigning to go on a
journey, and the road always led past the gentleman's house,
and he, not being altogether foolish, perceived his intent, and
took such order that when the canon came there he found the
wife no more, for the husband made her to bestow herself so
secretly that there could be no parley between them.   She, not
ignorant of her husband's jealousy, gave no sign that it was
displeasing to her, natheless she resolved to effect something,
for to lose the sight of her divinity seemed to her as hell.   So
one day, on the which her husband was away from the house,
she so dealt with the servants that she was left alone; and
forthwith taking what was needful, and with no fellow save
her brainsick rapture, she fared forth on foot to Autun.
There she arrived not too late to be recognised of her canon,
who kept her privily in his house for better than a year, for all
the excommunications and citations procured by her husband;
and he, having no other remedy, made complaint to the bishop,
who had as good an archdeacon as there ever was in France.
And such diligent search did he make for her through all the
canon's houses that he found her that was lost and clapped her
into prison, condemning the canon to a sharp penance.   The
husband, being advised that by means of the good archdeacon
and several other honest folk she was recovered, was content
to take her back on her oath that from henceforth she would
live virtuously, which the good man easily believed, for he
loved her greatly.   And being received again into his house,
she was entreated as honourably as afore, save that her husband
gave her two ancient bedchamber women, one of whom was
always with her.   But however kindly he might use her, the
wicked love she had for the canon made her deem all rest as
torment ; and though she was a mighty pretty woman, and he
a strong burly man, of a sanguine complexion, yet they had no
children, for her heart was ever seven long leagues from her body.

Yet this she dissembled so well that her husband conceived
that all that was past was forgotten of her as it was forgiven of
him.   But when she saw that her husband loved her as greatly
as ever, and had no suspicions, she craftily feigned to fall sick,
and so persisted in her cozenage that he was exceeding afraid,
sparing nothing to succour her.   Natheless she played her part
so well, that he and all his house thought that she was sick
unto death, and growing by slow degrees weaker and weaker;
and she, seeing him to be as sorry as he should have been glad,
prayed him to give her authority to make her will, and this he
willingly did, weeping the while.   And having power to devise,
though she had no children, she gave to her husband all that
she was able, asking his pardon for her offences against him;
then the parson being come she confessed and received the holy
Sacrament of the altar with such devotion that all wept to see
so glorious an end.   And when it was evening she prayed her
husband to send for extreme unction, since she grew so feeble
that she scarce hoped to take it alive; so he sent with all haste
for the parson, and she, by her great humility in the reception
of it, made all present to praise her.   So, having discharged
these holy mysteries, she said to her husband, that God having
given her grace to receive all the rites of Holy Church, she was
so quieted in her mind that she would fain rest awhile, and
prayed her husband to do the like, and indeed with all his
weeping and watchings he stood in sore need thereof.   And
when her husband and all his people with him were gone out,
the two old women who had guarded her so long in health,
not fearing now to lose her, save by death, went to sleep at
their ease.   And so soon as she heard them snoring, she arose
in her shift and went out of the room, listening whether any
one in the house was stirring; and having her loins girded and
her staff in her hand, she sallied forth by a little garden gate
that was not shut, and while it was night, in her shift alone
and with bare feet, she made her pilgrimage to the saint at
Autun, who could raise her from death to life.   But since it
was a long journey she could not accomplish the whole space
of it before the day began to dawn.   Then looking all along
the road she saw two horsemen riding furiously, and, thinking
it was her husband who sought her out, she hid her body in
a marshy place, with her head amidst the rushes, and as

her husband chased by he said to his servant, in a manner of despair : "Alas! the wicked woman! Who would have thought that, under the holy sacraments of the church, she would have concealed so foul and abominable a deceit!" The servant replied : "Since Judas, who received the same bread as she, feared not to bewray his master, do not esteem it a strange thing for a woman to do the like." Then her husband passed on ; and his wife tarried amidst the rushes, more glad to have deceived him than when she esteemed herself as a slave in her good bed at home. The poor husband made search through all the town of Autun, but he perceived that of a certainty she was not entered therein, wherefore he went back making great complaint of her and his loss, and threatening her with nothing less than death if he found her. But of this she had no fear in her mind, no more than she had of the cold in her body, though the place and the season should have sufficed to make her repent of this her damnable pilgrimage. And if we knew not how the fire of hell burns up them that are filled with it, we should justly find it a marvellous thing that this wretched woman, coming out of a warm bed, was able to stay a whole day in the bitter cold. Yet she lost not heart for the journey, but so soon as it was night fared forth again upon her way; and when they were about to shut the gates of Autun this pilgrim arrived there, and went straight to the shrine of her saint, who scarcely was able to believe that it was she, so astonished was he at the sight of her. But when he had made careful examination of her he found that she had flesh and bones, which a spirit hath not, and so assuring himself that she was no phantom, from henceforth they were in such good accord that they lived together fourteen or fifteen years. And though for some time she abode with him privily, at last she lost all fear, and worse than this, gloried to have such a sweetheart, so that she set herself in church higher than most of the honest women in the town, the wives of officers and other folk. And by the canon she had children, notably a daughter who was married to a rich merchant, and after so magnificent a sort that all the women in the town murmured at it, but had not authority to take any order in the matter. Now it came to pass that at this time Queen Claude, wife of Francis the First, passed through Autun, having in her following the Regent, mother to the King, and also her daughter the Duchess of Alençon. And the Queen had a servant, named Perrette, who came to the aforesaid Duchess, and said to her : "Mistress, hear me, I entreat you, for so you will do better than to go to the service at the church." The Duchess willingly gave ear to her, knowing she would not say aught that was not good, so Perrette forthwith told her how she had taken to her a little girl to help in the washing of the Queen's linen ; and on asking her the news of the town, she spoke as touching the grief of the honest women to see the canon's strumpet thus going before them, and made some relation of the woman's life. And the Duchess went presently to the Queen and the Regent, and recounted to them this history, and they, without any form of law, cited this poor wretch before them, who by no means hid herself away. For her former shame was changed into boasting that she kept the house of so rich a man, and no whit afraid or shamefaced, she came into the presence of the aforesaid ladies, who marvelled at this impudency, so that at first they knew not what to say. But afterwards the Regent remonstrated with her in such sort as should have made a woman of any understanding weep. But she did none of this, and with unspeakable audacity answered them : "I pray you, ladies, touch not mine honour, for, praised be God, I have lived with the canon so honestly and virtuously that no living soul can cast anything in my teeth. And let no one think that I do anything against the will of God, since for these three years past he hath not known me, and we dwell together as chastely and lovingly as two little angels, and never a thought nor a word betwixt us to the contrary. And whosoever shall sunder us will commit a great sin, insomuch as the good man, who is hard on his eightieth year, cannot live without me, who am but forty-five." You can conceive what fashion of discourse the ladies used with her, and the remonstrances which they made; but for all that her heart was not softened by their words, nor by her own years, nor for the company she was in. And to humiliate her the more they sent for the good archdeacon of Autun, who condemned her to a year's imprisonment on bread and water. Then the ladies sent for her husband, who, by reason of their exhortations, was content to take her back, after that she had performed her penances. But being a prisoner, and advised that the canon was resolved to be altogther quit of her, she thanked the ladies for that they had thrown the devil from her back, and repented her so heartily, that her husband, in place of waiting for a year, came and asked her of the archdeacon in a fortnight, and they lived in perfect peace and contentment ever after.

"Behold, ladies, how the chains of St. Peter are by evil ministers converted to the chains of the devil, and so hardly are they to be broken that the sacraments, which make Satan to flee away, are the means whereby he dwells the longer in their bodies. For the best is that which, when it suffers corruption, becomes the worst." "Truly," said Oisille, "the woman was a wretch, but she was sufficiently punished by coming before such judges as the ladies you have named, since the very look of the Regent was so virtuous, that an honest woman deemed herself unworthy to stand before her eyes, and was afraid. She on whom her regard was kind took great praise to herself, knowing that this lady looked on wanton women with but small favour." "This would be goodly work," said Hircan, "that one should have more fear for the eyes of a woman than for the Holy Sacrament, that if it be not received in faith and charity, is for everlasting damnation." "I promise you," answered Parlamente, "that they who have not God in their hearts are more afraid of the powers temporal than spiritual. And I suppose that this poor soul cleansed her ways more for her imprisonment and the loss of the canon than for any remonstrances that were made to her." "Yet you have forgotten," said Simontault, "the efficient cause that made her return to her husband. And this was that the canon was eighty and her husband younger than she, so this good dame came off best in all her battles; but if the canon had been a young man, she would not have forsaken him. Nor would the reproaches of the ladies have been of more avail than the sacraments she had received." "Yet," said Nomerfide, "she did well, methinks, not to confess her sin too easily, for such offences should be told with all humility to God, and stiffly denied before men; since, though the accusation be a true one, by force of lying and swearing, some doubt may be engendered in the minds of the judges." "Natheless," said Longarine, "a sin cannot be done so secretly that it shall not be revealed, if God do not hide it in them that for love of Him truly repent thereof." "And

what say you," said Hircan, "to them that no sooner sin than
they make proclamation of it?" "I find this a strange thing,"
said Longarine, "and a sign that the sin is not displeasing to
the sinner. And as I have told you, unless it be for the grace
of God, it cannot be denied before men; and some there are
who, taking pleasure in such discourse, blaze abroad their vice;
and others who, by contradicting themselves, accuse themselves." "If you know any example of this," said Saffredent,
"I give you my place for the telling of it." "Listen, then,"
said Longarine.

NOVEL LXII.

A notable slip of a lady, who beginning her story as if of another, ended it of herself.

In the time of King Francis the First there was a lady of
the blood-royal, fulfilled with all honour, virtuousness, and
beauty; knowing well how to tell a story with grace, and also
to laugh when one was told her. This lady, being at one of
her country houses, all her neighbours and retainers came to
see her, and recounted as many tales as were in their minds for
her contentment. And with the rest there was a dame who
determined not to be behind the others, and said to her: "Mistress, I can tell you a fine story, if you promise me not to speak
of it elsewhere; and it is a true one, that I will swear upon my
conscience. And this is the manner of it. There was a married
woman, who lived virtuously with her husband, though he was
old and she young; and a gentleman who was their neighbour,
seeing her wed to this old man, became amorous of her, and
pressed her hard for several years, but never had he any reply
from her that was not fitting for an honourable woman to make.
But one day this gallant conceived the humour that, if he could
take her unawares, she might mitigate in some degree her
asperity towards him, and having striven a long while with the
fear of danger, his love for the lady cast out all fear, and he
determined to find a place and a time to his purpose. And he
kept such good watch, that one morning, when the husband of
the lady went to another of his houses, and for the avoidance of
the heat set forth at daybreak, this young brisk entered his
mistress' house and found her a-bed and asleep, and her women
gone out of the room. Forthwith, without having the sense to

bolt the door, he got into the lady's bed as he was, booted and spurred, and mighty wrathful was she when he awoke her. But whatsoever remonstrances she could use with him availed nothing, and he took her by force, saying that if she called out he would tell all and singular that she had sent for him, whereat she was so afeared that she durst make no noise or alarm. Then hearing her women coming he arose hastily, and nothing would have been known of the matter had not his spur, fixing itself in the sheet, drawn all the bedgear to the ground, and left the lady stark-naked on the bed." So far did she devise her tale of another, but must needs say to make an end of it: "Never was woman so astonished as I when I found myself stark-naked." The worshipful lady, who so far had heard the tale unmoved, could not refrain from laughter at this conclusion, and said: "So far as I can see, you are well authorised to tell this history." The poor woman did what she could for her honour, but it had taken so far a flight that it could not be whistled back.

"I assure you, ladies, that if the doing of such an act were any great displeasure to her, she would have willingly lost the remembrance of it. But, as I told you, the sin will be declared by the very sinner, if it be not covered with the cloak that is said by David to make one blessed." "In good faith," said Ennasuitte, "this was a stupendous folly, to make others laugh at her own expense." "I think it not strange," said Parlamente, "that the word followed on the deed; for it is easier to say than to do." "Verily," said Geburon, "I find no sin at all in her. She was a-bed and asleep; he threatened her with death and shame; Lucreece, who hath been so belauded, did no more." "I confess," said Parlamente, "none is so righteous as to be beyond a fall, but when the deed is hateful so also is the memory of it, for to blot it out Lucreece killed herself, whilst this wanton would move others to laughter with it." "Yet, methinks," said Nomerfide, "she was an honest woman, since ofttimes she was entreated and always refused; so that the gentleman was forced to use cozenage to betray her." "What is this you say?" answered Parlamente; "think you that a woman can give a quittance to her virtue and let it go, when she has two or three times refused? If this were so many a slut would be esteemed an honest woman; for many an one

hath withstood him to whom her heart is given; some for fear
of shame, others to make themselves more vehemently desired.
Wherefore no account should be made of a woman, if she have
not steadfastly resisted to the end." "And if a young man
should refuse a pretty girl," said Dagoucin, "would you reckon
this great virtue?" "Truly," said Oisille, "if a young man,
sound in body, did this thing I should think it matter of admiration, but mighty hard to be believed." "Yet," answered
Dagoucin, "I knew one who refused that which all his fellows
most desired to gain." "I pray you," said Longarine, "take
my place for the telling of the story, but be mindful that we
are here present to speak nothing but only the truth." "I promise you," answered Dagoucin, "to tell the plain truth, with
no colour nor disguise."

NOVEL LXIII.

The admirable chastity of a young lord.

In Paris town there lived four girls, two of whom were
sisters, of such a fresh youth and beauty that they had but to
pick out from all the gallants. But a gentleman, who was
made provost of Paris by the then King, perceiving that his
master was young and of an age to desire such company, did
so practice with all the four, that, each one thinking herself
meat for the King, they all agreed to what the provost asked
them. And this was to be present at a feast, whither he had
bidden his master, to whom he made known the device, who
found it a very pleasant one, as did also two other great personages of the Court, and the whole three of them were agreed
to have a share in it. But as they were seeking for a fourth
there came to them a fine and noble gentleman, younger by
ten years than the rest, and they bade him to the feast, to
which he consented with a cheerful countenance, though he had
no desire for it in his heart. For on the one hand he was
married to a wife that bore him brave children, and with whom
he lived in such contentment that he would not for anything
have her take inward discontents concerning him; and on the
other hand he was the lover of one of the fairest ladies in all
France, whom he loved so well that all women beside seemed
to him ugly in comparison. And from his earliest youth before

that he was married, he could not be made to resort with other women, howsoever beautiful they might be; and took more delight to see his sweetheart and love her with a perfect love, than to have all that another woman could give him. Now this lord came to his wife and told her in secret the undertaking his master had in hand, and that he would rather die than perform what he had promised; for in like manner, as there was no man living whom he dared not attack in a rage, so he would rather die than murder another without cause and in a manner of premeditation; nor no more would he break his marriage vows by coveting another woman. Thereupon his wife loved him all the more, perceiving such virtuousness to dwell in him who was young, and asked him in what fashion he would excuse himself, inasmuch as princes take it ill in them who praise not their pleasures. But he replied to her: "I have always heard that the wise man keeps a journey or a sickness up his sleeve, to aid him in his hour of need. Wherefore I am resolved to feign sickness four or five days before, and by your countenance you can give me good help in my dissembling." "Verily," said his wife, "a pious hypocrisy, wherein I will not fail to assist you with the saddest face I can put on me; for he who can escape the wrath of God and the rage of his prince, is happy indeed." As they had determined, so it was done, and the King was very sorry to hear through the wife the sickness of her husband, which sickness lasted no long time, for, upon some intervenient business, the King forgot his pleasure to be mindful of his duty, and set forth from Paris. But one day, remembering the undertaking which had not been brought to an end, he said to the young lord: "We were mighty foolish to have gone so incontinent, without a sight of the four girls that were assured for the prettiest in my whole kingdom." And the lord replied to him: "I am glad you failed in this matter, for I feared that I alone, through my sickness, should have no part in that brave venture." And the King never discovered how the young lord had dissembled with him, and he from henceforth was more beloved of his wife than ever he had been.

Forthwith Parlamente fell to laughing, and said: "Had he done this for the love of his wife alone, it would have been still better. But as it was, he was worthy of great praise." "Methinks," said Hircan, "'tis no great praise for a man to keep his body in chastity for the love of his wife; for, upon many causes, he is well-nigh constrained to do so. God commands him, his oath binds him, and more than this, nature, when satiate, is not as obnoxious to temptation as when its desires are unappeased. But when a man, for his freewill love of his mistress, of whom he has not the enjoying, nor other contentment, save seeing and speaking with her, and often getting no favourable replies, remains so firm and steadfast that, come what may, he will show no fickleness, then I maintain 'tis an admirable and miraculous chastity." "There is nought of the miracle in it," said Oisille, "for when the heart is entirely addicted, all things are possible to the body." "Ay," said Hircan, "to bodies that have taken upon them the angelical nature." Oisille replied: "I would not speak of those alone, that by God's grace are all transformed into Him, but of these on this earth who are still within the fleshly tabernacle. And if you make search you shall find that men who have set their hearts and affections on gaining a perfect knowledge of the sciences, have not only forgotten the lust of the flesh, but also such things as are needful, I would say eating and drinking; hence comes it that they who love comely and virtuous women are so content to behold them and hear them speak, and have their spirits so at rest, that the flesh is voided of all desire. And they who know not such contentment are the carnal, shut up within their own fatness, and ignorant whether they have a soul or no. But when the flesh is subject unto the spirit, a man has no thought for the imperfections of the body, and is, as it were, insensible to them. And I knew a gentleman who, to show that he loved his mistress more than any of his fellows, made proof of the same by holding his fingers in the flame of a candle, and, steadfastly looking upon the lady, remained so firm that he was burnt to the bone, and persisted that he had felt no pain." "Methinks," said Geburon, "that the devil, whose martyr he was, should have made a St. Lawrence the Less out of him; for there are few so consumed by the flame of love that they fear not that of the smallest taper, and if a lady had made me to endure so much for the sake of her, I should have asked a great reward, or put her altogether out of my brain." "You would then," said Parlamente, "have your hour after the lady had had hers; like a certain gentleman of Valencia, in

Spain, whose story was told me by an honest captain." "I pray you," answered Dagoucin, "take my place and recount the tale to us, for I am assured it will be a pleasant one." "By this history, ladies," said Parlamente, "you will learn to think twice before you refuse a man, and not to trust that the present time will remain ever as it is, and so, knowing that it is subject to mutation, you will take thought for the future."

NOVEL LXIV.

A lady delaying to wed her lover, drove him into such inward discontent that he turned friar, and would have no more commerce with her.

In the city of Valencia there lived a gentleman who, for the space of five or six years, had so loved a lady that neither the honour nor the conscience of the one nor the other was wounded; for his intent was to take her to wife, and he could well do so inasmuch as he was comely, rich, and of a good house. And when he declared his love to her he also told her he was minded to agree with her as touching their marriage, and to have the counsel of her kinsfolk on it. And they, being gathered together to this end, found the marriage a very reasonable one, provided that the girl was well inclined to it; but she, either thinking to make a better match, or willing to dissemble her love for him, raised some difficulties, so that the company departed, not without regret, that she had not been able to come to a conclusion, for they knew the parties were in every way well suited. But the gentleman sorrowed most of all, for he could have borne the mishap patiently if he had thought that it was the fault of the kinsfolk and not of herself; but knowing the truth, that was worse to him than death, without a word to his sweetheart or any other he betook him to his house. And after that he had taken order with his affairs he went to a solitary place, where he laboured to forget this love, and turned it all to love of Our Lord, whose due it was. And during this time he had no tidings of the lady nor her kin, wherefore he was resolved, since he had failed to gain the happiest life he could hope for, to take to himself the most austere and offensive that could be imagined. And with this mournful thought, that was fit to be called despair, he became a monk in a religious house of St. Francis, not far from the dwellings of several of his kinsmen, who, knowing his intent, did all that was in their power to obstruct the same, but it was so stiffly rooted in his heart that no endeavour could turn him from it.   Yet, knowing the cause of his sickness, they thought to find the medicine for it, and came to her who was the reason of his sudden devotion.   She, mightily astonished and vexed at this mischance, having intended by her refusal only to make trial of his good will and not to lose it for ever, of which latter she was plainly in danger, sent him an epistle, the which, poorly translated, is somewhat as follows :

> " Since love, if 'tis not proved to be
> Steadfast and full of loyalty,
> Is nothing worth ; I did desire
> To purge thee with assaying fire,
> And win a love that should endure
> In constancy, abiding sure
> Throughout our lives.   And thus I say
> I raised some causes of delay,
> Before the binding of that chain
> That lasteth while life doth remain.

> " And now, dear sweetheart, thou that wast my all
> Art passed into the life monastical ;
> Whereat I sorrow so that I must speak,
> And by these words the woeful silence break.
> Come, then, dear love, in whom I have my breath,
> And losing whom I do but long for death ;
> Oh, turn thine eyes to me, and come away
> From cloisteral paths ; leave cord, and cowl, and grey ;
> And broken slumbers and austerity,
> So shalt thy heart have that felicity
> Ofttimes desired.   For now it is no less
> Than 'twas before, and I myself address
> To keep for thee alone this happiness.
> Oh, then return, and thy true sweetheart wed,
> That we may lie in one devoted bed,
> And call to our remembrance yet once more
> The love delight we two enjoyed afore.
> For this was my desire, I would but try
> To make more sure thy faith and constancy ;
> And since these and thy love are plainly shown,
> Come back, dear love, and make me all thine own."

This letter, carried by a friend of hers, who made all the remonstrances that were in his power, was received and read of the gentleman friar with so sad a countenance and with such sighs and tears, that it seemed as if he would burn and drown the poor epistle.　And to it he made no reply, but only said to the messenger that the mortification of his passion had cost him so dear that he had lost all desire of life and fear of death. Wherefore he required her who was the cause of it, since she had not been minded to appease his great love and desire, no more to torment him, but to be content with the evil she had done, for which there was no remedy but to seek out so harsh a life that by continual penance he might forget his grief.　And he trusted, through fasts and disciplines, so to weaken his body that the expectation of death should be to him his sovereign comfort, but above all would have no tidings of her, since the mere thought of her name was purgatory to him.　The gentleman returned with this sad reply and bore it to the lady, who grieved sorely at the hearing of it.　But love, that will hope unto the last, made her conceive that if she could visit him, sight and speech would avail more than writing, so with her father and those near akin to her she went to the monastery where he was, having neglected nothing that might increase her beauty. For she thought that if he did but once see her and hear her voice, the fire of love that had so long dwelt in his heart would surely be rekindled and burn more ardently than before.　So coming into the monastery towards the close of evensong, she sent for him to a chapel by the cloisters, and he, who knew not who desired to see him, went forth to the fiercest fight he had ever been in.　And when she saw him thus sallow and lean-looking that he was scarcely to be known, but nevertheless full of no less admirable a grace than afore, love made her stretch forth her arms to embrace him, and pity for the estate he was in so enfeebled her heart that she fell to the ground in a swoon. But the poor monk, who had in him some share of brotherly love, raised her up and set her on a seat in the chapel.　And though he stood as much in need of help himself, he feigned to be ignorant of her passion, fortifying his heart with the love of God against the occasions present to him, in such wise that by his face he might be judged not to perceive what was being done under his eyes.　And when she was recovered from her swoon, turning those glorious and pitiful eyes upon him with such an aspect as would have softened a rock, she did all she was able to persuade him to come out from the place where he was. To this he replied very soberly and virtuously; but at last the heart of the poor monk was so melted by her tears, that he saw Love the cruel bowman, whose sorrows he had so long borne, holding his gilded arrow ready for the giving a new and a more deadly wound; and so fled from before Love and his sweetheart as one whose surety was only in flight. And when he was shut up in his cell, not willing to let her go without clearly resolving her, he wrote a few words in the Spanish tongue, which seem to me so goodly in the matter, that, lest I diminish at all the beauty of them, I will leave them untranslated. This message he sent her by a little novice, who found her still in the chapel, and so despairing that if it had been lawful she also would have turned friar. But when she saw the manner of the writing: *Volvete don venesti, anima mia, que en las tristas vidas es la mia,** she knew that all hope was lost, and determined to follow the counsel of him and her friends, and going home to lead a life as melancholic as that of her lover was austere.

"You see, ladies, how the gentleman avenged him on his cruel sweetheart, who, thinking to make trial of him, drove him to such despair that when she would have taken him back she could not." "I am sorry," said Nomerfide, "that he would not leave his habit to be betrothed to her, for I think it would have been a perfect marriage." "In good faith," said Simontault, "I account him very wise, for whosoever hath well considered the estate of marriage will find no less trouble in it than in the austerity of a monastical life; and he that was so enfeebled with fasts and abstinences feared to take this lifelong charge upon him." "Methinks," said Hircan, "she did wrong to tempt so weak a man to wed, for 'tis too much for the lustiest of us. But if she had offered love to him, with no dues except free-will offerings, the friar's cord would soon have been untied. And since to take him out of purgatory she promised him hell, I say he had good cause to refuse her and make her to feel some of that anguish she had given him." "In sooth," said Ennasuitte, "there be many that, upon thinking they can do better than their neighbours, do worse, nay rather

* Return whence thou camest, O my soul, for amidst the sad lives is my life.

what is most repugnant to their inclinations." "Verily," said
Geburon, "though 'tis not altogether german to our discourse,
you call to my mind the case of a woman who did the contrary
to her desires, whence arose a great uproar in the church of
St. John at Lyon." "I pray you," said Parlamente, "take
my place and tell it us." "My tale," answered Geburon,
"shall not be so long nor so pitiful as Parlamente's."

NOVEL LXV.

A very admirable miracle, which may serve as an example of all others.

In the church of St. John at Lyon there is a gloomy chapel,
and in it a stone sepulchre to the mighty dead, whose figures
are carven on it to the life, and around are men at arms devised
as if asleep. And one day, during the heat of summer, a soldier
walking about the church was fain to slumber, so, seeing this
chapel that it was cool and shady, he was minded to keep guard
over the sepulchre like his fellows in arms, amidst whom he
laid himself down. Now it came to pass, as he was sleeping
most soundly, an old woman, very devout, came thither, and
having told her beads with a lighted candle in her hand, desired
to fix the same to the sepulchre. And perceiving that the
sleeping soldier was nearest to her, she would have set her
candle on his forehead, thinking him to be of stone. But the
wax not holding to the stone, the good woman, thinking its
coldness was the cause, thrust the flame against his forehead, so
as to make her taper stick to it. Then did the image, that was
not altogether without feeling, begin to cry out, whereat the
old woman was so afraid, that she began to proclaim a miracle,
and with such a voice, that all the priests within the church ran,
some to ring the bells, and others to see the miracle. And the
good woman led them to see the image that had moved, which
was to a few a matter for laughter, but the most part were not
content with this, being determined to make this sepulchre
bring them in as many pieces as the speaking crucifix on their
pulpit; but the design came to an end by reason of the old
woman's folly being publicly known.

"If all knew the follies of these devout women, they would
not be accounted holy, nor their miracles the truth. And

2 A

henceforth, ladies, have a care to what saints you give your candles." "'Tis a great marvel," said Hircan, "that whatsoever they do, women always do ill." "Was this ill done," said Nomerfide, "to bring candles to the sepulchre?" "Ay," answered Hircan, "inasmuch as she burnt a man's forehead, and no good is to be esteemed good if it be conjoined with evil. And are you of opinion that this woman thought she was offering a brave gift to God by setting up her poor taper?" Then said Oisille: "I make no account of the worth of the gift, but only of the heart of the giver. Perchance this poor woman had greater love for God than they that give fine torches, since, as it is written in the Gospel, she gave of her penury." "Yet I do not believe," said Saffredent, "that God, who is sovereign wisdom, can take pleasure in the foolishness of women; for, notwithstanding that He delights in simpleness, I see in the Scripture that He despises the ignorant; and though we be commanded to be as harmless as doves, none the less are we charged to be as wise as serpents." "As for me," said Oisille, "I do not deem to be ignorant her who bears her torch or taper before God, making amends for her sins, humbly kneeling upon her knees, with candle in hand, before her Lord, and to Him confessing her unworthiness, craves, with steadfast hope, mercy and salvation." "Would to God," said Dagoucin, "they were all as you, but I do not believe these poor foolish women offer their candles with like intent." Oisille replied to him: "They that speak least know most of the love and will of God; wherefore it is not good to judge any save only oneself." Ennasuitte, laughing, said to her: "'Tis no strange thing to affright a sleeping knave, for women of as low estate have given alarm to great princes, and without the putting of a candle to their foreheads." "I am persuaded," said Geburon, "that you know some history which you would tell us. Wherefore take my place, if such be your pleasure." "My tale shall not be long," said Ennasuitte, "but if I can tell it as it fell out, you shall have no desire to weep."

NOVEL LXVI.

A lord and lady sleeping together were mistaken by an old dame for a prothonotary
and a servant maid, and were sharply reproved of her.

During the year in which my lord of Vendôme espoused
the Princess of Navarre, the King and Queen their father and
mother having been feasted at Vendôme, went into Guienne
with them.   And tarrying in the house of a gentleman, in the
which were many fair maids, they danced for so long a time in
this good company, that the bridegroom and his bride grew
weary, and went to their chamber.   There they threw them on
the bed in their clothes, the doors and windows being shut, and
no one remaining with them.   But in the midst of their slumbers
they were awakened by the opening of a door, and my lord of
Vendôme, drawing the curtain, looked to see how it was, supposing it to be one of his .friends endeavouring to take him by
surprise.   But in the stead thereof he beheld entering in a tall
old bedchamber woman, who for the darkness of the room knew
them not, but seeing them mighty close to one another, fell to
crying ; " Ah! thou nasty wanton strumpet, 'tis a long time
that I have suspected thee for what thou art, but for want of
proof have not told my mistress !   Now are thy wanton ways
so manifest, that I am determined to cloak them no more.   And
thou, apostatical wretch, who hast brought such shame upon
this house, by leading the poor wench astray, were it not for
the fear of God, I would beat thee soundly where thou liest.
Arise, in the name of the devil, arise, for it seemeth as if there
were no shame in thee !"   My lord of Vendôme and his
Princess, to make this discourse last the longer, hid their
faces against one another, and laughed so heartily that they
could not speak a word.   But the old woman, perceiving that
for all her threats they would not budge an inch, came near to
them to have them forth by the arms.   Then she knew both
by their faces and their dress that they were not what she
sought for ; and recognising them, threw herself on her knees,
entreating them to pardon her for disturbing their rest.   But
my lord of Vendôme, willing to learn somewhat more on the
matter, arose incontinent, and would have the old woman tell
him for whom she had mistaken them.   This at first she would

not confess, but having obtained their oath never to reveal it, she declared it was a girl of the house, on whom a protho-notary was amorous; and said she had watched them a long while for her displeasure that her mistress put her trust in a man that would bring this shame upon the house. With this she left the Prince and Princess with closed doors, as she had found them, and they were mighty merry over the case. And though they told the story again, yet they would never name the persons concerned in it.

" And so the good woman, thinking to execute a righteous judgment, made that manifest to strange princes, of which the servants of the house had never heard a word." " I shrewdly suspect," said Parlamente, " whose house it was, and who was the prothonotary, for he has governed many a lady's house for her, and when he is not able to gain the favour of the mistress, he will have that of her maids; but, for the rest, he is a good and honest gentleman." " Wherefore say you *for the rest*," said Hircan, " since it is for what you have told of him that I esteem him an honest gentleman?" Parlamente replied: " I am per-suaded you know the sickness and the sick man, and that if he stood in need of defence, you would be his master attorney; but I would not willingly trust to a man who cannot manage his own passages without servants being advertised of them." "Think you," said Nomerfide, " that men care who knows, if they can but attain their ends? Trust me, if none other were to speak of it, by their own mouths they would proclaim what they had done." Hircan said to her in anger: " It needs not that men should tell all they know." But she, blushing, replied to him: " Perchance that same would not be altogether to their advantage." " By this discourse of yours," said Simontault, " it would seem as if men took pleasure in the hearing evil of women, and I am assured you place me among such. Where-ore I desire greatly to speak well of one, that the rest hold me ot as an evil speaker." " I give you my place," said Enna-suitte, " but pray you have your natural disposition under control, so that you may quit you worthily in our honour." Then began Simontault: " 'Tis no new thing, ladies, to hear some virtuous deed of yours, not worthy of forgetfulness, but rather fit to be written in letters of gold, for an ensample to women, and an admiration to men, seeing in the weaker vessel

that which is repugnant to weakness. Wherefore I tell you
this that I have heard from the lips of Captain Robertval and
from several of his fellowship."

NOVEL LXVII.

How a woman trusted in God amidst the lions.

Captain Robertval once made a sea voyage, with certain
vessels over which he was set by the King his master, to the island
of Canada, where he was determined, if the air of the country
should be found wholesome, to abide, and to build towns and
mansions; and as to the beginning he made all men are advised ·
of it. And that Christianity might be spread abroad throughout
the land, he took with him all manner of mechanicals, amongst
whom there was one so vile, that he betrayed his master, and
put him in danger of being taken by the folk of the country.
But God willed that his undertaking was brought to light before
any hurt could befall the captain, who made seize this wicked
traitor, and would have punished him according as he had deserved.
And this had been done were it not for his wife, who, having
followed her husband through all the dangers of the sea, would
not leave him to perish, but by her tears and lamentations
worked so with the captain and all his company, that as much
for pity of her as for the services she had done him, he granted
her desire. And this was for the husband and wife to be left on
a little island in mid-ocean, where dwelt no people, but only
ravening wild beasts; and it was likewise granted that they
should take thither such things as were needful to them. So
the poor folk, finding themselves all alone amid the fierce brutes,
had no help but in God, who had always been the steadfast
hope of the wife; and she, gaining from Him all her consolation, carried for her safeguard, comfort, and nourishment the
New Testament, in which she read without ceasing. And as
to temporals, she and her husband laboured to build them as
good a house as they were able, and when the lions and other
beasts came near to devour them, the husband with his arquebuss, and she with stones, made so stout a defence, that they
not only kept them at a distance, but very often killed some that
were good provaunt; so with such meats and the herbs of the
island they lived some time, after their bread had failed them.

At length the husband could no more bear with such victuals, and for the water he drank became so swollen that, after a few days, he died, having no servant nor consoler save his wife, who was to him both parson and physician; thus passed he from that wilderness to the heavenly country. And his poor wife, left alone, buried him in the earth as deeply as she could, but yet the beasts straightway smelt him out and came to devour the flesh of him; and she in her little hut shot at them with her arquebuss, so that her husband's body should not have such a sepulture. So living as to her body the life bestial, as to her soul the life angelical, she spent her time in reading of the Scriptures, in prayers and in meditations, having a joyful and contented mind within a body that was shrunken away and nigh amort. But He who never forsaketh His own, and who, when there is no hope in man, showeth His strength, did not allow that the virtue he had set in this woman should be hid from men, but willed rather that it should be made manifest unto His glory. So at the end of some time one of the ships of the armament passing by the island, the folk that were in it saw a smoke that put them in mind of them that had been left there, and they determined to see how God had dealt with them. The poor woman, seeing the ship draw near, went down to the strand, where she was when they came. And after praising God for it, she brought them to her hut, and showed them what manner of victuals she had eaten during her stay; the which would have passed their belief, had they not known that God can as well feed His servants in a wilderness as at a prince's feast. And since she could not abide in such a place, they took her with them to Rochelle, whither after their voyage they came, and made known to all that dwelt therein her faithfulness and patient long-suffering. And on this account she was received by all the ladies with great honour, and they with goodwill gave her their daughters that she might teach them to read and write. And in this honest craft she earned a livelihood, always exhorting all men to love Our Lord and put their trust in Him, setting forth by way of example the great compassion he had shown towards her.

"Henceforth, ladies, you cannot deny that I laud and magnify the virtues that God hath placed in you, the which show themselves the more as the subject is of small account."

"We are in nowise sorry," said Oisille, "that you praise the grace of Our Lord, for in truth all virtue doth come from Him; and the work of man is no more esteemed of God than that of woman, since neither the one nor the other, by their own heart and will, can do anything but plant, and God alone giveth the increase." "If you have well read the Scriptures," said Saffredent, "you will know that it is written: 'I have planted and Apollos watered,' but St. Paul sayeth not that women have put their hands to the work of God." "You would fain follow," said Parlamente, "the evil example of them that take the Scripture that is for them, and leave that is against them. If you read St. Paul to the end you will find that he commends himself to the ladies who have greatly toiled with him in the work of the Gospel." "Howsoever that may be," said Longarine, "this woman is worthy of all praise, as much for her love for her husband, for whom she put her life in jeopardy, as for her faith in God, who, as we have seen, did by no means forsake her." "As to the first," said Ennasuitte, "I suppose there is no wife here present who, to save the life of her husband, would not do the like." "I do believe," said Parlamente, "that some husbands are such beastly folk, that their wives should not find it strange to live amidst the beasts." Ennasuitte, taking this to herself, must needs say: "Save in the matter of biting, the company of beasts is as pleasant to me as that of man, who indeed are choleric and hardly to be borne. But still I maintain that, if my husband were to be in such a case, I would not forsake him for the fear of death." "Beware," said Nomerfide, "of loving too much; too great a love shall deceive both you and him, and love that is without knowledge ofttimes engendereth hatred." "You have not, methinks," said Simontault, "brought the discourse to this, without having some example for a confirmation thereof. Wherefore, if you know of such, I give you my place for the telling of it." "So be it, then," said Nomerfide, "and as is my wont, my story shall be a short and merry one."

NOVEL LXVIII.

An apothecary is made to take his own prescription.

At the town of Pau, in Bearn, lived an apothecary named
Master Etienne, who had to wife an honest woman and a good
housekeeper, and fair enough to have contented him. But as
he tasted a diversity of drugs, so also did he of women, to the
intent that he might be able to speak with more weight on
every kind of complexion, whereat his wife was so anguished
that she lost all patience, for he never had to do with her save
in Holy Week, as a matter of penance. And one day, when
the apothecary was in his shop, and his wife hidden behind,
listening to what he said, there came in a woman, gossip to the
apothecary, and smitten with the same disease as his wife. And
she, sighing, said to him: "Alas, gossip, I am the most wretched
of all women, for I love my husband more than myself, and do
but think how best I may serve and obey him; yet is all my
labour lost, since he loves more than me the nastiest, vilest slut
in the town. And I pray you, gossip, if you know any drug
that will change his complexion, give it to me, for if I be kindly
entreated of him, I do assure you I will return you all the
recompense in my power." The apothecary, consoling her,
said he knew a powder that, if she gave it to her husband with
his broth or roast, like powder of cinnamon, would cause him
to make her very good cheer. The poor woman, desiring to
behold this miracle, asked what it was, and whether she could
obtain it. He declared there was nothing like the powder of
cantharides, of which he had good store; so before they parted
she would have him make ready some of this same powder, and
took of it as much as she needed, and many a time afterwards
did she give him thanks, since her husband, being a lusty man,
and not taking too much thereof, was none the worse for it.
The wife of the apothecary heard all their discourse, and
thought within herself that she stood in as sore need of this
nostrum as her gossip. And knowing the place wherein her
husband had put the remainder of the powder, she was minded
to make use of it, when she should see her opportunity, and this
fell out in three or four days, when her husband, feeling a coldness in his belly, entreated her to make him a mess of pottage;

but she answered that a roast with cinnamon powder would be
more wholesome for him.   He therefore bade her forthwith
make one ready, and to take the cinnamon and the sugar from
the shop, which she did, in nowise forgetting to put in all the
powder he had not given his gossip, having no regard for dose,
weight, nor measure.   Her husband ate the roast, and found it
very good, but soon after he felt the effects, which he was fain
to satisfy with his wife, but to no avail, for in such sort did the
fire burn him, that he knew not on which side to turn, and said
to her that she had poisoned him, asking what she had put in
the roast.   She confessed the truth to him, telling him she had
as great a need to use the powder as had his gossip.   The poor
apothecary was not able to pelt her with aught save railing
words, for indeed he was too sick; but he drove her from
before his face, and sent for the Queen of Navarre's apothecary
to visit him.   And he gave him all the remedies fit to cure him,
the which was done in a short time, and he sharply rebuked
him that he had been so foolish as to give to another drugs that
he would not take himself, telling him that his wife had done
well, since she desired by that means to be the more beloved of
him.   And so the poor man was compelled to bear his sorrows
with long suffering, and to confess he was well punished by
falling into the pit he had prepared for another.

"Methinks, ladies, this woman's love was great without
knowledge."   "Call you it love for her husband," said Hircan,
"to do him a hurt for the pleasure she hoped to get from him?"
"I suppose," said Longarine, "her intent was only to recover
his love, that she deemed had strayed away.   To accomplish
this a woman will do all things."   "Yet," said Geburon, "in
the matter of eating and drinking, a woman should for no cause
give to her husband that of which she is not assured both by
her own experience and the writings of the learned; natheless,
one must pardon ignorance.   This woman was to be excused;
for the most blinding of all passions is love, and the most blinded
of all mortals is that woman who has not strength to order discreetly so weighty a matter."   "Geburon," said Oisille, "you
fall from your good custom, to make yourself appear of one
mind with your fellows.   But are there not women that have
borne both love and jealousy with patience?"   "Ay," said
Hircan, "and pleasantly withal; for the most discreet are they

that have as much delight to make a mock of their husband's doings as their husbands have to cozen them, and if it please you to give me your vote, to the end that Mistress Oisille may bring this day to an end, I will tell you of a husband and wife that are known to all this company." "Begin, then," said Nomerfide. And Hircan, laughing, began thus:

NOVEL LXIX.

A pleasant device of a serving maid, whereby she rid her of her master's solicitations.

At the castle of Odoz, in Bigorre, there dwelt an Italian named Charles, Master of the Horse to the King, who had to wife an honourable gentlewoman, but she having borne him several children was grown old. He likewise was no longer young, and lived with her in peace and quietness. Now and again he would hold parley with the maid servants, his good wife showing no sign of wrath, but giving them their dismission when she found them too familiar in her house. One day she took a good and discreet girl into her service, to whom she discovered her husband's complexion, and how she sent her servants away so soon as she found them to be wantons. This maid, so as to remain in the service and favour of her mistress, determined that she would be an honest woman, and though her master often endeavoured to gain her, she gave no heed unto him, but told all to her mistress, and they diverted themselves together with his foolishness. But on a day that this girl was sifting meal in the bolting-room at the back, having her surcoat drawn over her head after the fashion of the country (and this is like a chrisom-cloth, but covering all the body and the shoulders behind), her master, finding her in this gear, came and pressed her very hard. She, who for fear of death would not have consented, made pretence to agree with him, but natheless asked leave first to go to her mistress to discover whether she was busied in any way, to the intent that they should not both be taken in the fact, the which he granted her. Then she prayed him put her surcoat over his head, and bolt whilst she was away, so that his wife should not hear the noise of the bolter cease. This he did gladly, since he hoped to have that he craved of her. The servant, being by no means of a

melancholic complexion, ran to her mistress, and said to her :
" Come and see your husband, whom I have taught to bolt, so
as to be rid of him." The lady made great haste to see this
new servant of hers, and beholding her husband with the surcoat drawn over his head, and the bolter in his hands, she fell
to laughing mightily, and clapping her hands, called out : " Well
done, wench ; and what monthly wage would you have for your
toil ?" The husband, hearing her voice, and knowing he was
deceived, threw surcoat and bolter to the ground, and ran at
the girl, calling her wretch again and again ; and if his wife
had not come between them, he would have given her a good
quarterage. But at last the tumult was set at rest to the contentment of all, and henceforth they lived together very peacefully.

" What say you, ladies, to this wife ? Was she not wise
altogether to make her husband's pastime her own likewise ?"
" 'Twas but poor pastime," said Saffredent, " for the husband
to fail in his undertaking." " I do believe," said Ennasuitte,
" that it was more pleasure for him to laugh with his wife
than, at his age, to kill himself with the maid." " Yet," said
Simontault, " I had been sorely vexed to have been found
wearing that fine chrisom-cloth." " It has been told me," said
Parlamente, " that it is not to be imputed to your wife if she
found you not in gear very like to it, and thenceforth she has
had no rest." " Be content with the charges of your own
house," answered Simontault, " and do not curiously inquire
into mine. For had it been even as you say, she would never
have perceived it through wanting anything I could give her,
and indeed she has little cause to complain of me." " Honest
women," said Longarine, " want nothing but only the love of
their husbands, wherein alone is their contentment ; and they
that have bestial appetites can never satisfy them and keep their
honour unspotted." " Call you it a bestial appetite," said
Geburon, " when a woman desires of her mate that which by
right belongs to her ?" Longarine replied to him : " I say that
a chaste woman, whose heart is full of true love, takes more
delight in being perfectly beloved than in all the lusts of the
flesh." " I am of your opinion," said Dagoucin, " but these
gentlemen here will neither give ear to it nor confess that it is
true. I think that if reciprocal love does not suffice a woman,

what her husband alone can do will never satisfy her ; and forsaking the virtuous love of women she is fulfilled with the infernal lust of the beasts." "Truly," said Oisille, "you call to remembrance the case of a fair lady married to a noble husband who, falling from this virtuous affection, became more carnal than the swine, and more cruel than the lions." "I pray you, mistress," said Simontault, "to tell it to us, and so bring this day to an end." "I cannot," said Oisille, "and for two reasons : the one for its exceeding length, the other for that it is not of our time, but was written by an author well worthy of belief, and we are sworn to set forth nothing here that has been written." "You speak truth," said Parlamente, "but knowing what tale it is, and that it is written in the old fashion of speaking, I am persuaded that, save us two, nor man nor woman here present has heard it ; wherefore it will stand for new." And at this all the company prayed her to relate it, and to have no fear for the length, since there wanted still a good hour to evensong-time. So at their desire Mistress Oisille began after this sort :

NOVEL LXX.

In the which is shown the horrid lust and hatred of a Duchess, and the pitiful death of two lovers.

In the Duchy of Burgundy there was a Duke, an honourable and excellent prince, who had a woman to wife from whose beauty he took such contentment, that he made no account of her complexion, only striving to do her pleasure, the which affection she very craftily feigned to return to him. Now the Duke had in his household a gentleman, so fulfilled with all the graces that are to be looked for in a man, that he was beloved of the whole house, and notably by the Duke, who from his childhood had reared him near his person ; and seeing him so virtuous took a great liking for him, and from time to time trusted him with such of his occasions as were fitting to his youth. The Duchess, whose heart was not inclined towards chastity, not contenting herself with the love her husband had for her and the kindness he used in their conversation, looked often upon this gentleman, and found him so mightily to her taste that she grew to love him with a love that passed all

reason. And of this she did every day endeavour to inform
him, by sweet and pitiful looks, conjoined with a passionate
manner of feature and much sighing. But he, who had made
virtue his sole delight, could not conceive of vice in a lady who
had such small temptation thereto; so that the languishing eyes
and sheepish looks of this poor wanton brought her no harvest
save a mad despair. And this one day pricked her so shrewdly,
that forgetting she was a woman to be entreated and yet to
refuse, and a princess who should be adored of such servants
and yet have them in disdain, took upon her the spirit of a man
far gone in love, to ease her of this fire she could no longer
bear. So when her husband was at the council board, whither
the young man by reason of his age did not yet go, she made
him a sign to come to her; and this he did, thinking she had
some charge to lay upon him. But taking him by the arm, as
a woman who is weary of too much idleness, she led him to a
gallery, and then said to him: "I marvel that you who are
handsome, young, and full of grace, have lived so long in this
company and yet have never loved." And looking upon him
as pleasantly as she was able, she stopped short, and he
answered: "Madam, if I were worthy that your highness
should look down on me, it would be more a matter of astonishment to see one so unworthy as I am, offer his service and
be refused and mocked." The Duchess, hearing this discreet
reply, loved him more than ever, and protested that there was
not a lady in the Court who would not deem herself happy to
have him for a lover, and that he might well essay such an
undertaking, for he would without doubt bring it to an honourable completion. The gentleman kept his eyes lowered all the
while, not daring to look upon her face, that was hot enough
to have melted an icicle, and just as he would have excused
himself, the Duke came to require the Duchess at the council
board on some affairs that concerned her; and with great regret
she went thither. But the gentleman made no sign that he
had understood the words she had spoken to him, whereat she
vexed sore, not knowing wherefore he kept silence, save it were
on account of foolish fear, of which she deemed him to have
too much. A few days after, seeing that he made no account
of her speech, she resolved to put from her the thought of fear
and shame, and open her mind to him, being persuaded that a

beauty like to hers could get none but a good reception; natheless it would have been greatly to her liking to have had the
honour of being entreated. But she let honour go for the sake
of pleasure, and having several times made trial of discourse
like to what had gone before, and getting no reply to her taste,
she one day took him by the sleeve, and said she would speak
with him on certain weighty matters. The gentleman, humbly
and reverently as was befitting, followed her to a deep window
recess whither she had gone; and when she perceived that
none in the room could see them, in a trembling voice, halfway
betwixt desire and fear, she went on with her former discourse,
chiding him that he had not yet chosen any lady in the company, and assuring him that on whomsoever the lot might fall
she would give him her help so that he should be entreated
kindly. He, not less troubled than astonished at her words,
replied: " Madam, my heart is such that, were I once refused,
I should have no more joy in the world, and I know myself to
be so lowly that there is not a lady of the Court who would
deign to accept me as her lover." The Duchess, blushing, for
she thought he was well-nigh won, swore to him that she knew
the prettiest of all her ladies would gladly have him, and render
him perfectly content with her." " Alas! mistress," said he,
" I do not suppose there is a woman of this company so blind
as to be well affected towards me." The Duchess, perceiving
he would not understand her, drew up the veil a little from
before her passion, and for the fear his virtuousness gave her,
proceeded by manner of interrogation, saying to him: " If
Fortune had so favoured you that it was I who bore you this
goodwill, what then would you reply?" The gentleman at the
hearing of this thought he was dreaming, and falling on his
knees, said to her: " Madam, when it please God that I have
both the favour of the Duke my master, and of yourself, I shall
deem myself the happiest man in the world, for 'tis all I ask in
return for my loyal service, who more than any other am under
obligation to lay down my life for you. And I am persuaded
that the love you bear to my lord Duke is conjoined with such
chastity and nobleness of heart, that not only I, who am but a
worm of the earth, but the greatest prince and most gallant
gentleman in Christendom would be altogether unable to break
asunder the union between you two. And as for me, my lord

hath brought me up since I was a child, and hath made me to
be what I am; wherefore I would rather die than have any
thoughts unbecoming in a faithful servant towards any wife or
daughter or sister or mother of his."   The Duchess would
hear no more, but seeing herself in danger of being disgrace-
fully refused, she broke on a sudden into his words, saying to
him : "O boastful and foolish one, who would have you do
so?   Think you that the very flies in the air love you for your
beauty?   But if you were so daring as to address yourself to
me, I would show you that I nor love nor wish to love other
than my husband, and all the talk I have had with you has
been but a pastime for me, that I might know your mind, and
make a mock of you, as I do with foolish lovers."   "Madam,"
said the gentleman, "I have believed and do believe that all
this is as you say."   Then without listening for more she went
hastily away, and seeing that her ladies followed her, entered
her closet and grieved beyond all telling.   For on the one side
love, wherein she had failed, made her very sorrowful, and on
the other hate, both against herself for her folly and against
him for his wit, brought such fury upon her, that one hour
she was fain to lay violent hands on herself and die, the next
she would live to be avenged on him she accounted her mortal
enemy.

  After that she had wept a long while she feigned to be
sick, so that she should not sup with the Duke, the young
gentleman being commonly in waiting at supper-time.   The
Duke, who loved his wife better than himself, came to see her;
but so as the better to gain her end, she told him that she
thought she was great with child, and for that cause had a
defluction of rheum in the eyes, the which was great pain to
her.   So passed two or three days, the Duchess still keeping
to her bed, so sad and melancholic that the Duke plainly perceived that there was something else besides her greatness to
be mourned for.   And he came to lie with her at night, and
made her as good cheer as he was able, but for all that she
ceased not to sigh continually.   Then he said to her: "Sweetheart, you know I love you even as my life, and that when
your's fails mine will not endure; wherefore, if you would keep
me whole, I pray you tell me the cause of all your sighing, for
I do not believe that the reason you have given is sufficient."

The Duchess, seeing her husband to be minded towards her as she would have wished him, conceived that the time was come to take vengeance on her enemy, and throwing her arms about her husband wept, and answered him: "Alas, my lord, my greatest grief is to see you cozened of them that be so deeply pledged to guard your substance and honour." Hearing this, the Duke was very desirous to have the interpretation thereof, and besought her to tell him the truth without fear. And after several times refusing, at last she said: "Henceforth, my lord, I shall never wonder if strange peoples make war on princes, when they that are most of all indebted to them dare such a deed that the loss of goods is as nothing in comparison. I speak with respect to such a gentleman (and here she named him by his name), who having been fed by your hand, and entreated more as a son than a servant, has dared this miserable deed; namely, to lay siege to the honour of your wife, with which is bound up the honour of your house and lineage. And though by looks he hath long striven to acquaint me with his wicked intent, yet my heart, that takes account of none but you, perceived nothing; wherefore at the last he made it known to me by word of mouth. And to him I made a reply befitting mine estate and chastity, natheless I do so hate him, that I cannot endure to behold him, for which reason I have stayed in my chamber and lost the pleasure of your company. So I beseech you, my lord, keep no longer this pest near your person; for after such a crime, fearing lest I tell you of it, he may well do worse. This then is the cause of my grief, and methinks it is meet and right that you should forthwith take order with it." The Duke, who on the one hand loved his wife and esteemed that a great injury had been done him, and on the other hand loved his servant, whose faithfulness he had tried so well that he could hardly believe this lie for truth, was in great perplexity and wrathfulness. And he went to his chamber, and charged the gentleman no more to appear before him, but to begone to his lodging and tarry there for some time. He, not knowing the reason, was sorely vexed, thinking that he had deserved the very contrary to this ill treatment, and well assured of his thoughts and deeds, sent a fellow of his to speak to the Duke and carry a letter to him. Wherein he humbly besought him, that if by bad report he was estranged

from his presence, he would be pleased to grant a suspension
of judgment until he had heard from his lips the truth of the
matter, for it would be found that in no respect had he done
aught worthy of his displeasure.   Having seen this letter the
Duke's anger was somewhat appeased, and he privily sent for
him to his room, and with a wrathful countenance said to him:
"I never thought that my trouble with your nurture when you
were a child should have been converted to repentance for
having so far advanced you.   But now you have sought to do
me a worse thing than to take away my goods or my life; to
bring shame on the honour of her who is the half of me, and
so to make my house and lineage a byword for ever.   And
you can conceive that such a wrong pricks me so at heart, that
were I not in doubt as to whether it is the truth or no, you
would have been by now at the bottom of the moat, that I
might deal to you a privy punishment for a privy crime."   The
gentleman was no whit stumbled at this discourse, for his innocency gave him a firm and constant speech, and craved to be
informed who was his accuser, since such slanders should be
answered with sword rather than a word.   "Your accuser,"
said the Duke, "hath no arms save her chastity, for I will have
you know that it is my wife and none other who made this
thing manifest to me, and prayed to be avenged on you."   The
poor gentleman, hearing the crafty wickedness of the Duchess,
yet would not accuse her, but answered: "My lord, my lady
can say what she will; you know her better than I, and that I
have never been with her alone, save one time when she spoke
but very little with me.   Your judgment is as sound as any
prince in the world, wherefore, my lord, I entreat you declare
whether you have ever seen aught on my face that engendered
any suspicion.   For this fire of love cannot be kept secret
a long while and not be discovered of them that are afflicted
with the same disease.   And I entreat you, my lord, to believe
two things of me: the one, that I am so loyal to you that were
your wife the prettiest of all women, yet love would have no
power to bring a stain on my honour and fidelity; the other,
that even were she not your wife, she is the last woman on
whom I should grow amorous, and there is many another that
would come before her in my heart."   At the hearing of these
truths the Duke began to soften, and said: "I assure you that

2 B

I too never believed it; wherefore come into my presence again, and if it be discovered that the truth is with you, I will love you better than I ever did; and on the other hand your life is in my hands." For this the gentleman thanked him, submitting to all manner of pains and penalties if there should be found any fault in him.

The Duchess, seeing the gentleman in waiting as was accustomed, could not patiently bear it, but said to her husband: "You will get but your deserts, my lord, if you are poisoned, since you put more trust in your mortal enemies than in your friends." "Prithee, sweetheart, trouble not yourself as to this matter, for if I find that the truth is even as you have told me be certain that he will not live four-and-twenty hours after; but he hath so sworn to the contrary effect, that I, not having perceived myself any fault in him, cannot believe it without some sure proof." "In good faith," she said, "your kindness makes his wickedness the greater. What more proof would you have than to see a man like him remain so long and not be reported to be in love? Trust me, my lord, that without the great desire he had to be my lover, he would have found a mistress before now; for never did a young man live in such a company in this manner, without aiming at so high a mark that he was content with the mere hope of attaining thereto. And since you are persuaded that he is telling you the truth, put him to the oath as to his love, for if he loves another I am content that you should credit him; but if not believe that I speak the truth." The Duke found the conclusions of his wife good, and took the gentleman with him to the chase, and said to him: "My wife still persists in her judgment concerning you, and gives me a reason that makes me very suspicious—namely, that so comely and young a man was never before seen without a sweetheart for any length of time, and this doth cause me to believe that your intent is as she affirms, and that the expectation you have of her doth give you so much contentment, that you have no thought for other women. Wherefore as a friend I entreat you, and as a master charge you to tell me, whether you love any lady or no." The poor gentleman, to whom this secret was as dear as life, was nevertheless constrained, by reason of his lord's jealousy, to confess that of a truth he loved a woman whose beauty was so great that the

comeliness of the Duchess and the ladies of her Court was but
ugliness in comparison.   But he besought him never to require
her name at his hands, since the love betwixt him and his
sweetheart was of such sort that none could do it a hurt save
the one who first made it known.   The Duke promised not to
press him as to this matter, and was so content with him, that
he showed him more kindness than ever he had before.   This
the Duchess very plainly perceived, and with her wonted craft
set herself to find out the cause thereof.   And the Duke concealed it not from her, whereby to her lust of vengeance was
conjoined a bitter jealousy, that ·made her entreat the Duke to
require his sweetheart's name of the gentleman.   For she would
have .him believe 'twas all a lie, and the best means to discover
it would be to demand proof of the story, and if he could not
name her he esteemed so beautiful it would be exceeding foolish
to put any trust in his words.   The poor lord, whose mind was
swayed by his wife at her pleasure, went forth and walked
all alone with the gentleman, telling him that he was in greater
trouble than afore, for he strongly suspected that he had given
him this excuse to prevent the discovery of the truth ; wherefore
he prayed him to declare the name of her he loved so much.
The gentleman entreated him not to be the occasion of his
doing such a sin against his mistress—namely, to break the
promise he had made and kept for so long awhile, and cause him
to lose in a day that he had preserved for more than seven
years ; and said he had rather die than do this wrong to her
who was so faithful to him.   The Duke, finding that he was
not willing to tell him, grew most furiously jealous, and said to
him : "Choose then one of two things : either tell me the
name of your mistress or be banished from the lands over
which I have authority, and if I find you in them eight days
after, I will put you to a cruel death."   If ever grief took hold
on the heart of faithful lover, then did it on this poor gentleman, who might well say *Augustiae sunt mihi undique*, since on
the one hand if he told the truth he would lose his sweetheart
if she came to know that he had broken his promise ; and on
the other, if he told it not, he would be banished from the lands
wherein she dwelt, and would no more have the means of seeing
her.   So, pressed hard on either side, there came a cold sweat
upon him as on one who is dying of a broken heart, which

being seen of the Duke, was esteemed by him a proof that
the gentleman's only mistress was his own wife, and he thought
that, because he was not able to name any other, he was in such
piteous case, wherefore he harshly said to him : " If your words
were true, you would have none of this difficulty to declare her
name, wherefore I believe that your sin is tormenting you."
The gentleman, pricked by this speech, and driven by his love
for his master, resolved to tell him the truth, being persuaded
that he was so honourable a man that he would on no account
reveal it.   So throwing himself on his knees before him, with
clasped hands, he said : " My lord, both what I owe you, and
the great love I bear you, do more urge me than any fear of
death ; for I see you in such imagination and false judgments
concerning me, that to set you at rest I am determined to do
what no torment could have compelled me.   And I entreat
you, my lord, to swear and promise, on your faith as a Christian
prince, never to reveal the secret that, as it is your pleasure, I
am constrained to make known to you.   Forthwith the Duke
swore all the oaths he could call to mind that never by his lips,
his pen, or his countenance, would he reveal this thing to any
living soul.   The young man, being assured of so virtuous a
prince, straightway put the first stone to the building of his
woes, and said to him: " It is seven years ago, my lord,
that, knowing your niece the Lady of Vergier was a widow
and had no kindred, I set myself to gain her favour.   And
since I came not of a house that I should wed her, I was content to be received as a lover, and this was granted me.   And
it has pleased God that hitherto our passages have been ordered
so discreetly, that we two alone are advertised of them, and
now, my lord, you also are of our privity, and in your hands I put
my life and my honour, entreating you to keep our secret, and
to make no less account of your niece, for I think in the round
world there is none to be compared to her."   At this the Duke
was glad, for knowing the great beauty of his niece, he made
no doubt she was more pleasant than his wife, but yet could
not understand how such a matter should be conducted without
ways and means, and so prayed the gentleman tell him how he
visited her.   The gentleman showed him how his lady's chamber
opened out to the garden, and how, on the appointed day, she
would leave a little door open through which he passed, and

waited till he heard the barking of a little dog, that his mistress
sent into the garden when all her women were asleep.   Then
he went in and talked with her all the night, and, before he
set forth, she set him a day on which to see her again, and he
never failed to keep the appointment without some urgent
cause preventing him.   The Duke, who was mighty inquisitive,
and who in his time had been a hot gallant, as much to satisfy
altogether his suspicions as' to hear more of so strange a case,
prayed him the next time he visited his mistress to take him
also, not as a master but as a companion.   The gentleman,
having gone thus far, granted him his desire, telling him that
very day was appointed for their meeting, whereat the Duke
was in such delight as he would not have exchanged for a
kingdom.   And feigning to go to rest in his closet, he made
bring two horses for him and the gentleman, and all the night
they fared upon their way from Argilly, where dwelt the Duke,
to La Vergier.   And leaving their horses without the park,
the gentleman led the Duke into the garden by the little door,
praying him to remain behind a walnut-tree, where he could
judge whether his tale were true or no.   He had not been in
the garden a long while before the dog began to bark, and the
gentleman walked to the tower, where his lady failed not to
come out to him, and with a kiss said it seemed a thousand
years since she had seen him last, and then they entered the
tower together and shut the door upon them.   The Duke,
having seen the whole mystery, was more than satisfied, and
had not to wait there long, for the gentleman told his mistress
that he must return earlier than was his wont, for that the
Duke was going a-hunting at four of the clock, and he dared
not fail to be with him.   The lady, who preferred honour
before pleasure, would by no means keep him from his duty,
for the thing of which she made most account in their virtuous
love was that it was secret from all men.   So the gentleman
set forth at one hour after midnight, and the lady, in her mantle
and kerchief, went some way with him, but not so far as she
wished, for he made her turn back lest she should see the
Duke, with whom he returned as he had come to the castle of
Argilly.   And as they were upon the way the Duke swore continually to his servant never to reveal the secret ; and so loved
and trusted him that there was no one at Court more in his

favour, whereat the Duchess became mightily enraged. But
the Duke straitly charged her never more to speak on this
matter, for he knew the truth and was pleased with it, inasmuch as the lady was more loveable than she. At this the
Duchess was so cut to the heart that she fell into a sickness
more grievous than a fever; and the Duke going to see her
and console her, could effect nothing if he would not tell her
the name of the Beloved Lady, and she used such importunity
with him that he went from her room, saying: "If you talk to
me again after this sort, we will part from one another." These
words made the sickness of the Duchess to increase, and she
feigned to feel the child moving in her womb, whereat the Duke
rejoiced so much that he came to lie with her. But at the
moment in which she perceived him to be most amorous on
her she turned away from him, saying: "I beseech you, since
you have no love for wife nor child, leave us to die together."
And with these words she poured forth such tears and lamentations that the Duke was in great fear lest she should mis-
carry; wherefore, taking her between his arms, he entreated
her to tell him her desire, since all things were in common
between them. "Alas, my lord," she replied, weeping, "how
can I hope that you will do for me a thing at all difficult when
you refuse that which is most easy and reasonable—namely, to
tell me the mistress of the most wicked servant you ever had in
your house? I thought that you and I were but one heart, one
soul, and one flesh, but since you hide from me your secrets, I
am persuaded I am to you as a stranger and one not akin. Alas!
my lord, you have told me many a secret and weighty matter,
of which you have never heard that I spoke; you know by
such sufficient trial that my will is altogether your own, that
you ought not to doubt that I am more you than myself. And
being you have sworn to tell no other the secret of the gentleman, you will not break your word in telling me, for I am not
and cannot be other than yourself: I have you in my heart, I
hold you in my arms, and your child, in whom you live, is in
my womb; and yet I cannot have your heart, as you have
mine! But the more I am loyal and faithful to you, the more
are you cruel and severe with me; and this it is that makes
me a thousand times a day to desire, by a sudden death, to
deliver your child from such a father, and myself from such a

husband.   And this I hope will fall out soon, since you prefer
a faithless servant before such a wife as I am to you, and before
the mother of your child, that will without doubt perish, since I
cannot learn of you what I greatly desire to know." So saying
she threw her arms about her husband and kissed him, watering
his face with her tears and lamenting in such wise, that the
good prince, fearing lest he should lose his wife and his child
together, determined to tell her the whole truth. But before he
did so, he swore to her that if ever she revealed it to a living soul
she should die by his hand, to which she agreed and accepted
the penalty.   Then the poor cozened husband told her all that
he had seen from beginning to end, at which she feigned to be
pleased, but in her heart was very wrath. Natheless, for fear
of the Duke, she dissembled her passion as well as might be.

And it came to pass that on a great feast-day the Duke
held his court, bidding to it all the ladies of the land, and
amongst the rest his niece. And the dances having begun,
each gladly did his duty therein; but the Duchess being in
torment to see the beauty and grace of the Lady of Vergier,
could neither rejoice with the rest nor so much as conceal her
spleen.   For having made all the ladies to sit around her, she
began to discourse concerning love, and perceiving that the
Lady of Vergier said nothing, she asked her with a heart black
with jealousy: "And is it possible, fair niece, that your beauty
is without a friend or follower?"   "Mistress," replied the
Lady of Vergier, "my beauty hath not gained me such; for
since the death of my husband I have willed to have no lovers
save my children, with whom I am content."   "Fair niece,
fair niece," replied the Duchess with an abominable spitefulness,
"there is no love so secret as not to be revealed, nor little dog
so well trained and instructed whose bark cannot be heard."   I
leave to your imagination, ladies, what pain the poor Lady of
Vergier felt at her heart, hearing a thing so long concealed
made thus manifest to her great shame ; her honour, so carefully
guarded and so woefully lost, was a torment to her, but still
more her suspicion that her lover had broken his promise, the
which she had never looked for except he were to love some
lady prettier than she, who by her enchantments should cause
him to make all known to her. Yet so great was her prudence
that she made no sign, and replied laughing to the Duchess

that she understood not the language of the beasts. But under this wise concealment her heart was so full of sadness that she arose, and, passing through the chamber of the Duchess, entered a closet whither the Duke, as he walked up and down, saw her go in. And when she found herself in a place where she thought to be alone, she let herself fall upon a bed as one who swoons away, so that a lady who was lying by the bedside to rest herself, arose and looked through the curtain to see who it was; and finding it was the Lady of Vergier who thought herself alone, she durst not do anything, but kept still and listened to what she said. And the poor lady with a dying voice began her plaint, saying: "Ah, hapless one! what word is this that I have heard? What sentence of death hath been passed upon me? What final judgment have I received? O my beloved, my beloved, is this the reward of my chaste and honourable affection? O heart of me, what dangerous choice hast thou made; for the most loyal the most faithless, for the truest a deceiver, for the most secret a scandalous man? Alas! can it be that this thing that was hidden from the eyes of all men hath been revealed to the Duchess? My little dog that was the only help of our long love was too well taught; it was not thou that hath discovered me, but he whose voice can be heard above the barking of the dog, and whose heart is more thankless than the heart of the beast. He it was who, against his oath and promise, hath made manifest our happy life that did hurt to none, and endured for many a year. O my beloved, my beloved, who alone art in my breast, in whom alone I live, was it needful for thee to declare thyself my mortal enemy, and to cast my honour to the four winds, my body to the earth, and my soul to its eternal rest? Hath the Duchess, then, so great beauty that it hath changed thee as did the beauty of Circe? Art thou, then, become from virtuous vicious, from good evil, and from a man a ravening beast? O my love, my love, though thou hast broken thine oath, yet will I keep mine. Never more will I see thee, after that thou hast noised our love abroad; but since I cannot live without the sight of thee, I submit willingly to mine anguish, and seek no cure for it either in reason or in medicine; for death alone shall bring it to a close, and be sweeter to me than to tarry in the world without love, without honour, or delight. Nor war nor death

hath taken my lover from me, nor sin nor fault of mine hath
robbed me of mine honour or contentment; 'tis cruel chance
that rendereth him who of all had most cause for gratitude
ungrateful, and maketh me to receive the contrary to what I
have deserved. Ah, my lady Duchess, what delight it was to
mock me and my little dog; enjoy, then, that which belongs
alone to me. Make her to be a jest who thought, by concealment and virtuous loving, to be freed from all such jesting.
How hath this word pierced through my heart, that I redden
with shame and grow pale with jealousy. Alas! my heart, 'tis
time thou wast no more. Love burneth thee as with fire,
jealousy and wrong are on thee as a frost of death, and sorrow
and shame will not have me give thee any comfort. Alas!
poor soul, that for adoring the creature forgot the Creator,
thou must return into the hands of Him from whom an idle
love drew thee awhile away. Be of good courage, O my soul,
for thou shalt find a kinder Father than was the lover who
made Him to be forgotten. O God, my creator, true and
perfect love, by whose grace my love was unspotted from sin,
save that of loving too much, I entreat Thee of Thy mercy
receive the soul of her who repenteth, for that she hath broken
Thy first and most righteous commandment. By the merits of
Him whose love passeth all understanding, pardon the sin that
I by too great love have committed, for in Thee alone do I put
my trust. And farewell, O my lover, whose name doth break
my heart." And forthwith she fell backward, and her face
became white as death, her lips blue, and her extremities cold.
And at that moment her lover came into the hall, and saw the
Duchess dancing amid the ladies, and looked on every side for
his mistress, but not seeing her, entered the chamber of the
Duchess. There he found the Duke sauntering up and down,
who, guessing his intent, whispered in his ear: "She is gone
into that closet, and methinks she looked somewhat sickly."
The gentleman asked if it was his pleasure that he should go after
her, and the Duke prayed him to do so. And when he was
come into the closet he saw the Lady of Vergier standing at the
threshold of death, and he threw his arms about her and said:
"What ails you, sweetheart? Would you leave me, then?"
The poor lady, hearing that voice she knew so well, took a
little strength, and, opening her eyes, looked on him who was

the cause of her death, but upon that look love and sorrow swelled so within her that with a pitiful sigh she gave up her soul to God. The gentleman, with scarce more life in him than the dead woman, asked of the lady that was by the bed after what sort this sickness had come upon her. And she told him all the words that she had heard. Then he knew that the Duke had revealed the secret to his wife, and, embracing the body of his sweetheart, he for a long while watered it with tears, saying thus : " O traitorous and wicked lover that I am, wherefore has not the punishment of my treachery fallen upon me, and not upon her who is innocent? Wherefore did not thunder from heaven overwhelm me on the day that my tongue revealed the secret of our virtuous love? Wherefore did not the earth open and swallow me up, faithless that I am? O tongue, mayest thou be punished as was the tongue of the rich man who in hell lifted up his eyes being in torment. O heart, too, fearful of death and banishment, mayest thou be torn for ever of eagles as was the heart of Ixion.* Alas! my love, the woe of woes, and the bitterest of all woes, hath over-taken me. Thinking to keep you, I have lost you for ever ; thinking to live with you a long while in virtuous contentment, I cast my arms about your dead body ; and dying, you were displeased with me, my heart, and my tongue. O most loyal and faithful of all women, I do condemn myself for the most disloyal, fickle, and unfaithful of all men. Would that I could impute the blame to the Duke, in whose promise I trusted, hoping thereby to prolong our days in happiness, but alas! I should have known that none could keep my secret better than myself. The Duke was more justified in that he revealed it to his wife than I who revealed it to him. I accuse myself alone of the greatest wickedness that ever fell out between lovers. Would that I had endured to be cast into the moat, as he threatened me ; then, my love, you would be still alive, and I should have met with a glorious death, in keeping of the law of love. But I broke my promise and remain alive, and you, by reason of your perfect love, are dead ; for the purity of your heart could not bear to know the wickedness of your lover, and suffer you to live. O God, why hast thou made me man, with

---

* There appears to be some confusion here between Ixion (who was bound to a wheel) and Prometheus (whose *liver* was torn by a *vulture*).

love so light and heart devoid of knowledge? Why madest
Thou not me the dog that served his mistress faithfully?
Alas! my little friend, my joy at your bark is turned to bitter
grief for that another has heard it. Yet, dear sweetheart,
neither the love of the Duchess nor of any other woman could
make me vary, though several times in her wicked craftiness
she prayed and entreated me; but my folly hath overcome me,
who thought by it to establish our love for ever. Yet though
I was foolish, none the less am I worthy of blame, for I revealed
the secret of my mistress, and I broke my promise to her, and
for that alone I see her dead before mine eyes. Alas! sweetheart, will death be more cruel to me than thee, whose love
hath ended thy life? I believe that it will not deign to touch
my wretched, faithless heart, for life with dishonour and the
recollection of what by mine own fault I have lost will be
harder to bear than ten thousand deaths. And if any, by
malice or mischance, had slain you, forthwith would my sword
been in my hand to avenge you; so it is right that I should
not pardon that murderer who is the cause of your death by a
more wicked deed than the stroke of a sword. And if I knew
a more infamous executioner than myself, I would pray him to
put to death your traitorous lover. O love, by my love that
was without knowledge I have done you a displeasure, thus it
is that you will not succour me as you succoured her who kept
all your laws. Nor is it befitting that I should die so honourable
a death, but rather that mine own hand should slay me. Since
with my tears I have washed your face, and since with my
tongue I have besought your forgiveness, now with my hand
I will make my body like to yours, and send my soul whither
you are, for I know that a virtuous love hath no end in this
world nor in the next." And then rising from beside the body,
he drew his dagger, and like a madman dealt himself a violent
blow therewith, and, falling back, took his sweetheart in his
arms and kissed her in such wise that there seemed to be in
him more of love than death. The lady, seeing the blow, ran
to the door and called for help; and the Duke, hearing the
cry, and fearing for them that he loved, came the first into the
closet, and, beholding the pitiful pair, essayed to draw them
apart, so that the gentleman, if it were possible, might be
saved. But he held his sweetheart so firmly, that till he was

dead they could not be sundered. Yet hearing the voice of
the Duke speaking to him, and saying: "Alas! what is the
cause of this?" with a terrible look he replied to him: "My
tongue and yours, my lord." So saying, he gave up the
ghost, with his face close to that of his mistress. The Duke,
desiring to know more, constrained the lady to tell him what
she had heard and seen, and this she did, sparing nothing.
Then the Duke, knowing that he himself was the cause of it,
threw him on the dead lovers, and with tears and very sorrowful
lamentations, and ofttimes kissing them, asked pardon for his
sin. And after, in furious fashion, he arose, and drew the
dagger from the gentleman's body; and as a wild boar,
wounded by a spear, rushes madly against his enemy, so went
he to seek her out who had wounded the very depths of his
heart. And he found her dancing in the hall, more gay than
she was wont to be, for the thought that she had avenged her
on the Lady of Vergier. So the Duke took her in the middle
of the dance, and said to her: "You took the secret upon
your life, and upon your life fall the punishment." So saying,
he seized her by the hair, and struck her with the dagger
through the throat, whereat all the company were astonished,
and each thought the Duke was beside himself. But having
fulfilled his intent, he gathered together into the hall all his
servants, and recounted the honourable and pitiful history of
his niece, and the evil his wife had done to her, and all present
wept at the hearing of it. And the Duke ordained that his
wife should be buried in an abbey that he had founded, in part
for satisfaction of his sin in putting her to death; and he made
build a fair sepulchre where the bodies of his niece and the
gentleman were laid together, with an epitaph showing forth
their tragical history. And the Duke led an armament against
the Turks, wherein God so favoured him that he gained both
honour and profit, and found when he returned that his eldest
son was fit to take the lordship upon him, and so, leaving all,
he became a monk in the abbey where the bodies of his wife
and the two lovers were buried, and there with God passed
happily the remnant of his days.

"Such, ladies, is the story you would have me tell you, the
which I see plainly by your eyes you have not heard without
compassion. Methinks you would do well to set it before you

for an ensample, lest you put too much your affections on men, for howsoever good and virtuous they be, there is always at the end an aftertaste of trouble. And you know that St. Paul warns even such folk as be married that they love not one another to excess. For the nearer the heart to earthly things the farther is it from heavenly things, and the more difficult the chain to be broken. Wherefore I beseech you, ladies, pray to God for His Holy Spirit, whereby your hearts shall be so inflamed with His love, that when·you die it will be no pain to leave that which is dear to you upon earth." "Since their love was so honourable," said Geburon, "as you say it was, what need was there to use such concealment?" "For that," said Parlamente, "the malice of men is so great, that they are not able to conceive how passionate love can be conjoined to virtue, since they esteem men and women vicious, as they themselves are. On this account, if a woman have a dear friend, beyond her most immediate kin, she must speak with him secretly, if she would speak with him long. For a woman's honour is as much made matter of dispute through a virtuous as through a vicious love, since men judge but by appearances." "But," said Geburon, "when the secret is discovered it fares so much the worse with them." "I confess that it is so," said Longarine, "wherefore 'tis better not to love at all." "We appeal from that sentence," said Dagoucin, "for if we thought the ladies were without love, we should be without life. I speak of them who live but to gain love, and though they have no good success, yet does hope sustain them, and make them to do a thousand valorous deeds, till old age converts these honourable pains into others. But if we conceived that the ladies loved us not, in place of warriors we should have to turn hucksters, and instead of winning honour think only how to keep up riches." "Then," said Hircan, "you would maintain that, if there were no women, we should become cowards? As if we had no heart save what they gave us! I am altogether of the contrary opinion, and believe that there is nothing that weakens the heart of a man so much as the excessive loving or resorting with women. And for this cause the Jews would not have a man go to the wars during the first year after his marriage, for fear lest his love for his wife should draw him from the danger he ought to seek out."

"I esteem," said Saffredent, "this ordinance without sufficient reason, insomuch as there is nothing that makes a man go abroad from his house so much as marriage, for the wars without are not harder to be borne than those within, and I believe that to make man desire to go to far countries and forsake his hearth he must first be wed." "It is true," said Ennasuitte, "that marriage takes away from them the care of their houses, since they trust the hearth to the wife, and think of nothing but honour, being persuaded that the woman will have due care for the profit." Saffredent replied to her: "Howsoever that may be, I am glad that you are of my opinion." "But," said Parlamente, "you dispute not concerning that which is most weighty of all : wherefore was it that the gentleman, who was the cause of all the woe, did not die so soon as she who was innocent?" Nomerfide replied: "'Tis because women love better than men." "Rather," said Simontault, "is it because the jealousy and despair of women break their hearts, without their knowing wherefore, while the wisdom of men make them to inquire as to the truth. This done, they show the greatness of their souls, as did this gentleman, who having heard what was the cause of his sweetheart's death, manifested his love towards her, and spared not his own life." "Natheless," said Ennasuitte, "she died of true love, for her steadfast and faithful heart could not endure to be so shamefully deceived." "The reason of it was jealousy," said Simontault, "that would give no room to reason, and she believed evil of her lover of which he was not guilty. Moreover her death was constrained, for she could not help it; while her lover, after that he knew what wrong he had done her, of his free will put himself to death." "Yet," said Nomerfide, "the love must needs be great to cause such sorrow." "Do you have no fear," said Hircan, "for you will never come to your death through such a fever." "No more," answered Nomerfide, "than you will kill yourself after discovering your fault." Parlamente, who suspected this dispute to be at her expense, said to them, laughing: "'Tis enough that those two died for love, without two others proceeding to battery and assault for love also. And there is the last bell for evensong, so we must begone whether we will or no." Thereupon the company arose and went to hear evensong, forgetting not in their prayers the souls of the true lovers, for whom the monks, of their goodwill, did sing a *De Profundis*. And while they supped their talk ran on nothing but the Lady of Vergier, and after diverting them together for a while, each went to his chamber, and so put an end to the Seventh Day.

DAY THE EIGHTH.

ON THE EIGHTH DAY RELATION IS MADE OF THE MOST LECHEROUS CASES THAT CAN BE CONCEIVED.

PROLOGUE.

When morning was come they made inquiry as to how their bridge was being forwarded, and found that in two or three days it would be finished. At this certain of the company were sorry, for they would have had the work last much longer, that this pleasant life might last also; but seeing that there were not more than two or three days left to them, they resolved to lose no time, and prayed Oisille to give them their spiritual refection as she was wont. And this she did, but kept them longer than afore, for she wished before they departed to bring to end the Epistle General of St. John. And in the expounding of it she quitted herself so well, that it seemed as if the Holy Ghost, full of love and sweetness, spoke by her mouth. So, all enflamed with this heavenly fire, they went to hear high mass, and afterwards while they were at dinner spoke together of the day that was past, calling on one another to make this as fine. And to that intent they went apart, each one to his chamber, until the time was come for them to go to their Recounting-House on the Board of Green Grass, where they found the monks already come and in their accustomed place. When all were seated it was asked who should make a beginning, and Saffredent said: "Since you have done me the honour to let me begin two days, methinks we should do a wrong to the ladies if one of them did not also begin two." "If that be so," said Oisille, "we should have to stay here a long time, or one of you and one of us would have to go without a day." "As for me," said Dagoucin, "if I had been chosen I should have given my place to Saffredent." "And I," said Nomerfide, "should have given mine to Parlamente, since I am so accustomed to obey that I know not how to command."

To this all the company agreed, and Parlamente thus began :
" The days that are passed have been filled with such discreet
stories, that I am of opinion that this day should be made up of
the most wanton follies that we can devise. Wherefore, to set
you an ensample, I will begin."

NOVEL LXXI.

How a wife was brought back from the grave and gate of death by seeing her husband
attempt the servant maid.

In the town of Amboise there lived a man named Brim-
baudier, saddler to the Queen of Navarre, and one whom from
the colour of his visage worshipped Bacchus rather than Diana.
He had to wife an honest woman, who governed his household
discreetly, and he was well content with her; and one day it
was told him his wife was sick unto death, whereat he manifested very great sorrow, going with all speed to succour her.
And he found the poor woman in such case that she had more
need of the parson than the physician, and her husband's
anguish was pitiful to behold. But to represent it well it
would be needful to speak thickly as he did, and still better to
paint one's face in the similitude of him. After that he had
done for her all that was in his power, she asked for the cross,
and it was brought her. Seeing this the good man threw
himself on a bed, quite desperate, and crying in his thick voice :
·' Alas, alas! I shall lose my poor wife. What shall I do, unhappy wretch that I am ?" and much more to the same intent.
At last, perceiving that there was no one in the chamber except
a mighty pretty servant maid, he called her in a low voice to
him, and said to her : "Sweetheart, I am dead, nay worse than
dead, to see your mistress thus passing away. I know not
what to do nor say, save that I put me in your hands, and pray
you take the charge of my house and my children. Here are
the keys that hang by my side. Prithee have a care to the
household, for I can no more avail anything." The poor girl
comforted him, and bade him not despair, and if she lost her
mistress there was no need for her to lose her good master.
He replied : "Sweetheart, it skills not talking, for I am at the
point of death. See how cold is my face; put your cheeks
close to mine to warm them." So saying he laid his hand

to her breasts, at which she would have made some difficulty, but he prayed her not to be afraid, since it was necessary they should be very near to one another. Thereupon he took her in his arms and threw her on the bed. His wife, who had no company but the cross and the holy water, and had not spoken for the last two days, began with her weak voice to cry out as loudly as she was able: "Ah! Ah! Ah! I am not dead yet." And threatening them with her hand, she called out : " Villain, strumpet, I am not dead yet." The husband and the servant, hearing her voice, arose, but so great was her wrath against them that the catarrhous humour which had hindered her speech was dissolved, and she poured out her anger in railing and calling them every evil name she could imagine. And from that hour she began to amend, and grew quite whole, often reproaching her husband for the small love he had for her.

"You see, ladies, the hypocrisy of men, and how readily they console them for the loss of their wives!" "How do you know," said Hircan, "that he had not heard that this was the best cure for his wife's disease? For since by kind treatment he could do nothing, he would try whether the contrary would avail anything, and had very good success therein. And I marvel that you, being women, have manifested the complexion of your kind that is recovered by ill-treatment rather than good." "There's not a doubt on it," said Longarine, "such a cure would have raised me not only from my bed but from the very grave." "But what wrong did he to her," said Saffredent, "to take some small consolation when he thought she had been dead? For it is well known that the bonds of marriage endure but for life, and afterwards one is loosed from them." "Ay," said Oisille, "loosed from one's oath, but in a steadfast heart love always remains. And his grief was soon forgotten, since he did not wait till she had breathed her last." "But what is most marvellous in mine eyes," said Nomerfide, "is that, seeing death and the cross before him, he had no fear to do God a displeasure." "A brave reason!" said Simontault. "You would not marvel then at wantonness, if it were done far from the church and the cemetery?" "Make a mock of me," said Nomerfide, "as you will, yet to think upon death makes the heart to grow cold, be it never so young." "I

should be of your opinion," said Dagoucin, "had I not heard
to the contrary from a princess." "That is to say," said Parlamente, "that she recounted to you some tale. Wherefore,
if it be so, I give you my place for the telling of it." And
Dagoucin began thus:

NOVEL LXXII.

The case of a monk and a nun that wrought abominations in the presence of the dead.

In one of the fairest towns in France there is an hospital,
well endowed—namely, with a prioress and fifteen or sixteen
nuns, and in another part of the building a prior and seven or
eight monks. And these day by day sang their offices, and
those were content with paternosters and the Hours of Our
Ladye, since they were altogether occupied in the service of
the sick. One day there was a poor man at the point of death,
and all the nuns were around him, who, after they had done all
that was in their power for his health, sent for one of the
monks to confess him. Then seeing he still grew weaker,
extreme unction was given him, and little by little he lost the
power of speech. But insomuch as he tarried a long time and
did not pass, and seemed able to hear them, each of the nuns
set herself to speak to him after the best sort she could, whereat
at length they grew weary; and when night was come and he
was still alive, one by one they went away to bed. And there
remained, for the making of the body ready for burial, but one
of the youngest nuns and a monk, whom she feared more than
the prior or any other by reason of the great austerity of his
words and life. And when they had duly chanted their hours
in the dead man's ear they saw that he was dead, so they made
him ready for burial. But in the exercising of this last work of
mercy the monk fell to speaking on the miseries of this life and
the exceeding happiness of death, and while he discoursed to
this effect it struck midnight. The poor girl listened with due
attention to his words, and looked on him with tears in her
eyes, whereat he took such delight that, speaking of the life to
come, he began to embrace her, as if he desired to carry her in
his arms to Paradise. She, accounting him for the most devout
of all the monks, durst not refuse him, and perceiving this,
speaking of God all the while, he did on her the work that the

devil had of a sudden put into his heart; for before he had
never attempted any such thing.　And he persuaded her that
a sin that is done in secret is not imputed to men by God, that
two people with no ties could do no offence in this manner, if
there was no scandal, to the avoidance of which she must take
heed to confess to none but him.　So they departed thence,
she going first; and passing through the Ladye Chapel, she
would say her prayers therein, as she was wont.　But when
she began : "Virgin Mary," she remembered that she had lost,
on no love nor compulsion, but through a foolish fear, the style
and title of virginity, and so bitterly did she weep that it seemed
as though her heart would break.　The monk, hearing the
noise of her lamentation from afar, feared lest she was converted and his pleasure lost to him, and coming to her found
her with her face to the ground before Our Lady.　Therefore
he sharply rebuked her, and said that if she made it a matter
of conscience, she might confess to him, and be quit of him if
she would; for one way or the other there was no sin.

The foolish nun, thinking to make satisfaction before God,
went to confession, but for penance he only swore that she
sinned not at all to love him, and such a petty fault could be
washed away with holy water.　She, trusting more in him than
in God, returned at the end of some time to his obedience, in
such sort that she became great with child.　At this sorely
vexed, she prayed the prioress to drive away the monk from the
convent, since he was so crafty that he would not fail to seduce
her.　The prior and the prioress, who dwelt in good accord
together, made a mock of her, telling her she was big enough
to defend herself against a man, and that he of whom she spoke
was too devout to do such a deed.　At last, driven by the gnawing
of her conscience, she craved leave of them to go to Rome, for
she thought, if she could but confess her sins at the feet of
the Pope, her maidenhead would come back to her.　This the
prior and the prioress granted her with a good will, for they
had rather that against their rule she should go on a pilgrimage,
than continue within the convent with her present scruples.
And they feared also lest in her despair she should blaze abroad
the life that was led in the convent, and so he gave her money
for her journey.　But God willed that she should be in the
rood-gallery of the church of St. John at Lyon, after evensong;

and there was also in the church the Lady of Alençon, who was afterwards Queen of Navarre, who was privily performing a nine days' devotion, having with her three or four of her women. And she, kneeling on her knees before the rood, heard some one mounting the stair to the loft, and by the light of the lamp perceived that it was a nun. And to the end that she might hear her devotions the Duchess withdrew herself to a dark corner hard-by the altar. But the nun, who thought she was alone, fell on her knees, and beating her breast, wept so that it was pitiful to hear her, crying all the while: "My God, my God, have mercy upon me a sinner!" The Duchess, so as to come at the root of the matter, drew near to her and said: "Sweetheart, what ails you, and whence come you, and what brings you hither?" The poor nun, who knew her not, answered and said: "Alas, sweetheart, so great is my woe that I look to God alone, and pray Him to grant me the means of speaking to the Duchess of Alençon, since I am assured if there be cure for my sickness she will find it out." "Sweetheart," said the Duchess, "you may speak to me as to her, for I am of her most familiar acquaintance." "Nay," said the nun, "no other than she shall be advertised of my secret." Then the Duchess told her that she might speak freely, since she had found that she sought for; and the poor woman threw herself at her feet, and told her the whole matter, as you have heard it, and how she fell into her mischance. The Duchess comforted her so well that she still left her a continual repentance for her sin; but put out of her brain the intent to go to Rome. And so she sent her back to her priory with letters to the bishop of the diocese charging him to drive away that shameful monk.

"This story the Duchess herself told to me, and by it you can see, ladies, that Nomerfide's nostrum is not fitting for all sorts and conditions. For these two touching the dead were not less touched by lust." "Verily," said Hircan, "this was a thing that never man did before, namely, to speak of death and to do the works of life." "Sin is no work of life," said Oisille, "for 'tis well known that sin brings death." "Trust me," said Saffredent, "the poor folk thought nothing of theology or the like. But as the daughters of Lot made their father to be drunken that the race of man might be continued, so they would fain have repaired what death had done by making a new man in the place thereof; wherefore I see no ill in the affair save the tears of the nun, who still wept and still came back to the cause of her weeping." "I have known many like her," said Hircan, "who at the same time bewail their sins and rejoice in their pleasures." "I suspect I know," said Parlamente, "of whom you speak, but their rejoicing hath lasted so long that it were time for the lamentation to begin." "Hush, mistress," said Hircan, "the tragedy that began with laughter is not yet ripe for its end." "To change the matter of my discourse," said Parlamente, "methinks Dagoucin hath departed from our fixed resolve and ordinance, namely, to tell none but pleasant tales, while his was very pitiful." "You have said," answered Dagoucin, "that we should only speak of wantonness; and I, methinks, have not failed to do so; but that we may hear some more pleasant case I give my vote to Nomerfide, in the hope that she may repair my fault." "And I have a tale ready," said she, "meet to follow yours, since it too runs on death and the monks. Wherefore, if it be your pleasure, give ear."

[Here end the Novels of the late Queen of Navarre, since no more of them can be found.—*Note at the end of the edition of* 1559.]

[*The following novel, which, we regret to say, was accidentally omitted in the course of printing the "Heptameron," should be read after Novel XI. It took the place of the eleventh novel in Gruget's edition of 1559, and by the best critics is considered not to have come from the pen of Margaret.*]

THE FRUCTIFYING DISCOURSE OF A CERTAIN GREY FRIAR.

Near the town of Bleré, in Touraine, there is a village called St. Martin le Beau, to which place a friar of the monastery of Tours was invited that he might preach the Advent and Lenten sermons. And he, having more rhetoric than learning, was sometimes at a loss for matter wherewith to complete his hour's lecture, and in place thereof fell to telling tales, which altogether satisfied the good folk of the village. So on Maunday Thursday, as he discoursed upon the Paschal Lamb, and showed them how it was wont to be eaten at night, he saw before him certain fair maids of Amboise, who had lately come to St. Martin's to spend Easter, and to stay there some few days afterwards. And being minded to make a figure before them he asked all the women there present if they knew not what it was to eat raw flesh at night. " For," said he, " if you are ignorant, I will teach you the manner of it." The young men of Amboise, who were there with their wives and daughters and nieces, knowing not the humour of this pilgrim father, began to be offended thereat; but when they had heard more their offence was turned to laughter, notably when he said that in eating of the lamb it was needful for a body to have his loins girded, his feet in his shoes, and his hand on his staff. The friar, seeing that they laughed, and suspecting the cause thereof, rejoined straightway: " Well, then, his shoes on his feet, and his staff in his hand; is it not the same?" Whether this was received with laughter I leave you to determine; and indeed the very ladies could not refrain therefrom, so that he held forth to them on other pleasant matters. And perceiving that the hour-glass was well-nigh run out, not wishing them to depart in a bad humour with him, he said: " Verily, fair ladies, when you erelong hold parley with your gossips, you will ask, ' Who is this master friar that speaks so boldly? 'Tis a good fellow, I warrant me.' Verily, verily, I say unto you, be not astonished if my speech be thus assured, for I am of Anjou, and your servant." So saying he made an end to his preaching, leaving his hearers more ready to laugh at his idle talk than to weep at the memory of Our Lord's passion at that time had in remembrance. And his feast-day sermons were in no way inferior to these; for you know that such brethren do not forget to go about begging for their Easter eggs, and not only eggs but many other things, such as linen, yarn, chitterlings, hams, chines, and the like dainty pickings. And on Easter Tuesday, amidst his exhortations in which such folk do abound, he said: "Fair ladies, it is my bounden duty to thank you for the liberality which you have used towards our poor monastery. Yet I must needs tell you that you have not duly considered our necessities; for the greater part of your gifts doth consist of chitterlings, whereof we have no need; for, God be thanked! our monastery is full of them. What, then, shall we do with such a multitude of chitterlings? · Why, ladies, I will resolve you. Do you but mingle your hams with our chitterlings, and your alms will be exceeding acceptable." From this in his discourse he lighted on scandal; and after he had given some few examples thereof, he put himself into a great heat, and cried aloud: "Verily, people of St. Martin, I marvel at you in that you are offended at a small thing, and without a cause, telling tales of me and saying: ' 'Tis a strange matter, but who would have believed that the good father had got his landlady's daughter with child?' Truly this is great matter for wonderment that a monk hath got a wench with child! But consider, I pray you, would it not have been been still more admirable if the wench had got the monk with child?"

"Such, ladies, was the fare wherewith this good shepherd nourished his Master's flock. And so shameless was he that after he had sinned, he must needs make relation of his sin in the pulpit, where nothing should be proclaimed that doth not serve for the edification of the people; and, above all, for the glory of God." "Truly," said Saffredent, "this was a master monk, and as much to my liking as Brother Anjibaut, on whose back was laid all every merry case related in good company." "As for me," said Oisille, "I see no cause for laughter in his discourse, especially at such a season." "You forget, mistress," said Nomerfide, "that in those days (though 'tis no long time since) the good folk of the villages, and for the matter of that the townsfolk also, who esteem themselves of readier wit than other men, did much more esteem such orators than them that preached the Gospel in pureness and simplicity." "Howsoever that may be," said Hircan, "he did not amiss to ask hams in place of chitterlings, for there is more eating on them. And if any devout woman had understood him to speak by way of amphibology, as I believe he intended, neither he nor his fellows would have fared ill; nor yet the wench who filled her bag thereby." "But consider," said Oisille, "the impudency of him, who would gloze the text in this fashion, thinking he had to do with brute beasts like himself; and would fain corrupt poor maids by teaching them the manner of eating raw flesh at night." "But you forget," said Simontault, "that he saw before his eyes those young tripe-sellers of Amboise, in whose buckets he would with hearty goodwill have washed his ——. Shall I name it? Not so; but you understand my intent. And he would fain have made them taste it, not roasted, but all stirring and frisking, so that they might enjoy it the more." "Fair and softly, Sir Simontault," said Parlamente, "you forget yourself; "have you altogether laid aside your accustomed modesty?" "Not so, mistress," answered he; "but the rascal monk made me go somewhat astray. Wherefore that we may return to the right path, I pray Nomerfide, who caused me to wander, to give her vote to some one, that the company may forget our common fault." "Since you make me a partaker in your error," said Nomerfide, "I will address myself to one well fitted to repair it. And that is Dagoucin, for so discreet is he, that he would rather die than tell a wanton case."

www.ingramcontent.com/pod-product-compliance
Lightning Source LLC
Chambersburg PA
CBHW032317280326
41932CB00009B/846